MODERN RHETORICAL CRITICISM

SECOND EDITION

Roderick P. Hart
University of Texas at Austin

Allyn and Bacon

Boston   London   Toronto   Sydney   Tokyo   Singapore

To Kate and Chris
Rhetor, Critic

Vice President, Humanities: Joseph Opiela
Series Editor: Carla Daves
Marketing Manager: Karon Bowers
Series Editorial Assistant: Andrea Geanacopoulos
Cover Administrator: Suzanne Harbison
Composition and Prepress Buyer: Linda Cox
Manufacturing Buyer: Suzanne Lareau
Editorial-Production Service: York Production Services

Library of Congress Cataloging-in-Publication Data

Hart, Roderick P.
    Modern rhetorical criticism / by Roderick P. Hart. — 2nd ed.
      p.   cm.
    Includes bibliographical references and index.
    ISBN 0–205–19665–9
    1. Rhetoric. 2. Criticism. 3. Persuasion (Rhetoric)
  4. Literature—History and criticism—Theory, etc. I. Title.
PN175.H37 1996
808—dc20   96–41568
                                     CIP

Printed in the United States of America
10 9 8 7 6 5 4 3 2 1   01 00 99 98 97 96

CONTENTS

Unit 3
SPECIALIZED FORMS OF CRITICISM

PREFACE

The study of rhetoric is an old one. It was studied by the ancient Greeks and Romans, by medieval courtiers, by Renaissance theologians, and by political thinkers in the emerging democracies of the eighteenth century. Each sensed that something special, something powerful, happened when a firebrand mounted a public platform or entered a church pulpit or hand-delivered a scathing editorial. This power continues to be unleashed today, and so rhetoric is once again being studied with gusto. Here is why: Adolf Hitler's Big Lie, 20-second radio commercials, computerized mailing lists, the Gingrich Revolution, televised evangelism, the politicized novel, time-sharing apartment sales, the resurgence of state militias, AIDS awareness campaigns, taxpayers' protest rallies, the merchandising of professional baseball, MTV videos, advocacy journalism, Weight Watchers International, soap operas, and H. Ross Perot. All of these characters and events collect in the rhetorical arena. All of them change people's lives. To ignore them is to risk one's political, moral, and financial security.

Modern Rhetorical Criticism is a comprehensive, up-to-date guidebook to public rhetoric. It is written for those taking coursework in rhetorical criticism and for students of literary criticism interested in the rhetorical approach to ideas. Its goals are threefold: (1) to broaden the reader's conception of persuasion so that its uses in law, politics, religion, and commerce are seen as different in degree—not in kind—from its less obvious uses in literature, science, education, and entertainment; (2) to survey the major critical studies of rhetoric produced in the United States during the past thirty years; and (3) to equip the reader with the critical tools and attitudes needed to see how rhetoric works its magic.

Any book is necessarily selective. So, the reader will not find in *Modern Rhetorical Criticism* a complete history of rhetorical thought or of the rival schools of criticism making up that history. Rather, the book emphasizes the more recent, U.S. tradition of critical inquiry. Unlike the European tradition which has been popular among students of literature and which has focused largely on stylistic matters, the American tradition (beginning in the early 1900s) has featured public debate, thereby emphasizing the spoken word. And in an era of electronic mass media, an era that has given to public speech a kind of power never before witnessed in human history, such an emphasis seems especially warranted. Each day, after all, the mass media entice us to remember some things and not other things, to spend money on this product and not that one, to grieve about these circumstances and to ignore those. Such enticements lie at the heart of rhetoric. We ignore them at our peril.

The book begins with two overview chapters, one on the nature of rhetoric and one on the nature of criticism. These introductory discussions present the basic terminology of rhetorical study and show why criticism is so central to the intellectual life. Unit II pushes deeper into rhetorical texts themselves by providing the basic tools needed to understand the situations, ideas, arguments, structure, and style making up rhetorical exchanges and to see how the electronic media have fundamentally altered those exchanges during the last forty years. Finally, Unit III treats more ambitious forms of analysis—those dealing with role, culture, and drama—and also shows why certain recent schools of criticism—feminism, Marxism, and postmodernism—must be understood by anyone hoping to produce intelligent criticism today.

The second edition of *Modern Rhetorical Criticism* differs from the first in several ways. It includes two completely new chapters, one on Analyzing Media and one on Feminist Criticism. The former chapter surveys how the mass media can be studied from a rhetorical vantage point, especially in such areas as popular entertainment, mass advertising, and televised news coverage. The chapter on Feminist Criticism focuses on five approaches—to policy, to narrative, to representation, to performance, and to biology—that have made feminist studies one of the most dynamic and challenging areas of investigation today.

Also, this new edition of *Modern Rhetorical Criticism* updates the research in the other subdisciplines of criticism, as well as provides new tools for dissecting messages. In addition, new examples of actual criticism are provided so that theory is continually made practical for the reader. Finally, a fresh chapter on Continental Criticism brings the European voice to rhetorical studies, thereby supplementing the traditional focus guiding rhetorical/textual studies in the United States.

Several features make this book unique. For example, besides presenting a wide array of critical techniques and summarizing hundreds of critical studies, the book contains numerous pieces of original criticism. Sometimes, the texts analyzed are masterworks—patriotic oratory, Shakespeare's plays, congressional debates, Orwell's *Animal Farm*—and sometimes they are more practical: Army recruitment literature, bureaucratic propaganda, stand-up comedy, junk mail circulars. These sample analyses are intended to show how genuinely creative criticism "opens up" a text that the persuader has (consciously or unconsciously) wrapped up tightly.

Two other features make *Modern Rhetorical Criticism* distinctive:

Critical Probes: Specific, concrete questions that can be asked of a given text are scattered throughout the book. These probes are, essentially, the critic's tools. When used insightfully, which is to say, when used carefully, patiently, and imaginatively, these questions shed light on textual matters often ignored by the average listener or reader.

Chapter headnotes: Each chapter begins with a sample persuasive message that graphically previews the chapter's content. These headnotes range from holocaust revisionism to Broadway lyrics, from contemporary funeral prayers to children's textbooks, and from avant garde poetry to social protest rhetoric.

The very existence of *Modern Rhetorical Criticism* shows how important rhetorical inquiry has become during the past thirty years. In colleges and universities, more and more academic courses are devoted to rhetorical matters. When taught in academic Departments of Speech or Communication, they bear such titles as Speech Criticism, Contemporary Public Address, Political Communication, Persuasion and Propaganda, Rhetoric and Media, or Historical/critical Research Methods. In Departments of English, they fall under such headings as Rhetoric and Literature, Text and Language, Stylistics, Rhetoric and Genre, or Advanced Composition and Exposition. Moreover, sociologists, anthropologists, political scientists, historians, and religious scholars have all demonstrated increasing interest in rhetorical issues. But no matter what such courses are called, they tend to tell the same tale: Rhetoric has always been with us and always will be. As Humpty Dumpty might have said, the only important question is: Who will become rhetoric's master? *Modern Rhetorical Criticism* hopes that it will be the reader.

ACKNOWLEDGMENTS

Any author hoping to write a competent book does not do so alone. I have hardly been alone. Professor Carroll Arnold of Pennsylvania State University started me on this journey some thirty years ago. His influence, and the influence of Professor Richard Gregg, have been profound, even if those influences may seem indistinct to them at this late date.

More recently, I have benefited from the help of my colleagues in rhetorical studies at the University of Texas, especially Rick Cherwitz, Dana Cloud, and Ron Greene. Two former colleagues—David Payne and Joanne Gilbert—made special contributions to this book by helping me with two of the chapters. Another former colleague, Kathleen Jamieson, reads everything I write and sometimes approves of it. These people directed me away from certain pitfalls, but I alone am responsible for the pitfalls into which I may have fallen.

I appreciate the help of Vidula Bal, Hannah Gourgey, Cindy Smith, and Mary Triece, who helped make the nettlesome aspects of writing this book less nettlesome. I also wish to thank, once again, Professors Edwin Black, Suzanne Daughton, Bruce Gronbeck, David McLennan, John Pauley, Deborah Smith-Howell, and Kerry Strayer who gave me the benefit of their counsel for the first edition of *MRC*. Deborah Smith-Howell also read this second edition, and David Payne contributed especially to the chapter on Dramatistic Criticism. Above all, I am thankful to my family, especially to my mother, who is the best rhetorical critic I know, and to my wife who is, simply, the best.

Chapter 1

THE RHETORICAL PERSPECTIVE

Because as they cut it was that special green, they decided
To make a woman of the fresh hay. They wished to lie in green, to wrap
      Themselves in it, light but not pale, silvered but not grey.
Green and ample, big enough so both of them could shelter together
In any of her crevices, the armpit, the join
Of hip and groin. They—who knew what there was to know about baling
The modern way with hay so you rolled it up like a carpet,
Rather than those loose stacks—they packed the green body tight
So she wouldn't fray. Each day they moulted her to keep her
Green and soft. Only her hair was allowed to ripen into yellow tousle.

The next weeks whenever they stopped cutting they lay with her.
She was always there, waiting, reliable, their green woman.
She gathered them in, yes she did,
Into the folds of herself, like the mother they hadn't had.
Like the women they had had, only more pliant, more graceful,
Welcoming in a way you never just found.
They not only had the awe of taking her,
But the awe of having made her. They drank beer
Leaning against the pillow of her belly
And one would tell the other, "Like two Adams creating."

And they marveled as they placed
The cans at her ankles, at her neck, at her wrists so she
Glittered gold and silver. They adorned what they'd made.
After harrowing they'd come to her, drawing
The fountains of the Plains, the long line
Of irrigating spray and moisten her up.
And lean against her tight, green thighs to watch buzzards
Circle black against the pink stain of the sunset.

What time she began to smolder they never knew—
Sometime between night when they'd left her
And evening when they returned. Wet, green hay
Can go a long time smoldering before you notice. It has a way
Of catching itself, of asserting that
There is no dominion over it but the air. And it flares suddenly
Like a red head losing her temper, and allows its long bright hair
To tangle in the air, letting you know again
That what shelters you can turn incendiary in a flash.
And then there is only the space of what has been,
An absence in the field, memory in the shape of a woman. [Macdonald,
        1985:75–6]

This is not a book about poems. It is a book about rhetoric. It is also a book about criticism. It is a book that invites careful attention to the messages of daily life. The book encourages us to pick and probe at messages designed to influence human thoughts and actions. Because it is a book about **rhetoric,** it is a book about *the art of using language to help people narrow their choices among specifiable, if not specified, policy options* (not a very sophisticated definition, perhaps, but one that has its intuitive attractions). For example, we know, intuitively, that the poem above involves a special use of language. But is it language designed to *narrow* the choices of other people? Not in any obvious sense. Our day-to-day experience with obvious forms of rhetoric—advertising, political speeches, televised evangelism—tells us that if poet Cynthia Macdonald is attempting to persuade us of something specific, she has chosen a strange tack indeed.

Admittedly, Macdonald uses language well—beautifully, in fact. She paints her pictures with dexterity, making us see the plain beauty of the bountiful pasture she describes, making us hear the casual conversations of the laboring brothers, making us feel the alternating softness and hardness of the carefully baled hay, making us smell the acrid smoke of the Hay Lady as she gives up her all. Poet Macdonald also evokes rich feeling states: the sense of almost womb-like comfort provided the tired farm hands by the Hay Lady; the wonder of watching nature's earthen blackness blend into the "pink stain" of her sunsets;

the sadness that all humans experience things close to them—pets, people, bales of hay—expire. Macdonald, then, gives us precisely what a good poet often gives us—old thoughts thought anew, old feelings felt anew—but she does not give us rhetoric.

But what if Macdonald had chosen to end her poem differently? What if she had concluded in the following manner:

> But woman is neither hay nor memory,
> Not pillow not whore not kindling.
> She is woman, and she is woman supreme,
> All farmhands take note.

This would have been a jarring, discordant conclusion to Macdonald's poem. Our addition here changes the "tone" of her work by introducing a new kind of obviousness. Our addition also draws a "moral" from Macdonald's story and "summarizes" things she left unsummarized. Finally, our addition adds a sinister element to Macdonald's poem with its stark warning in the last line.

In the language of this chapter, our addition has made the poem "more rhetorical." Unlike poetry, rhetoric is often concerned with specificity, with drawing conclusions, and, yes, with warnings. The shift in "tone" we have attempted here is a shift both in worldview as well as language. It is therefore not surprising that our addition brings a forceful, staccato quality to the poem that seems rather blunt when compared to Macdonald's own delicate rhythms.

The following speaker makes things blunter still when offering his "Kudos for Condos":

> Mr. Speaker, two decades ago, a group of men and women took advantage of a new idea in American real estate by completing the first condominium conversion in the United States. Now, as the residents of this building prepare to celebrate its twentieth anniversary, they can look back proudly at having set the standard that all other real estate conversions would do well to emulate.
>
> This historic building is located at 9410 64th Road, in Rego Park, Queens County, New York. Its residents have had true success by allowing tenants a real choice; in fact, one tenant who decided not to buy his apartment lived on under rent-control protection for almost twenty years.
>
> Mr. Speaker, in the story of this modest structure in Rego Park and of the creative people who transformed it, I think we can see a truly American spirit of inventiveness and the can-do-ethic. It is precisely this kind of innovation to meet challenges that has allowed this nation to sustain such a tremendous history of growth.
>
> As always, it was the people involved in this enterprise who made the difference. David Wolfenson was the landlord of the building twenty years ago; it was his initiative that started the entire process. Edward Schiff gave the expert legal advice necessary to complete the project; twenty years later, he still represents both sponsors and tenant groups.

> Mr. Speaker, I call now on all of my colleagues in the U.S. House of Representatives to join me in congratulating the men and women of 9410 64th Road on the twentieth anniversary of their successful conversion, and in wishing them the best of luck for the future. [Ackerman, 1986:16]

Any person of aesthetic sensibility will be almost embarrassed by the stark contrast between Cynthia Macdonald's mellifluous lines and Representative Gary Ackerman's crass lionizing in the halls of the U.S. Congress. In contrast to Macdonald, who demands thoughtful reconsideration from her readers, Ackerman makes us squirm with his tedious pontificating ("they can look back proudly . . ."), his tiresome cliches ("a truly American spirit of inventiveness . . ."), and his ponderous overstatements ("it is precisely this kind of innovation to meet challenges that . . ."). Unrequired pontificating, tiresome cliches, ponderous overstatements—this is rhetoric. Or at least some of it. The worst of it, perhaps. But each day, in each profession, people like Gary Ackerman produce rhetoric, much of it trivial, some of it important, all of it purporting to help others sort through their choices.

Modern Rhetorical Criticism invites us to study why the *Congressional Record* is filled with such stuff, why Representative Ackerman's constituents were flattered by his blandishments, and why his colleagues in the House smiled benignly when he read his remarks into the *Record*. Because he operates as something of a classic persuader here, Ackerman tries to "cut off" the many options for response available to his audience. Ackerman's **policy options** are clearly specified ("let's cheer for condos"), whereas Cynthia Macdonald never tells her audience exactly what she expects them to *do* as a result of reading her poem. (Even our addition to her poem is similarly veiled when it tells all farmhands to merely "take note," whatever that may mean.) This lack of specificity is what makes reading verse such a pleasure: It gives us room to wander; it permits a vacation from choosing between this concrete possibility and that concrete probability. Congressman Ackerman, in contrast, is all business.

But must all rhetoric be as pedestrian and self-serving as Gary Ackerman's? Clearly not. Human history has been written by great persons authoring great orations for social betterment. Often, these great statements have seemed more poetic than pragmatic, as satisfying to the heart as to the head. Consider, for example, the remarks that holocaust survivor and Nobel laureate author Elie Wiesel made when accepting a Congressional Medal of Honor from President Ronald Reagan in April of 1985, shortly after Mr. Reagan had unwisely accepted an invitation to speak at a German cemetery where Nazis were buried:

> Today is April 19, and April 19, 1943, the Warsaw ghetto rose in arms against the onslaught of the Nazis. They were so few and so young and so helpless, and nobody came to their help, and they had to fight what was then the mightiest legion in Europe.

Every underground received help except the Jewish underground, and yet they managed to fight and resist and push back those Nazis and their accomplices for six weeks, and yet the leaders of the Free World, Mr. President, knew everything and did so little of nothing, or at least nothing specifically to save Jewish children from death.

You spoke of Jewish children, Mr. President. One million Jewish children perished. If I spent my entire life reciting their names, I would die before finishing the task.

Mr. President I've seen children, I have seen children being thrown in the flames—alive! Words, they die on my lips. So I have learned, I have learned, I have learned the fragility of the human condition.

And I am reminded of the great moral essayist, the gentle and forceful Abe Rosenthal, having visited Auschwitz, once wrote an extraordinary reportage about the persecution of Jews, and he called it, "Forgive Them Not Father, for They Knew What They Did."

I have learned that the Holocaust was a unique and uniquely Jewish event, albeit with universal implications. Not all victims were Jews. But all Jews were victims.

I have learned the danger of indifference, the crime of indifference. For the opposite of love, I have learned, is not hate, but indifference.

Jews were killed by the enemy but betrayed by the so-called Allies who found political reasons to justify their indifference or passivity.

But I've also learned that suffering confers no privileges. It all depends what one does with it.

And this is why survivors of whom you spoke, Mr. President, have tried to teach their contemporaries how to build the ruins, how to invent hope in a world that offers none, how to proclaim faith to a generation that has seen it shamed and mutilated, and I believe, we believe, that memory is the answer, perhaps the only answer. [Wiesel, 1985:22]

This is hardly Ackerman-like discourse. A great man, not an average man, is speaking. And he is speaking of great matters, not of expedient matters. Like poet Macdonald, Wiesel conjures up word-pictures that galvanize, draws on our psychic histories, uses language that sears the emotions. But there is an awkwardness to Wiesel's language also. He repeats himself frequently, begins sentences and then begins them again, uses more words than he really needs for clear communication. Wiesel's message could use a good editing: greater specificity, less choppiness, fewer cliches.

But to call for such changes would be to miss the point of this rhetorical exchange, for Elie Wiesel had no intention of producing poetry that day. He wanted one thing: to get Ronald Reagan to cancel his trip to the Nazi graves. Wiesel's eloquence derived from the emotional investment he made in his message, from his personal experiences during the war, and from his clarity and forthrightness of expression. All of this made for an *artistry* not seen in Representative Ackerman's speech on condos but it also made for an *insistence* not apparent in Cynthia Macdonald's poem. In short, Elie Wiesel mustered as much artistry as his insistence would allow.

Modern Rhetorical Criticism will probe these subtleties of human interaction. The book presents practical techniques for uncovering the wishes and schemes hidden in public discourse and shows how important answers can be gotten if the right questions are asked of a text. It details a number of theoretical perspectives for "taking apart" the messages we hear each day so that we can better appreciate why, rightly or wrongly, the Gary Ackermans of the world far outnumber the Elie Wiesels and the Cynthia Macdonalds. But before considering these perspectives, let us consider what rhetoric is and what it is not.

THE ARTS OF RHETORIC

The premises in this chapter are threefold: (1) Rhetoric is a special sort of human activity; (2) it takes a special kind of talent to understand it; and (3) by understanding it, one acquires a special perspective on the world itself. We can get some sense of the special nature of rhetoric by contrasting the messages above. After reading Macdonald's poem, for example, each reader has a unique set of feelings and expectations. Macdonald develops many images, sets off many associations. She seems to demand nothing in particular from us as readers. Ackerman, in contrast, clearly seeks universal agreement from his listeners about a narrowed set of choices. He takes pains to provide a common background for his listeners, uses language in highly conventional ways, mentions specific names and dates and places, is obvious when identifying good ("innovation") and evil (the lack of a "real choice" in housing), tells his listeners what he wishes them to do next (i.e., applaud).

There is also a purposefulness in Ackerman's remarks that is missing in Macdonald's poem. Ackerman seems less patient than Macdonald; he is almost boorish in his concern that we get his story straight. Macdonald, in contrast, seems more willing to let us find our own story within her story. She wants us to be different after reading her poem but she seems content to let *us* explore the dimensions of that difference. Both rhetoric and poetry tell a story, but the rhetor (i.e., one who uses rhetoric) takes special pains to be sure that the moral of the story is clear to the audience.

But, shorn of the addendum we created above, what is the moral of Cynthia Macdonald's story? Is she operating as some sort of naturalist, innocently employing imagery drawn from primitive life forces, hoping only that in reading the poem we will come to re-appreciate the essential connectedness of the human and natural worlds? Or could she be a retrograde sexist, heralding a masculine world of physical dominance in which women become pliable objects to be freely manipulated by men? Or is she an avant-garde feminist, surrealistically describing a world in which Man (the laborers) is deceived into believing that he can "possess" Woman (the Hay Lady) who suddenly, and imperiously, leaves for parts unknown?

All of these interpretations are possible, and they are the sorts of things that critics debate about. But the important thing to note here is that *the poet herself does not resolve these disputes.* The poet keeps her own counsel, content to provoke such questions in her readers but not to answer them.

Like poetry, rhetoric is an art. Like poetry, rhetoric creates a story out of nothing, using symbols to bring to life feelings we had forgotten we had, plans we had not yet considered. As we see in Ackerman's speech, rhetoric uses common ideas, conventional language, and specific information to change listeners' feelings and behaviors. The story rhetoric tells is always a story with a purpose; it is never told for its own sake.

Given our definition of rhetoric above, every rhetorical task involves five basic moves: (1) the speaker tries to exert change by using **language** rather than non-symbolic forces (like guns or torture); (2) the speaker must come to be regarded as a **helper** rather than an exploiter; (3) the speaker must convince the listener that new **choices** need to be made; (4) the speaker must **narrow** the listener's options for making these choices, even though (5) the speaker may become subtle by not **specifying** the details of the policies advocated.

Thus, the user of rhetoric peddles choices, even though most people naturally resist making choices unless forced to do so. And if forced to do so, people also naturally resist having their search for a solution prematurely constrained by someone else. So persuasion takes work: The speaker must "help" without appearing gauche or paternalistic and the speaker must establish that the world is not yet fundamentally right (hence requiring new choice-making by the listener) but that it can soon be set right by making the (narrowed) choice the speaker endorses.

The average television commercial tells this tale a thousand times daily, with New Bride being driven to despair (and choice) by the ring-around-the-collar spotted by Handsome Husband. Mature Neighbor quickly arrives on the scene with her bag of groceries *and* a box of new Narrowed Choice. Marital bliss is quickly restored, we are led to believe, and choice-making recedes into the background until crabgrass strikes fifteen minutes later. Not all persuasion is this predictable, of course, but all of it involves the art of managing choices.

But if rhetoric is an art, it is an art far different from the arts of poetry and painting. It is an art with these characteristics:

1. A cooperative art. Rhetoric is an art that brings speakers and listeners together. It cannot be done in solitude. To speak by oneself in a closet is of course possible but hardly normal. Rhetoric makes little sense unless it is made for others. After all, it is the reactions of other people that will be its measure: their votes, their purchases, their conversions, their affection. And so rhetoric is a transactive art because it brings two or more people together in an atmosphere of potential change.

By sharing communication, both speakers and listeners open themselves up to each others' influence. In that sense, communication is not something that is *done* to others. Rather, it is something that people choose to do to themselves by consenting to communicative contact. By agreeing to rhetorical exchange, says Arnold [1972:16], people acknowledge their dependence on one another. In the world of rhetoric, a speaker succeeds only when he or she can induce listeners to "contribute" their knowledge, feelings, and experiences about the matter in question. The rhetorical critic studies such invitations to cooperate.

2. *A people's art.* Rhetoric is an ordinary art. Its standards of excellence are the standards of ordinary people. Rhetoric is rarely as graceful or as lilting as poetry because the people for whom it is made are too busy to bother with grace and lilt. Rhetoric works within the constraints of everyday logic, the logic of people who live in condos and like them. The heroes in rhetorical history are people like Louisiana populist Huey Long, who severely mangled the King's English whenever he spoke but who was loved by his constituents because of it, not in spite of it. Rhetoric is often neither pretty nor fetching, although it can be both. At times it is even heavy-handed, although it tries never to be seen as such. At its best, rhetoric is ordinary language done extraordinarily.

3. *A temporary art.* Normally, rhetoric is rooted in the age of its creation. The people who create rhetoric speak today's language, not yesterday's. Such speakers use timebound examples, timebound statistics, timebound jargon, caring little how it will sound tomorrow. That is why most of the rhetoric we hear each day sounds more like Gary Ackerman's than Abraham Lincoln's. Or, more precisely, that is why only one or two of Lincoln's speeches continue to be reread today. The remainder of his speeches dealt with issues and personalities that no longer concern us. Only on a few occasions did he turn rhetoric into poetry. Like Elie Wiesel, Lincoln knew that most rhetoric was meant to be consumed, not savored.

4. *A limited art.* As Bitzer [1968] reminds us, rhetoric is deployed only when it can make a difference. Rhetoric cannot really move mountains, which is why so few people stand at the bases of mountains to orate. Similarly, Bosnian Serbs normally cannot move Bosnian Muslims by speaking to them, and that is why, sadly, they often do not try. Neither of these situations is "rhetorical" in Bitzer's sense because human discourse cannot seem to change them. Rhetoric can do much, but it cannot do everything.

5. *A frustrating art.* There are no laws of rhetoric. There are important rules of thumb but little else. To be effective in persuasion one must have a delicate touch, an ability to use the right argument and the deft phrase at precisely the right time. When deciding what to say, the rhetor always swims in a sea of uncertainty because (1) people normally argue only about uncertain matters (e.g., Should euthanasia be permitted?) rather than about that which is fixed (e.g., the inevitability of death) and because (2) people are so complex, so changeful, and so ornery about so many matters. Thus, when stumping for more funding for the space shuttle, a NASA spokesperson must often leave the best scientific arguments at home because it is ordinary citizens and their rep-

resentatives, not scientists, who fund space missions. Rhetoric, then, deals with the probable, the best case that can be made under limited circumstances. It is used to decide the undecided question and to solve the unsolved problem [Bryant, 1972:20–1]. People talk when they can think of nothing else to do but feel that they must do something.

6. *A generative art.* Contemporary writers [e.g., Cherwitz and Darwin, 1995] tell us that rhetoric produces most of what passes for everyday knowledge. They claim that rhetoric helps us learn what other people think (e.g., whether or not space funding should be increased) and also to learn our *own* minds about things (e.g., an old dictum claims that one never really knows something until one can teach it to someone else). By arguing with one another we produce what is called "social knowledge," the sort of knowledge that determines much in human affairs.

Today in the United States, for example, witches are no longer burned, blacks are no longer limited to plantation employment, and Japanese-Americans are no longer interned. But in other eras, *when other arguments prevailed,* such "truths" were taken for granted and, more important, were used as the basis for social policy. So rhetoric never produces True Truth. It produces partial truth, truth for these times and these people. As Johnstone [1969:408] says, "the only way to tell whether what I have is a truth or a falsehood is to contemplate its evocative power," that is, its power to secure the agreement of others. And lest we think that such social knowledge is not really knowledge, we need only reflect upon the comparatively recent history of witches, blacks, and Japanese-Americans.

THE RANGE OF RHETORIC

One way of understanding rhetoric is to consider what it is and what it is not or, better, *how much* of a thing it is and *how much* of another thing it is not. In Figure 1.1, "the rhetorical" is depicted as an area bordering on other domains but one that is nonetheless special. For example, rhetoric resembles science in that both the scientist and the rhetor want to be taken seriously. The persuader wants listeners to believe that calamity will in fact strike unless the speaker's warnings are heeded. Like the scientist, the persuader marshalls evidence (e.g., the testimony of experts, certain statistical trends, etc.), uses this evidence to comment on some real, not imagined, feature of the observable world (e.g., "overpopulation will inundate the infrastructure of this city"), and then employs this package of arguments to support a policy recommendation (e.g., "We must put an immediate moratorium on building permits.")

But even though both the scientist and the persuader seek to make things demonstrably true, the persuader is willing to treat the perceptions of *ordinary people* as the acid test of demonstratedness. The scientist, in contrast, normally is expected to meet a more exacting standard of truth (empirical verifiability,

FIGURE 1.1 Realm of the Rhetorical

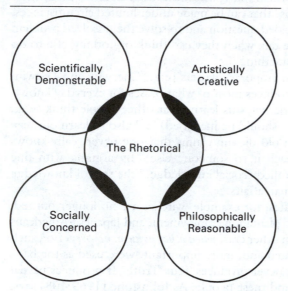

the judgments of experts, experimental replication, etc.), while the persuader's truth is often fifty-one percent truth: the majority judgment of ordinary citizens. For most persuaders on most issues, fifty-one percent truth is judged sufficient.

As we have mentioned above, the persuader, like the poet, is artistically creative. Both work with symbols to breathe life into ideas. Neither uses tangible tools (like pickaxes) to change tangible phenomena (like rocks). Rather, both the artist and the persuader use their imaginations to engage their audiences' imaginations. But as we have noted before, the persuader's creativity is often exercised in behalf of decidedly short-term gains (i.e., assent on the particular issue at hand) and the persuader, because he or she is a "narrower," is unlikely to give listeners the intellectual freedom normally permitted them by the artist. It is also true that the imagination of the persuader is not likely to be as uncontrolled as that of the traditional artist because, as we have said, rhetoric is a *social* art. It does little good for the rhetor to take flights of fancy unless the audience can come along as well.

The persuader also tries to be philosophically reasonable, to ensure that an argument makes the kind of *patterned* sense it must make to be understood by others. The rhetor typically avoids the incomplete mental image, the sudden self-interruption, or the discordant use of language that lends excitement to more purely artistic endeavors. It is also true, however, that the persuader typically uses what works and is less scrupulous in argumentation than the philosopher. The rhetor uses, in Aristotle's terms, all the means of argument available, not just those recommended in the logic books.

As we shall see in Chapter 5, there is a special logic to persuasion, a "psycho-logic," and it is to these informal methods of reasoning that the practical speaker most often pays homage. Thus, as Windt [1972] points out, it even makes "sense" at times for certain speakers (e.g., radical antiwar protesters) to stomp their feet and to act crazed. The logic of persuasion is sometimes a curious logic.

Finally, the persuader is socially concerned, at least in part. The persuader is a public person, seeking to change not just one life but many lives. When abandoning solitude, the persuader promises that many people's lives will be improved in some important way. But the persuader is not a social worker. As McGee [1975] says, persuaders present *their* versions of what "the people" believe, often taking great liberties with public opinion when doing so. Thus, the persuader's social concern is limited to his or her private version of the ideal life, a life in which everyone owns a Ford automobile or votes a straight Socialist ticket or gives witness to Biblical truths. The persuader wants to make a particular kind of change, a public change. Those who dream social dreams needs the aid of others.

Because it borders on so many worlds, the realm of rhetoric is powerful. The rhetor draws on each of these worlds and yet steps back from each simultaneously, seeking to become a poet, but a poet of practical consequences, a scientist, but a scientist unencumbered by footnotes. The persuader also becomes an easy-going logician and a social worker with an eye on the bottom line. By blending these roles skillfully as, say, Barbara Bush and Hillary Clinton did when serving as First Lady, persuaders become highly influential. For this reason alone they bear watching. Watching them is the job of the rhetorical critic.

The definition of rhetoric provided above is obviously a generous definition, one designed to encompass a variety of messages. Included within this broad definition would be the television docudrama, the cooing of lovers on a park bench, the scientific treatise, the invocation at the City Council meeting, the reprimand from the boss at work, the presidential address, the college lecture, the adolescent's whining during dinner, the blockbuster movie, the top sergeant's welcome to boot camp, the Diet Coke commercial, the psychiatrist's counseling session, and much else.

All of these situations require the use of language and all of them can result in both obvious and nonobvious forms of influence. Indeed, it is a hallmark of the critical perspective that all messages be examined carefully, especially those that seem to lie outside the realm of rhetoric. Currently, rhetorical critics are launching just such investigations into such seemingly nonrhetorical areas as aesthetics, science, philosophy, and friendship-formation in order to witness subtler forms of persuasion.

Indeed, the most basic job of the rhetorical critic is to be able to discover *when* rhetoric is being used in the first place. Persuaders, after all, do not always own up to their profession. Often, they would like to be mistaken for a scientist or a poet or a philosopher. By keeping a sharp eye peeled for the essential features of rhetoric, however, the critic can discover when rhetoric has come to call.

Normally, three features make a message rhetorical: (1) delineations of the good, (2) resonance for a particular audience, and (3) clear or clearly implied policy recommendations ("policy" being conceived here in its broadest sense, including proposals of marriage, requests for repentance, voter solicitations, and much else.)

For example, Table 1.1 presents three similar-yet-different lists of events ranging from the obviously rhetorical to the less obviously rhetorical. As one moves from right to left, notice how the events change in subtle yet important ways, increasingly lending themselves to more immediate and more powerful rhetorical uses. In the case of the photographs, for example, it is not hard to imagine how the picture of an Appalachian shack could be used in the hands of a community activist seeking federal funding. Such a picture presents a special invitation to the viewer to think *now* about matters of right and wrong. The fact that this is an "American" shack makes Americans especially uncomfortable because it calls into question certain aspects of the national dream. Perhaps because of this audience resonance, the policy recommendations

TABLE 1.1 Types of Rhetorical Events

Messages	More Obviously Rhetorical	Uncertain	Less Obviously Rhetorical
Photographs	An Appalachian shack	The White House	A South Sea hut
Telephone call	From Handicapped Workers of America	From a son at college	From a rich friend
Drama	Guerrilla theatre	Off-Broadway drama	Broadway musical
Signs	On a highway billboard	At an hourly parking lot	On a restroom door
Commercials	About hamburgers from Wendy's Restaurants	About drugs, from the National Basketball Association	About Picasso from the National Museum of Art
Magazines	*Michigan Militia Report*	*Harpers*	*Time*
Guided tours	At Budweiser plant	At Lincoln Memorial	At Yellowstone National Park
Humor	Political jokes	Ethnic jokes	Animal jokes
Poetry	Langston Hughes	Wallace Stevens	E.E. Cummings
Trip directions	From Big Al to his car lot	From a new boyfriend to his lake cabin	From Rand McNally to Salt Lake City
Statistics	From International Association of Oil Producers	From Mobil Oil Corp.	From U.S. Department of Energy
Music	Folk songs	Church hymns	Rhythm and blues
Football	Half-time pep talk	TV color commentary	Cheerleaders' cheers
Storytelling	Religious testimonials	Folklore	Fairy tales

seem to jump out of the picture for many Americans—"Let us put a stop to this kind of poverty" or "Why don't those people get a job and live better?"

The picture of the White House is more ambiguous. One can imagine the photograph being used in patriotic ways in the United States ("the seat of our democracy") and quite differently in Iraq or Iran ("home of the jackal"). It could be used for comedic effect on The Comedy Channel ("The Prez's house") or for purely crass boosterism on a multicolored flyer ("Bring your convention to Washington. Hotel rates have never been lower.")

The South Sea hut, in contrast, might lend itself to any number of case-makings. Previous rhetoric in the U.S. culture, at least, seems not to have marked it yet for special use and hence the image makes fewer immediate and specific demands on us (Should it be used for a travel brochure? In connection with religious missionary work? As a symbol of exploitation in the Third World?).

As one moves from right to left in Table 1.1, one gets the feeling that (1) the speaker's exact purposes for persuasion become less ambiguous, (2) perhaps as a result, the emotions of the speaker lie increasingly close to the surface, (3) increasingly specific "policies" are being recommended to the audience or at least broadly hinted at ("Give now," "Commit yourself fully," "Follow the Word"), (4) the question of essential good and evil has become less of a question, and (5) finding an "ideal audience" for the message would become easier because fewer and fewer people can fill the bill as the rhetoric heats up. In short, as we move from right to left, things become more rhetorical.

This is not to say, of course, that we should turn our backs on less obvious rhetoric. Indeed, critics have become increasingly interested in these subtler messages precisely because most people (that is, most potential audience members) are oblivious to the *hints* of good and evil or *implied* policy recommendations buried within them. Thus, for example, critics have looked at the range of meanings provided by Garrison Keillor's "Prairie Home Companion" [Foss and Foss, 1994], at sanitized racism in letters-to-the-editor [Lacy, 1992], at the rhetoric of *Donahue* [Priest and Dominick, 1994], and at the very careful language used by the Supreme Court when making abortion decisions [Sullivan and Goldzwig, 1995]. Throughout this book, we will look for rhetoric in all of its haunts and hideways.

THE FUNCTIONS OF RHETORIC

Thus far, we have discussed what rhetoric is and what it is not, where it can be found, and what shapes it takes. It now remains for us to examine what rhetoric *does*, how it functions in human society. Of course, we will be studying the uses of rhetoric throughout this book but here, briefly, we can examine some of its less frequently noticed uses.

1. Rhetoric unburdens. People who make rhetoric do so because they must get something off their chests, because the cause they champion overwhelms their natural reticence. Such people refuse to let history take its slow, evolutionary course and instead try to become part of history themselves. The history they make may be quite local in character (e.g., picketing a neighborhood abortion clinic), but rhetorical people typically do not hang back. They sense that the world around them is not yet set and so they approach it aggressively, often convinced that they can make a difference, always convinced that they must try.

On occasion, however, the need to speak produces ambivalence. For example, cult-leader Charles Manson, who once engineered a series of horrible crimes in California (known as the Tate-LaBianca murders) and who is still serving a life-sentence in prison, seems especially conflicted about such matters. After having been in jail for many years, Manson finally consented to an interview with journalist Keven Kennedy and his remarks tell us much about his rhetorical mindset:

> Kennedy: Do you want to be released from prison?
> Manson: Released? I just want to be left alone. You see, I dismissed the world a long time ago. Really I did. I dismissed it. It's gone from my mind. It comes over and says, "You pay me some attention." I say, "No." "Will you accept our God as being *the* God?" I say, "All right. I'll accept anything. Now, can I get on with my business?" [Manson, 1985:28]

At this point in the interview, Manson appears to have quit the business of leadership. He seems unwilling to make the sorts of adjustments communication requires. But less than two minutes later Manson had this to say:

> Manson: I just learn to reflect people back at themselves. Because man is not working—why tell anybody? If you start informing people that are misinformed, you'd spend the rest of your life informing people that are misinformed. *I would feel that I had achieved something if we could stop the misinforming of people and inform them properly.* [Manson, 1985:29, italics mine]

In this latter statement, Manson captures the rhetorical person's basic instinct: to become less anonymous and "inform them properly." Although his years in prison have no doubt quelled his ardor for social contact, Manson's leadership needs lurk just beneath the surface. While he seems to have lost a bit of heart over the years (for which we may all be thankful), even the fifty-year old Charles Manson harbors the persuasive instinct.

In a sense, then, communication is a kind of arrogant imposition on other people. When A tries to persuade B, for example, A affirms that (1) something is wrong in B's world and (2) that A can fix it. Thus, if it is true that the poet is an escapist, it is also true that the rhetor is an infiltrator. Naturally, the arrogance of the rhetorical act is normally well disguised by the practicing persuader who is, after all, only there to "help" ("You owe it to *yourself* to sign this contract," "The *handicapped* do indeed appreciate your contribution,"

"Do this for the *Lord's* sake"). Still, a rhetorical engagement is no less intrusive just because its intrusions have been camouflaged.

2. *Rhetoric distracts.* When speaking, a speaker wants to have all, not just some, of our attention. To get that attention, the speaker must so fill up our minds that we forget, temporarily at least, the other ideas, people, and policies important to us. Naturally, we do not give away our attention freely, so it takes rhetoric at its best to sidetrack us. One way of doing so is for the speaker to control the premises of a discussion. As McCombs and Shaw [1972] demonstrated some years ago, the power of the mass media derives not so much from their ability to tell us what to think but what to think about. When choosing to report on industrial lead poisoning, for example, a local TV station simultaneously chooses *not* to cover the crowning of the Apple Queen or the win-loss record of the local Double A farm club. By "setting the agenda" in this fashion, by controlling the premises pertaining to newsworthiness, the media can thus influence any conclusions drawn from those premises.

So the rhetor asks listeners to think about this topic, not that one, to try out this solution, not that endorsed by the speaker's opponent. In this sense, rhetoric operates like a good map. Maps, after all, have a distinctive point of view: They "favor" interstate highways (by coloring them a bright red) over rural roads (often a pale blue); they emphasize urban areas (blotched in yellow) over small towns (a small dot); they adapt their appeals to vacationers (by highlighting Yosemite) rather than to truckers (no diners are listed). Like the rhetor, the roadmap bristles with integrity, implying by the precision of its drawings that it provides the complete story: all the highway news that's fit to print.

Rhetoric, too, tries to narrow our latitudes of choice without giving us the feeling that we are being thereby hemmed in. Rhetoric tries to control the *definition* we provide for a given activity ("Your church offering isn't a monetary loss; it's a downpayment on heaven") as well as the *criteria* we employ to solve a problem ("Abortion is not a religious issue; it's a legal one"). By also emphasizing one speaker *category* over another (e.g., Bill Clinton as commander-in-chief vs. Bill Clinton as favorite patron of McDonald's), persuaders invite us to focus on this and not that, on here and not there, on now and not then.

3. *Rhetoric enlarges.* In some senses, modern persuaders are like the heralds of old. They move among us singing the siren song of change, asking us to consider a new solution to an old problem (or an old solution to a problem of which we were unaware). Rhetoric operates, then, like a kind of intellectual algebra, asking us to equate things we had never before considered equatable. Thus, for example, Adolf Hitler rose to fame (and infamy) by linking German nationalism with increased militarism and Germany's economic woes with Jewish clannishness. These were corrupt equations but for him they were useful ones.

Often, the **associations** encouraged by rhetoric are no less sophisticated, or honorable, than those created by Hitler. Nevertheless, these linkages are the workhorses of persuasion. So, for example, some manufacturers of personal computers now virtually assure unwary parents that computing skills will translate instantly into educational achievement for their children. It is interesting to note that persuaders rarely ask for major expansion of their listeners' worldviews. They imply that only a slight modification is in order. Persuasion moves by increments of inches.

Often, persuaders **disassociate** ideas in order to expand the viewpoints of their listeners. So, for example, Bankamericard changed its name to Visa in the early 1970s so that the more international flavor of the new name would offset the growing anti-Americanism found in Western Europe at the time. Similarly, during the neophyte's first meeting at Alcoholics Anonymous, an attempt is made to break the now-intimate connection between that person's self-image and the use of stimulants. Naturally, the alcoholic, like all listeners, initially resists such "enlarging" perspectives. It becomes the persuader's task to demonstrate that any such alterations are a natural extension of thoughts and feelings the listener *already* possesses and that any such new notions can be easily accommodated within the listener's *existing* repertoire of ideas. That is why rhetoric is called an art.

4. *Rhetoric names.* To understand the power of rhetoric we must remember that creatures and noncreatures alike (people, frogs, rocks, bicycles) are born without labels. People are, as best we know, nature's only namers. And they name things with a vengeance: Orville Reddenbacher's Popcorn; Sri Lanka; black holes; the Utah Jazz; Nirvana. People take their naming seriously: Newly enfranchised Americans anglicize their names to ward off discrimination; professional women often retain their maiden names to avoid being seen as the captives of their mates; fights sometimes erupt when black youngsters play a name-calling game known as "the Dozens."

No doubt, naming is as important as it is because meaning is such a variable thing. A tornado-ravaged town, after all, is but wind and torment until it is publicly labeled by the appropriate public official as "a Federal Disaster Area." Some executions spawn massive religious movements (e.g., the death of Jesus Christ) or excite political passions (e.g., the Rosenbergs during the 1950s), while other executions are met with mere curiosity (e.g., that of Gary Gillmore, the first person to be executed in recent times). The facts in each of these capital punishment cases were different, of course, but so too was the rhetorical skill of the partisans who labeled the executions.

The naming function of rhetoric helps listeners become comfortable with new ideas and provides listeners with an acceptable vocabulary for talking about these ideas. Through rhetoric, "white flight schools" are transformed into "independent academies," "labor-baiting" becomes the "right-to-work," a "fetus" is seen as an "unborn child," "suicide" is replaced by "death with dignity," and a vague assemblage of disconnected thoughts and random social trends is decried as "secular humanism." A major challenge for the rhetorical critic, then, is to study how namers name things and how audiences respond to the names they hear.

5. *Rhetoric empowers.* Those who decry the art of rhetoric often do so because its users embrace many truths, not just one. Traditionally, teachers of rhetoric have encouraged speakers to consider alternative modes of saying things and not just to utter the first thought that comes to mind. This attitude sometimes brings censure to rhetoric. Those who embrace absolute standards of right and wrong have always had problems with rhetoric because, above all, rhetoric encourages flexibility. Flexibility, in turn, provides options: to address one listener or several; to mention an idea or avoid it; to say something this way and not that way; to tell all one knows or only just a bit; to repeat oneself or to vary one's responses. Rhetoric encourages flexibility because it is based on a kind of symbolic Darwinism: (1) speakers who do not adapt to their surroundings quickly become irrelevant; (2) ideas that become frozen soon die for want of social usefulness.

Such flexibility, in turn, permits continual growth, for the individual as well as for society. Rhetorical theorists contend that there are as many ways of making an idea clear to listeners as there are listeners [Hart and Burks, 1972]. Moreover, because it encourages adaptability, rhetoric permits personal evolution for speakers as well. 1960s conservative Barry Goldwater, 1970s radical Tom Hayden, and 1980s businessman Ross Perot continued to be prominent in the 1990s not because they changed their beliefs fundamentally, but because as they matured they found new *ways* of telling their truths.

Social power, then, often derives from rhetorical strength. Grand ideas, deeply felt beliefs, and unsullied ideologies are sources of power too, but as the philosopher Plato told us, none of these factors can be influential without a delivery system, without rhetoric. Purity of heart and a spotless record for integrity are assets to a political speaker but they are hardly enough to sustain a campaign unless those qualities are *shared* with the voters. As Bryant [1972:23] remarks, if they are to be used with confidence "a bridge or an automobile or a clothes-line must not only *be* strong but must *appear* to be."

6. *Rhetoric elongates.* What does rhetoric make longer? Time. Time, that most precious of all substances, can be extended— or, more accurately, seems to be extended—when rhetoric is put to use. Consider the Reverend Martin Luther King, Jr. When he came on the scene in the 1960s, King no doubt knew that civil rights laws would not be enacted just because he mounted the public platform. *But King succeeded in making the future seem to be the present* because his appeals reached so deeply into people's souls and because his futuristic images were painted so vividly: "I have a dream . . . that one day, right here in Alabama, little black boys and black girls will be able to join hands with little white boys and white girls as sisters and brothers. I have a dream today!" [King, 1964:374].

Naturally, King's speeches did not cause immediate legal and social changes. But for his followers, the devastations of the past commanded less of their attention when they listened to him describe future possibilities. In his presence, listeners lingered in the future and felt better because of it. As Hart [1984a:764] says, rhetoric can become a "way station for the patient."

Most persuaders sell the future when trying to move listeners to a better place, a happier circumstance. Whether it is more robust health through Herbalife, a slimmer figure with Lean Cuisine, or fewer taxes with Bob Dole, rhetoric transports us, momentarily at least, across the boundaries of time. Admittedly, this is a kind of surrogate or false reality. But genuinely effective rhetoric makes such criticisms of literal falseness seem small-minded. When tempted with visions of untold wealth via Amway or a glorious afterlife via Jesus, many people relax their guards.

It is also true that rhetoric can be used to appropriate the *past*. When doing so, of course, skilled persuaders do some historical housecleaning. Thus, as Warner [1976] tells us, most patriotic celebrations in the United States omit from their oratory stories of ethnic or religious persecution. The Fourth of July speaker steers clear of these unquestionable historical facts, because ceremonial rhetoric has its own, upbeat, story to tell. Rhetoric tells a *selective* history, taking us back in time for a brief, heavily edited, tour of history. But as the good eulogist knows, not everything about the dearly departed needs to be told at the funeral. The eulogist reminds us of the deceased's grandest virtues, his or her most endearing qualities, because only the best of the past can make the present seem less tragic. So, while rhetoric often tells literal lies, most of us would have it no other way.

CONCLUSION

In this chapter, we have covered the essentials of rhetoric. We have seen that rhetoric has features not found in other creative arts like painting and music and poetry. Rhetoric's creations are practical creations, and because they are the creations of real people living in the real world, rhetoric is a controversial thing to study. Many people do not like rhetoric, which is to say, they like their own rhetoric best. But human beings have little choice but to use rhetoric if they wish the world to be different than it is. Jonas Salk may have invented a vaccine for polio, but no further vaccines will be discovered at the Salk Institute unless its fund-raising goes well. Neal Armstrong may have set foot on the moon, but he was permitted to do so only because congressional arms were twisted by the space lobby in the United States. Similarly, Americans who enjoy riding on an interstate highway system or watching rock videos should thank the structural and acoustic engineers who made such marvels possible but they should thank, too, the rhetorical engineers whose persuasive appeals generated the funding needed to nurture those inventions.

So rhetoric is with us, for both good and ill. It is with us because most worthwhile ideas come from *groups* of people working in concert. For religions to thrive there must be apostles. For ideas to be understood there must be teachers. For justice to be served there must be lawyers. To turn our backs on rhetoric would be to turn our backs on the sharing of ideas and hence any practical notion of human community. So rhetoric is with us because it must be with us.

But just because rhetoric exists and just because we must use it does not mean that it is easily understood. This book is dedicated to the proposition that rhetoric can and must be understood. The assumption here is that the more lenses available for viewing rhetoric, the greater will be our understanding. Thus, each chapter of this book will dissect persuasive messages. In some chapters, we will use wide-angled lenses to examine such broad features as setting and role and purpose, and in other chapters we will use more refined lenses when viewing argument, form, structure, and language. We will consider what various schools of criticism have to say about persuasion and then look at some of the fascinating things scholars have found about the many forms of rhetoric. But we should do none of that until we have an instrument for doing so. And so we will now examine a microscope suitable for examining rhetorical exchange: the critical perspective.

Chapter 2

THE CRITICAL
PERSPECTIVE

I would be most happy if you would attend a Cabinet luncheon next Tuesday the nineteenth. If you want to bring your press secretary and any other member of your staff I'll be glad to have them. If you can arrive at about twelve fifteen I'll have General Smith and the Central Intelligence Agency give you a complete briefing on the foreign situation. Then we will have luncheon with the Cabinet and after that if you like I'll have my entire staff report to you on the situation in the White House and in that way you will be entirely briefed on what takes place. I've made arrangements with the Central Intelligence Agency to furnish you once a week with the world situation as I also have for Governor Stevenson.
    Harry S. Truman [1952]

This letter was sent to Dwight D. Eisenhower who, when he received it (on August 14, 1952), was the Republican candidate for the U.S. presidency. Mr. Truman's letter bears the stamp of his efficient informality: "If you can arrive at about twelve fifteen," "I've made arrangements," "I'll . . . give you a complete briefing." Also in evidence is his vigor of expression and personal openness: "I'll be glad," "I would be most happy," "if you like I'll have my entire staff. . . ." Although Truman's prose is businesslike, its intent is clear: To put the good of the country above political partisanship by giving the Republican candidate the same information he had provided Democrat Adlai Stevenson somewhat earlier. Informal conversation, a light lunch, a cordial briefing. Who could ask for more? Dwight Eisenhower, for one:

Dear Mr. President:

Thank you for your offer to have me briefed by certain agencies of the Government on the foreign situation. On the personal side I am also grateful for your luncheon invitation.

In my current position as standard bearer of the Republican Party and of other Americans who want to bring about a change in the National Government, it is my duty to remain free to analyze publicly the policies and acts of the present administration whenever it appears to me to be proper and in the country's interests.

During the present period the people are deciding our country's leadership for the next four years. The decision rests between the Republican nominee and the candidate you and your Cabinet are supporting and with whom you conferred before sending your message. In such circumstances and in such a period I believe our communications should be only those which are known to all the American people. Consequently I think it would be unwise and result in confusion in the public mind if I were to attend the meeting in the White House to which you have invited me.

As you know, the problems which you suggest for discussion are those with which I have lived for many years. In spite of this I would instantly change this decision in the event there should arise a grave emergency. There is nothing in your message to indicate that this is presently the case.

With respect to the weekly reports from the Central Intelligence Agency that you kindly offered to send me, I will welcome these reports. In line with my view, however, that the American people are entitled to all the facts in the international situation, save only in those cases where security of the United States is involved, I would want it understood that the possession of these reports will in no other way limit my freedom to discuss or analyze foreign programs as my judgment dictates.

Very respectfully,

Dwight D. Eisenhower [1952]

Dwight Eisenhower as ungrateful wretch? Only a critic can tell for sure. This chapter focuses on the attitudes and skills needed to make sense of human discourse. We will see that there is always more to rhetoric than first meets the eye and that even a pleasant invitation for lunch can, in the hands of a wily politician, turn out to be more than it seems.

But what exactly is Mr. Eisenhower doing here? And why is he so rude? Most likely, he is using the Truman invitation to establish his independence as a presidential candidate and to offset what he sees as Truman's political ploy.

Although Eisenhower is careful to observe the amenities ("on the personal side I am also grateful"), he quickly points out that his role as "standard bearer of the Republican Party" makes special demands on him. Eisenhower seems worried that the act of chatting with an opposite-party incumbent might make it seem as if he, the candidate, were a mere child being summoned to the principal's office. So Eisenhower counterattacks by launching arguments about the Democratic party's failures of leadership and about his own vast experience as a world leader: "The problems which you suggest for discussion are those with which I have lived for many years." Also, by the very form of his letter (much longer than Truman's, less informal, more hortatory), Eisenhower tries to shift the momentum so that he, not Truman, takes the principled stand.

The astute critic will also note Eisenhower's veiled attack on Truman's motives who, Eisenhower implies, is using the letter to cover up his own rank partisanship (i.e., Ike's remarks about the Democratic candidate "with whom you conferred before sending [me] your message"). Ike also hints that the luncheon has been designed as a photo opportunity for *Truman* because there seems to be no real need for the discussion ("I would instantly change this decision in the event there should arise a grave emergency"). Finally, Eisenhower's clever use of language makes Truman seem sneaky and underhanded ("our communications should be only those which are known to all the American people") while Eisenhower himself emerges as open and honest, a man in charge: "I would want it understood that the possession of these reports will in no other way limit my freedom to discuss or analyze foreign programs as my judgment dictates." Rhetoric can be complicated stuff indeed.

Rhetorical criticism is the business of identifying the complications of rhetoric and then explaining them in a comprehensive and efficient manner. This definition implies several things: that rhetorical texts are complicated, that there is an orderly way of describing these complications, and that the best criticism describes them elegantly. So when confronting messages, the critic examines such factors as role, language, arguments, ideas, and medium to reduce the confusion persuaders intentionally or unintentionally create.

Thus, *Modern Rhetorical Criticism* is a guidebook to confusion. The book outlines methods for inspecting persuasive messages in order to see what news about people they might contain. Before considering critical techniques, however, we need to know something of the critical enterprise itself, an enterprise designed to expose the clever rhetoric of clever politicians like Harry Truman and Dwight Eisenhower. This chapter offers just such a perspective on cleverness.

THE PURPOSES OF CRITICISM

In the passage above, Dwight Eisenhower operates as both a persuader and a critic. As a critic, he dissects Harry Truman's message with care and, as a persuader, he slyly accuses Truman of using the luncheon to salve his own guilty conscience. Eisenhower portrays Truman's politeness as political manipulation

and refuses to become part of the President's elaborately staged demonstration of statesmanship. When responding as he did, Ike did what all good critics do: He examined rhetorical texts to account for *all* of their important
meanings, not just those the persuader featured.

Naturally, another critic might argue that it was Eisenhower who acted
ingenuously when transforming Truman's gracious luncheon invitation into
something sordid. In either case, the critic would be doing what all good rhetorical critics do: building an argument about social conditions by observing what
people say. Naturally, only a community of informed persons could judge
whether Eisenhower was the rhetorical criminal or the rhetorical victim here.
This community, the community of critics, would listen to the contrasting arguments, examine the evidence each offered, and then render its judgment. So that
is what rhetorical critics do. But why do they do it? There are several reasons:

1. Rhetorical criticism documents social trends. Rosenfield [1972:133]
sees the critic as a special sort of sports analyst who takes part in the swirl of life
but who also has perspective on it. Rosenfield distinguishes between the fan
who enjoys the game of persuasion and the expert commentator who both
appreciates and comments knowingly on it. Criticism therefore requires special discernment: the ability to stand simultaneously in the midst of and apart
from the events experienced. Like the sports commentator, the critic provides
an instant replay of the event, pointing out features that the too-involved fan
was unable to see because of the immediacy and excitement of the event itself.
The critic re-views the scene of the action, calling attention to features of persuasion that the listener saw but did not notice.

The good critic magnifies without distorting, focusing on rhetorical characteristics that, while humble, may nevertheless be important. Thus, for example, Hart [1978] noticed that the pamphlets issued by radical atheists were
raggedly produced, containing grammatical faults, typographical errors, and
even missing words. The following is an example of such rhetoric:

> By hypnotic methods, by imposing fear of God or devil, beliefs contrary to sci-
> ence, common sense are implanted into the subconscious minds of the children,
> and then by massive propaganda, which saturates the TV, the press, often schools
> and libraries, the victims are brain stuffed into accepting religion, on 'faith,' which
> is attempting to believe things which cannot be proven, and are contrary to com-
> mon sense, intelligence and reason.
> [Johnson: n.d.]

Although seemingly insignificant, such run-on sentences led Hart to conclude
that a hurried, telegraphic rhetoric is well suited to a group that has to make a
quick impression on its hard-to-get readers. He went on to describe the philosophical worldview of the atheists, citing in each case the minor-but-important
features of the garbled style he noticed.

The good critic notices verbal trends, features that are too regularized to
be accidental and too suggestive to be unimportant. According to Farrell
[1980], the critic thereby treats messages as symptoms of some larger social

fact. The critic says: "I see a bit of 'X' here and am willing to bet that there is more 'X' to be found in society at large." So, for example, Leathers [1973] has shown that Radical Right persuaders often use the *nonexistence* of facts as proof of their existence (i.e., "you can't see It because 'they' won't let you, which only proves that It is there in massive quantities"). Leathers worries about the rhetoric he describes, fearing that such shoddy reasoning will become attractive to people who cannot or will not listen carefully to what they hear. Thus, the critic acts as society's vanguard, spotting in today's rhetoric the smoke that becomes tomorrow's fires.

As Brockriede [1974] has said, all rhetorical critics are arguers. Feminists argue that articles in popular magazines demean women. Physicians argue that beer commercials glorify alcoholism. Social activists argue that ethnic stereotypes in situation comedies undermine minorities. In each case, a critic is arguing that *regularized* features of rhetoric have become dangerous to society. In other circumstances, it is the absence of regularity that causes alarm: Appeals to national unity drop off in political campaigns and letters to the editor become self-centered rather than community-centered. Combining these perceptions, the critic might posit the rise of a new narcissism and then speculate about its consequences for society at large. In short, the critic's job is discover trends and then see where they lead.

2. *Rhetorical criticism provides general understandings via the case-study method.* By scrutinizing a small number of texts, the critic restricts the range of available insights. Even if a thousand televangelized sermons were collected for study, the critic would still be examining messages rooted in a peculiar political circumstance, in a specialized medium, and in a unique cultural backdrop. Even with such a large sample, the critic would still only have a sample, a mere whisper of history's religious utterances. Because the critic's focus is tight, the critic's challenge is to tell the largest story possible given the necessarily limited evidence available.

So the critic is a sampler, and samplers must be both modest and cautious and modesty and caution are not altogether bad. But modesty and caution do not ensure unimportance. What the critic gives up in *scope* is offset by the *power* of insight made available. What ensures this power? Choosing a provocative text for study, asking important questions of that text, and drawing intriguing conclusions. The critic is indeed a sampler, but that which is sampled—human discourse—is hardly trivial since people imbed in their talk some of their most complicated motivations. It is the critic's job to sort through these embeddings, finding evidence of the universal in the particular and yet, as Leff [1992] cautions, also respecting the integrity and particularity of each message/event.

The critic therefore operates like the anthropologist who sometimes finds in the smallest ritual the most complete depiction of tribal history and culture. The good critic never studies a particular text simply because it exists but because it promises to tell a story larger than itself. This means that no message is too modest for careful inspection. If ego-defense is in fact a powerful human motivation, both the advertisements on match covers and the character-sketches in the modern novel should bear witness to it. If human brutality is indeed on the rise, it might as well be evidenced in the interviewing styles of late-night radio commentators as in the rhetoric of the Ku Klux Klan. If gender animosity is in fact a universal feature of human history, it should be discoverable in the scripts of both soap operas and grand operas.

Like all research activities, criticism requires that one (a) *isolate* a phenomenon for special study (e.g.,the rhetoric of U.S. space exploration), (b) *describe* special aspects of that phenomenon (e.g., that rhetoric's heavy reliance on metaphors), (c) *classify* features of that phenomenon (e.g., its dependence on frontier metaphors vs. temporal metaphors), (d) *interpret* the patterns noticed (e.g.,"the American people are still not capable of thinking in terms of fixed borders"), and (e) *evaluate* the phenomenon (e.g., "Will the U.S. become extraterrestrial imperialists?"). These five intellectual skills are, of course, central to all forms of disciplined inquiry but they constrain the critic in particular ways, as we will see throughout this book.

3. *Rhetorical criticism produces meta-knowledge* (that is, explicit understanding of implicit realizations). There are many similarities between literary criticism and rhetorical criticism. Both require acuteness of perception, both demand textual exploration, and both expose human wants and desires as expressed in language. But there is also a major difference: While few of us speak poetry day to day, all of us, as Molière reminded us, speak prose. We are, all of us, persuaders of a sort, even if our rhetorical successes are normally modest. Because this is so, rhetorical criticism is criticism of life itself, of our own participation in the experience of living.

And because this is so, everyone is capable of doing rhetorical criticism without ever reading *Modern Rhetorical Criticism*. By having lived and talked for several decades or more, all of us have done the homework necessary to do criticism. Consider, for example, the following rather ordinary message:

> COM 390R. *Seminar in Contemporary Rhetorical Criticism*. May be repeated for credit when topics vary. Semester topics have included dramatistic criticism, content analysis, and methodologies for movement studies. Prerequisite: Upper-division standing.

What sort of message do we have here? Without question, a course description from a college catalog. But how do we know such a thing? How is it possible for a reader who has never opened the course catalog of the University of Texas at Austin to make such a perception? And why do we have such *confidence* in that perception? Why could we not possibly mistake this message for a chili recipe or a love letter or the lyrics to a rock song or the preamble to the Constitution or a page from Fodor's latest guide to Austria? Wherein lies the "implicit knowledge" necessary to identify this textual fragment? If we know this much about rhetoric, what else do we know that we don't know we know? And how do we know such things?

Last question first. We know such things because we are members of life's audience. We know it because each day, without effort or conscious attention, we are voracious consumers of messages. Each day, from dawn to dusk, we swim in a sea of rhetoric: commercials for underarm deodorants, letters from loved ones, newspaper editorials, political oratory, *People* magazine. Each year, from January to December, we process, discard, and reprocess a virtual blizzard of discourse. Each lifetime, from birth to death, we add to our extraordinary catalog of messages, constantly increasing the complexity and subtlety of our rhetorical knowledge. There is not a course description alive that could escape our detection.

Alas, the knowledge just described, while useful, is normally inert. While most people can identify messages accurately enough, few are able to explain *how we know what we know*. Few people pay attention to the details of their rhetorical experience. On reflection, however, on the doing of criticism, almost everyone can do so. For example, the form of our course description is revealing: no complete sentences, abnormal punctuation patterns, and inconsistent italicizing, all of which suggest a hurried, businesslike tone, a message totally uninterested in wooing its reader. In addition, its reasoning patterns are telegraphic. Concepts like "seminar," "credit" and "prerequisite" are never explained, creating a heavy demand on the reader to supply the ideas necessary to make logical sense of the message. The language is also formidable: excessive use of jargon, polysyllabic words, and opaque phrases (e.g., COM 390R).

Also revealing is what is not found in the text. Nobody runs or jumps or feels here. No *doing* is being done. This absence of verbs suggests institutionalization, hardly what one would expect from what is essentially a piece of advertising. But this is a special sort of advertising, advertising without adjectives. The topics mentioned are not "new and improved" topics, just topics; the movement studies are not "innovative and exciting," just plain vanilla. And much else is missing. There are no extended examples to help the reader see what the course will be like, no powerful imagery to sustain the student's visions of wonder while standing in the registration line, no personal disclosure by the author to build identification with the reader. It is almost as if this message did not care about its reader or, for that matter, even care about itself. It does nothing to invite or entice or intrigue. It does not unburden itself.

There is one thing that almost all college students know about such course descriptions: They cannot be "trusted." Students know that they are written by groups of people and therefore do not bear the marks of the instructor's personality. Students know that such descriptions are processed by a complex bureaucracy that impresses its rigidities onto them. Students know that they must sample the rhetoric of their peers and the rhetoric of the professor who will teach the course before signing up. These latter rhetorics, students reason, will have the color, detail, and humanity central to proper decision-making. And so course descriptions dutifully sit in college catalogs: unread, unrespected, unloved. A hard life.

Frequently, then, criticism reminds us of what we already know about the world. It asks us to compare each new message to the data bank of messages already accumulated over a lifetime of reading and listening. Criticism asks us to make our implicit knowledge explicit since only explicit knowledge can be used in practical ways. So rhetorical criticism is quite ecological: It invites us to become more active in retaining each day's messages so that they can later be recycled for use in understanding new messages.

4. *Rhetorical criticism invites radical confrontation with Otherness.* Perhaps this phrasing is a bit melodramatic, but criticism is a wonderful way to get outside of oneself. Naturally, most of us resist leaving our own perfect worlds to enter the strange, dark habitats of others. Our worlds are orderly, theirs chaotic; ours enlightened, theirs bizarre. But we also have wanderlust, a curiosity about the not-us, which is why vacationing in strange lands is such a prized experience. Rhetorical criticism can also be a kind of vacationing, a way of visiting the not-us by examining what they have to say. As with all vacationing, though, criticism requires preparation—attitudinal preparation. We must remember that all persons have reasons for doing what they do even if their reasons are not our reasons and that we cannot understand others unless we are willing to leave our own tastes, experiences, and prejudices at home. And if we are unable to leave them at home, we should at least store them in a seldom used suitcase when exploring.

This is not a moral injunction (criticize others as you would have them criticize you). It is an intellectual injunction, which says that one cannot *understand* others unless one appreciates how they reason and behave. But this injunction is not easy to follow. Consider, for example, the following streetcorner materials distributed each day in each city of the United States:

- *Jesus and Mary Speak to the World through Veronica Luken*
    (Our Lady of Roses Shrine, Bayside, New York)
- *Active Involvement for a Better America*
    (United States Jaycees)
- *Heard any Good Fag Jokes Lately?*
    (National Gay Task Force)
- *Marijuana in America: The Facts*
    (National Organization for the Reform of Marijuana Laws)
- *How to Strengthen Your Motivation to Succeed*
    (Weight Watchers International)
- *Fight Forced Busing*
    (National Socialist White People's Party)
- *Smoking in Public: Let's Separate Fact from Friction*
    (R. J. Reynolds Tobacco Co.)
- *Dear Recreational Vehicle Owner*
    (The Good Sam Club)

Many people's first response to this smorgasbord of texts is: "Only in America!" From the standpoint of criticism, this is actually a healthy response. At least initially, the good critic examines all rhetoric in a spirit of wonder rather than one of censure: What do R.V. owners have to say to one another? How does a tobacco company conceal its self-interest in a public service announcement? What do Weight Watchers know about motivation that I do not? And who, pray tell, is Veronica Luken?

Questions like these pull us into rhetoric and thereby pull us toward people, people who experience the world in special ways. If done well, criticism forces us outside the comfort and familiarity of how we think and feel. It asks, for example, why racists are racists. What experiences have made them so different? Why are they so afraid of integration? What *really* threatens them? Bus-riding? Black skin? Inferior education? Perhaps. But could it also be Rapid Change or Technological Advancement or Social Mobility or Mass Anomie or perhaps just Life-in-general? All of these are possibilities, and only careful, critical inspection of *Fight Forced Busing* could help us sort through them.

Because the rhetorical critic examines messages meant for other people at other times, it is hard to do criticism and remain provincial. Rhetoric bring us face-to-face with otherness. Thus, when examining texts the critic is almost always an intruder, an uninvited guest. The good critic remembers this and offers explanations of rhetoric as it was constituted, not as he or she would have had it constituted. The critic operates in this fashion not because it is nicer to do so but because it is smarter.

It is often not easy to be a good guest at someone else's party. Critics are people too, after all, who often feel strongly about the public matters they study. So it is useful to remember certain ground rules when doing criticism, ground rules that foster an enlightened sense of otherness:

(a) *All public messages make sense to someone.* Because rhetoric is a people's art, it is sometimes easy to feel superior to it. Despite their noxious appeals, however, someone must like the collection of once-athletic men shown congregating in bars during beer advertisements. Someone must appreciate their swagger and bravado. Someone must be able to love them despite their mangled grammar and soft-core sexism. It is the critic's job to presume such attractiveness and to discover why such commercials are attractive to TV audiences.

(b) *All criticism is autobiography.* This is George Bernard Shaw's famous phrase and it is as true today as it was at the turn of the century. Try as hard as they might, critics can never be completely objective about rhetoric. Nor should they be. But they should at least be *conscious of their subjectivity*, aware of the biases they bring to the critical task and willing to explain those biases when sharing their observations with others.

(c) *Description before evaluation.* The critical instinct—I like it/I hate it—is a powerful instinct. It rears up in us each moment of each day. But to make sense of something that is radically other, the critic must first get the lay of the land. Thus, the ultimate challenge is to explain rhetoric with which we disagree or to find flaws in rhetoric to which we are instinctively attracted. The good critic therefore tries to appropriate the psychology of the *natural* audience before asking: What does this message do for me?

(d) The good critic cannot be timid. Nothstine, Blair, and Copeland [1994] remind us that, because rhetoric is so powerful, the good critic cannot shrink from judgment. Each day, powerful individuals use rhetoric to feather their nests, to deny others their rights, to impoverish them. There are, to be sure, countervailing rhetorics but it takes a critic to know one from the other. Gaining such knowledge transforms criticism from an intellectual game to an engaged lifestyle and the student of rhetoric into a footsoldier in an age-old political battle. To engage in this battle, we must be able to think like the enemy.

Although these attitudes cannot solve all critical problems, they can be helpful guidelines. Rhetorical criticism puts us in direct touch with humanness because it examines what humans do most artfully—write—and most instinctively—talk. The critic of rhetoric therefore stands in a privileged place.

THE QUALITIES OF CRITICISM

Not all critics are born equal. There is no Declaration of Critical Independence to ensure that each critic will be perceptive. Even when examining a rich and suggestive piece of rhetoric, some people fail to appreciate its nuances. The gifted critic, on the other hand, can build a provocative story out of the humblest message. So, for example, Philipsen [1975] sat and listened each day to blue-collar youths in South Chicago, eventually using cues in their everyday talk to build a fascinating tale of what manhood meant, and did not mean, in such a community. To be sure, the rhetoric Philipsen examined was quite ordinary, so he had to be especially creative to find the truths hidden in its informality. But perceptiveness and creativity are not completely inherited. They can be nurtured. It is possible to become more perceptive as critics if we (1) adopt a useful set of critical attitudes and (2) ask the right sorts of questions when inspecting rhetoric. Each chapter in this book will suggest some of these questions but it is our job here to examine the characteristics of the ideal critic.

1. The good critic is skeptical. There is no other way to say it: The good critic does not take life at face value. Skeptics treat life on their terms, not on life's terms, and most assuredly, not on the persuader's terms. The good critic is one who stands back and watches, who will not be drawn into the pyrotechnics of rhetoric until fundamental questions about the speaker's motives have been resolved. Skepticism, however, need not lead to cynicism. The skeptic is one who insists on taking a second look at everything simply because there is always more to a story than first meets the eye. The cynic, on the other hand, is a skeptic gone sour, one who refuses to take even a first look because of past disappointments.

Two key presuppositions of the skeptic are that all rhetoric denies itself and that good rhetoric denies itself completely. There are, of course, a few forthright persuaders to be found—the used car dealer, the politician, the streetcorner evangelist—who tacitly admit to their status as persuaders. But even here there is legerdemain. The used-car dealer agrees to take less for the automobile because he "was young once too and remembers his first car." The politician is never the crass solicitor but one biding her time until canonization when her "dream for the nation becomes a reality for all people." And the evangelist is never motivated by personal ego when buttonholing passersby but is "compelled from afar to do the work of the Lord." These people do not wish to be seen only as persuaders; they wish to be seen as something more exalted in addition.

Still others deny the rhetorical function entirely. Lessl [1985] tells us that astronomer Carl Sagan wraps himself in the mantle of both poet and priest in order to "teach" his viewers about the value of space exploration. McMillan [1983] tells us that corporate managers weave politically tinged values into their "explanations" of company policy. Adams [1986] tells us that newscasters look to a geographical region's popularity with American tourists before deciding which natural disasters to "report." In each case, these teachers, managers, and reporters-turned-persuaders have sought to have direct, but unacknowledged, influence. They also tried to escape critical detection by holding up signs emblazoned with the statement "No persuasion here. Look elsewhere for objects of criticism." The good critic does not look elsewhere. The good critic does not even blink.

As Fisher [1989] and others explain, persuaders often use narratives to throw the critic off the persuasive scent. Story-telling, as Ronald Reagan well understood, signals a time-out: "Listen to this story as a story. You need not worry about argumentative propositions being advanced here." Most of us relax in the presence of narratives. Thus a "mere" story, *Uncle Tom's Cabin*, became one of the most potent pieces of civil rights rhetoric the United States has known. And thus business executives sell stock options during cocktail parties, those "time-out" events that advance rhetoric by denying its possibility. In some senses, then, the nonpersuader is the best persuader and the non-appeal the ultimate appeal.

2. *The good critic is discerning.* One need not be a genius to be discerning. Sherlock Holmes was not brilliant, but he was discerning. He knew when to pay attention (when others were not around), how to pay attention (by looking to the left when others looked to the right), and where to pay attention (by looking in the scullery kitchen rather than in the public parts of the mansion). Holmes' eyes took in no more information than did those of the local constable. But unlike the local constable, Holmes had better categories for sorting and storing the information he collected. Both noticed the brown shoes on the body of the deceased but Holmes also noticed the absence of scuff marks.

Holmes did so because he had a theory of scuff marks. To the constable, shoes were shoes, but to Holmes the way people scuffed their shoes was a function of the purposiveness of their walk, which was a function of their lifestyle, which in turn was a function of their social habits and, ultimately, their mental habits. And that is why a man wearing unscuffed shoes would never have died a natural death while roaming through the moors. *That* sort of person detests moors.

Like Holmes, the good critic is hard to distract. Concentration is a precious gift for a critic since persuaders try so hard to divert their audiences' attention. As a result, the good critic pays attention to textual details that most audiences ignore. Thus, by simply noticing the raw frequency of certain word choices, Hart [1986b] concluded that Ronald Reagan's first inaugural address was more ideological than was normal for a ceremony, a kind of rhetorical hangover from a very ideological campaign. Of course, Ronald Reagan himself did not assume that his choice of individual words would be of much interest to his listeners. He no doubt presumed that his lectern-thumping would be muffled by the colorful metaphors he used and by the pleasant stories he told. That is why, when examining the Reagan speech, it proved useful to look elsewhere.

Most good critics look elsewhere. To understand the routines of social power in the United States, for example, Whittenberger-Keith [1989] inspected neither economic charts nor voting patterns but manners books. To determine the extent of contemporary racism, Rainville and McCormick [1977] looked not at open-housing laws but at the descriptions of black and white athletes provided by sports' commentators. In both cases, the critics assumed that: (1) All texts are filled with data, even if some of these data seem irrelevant at first blush; (2) what is *not* present in a message is often more important than what is present; and (3) how an idea is phrased may sometimes be less important than the fact that the idea is mentioned at all. The good critic therefore asks questions of texts that audiences and poor critics rarely ask. But discernment should not be confused with eccentricity. Few critics ask how often the letter "E" is used in a passage because nobody has yet generated a *good reason* for doing so. Rather, the good critic has a sense for significance, a sense that matures as more and more discourse is examined. This was Sherlock Holmes's kind of sense.

3. *The good critic is imaginative.* Almost anyone can gather facts about a message. But it takes a good critic to know what to do with them. For example, most people have seen the late night public service announcements urging safe driving. Murray Edelman [1977] had observed them, too. But because he was both skeptical and discerning, as well as imaginative, Edelman thought harder than most people about this ostensibly innocent rhetoric. Although controversial, his conclusion about the safe-driving advertisements is provocative: Such campaigns place responsibility for highway safety completely on the driver and therefore deflect attention from a major source of highway carnage—automobile manufacturers. Not only did Edelman see rhetoric where there appeared to be none, and not only was he able to zero in

on just the right features of the texts he analyzed, but he was also able to link his observations to a larger story about how entrenched economic interests use persuasion to maintain positions of privilege.

One need not be a leftist to appreciate how Edelman operated here. The larger story he told—his theory—gave an enriched purpose to his inquiries. He did not investigate public service advertisements because he enjoyed them (who does?) but because when watching them late one night he was struck with a *general idea* about how political pressure operates in the United States. Naturally, this one analysis by Edelman could not establish some grand new law of political influence, but his case study did raise several general questions that he, and others, could try to answer by collecting more evidence. But it was the imaginative leap from data to theory that made Edelman's observation such an important one.

A message is worth analyzing if it tells a story larger than itself. This means that the good critic always has a rationale for examining a text. These rationales take many forms: (1) the study may be worth doing because the speaker has dealt with a **classic dilemma** (e.g., How can a president apologize for backing misguided legislation without losing his authority?); (2) the speaker may have dealt imaginatively with **unresolved tensions** (e.g., How can a president appeal to the farmers without losing the urban vote?); (3) the speaker may have addressed **projected problems** (e.g., How can a president make the nation comfortable with life in a financially uncertain world?); (4) the speaker's situation may be a **parallel instance** of a continuing one (e.g., How did early presidents change citizens' health habits?) or (5) the speaker may have been the first to confront some **unique circumstance** (e.g., What persuasive tools can a president use during an impeachment trial?).

There are, of course, countless such good reasons for doing rhetorical criticism. Notice that in all of the above instances, however, the critic has addressed issues of universal interest. Concern for the larger story, therefore, should animate each piece of criticism written. This same principle suggests several guidelines for developing a critical rationale:

(a) No message is inherently worthy of study. Just because a given text fascinates the critic does not mean that studying it will be worthwhile. Often, criticism becomes eccentric and too specialized because the critic fails to develop a clear reason for doing criticism. This produces scholarship-by-whim. Thus, when picking a text, the critic should be asking: *Why* does this message intrigue me? "Just because" is not a sufficient answer.

(b) The past speaks to us constantly. Examining the rhetoric of the past, even the rhetoric of the distant past, can be quite useful because it gives us perspective on the lives we live today. Naturally, as Wichelns [1972:43] reminds us, all rhetoric is "rooted in immediacy" and we therefore must be careful not to distort the past in a headlong rush to find within it contemporary relevance. But people are people. And cultures are cultures. And rhetoric is rhetoric. The past has much to teach us if we but open our ears to its voices.

(c) People who are larger than life may not be life-like. "Tabloid scholarship" [Hart, 1986a:293] presumes that persuasion by "great" persons will be especially worthy of study. This is a poor assumption. It is easy to become distracted by high-profile speakers like presidents and popes, people who often say interesting things but who are far removed from the lives most people lead. The good critic remembers that the messages of ordinary people are often highly suggestive because they better represent how persuasion functions in general.

(d) Imitation is not the sincerest form of flattery. All too often, critics fail to go far enough in their analysis because they merely "translate" a message rather than explain it. This is especially true for the beginning critic, who is tempted to latch on to an existing critical system and then superimpose it on an innocent piece of rhetoric. The result is criticism that succeeds only in finding new examples of old persuasive strategies.

No set of guidelines will ensure brilliant criticism. But the guidelines above will ensure that we ask *why* criticism is being done in the first place. Skepticism and discernment are central to good criticism, but unless the critic makes an imaginative leap from text to idea, criticism becomes wasted time and wasted paper. Persuasion is too interesting and criticism too productive to be overturned by unasked and unanswered whys.

THE STANDARDS OF CRITICISM

Evaluation seems to leap out of a word like criticism. Most people in daily life are "critics" in this sense when they complain about the local transit system or the tardiness of mail delivery. Normally, however, these everyday evaluations are not reflective. Few people are willing actually to visit the offices of the transit company, do a time-and-motion study of its operations, interview its personnel, pore over maps of urban geography, calculate the economies of scale produced by different routings, and then do the massive data synthesis necessary to determine if there is, in fact, sufficient reason to be perturbed by the late bus at the corner of Maple and First. So it is important to distinguish between general complaining and *reflective complaining,* better known as criticism. Equally, it is important to distinguish between gushing compliments and *reflective compliments,* which are also criticism. The judicious critic is therefore one who knows when and how to render an evaluation.

Most faulty critical statements result from premature evaluation, from judging the goodness or badness of a rhetorical message before having carefully inspected its pieces and parts, before having collected data sufficient to sustain the critical judgment. Another type of faulty evaluation occurs when the critic fails to explicate the standards used in the evaluation. We react differently to a critic who says "My mother is a terrific cook because she only buys food in yellow containers" than we do to one who argues "My mother is a good cook because she prepares tasty foods low in cholesterol." The first critic seems to be using absurd standards for judgment while the second seems more reasonable—reasonable, that is, in the eyes of other, reasonable people. In this connection, Black [1978:7] makes the critic's obligations clear:

> The person who hears a speech and says, "I like it," is not making a critical statement. He is reporting the state of his glands; he is speaking autobiographically. If we happen to like the person or if we are curious about the state of his glands, we may be interested in his report. Certainly his psychoanalyst would be interested in it. But neither the analyst nor we should confuse the statement with criticism. It is not criticism because, although it may be stimulated by an object, it is not *about* an object; it is a statement about the speaker's own feelings, and nothing more.

Rhetorical critics have used a variety of critical standards to evaluate the rhetoric they have studied. In addition to being plentiful, argue Rybacki and Rybacki [1991:9], the available standards for criticism change from age to age as well. Although we shall not detail these standards here, it is interesting to note their variety, any one of which can be used intelligently or foolishly. The judicious critic is one who knows which standard is being used and, most important, why. And the exceptionally judicious critic is one who gives fair attention to the many alternative standards by which persuasion may be evaluated, some of which are:

1. *The Utilitarian Standard:* Given the limitations of the situation, did the message do what it was intended to do? Did people react as the speaker hoped? Compared to other speakers on this topic in situations like this, did this speaker do as well as could be expected?

2. *The Artistic Standard:* Was the use of language exceptional? Did the message meet the highest standards of beauty and well-formedness? Did it so stimulate the imagination that it brought new ideas to life?

3. *The Moral Standard:* Did the message advance "the good" and encourage public virtue? Was there sufficient moral instruction by the speaker so that listeners were moved toward worthy, not just convenient, goals? Did it meet acceptable standards of right and wrong?

4. *The Scientific Standard:* Did the message accurately represent reality? Did the speaker's arguments have a factual base, and did conclusions follow directly from the evidence presented? Could the claims in the message be independently verified?

5. *The Historical Standard:* Was there anything in the message for "the ages"? Is it likely that the ideas presented and the values endorsed will outlast the speaker? Did the message set processes in motion that resulted in major social changes?

6. *The Psychological Standard:* Did the message purge the emotions of the speaker? The audience? Did the text calm important fears and anxieties? Were people so motivated by the message that social energy and personal commitments were renewed?

7. *The Political Standard:* Did the message advance the goals of the social groups the critic endorses? Will the "right" sort of people be advantaged

because of it? Will any harm be done to the most deserving people in society because this message was created?

Two things should be clear about this list of standards. First, it is no doubt incomplete—each critic can, and should, freely supplement the list. Whichever standard is chosen, the critic still has the obligation of defending the appropriateness of the choice made. A second important point is that messages that meet one standard may fail miserably in light of another. So, for example, a speech at a Billy Graham Crusade may succeed in increasing donations to the church (the Utilitarian standard) and, because its description of the afterlife is so masterful (the Artistic standard), the congregation's guilt over their indulgent lifestyles may be removed (the Psychological standard).

On the other hand, in describing sin the Reverend Graham may have grossly distorted the extent of the national drug problem (the Scientific standard) by making it seem as if it were only a problem for minority groups (the Political standard), thereby making it unlikely that anyone in the future would have much respect for the remarks he made (the Historical standard). Clearly, one must operate thoughtfully when choosing critical standards as well as when deploying them. Rarely do we have trouble deciding whether we like a thing or dislike it. Explaining why we feel this way takes something else. It takes a judicious critic.

CONCLUSION

Criticism can be complicated but it can also be highly rewarding. To look carefully at what people say and how they say it is to take the human enterprise seriously. People indeed are complex but they are also fascinating. One of the most fascinating things about them is their rhetorical natures. Communication is an attempt to build community by exchanging symbols. Since the building of community is what most makes people people, listening to what they have to say is to pay them the ultimate compliment. This is true even if we, as critics, sometimes listen more carefully than is normally expected—or desired. And in paying this much attention to what people say, we also pay attention to ourselves, which makes criticism the ultimate self-compliment as well.

There is nothing magical about good criticism. Good criticism is the art of developing and then using critical probes, which are nothing more than intelligent and specific questions to be asked of a given text. Dozens of these critical probes are distributed throughout this book. By using them in criticism, the critic cannot help but become more discerning. Also, because the subject matter here is rhetoric, this book no doubt will add to the reader's supply of skepticism. And because the work of professional critics will be examined throughout, the reader will be presented with many examples of judiciousness. But the imagination necessary for productive criticism will have to derive from another source, from inside critics themselves. Let us hope that imagination abounds for all who would be critics.

Chapter 3

ANALYZING SITUATIONS

["I wish I could sing!"] I speak to you as an American Jew. As Americans we share the profound concern of millions of people about the shame and disgrace of inequality and injustice which make a mockery of the great American idea. As Jews we bring to [this] great demonstration, in which thousands of us proudly participate, a two-fold experience—one of the spirit and one of our history.

In the realm of the spirit, our fathers taught us thousands of years ago that when God created man, he created him as everybody's neighbor. "Neighbor" is not a geographic term; it is a moral concept. It means our collective responsibility for the preservation of man's dignity and integrity.

From our Jewish historic experience of three and a half thousand years we say: Our ancient history began with slavery and the yearning for freedom. During the Middle Ages my people lived for a thousand years in the ghettos of Europe. Our modern history begins with a proclamation of emancipation.

It is for these reasons that it is not merely sympathy and compassion for the black people of America that motivates us. It is above all and beyond all such sympathies and emotions a sense of complete identification and solidarity born of our own historic experience.

[Friends], When I was . . . [in] . . . the Jewish community in Berlin under the Hitler regime, I learned many things. The most important thing that I learned in my life, and under those tragic circumstances, is that bigotry and hatred are not the most urgent problem. The most urgent, the most disgraceful, the most shameful, and the most tragic problem is *silence*. A great people which had created a great civilization had become a nation of silent onlookers. They remained silent in the face of hate, in the face of brutality, and in the face of mass murder.

America must not become a nation of onlookers. America must not remain silent—not merely black America, but all of America. It must speak up and act from the President down to the humblest of us, and not for the sake of the Negro, not for the sake of the black community, but for the sake of the image, [the dream], the idea, and the aspiration of America itself.

Our children, yours and mine, in every school across the land, every morning pledge allegiance to the flag of the United States and to the Republic for which it stands, and then they, the children, speak fervently and innocently of this land as the land of "liberty and justice for all."

The time, I believe, has come for us to work together, for it is not enough to hope together—for it is not enough to pray together—to work together, that this children's oath—pronounced every morning from Maine to California, from North and South—that this oath will become a glorious, unshakable reality in a morally renewed and united America. [Thank you.]

This chapter begins with a question: Who gave this speech? Here are several more: Can we be sure that this was, in fact, a speech and not an essay? If a speech, when was it given? Where? Under what social and psychological circumstances? What of the audience? Were they wealthy, middle class, or poor? Were they Jewish like the speaker, or were they religiously and ethnically diverse? How did they feel about the topic? Sympathetic or hostile? Excited or bored? What about the speaker? Male or female? Educated or noneducated? Of high status or low status? Young, middle-aged, or elderly? What was the speaker's occupation?

Such questions may seem bizarre. Few people, after all, must deal with mystery messages. Most texts come prepackaged, replete with the information needed to make sense out of them. Most messages are understandable because we confront them in their natural habitats: in a particular place, at a particular time. Besides, if we ever did happen upon a mystery message, surely there are reference books available to provide any information needed.

This chapter will presume that no such reference book exists. It will also presume that most persuasive messages contain information that normally slips past the unperceptive observer but still influences that observer. We will see here that every message contains "genetic markers" that reveal much about its parentage—where it came from and why. We will discover that since each persuasive message is produced in a unique rhetorical situation, thereby constituting a unique speech-act, *the situation itself can make a statement apart from the statements contained in the words of the message.*

In a sense, all criticism is a kind of guessing game, with the critic trying to shed light on the rhetorical shadows of a text. By inspecting a message carefully the critic turns presumed knowledge into tested knowledge. So, for example, how do we know that the speech above is, in fact, a speech? The clues are several. For instance, it would be presumptuous for a writer to pen the first sentence in the first paragraph since these remarks seem part of a *continuing* dialogue with somebody the speaker never identifies. While writers sometimes start in the middle of things, they rarely leave their readers without background clues for long, certainly not forever. But a speaker talking to a live audience could make such a reference if they had just shared some sort of musical experience, which seems to be the case here.

Also, the language in the message does not seem quite smooth enough for written composition. The sentences are often short—simple, declarative—and they contain few of the embedded clauses common to essay- or textbook-writing. There is also much direct address here ("we share," "our fathers taught us"), a feature often found in personal correspondence. But there is also much *formal* direct address here ("Friends . . .") that would be off-putting if found, say, in a loved one's postcard from Tahiti. The words in the passage are common ones, so the message could be a popular editorial, but the speaker ends by thanking the audience for their attention, something that writers never do. After all, while a writer can presume that time is being freely provided by readers (who can pick up or put down the printed matter at their leisure), the speaker is always aware that attention is a gift that busy and easily bored listeners give to speakers. And so we have a speech.

A contemporary speech? Possibly, although one gets very little flavor of today's hard-nosed pragmatism and P.A.C.-controlled politics here. There is no talk of funding possibilities, enactable legislation, or factual precedent. Rather, the speech seems to be a *beginning* ("The time . . . has come"). We hear of plans being made, not of victories being savored. Moreover, the speaker attempts to turn his individual listeners into some sort of collective ("our children, yours and mine"), as if he could not presume that they already shared the same priorities.

What else do we have? We have singing, Jews, Blacks, collective responsibility, repudiation of silence, pledges of allegiance from North to South, a post-World War II time-frame, and, most pregnantly, the Emancipation Proclamation. This is also a short speech, perhaps one of many given that day. Moreover, either the speaker is rudely ignoring local personalities and local conditions or is reaching out to a *national* constituency ("from Maine to California"). All in all, this sounds like the language of the 1960s, an era in which even political rhetoric sounded religious and in which a term like "great demonstration" had an ideological rather than a mercantile meaning. This sounds like the era of the gospel-singing Mahalia Jackson, who preceded our speaker, and of Martin Luther King, Jr., who spoke just after our speaker. The place: Washington, D.C. The scene: the Lincoln Memorial. The audience: some 200,000 civil rights marchers. The date: August 28, 1963.

And our speaker? What does the message/situation tell us? A male, no doubt, for few women addressed such large crowds in the United States in 1963. The mere *act* of speaking at a massive demonstration like this was an outward sign of power, and the roots of sexism held fast in 1963, even within the then-forming civil rights establishment. The language, too, is full of male forcefulness (e.g., when the speaker sets his own scene: "I speak to you as an

American Jew"). Also, the gentle paternalism (" 'Neighbor' is not a geographic term; it is a moral concept.") and historic persona ("During the Middle Ages, my people . . .") clearly suggest the thoughts of an older speaker (or a self-important younger one). Finally, even though the phrase "a rabbi" was removed in the first line of the fifth paragraph, the speaker himself signals his occupation with his scholarly distinctions ("not for the sake of the black community, but for the sake of . . ."), his spiritual exhortations ("a glorious, unshakable reality in a morally united America"), and his sermonic style ("in the face of hate, in the face of brutality, and in the face of mass murder . . ."). The speaker was Rabbi Joachim Prinz [1963], then national president of the American Jewish Congress and one of several speakers who shared the platform with Dr. King on that historic day in 1963.

So our critical work is done. But was it worth it? Would it not have been easier simply to look up the required information in a handy reference book? Easier, yes. More informative? Decidedly not. In the language of Chapter Two, use of a reference book would not have explained how we knew that we knew important distinctions between contemporary and noncontemporary speech, between male and female speech, between religious and secular speech, between private and public speech, between mature and immature speech, between formal and informal speech, and between speech and nonspeech.

In this chapter, we will come to understand that all messages "do" as well as say and that all messages bear the imprints of the social situations that produced them, thereby making rhetoric a *situated* art that can be understood only when text and context are considered simultaneously. In this chapter, we will see that the best reference book of all is that housed in the critic's personal library of rhetorical knowledge.

THE MEANINGS OF SPEECH-ACTS

A basic fact about speaking often goes unnoticed: It is an activity. That is, by addressing another, a speaker both says something *and does something*. Many critics miss this "doing" function in their headlong rush to study words. But as Hart [1987:xxi] has said, "by choosing to utter words to another, a speaker makes at least these decisions—to speak to A and not to B; to speak now and not then or never; to speak here and not there; to speak for this period of time, not longer or shorter. These rhetorical decisions contain 'information' for us as observers if we are wise enough and patient enough to track these decisions."

Daily life often teaches these lessons about speech-acts. Sometimes painfully: Despite his gift for storytelling, a guest overstays his welcome at a party; despite her good intentions, a young executive is fired for sharing classified information with a colleague in a public restaurant; despite their affability, a married couple insults their new neighbors by greeting them with a wave instead of an extended conversation. In each of these cases, the messages exchanged were innocent enough, but matters of place, timing, and relationship undid them.

Philosopher J. L. Austin [1970] has labeled this "extra" dimension of persuasion its **performative** character. Austin himself was particularly intrigued by situations whose performative features dominated its message features (e.g., if said in the right context, "I do" both communicates loving sentiments *and* gets one married.) But as Benjamin [1976] has observed, all rhetorical messages probably have important performative aspects to them, which is why the critic is urged to calculate a message's performative features *before* doing any sort of careful textual analysis.

Consider, for example, the furor aroused when a physician wrote a brief column in the illustrious *Journal of the American Medical Association*. The column was entitled "It's Over, Debbie" (1988) and vividly detailed a case of euthanasia performed by the author-doctor. Hyde [1993] has analyzed this letter and argues that its importance lay not in what it said but in *what the act of publishing it did*. Many doctors, after all, have done mercy killings but few have acknowledged doing so and fewer still have done so in public. Some journals had discussed euthanasia, but not in one of the most prestigious medical publications in the United States. In other words, "It's Over, Debbie" caused a ruckus in the medical community, even among physicians who never actually read the article.

All of this happened because texts act. They do so because they contain, according to Arnold [1974:38–43] and Hart et al. [1983:13–14], any number of "implicit understandings." That is, the agreement to communicate with another means at least these things:

1. The speaker feels something is wrong. This wrong thing may not be a calamity but even a friendly greeting to a passerby can be seen as an attempt to ward off the forces of alienation and to increase goodwill in society. Preachers preach and teachers teach because of the sin and ignorance they hope to offset. Politicians speak politics when they envision that their legislative mandate is in trouble. Indeed, politics is inevitably rancorous because it focuses on the most persistent of problems: poverty, disease, war, natural disaster. Even a speech at a happy event, such as a toast at a wedding, is designed to wave away nonhappiness for the couple. People talk when they are troubled and during all other moments they are quiet. The first question the critic must ask, therefore, is: What's wrong?

2. The speaker is not yet desperate. Rhetorical people are optimists; they believe that talk can change human affairs. By speaking, people signal hope to one another. Total desperation, in contrast, drives people away from rhetoric, away from human solutions and toward more "transcendent" remedies such as contemplation or narcotics. So where there is rhetoric there is hope, or so implies the person who takes the trouble to speak. It is for these reasons that nuclear arms limitation talks always make front-page headlines. The mere agreement to talk documents that hope abides.

3. *The speaker is committed.* To something. Not necessarily to the subject matter of the text. Perhaps just to himself or herself. Perhaps to the proposal being advocated. But speech, especially public speech, implies a dramatic sort of commitment primarily because of the substantial risks attendant to it. Often, these commitments are strongly emotional (e.g., for a social activist) and often these commitments to speak cost us time (e.g., a campaigning politician), money (e.g., a poorly paid campus evangelist), relationships (e.g., a lecturer traveling the country without her family), or sleep (e.g., a late-night television commentator). In each case, the speaker signals that speaking is worth what it costs.

4. *The audience is open to change.* Listening, too, is a commitment, a tacit acknowledgment that listeners are not set in their ways. To listen to a live speech, after all, is to interrupt what one is doing, to don coat and hat and dodge the raindrops, sometimes to stand in line for tickets, occasionally to be seated in uncomfortable surroundings, often to be confronted with strange thoughts and uncomfortable emotions. Satisfied teenagers have no need for education, satisfied citizens have no need for politics, satisfied people have no need for rhetoric.

McGuire's [1976] study of Catholic Pentecostals nicely demonstrates these implicit messages of listening. McGuire became interested in glossolalia—speaking in tongues—and in what such uncommon speech patterns meant to those who used them. Typically, scholars have been interested in the psychological features of tongue-speakers but McGuire felt that the *social agreements* among glossolalics and their listeners contained the richest story. By speaking in tongues, McGuire found, such persons signalled (1) that they spoke as God's "medium" and not for themselves as individuals, (2) because of their "surrendered" status they could use more metaphorical and poetic language than could ordinary worshippers, and (3) that their rapturous experience did not blind them to norms of common social politeness in church. McGuire also found that listening to glossolalia required congregation members to be unusually "active" as auditors. They listened to confirm, not to question, often reading much into the messages they heard. After one glossolalic experience, for example, "one woman testified to having 'laid hands upon' a leaking faucet to 'cure' it; another member's confirmation of a scripture reading involved an inaccurate hearing of a key word in the text; another testimony involved a detailed mathematical calculation of the number who would be saved on the Last Day" [McGuire, 1976:14–15]. In short, McGuire made sense out of the worship services by asking not what was being said but *what was being done.*

Thus, a key question for the rhetorical critic is this: By speaking on this topic to this audience in this setting at this time, what "news" is the speaker making? Sometimes, the "news" lies in the **speaker-topic** relationship, as when a liberal like Bill Clinton first discussed limiting affirmative action programs, thereby signaling that the program may have outlived its usefulness. At other times, the news lies in the **speaker-setting** relationship, as when Mr. Clinton shone during the 1992 presidential debate in Richmond, Virginia, where ordinary people, not the press, asked the questions. Or the story could lie in the **speaker-audience** relationship, as when President Clinton reluctantly, and belatedly, spoke to reporters about the politically dangerous Whitewater affair. In each of these situations, both a statement and a meta-statement was made by Mr. Clinton. It is this larger statement that the critic must examine in each instance of persuasion.

It would matter little, for example, what the pope said about papal infallibility should he ever agree to discuss it. The mere *fact* of his doing so would send an important message. Similarly, when the rock group, Public Enemy, retracted certain antisemitic statements made by their own Professor Griff, they silently acknowledged, according to Sloop [1994], the power of the liberal consensus in the United States. And as Brydon [1985:148] observed, the mere agreement of a political incumbent to debate a challenger can send a message of great strength or great weakness to voters, media personnel, and challenger alike. At times, not to speak is to say a good deal.

THE FUNCTIONS OF SPEECH-ACTS

Because the natural tendency of the critic is to be fascinated with words and their meanings, it is not always easy to focus on the "action" of a speech-act. This was less of a problem for Maurice Bloch [1975] and his colleagues, who studied the speaking activities of people in nontechnological societies. Because they were comparative strangers to the tribes they studied, the researchers could shift their attention from the words spoken to the speaking activities *as activities*. In his book, Bloch presents the work of ten different anthropologists who fanned out all over the world to study what political speechmaking "did" for the societies they studied.

One of these researchers studied the Merina of Madagascar and found the oratory to be depersonalized, bearing no distinctive stamp of the speaker. Indeed, even the orator's intonation patterns had been fixed by tradition, suggesting that for the Merina the act of speaking was, ipso facto, an act of tribal submission. In another case, among the Tikopia of the Solomon Islands, the chief of the tribe rarely showed up for the speaking activities, thereby ensuring that his authority could never be directly questioned by those in attendance. In the speeches of the Kaoleni of Kenya, researchers found few references to hierarchy or leadership, since to mention such matters would have been to call attention to sharp economic cleavages in that society.

The general impression one gets from such traditional oratory is one of *constraint*. Political speaking in such societies seems more a process of putting on a show than of solving problems in a direct and clinical fashion. Speaking generally about such traditional peoples, Bloch [1975:8] observes that "the orator's words are almost entirely not his own, in the sense that he sees them as handed down from the ancestors. He will have learned all the proverbs, stories and speech forms and his main aim is to repeat them as closely as possible." Bloch [p. 9] goes on to say that listeners in these societies also make clear social statements when they take part in such speaking events: "On these occasions if you have allowed somebody to speak in an oratorical manner you have practically accepted his proposal. . . . When someone speaks to you in this way there quite simply seems to be no easy way of saying 'no' or commenting on the substance of what is said." In short, Bloch and his colleagues found that such speech-acts were symbolic tokens of basic political structures. For them, speaking *was* political action.

Closer to home, Hart [1987] conducted a comprehensive study of the basic rhetorical decisions made by recent American chief executives. Rather than examine the texts of presidential messages, Hart simply recorded the date, place of delivery, occasion, topic, audience, and political circumstance of each of the presidential speeches delivered from 1945 onward. This amounted to a data base of some 10,000 speech events. By looking at the pattern of speech decisions made by the presidents—who they talked to, about what, when and where—he hoped to catalog the most basic functions of presidential discourse. The basic question Hart asked—What does speech do?—focuses on a fundamental set of meta-messages and therefore should be asked during any rhetorical inquiry:

1. *Speech situations index power.* Hart observes that the first audience addressed by Ronald Reagan after his assassination attempt consisted exclusively of press correspondents, suggesting how central the media now are to a president's image of strength. Also, even though Mr. Reagan opposed affirmative action, he spoke extensively to women's groups early in his administration, signaling how important such groups had become even to a conservative president.

2. *Speech situations index ego needs.* For example, Hart discovered that Lyndon Johnson gave an unusually large number of speeches in his home state, probably because Texas audiences confirmed for him that he had finally "made it" as a national figure (something he never seemed quite sure of himself). A reverse finding was that Richard Nixon never spoke in the state of Massachusetts while president, perhaps because he suffered from a "Kennedy complex" and felt threatened when speaking in the shadow of Harvard.

3. *Speech situations index social obstacles.* Hart concludes that the presidency is becoming more difficult since chief executives are increasingly delivering preplanned speeches to preselected audiences instead of putting up with the give-and-take of press conferences (George Bush was particularly fond of this tack). Also, the presidents sharply increased their regional speaking when Congress was controlled by the opposing party, no doubt because the chief executives hoped to build grassroots support for their legislation and to use that support for Congress-bashing (e.g., when Bill Clinton spent a great deal

of time in California just as the Republicans cut the defense spending on which California relied).

4. *Speech situations reveal speaker priorities.* Unlike any of the other chief executives, Jimmy Carter continued to speak extensively in the two months *following* his 1980 defeat for reelection. The reason? He was a dogged individual strongly committed to the policies the electorate had just repudiated. Similarly, Democrat Lyndon Johnson traveled unusually often to Republican states in order to enlist support for prosecuting the war in Vietnam, thereby showing how important such policies were to him.

5. *Speech situations reveal audience priorities.* Presidential speaking has now become a full-time business; the American people cannot get enough of their chief executive. Presidents now speak extensively during both election and nonelection years and during the summer months as well as during all other seasons of the year. For whatever reason, the American people seem to have developed an insatiable diet for presidential oratory.

6. *Speech situations reveal speaker-audience relationships.* Presidents are now spending more and more of their time speaking to private groups behind the closed doors of convention halls than to ordinary citizens in town squares. No doubt, such changes have been occasioned by alterations in patterns of political fund-raising, a fact also reflected in recently increased speaking activities in the Sun Belt, a part of the country undergoing great surges in population (and infusions of capital). In short, presidents use speech to flatter the people they must flatter.

Our concern in this section has been on *pre*-rhetorical analysis, not on words but on word-using. Because speech is always a situated activity, speakers must structure the right "configuration" of elements—audience, topic, setting, etc.—to have maximum impact. Shortly, we shall turn to a more detailed analysis of these elements; but before doing so let us consider the first question to be asked of any rhetorical event: *What act is being performed here?*

This is a simple question, but answers to it are normally complex. An elementary way of answering this question is to reduce the speech activity to one word, a gerund. Admittedly, such an approach is somewhat simplistic, but that is precisely its value: It reduces the speech-act to its most basic performative feature. Although the critic is free to choose any characterizing term for this purpose, Table 3.1 presents a starter's list, borrowing from the work of Gaines [1979] and supplemented by other suggestions as well.

The key move here is to describe, not to evaluate, the speech-act. Naturally, as with all criticism, the critic must be able to defend the characterizing term chosen for the speaking event in question. No doubt, different critics analyzing the same event would spot different "performances." That is as it should be, since this sort of exercise provides only a first, quite partial, glimpse of the event in question. But there is real utility in attempting this critical procedure, not for the answers derived but for the questions raised. It

TABLE 3.1 Available Terms for Characterizing Speech-Acts

activating	disputing	ordering
amusing	distracting	placating
angering	diverting	praising
announcing	edifying	promising
avoiding	enacting	refuting
calming	encouraging	reminding
challenging	enlightening	reporting
commencing	entertaining	requesting
confusing	escalating	retracting
consecrating	finishing	rousing
continuing	frightening	shocking
deceiving	humiliating	soothing
delaying	inciting	startling
demanding	inspiring	surprising
deterring	insulting	teaching
displaying	intimidating	warning
disposing	leading	

seems clear, for example, that our Rabbi at the Lincoln Memorial was not attempting to Amuse or Promise or Continue or Entertain or Surprise. Equally, it appears that he was not trying to Confuse or Deter or Escalate or Frighten or Startle.

But was he Commencing something or Continuing something? Was he Warning or Encouraging his television audience? Was he Soothing or Challenging the tired civil rights workers? Was he Inciting or Diverting or doing both at the same time? And what was he doing most often? Questions like these focus on the most general terrain of a speech-act and help orient any subsequent textual analysis. They also throw light on the overall architecture of the rhetorical act—who said what to whom and why—and thereby raise questions asked all too rarely but almost always profitably.

THE COMPONENTS OF SPEECH-ACTS

This section will consider how a critic can better understand a message by reckoning with its larger social situation. According to Bitzer [1968], a number of situational factors operate to suggest what can and cannot be said by a person in a given instance. Some of these suggestive factors lie within the speaker (e.g., knowledge, experience, psychological state) while others are external (e.g., the time of day, what others are saying, etc.). In either case, a message becomes a public record of how the speaker coped with the suggestions built into the rhetorical situation.

Figure 3.1 captures the most basic of such factors. Several features of the model are worth noting:

1. The model situates the message within an array of social forces. No piece of discourse can be understood outside of its natural habitat. While an ancient poem may delight persons living generations later, that is rarely the case with rhetoric. Old rhetorical messages seem to warn subsequent readers: "You really should have been there." Thus, Arnold [1968] notes that when the parliamentary speeches of William Butler Yeats were anthologized, the editor provided the situational details necessary to makes sense out of the speeches. In contrast, collections of Yeats' poems rarely contained such situational markers.

2. The model describes a system of elements. Any speech-act is always more than the sum of its parts; to change one element is to change the whole. Anyone who has seen the "same" newsmagazine audience put to sleep by a discussion of the national deficit and electrified one week later by a Michael Jackson/Lisa Marie Presley interview knows that changing *one* element of a rhetorical system can produce changes throughout that system.

3. All situational elements operate within a unique cultural boundary. It is often hard to see the effects of culture on human interaction. Nevertheless, the critic must try to do so since culture penetrates all message-sending and all message-receiving. The themes found in a *Die Hard XXI* film may seem quite

FIGURE 3.1 Elements of a Rhetorical Situation

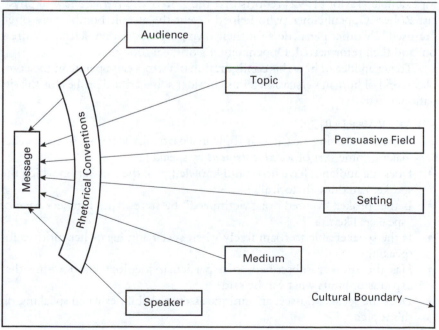

universal to the average American moviegoer but it takes only the slightest cultural sensitivity to be able to trace its sexism and nationalism to a long cultural history of conservative U.S. values.

4. *A message is the visible record of a complex interaction.* The rhetorical critic focuses heavily on message cues because that is all that is left after a dynamic human encounter has occurred. One way of tracking this complexity is to compare two versions of the "same" text. This approach was taken by McMullen and Solomon [1994] who found that the feminist themes in Alice Walker's book *The Color Purple* were replaced by a more general, and more popular and hence lucrative, never-say-die emphasis by director Stephen Spielberg when the book was turned into a movie.

5. *The message is the rhetorical critic's touchstone.* Anthropologists may study social settings, sociologists may study audiences, psychologists may study media effects, philosophers may study human thought, and historians may recount the careers of great speakers. But it is the rhetorical critic who uniquely examines the marks *left on messages* by these various forces.

Our model, then, conceives of messages as repositories of information about situational elements. As Branham and Pearce [1985:25] observe, text always implies context and context always implies text, which is why, they argue, the off-color jokes of comedian Lenny Bruce could be shocking in the uptight 1950s and seem almost quaint thirty years later. One way of discovering the context within the text is to inquire into the **intertextual** aspects of a message—the bits and pieces of previous texts "deposited" into a new text. So, for example, Taylor [1992] reports that the *Letters and Recollections* of physicist Robert Oppenheimer (who helped invent the atomic bomb) were often "re-used" by other persuaders for their own purposes as they selectively drew on, and then reformatted, Oppenheimer's original thoughts.

To get an idea of how this configuration of factors can operate in the complex world of human persuasion let us consider some critical probes for the situational analyst:

SPEAKER VARIABLES
- Besides discussing a particular topic in a particular location, is the speaker making some sort of *social statement* by speaking?
- Does the audience have first-hand knowledge of the speaker on which the speaker can draw rhetorically?
- Is the speaker "sainted" or "victimized" by stereotypes listeners have of "speakers like this"?
- Is the speaker able to roam freely when specifying his or her motives for speaking?
- Has the speaker subscribed to a particular ideology or doctrine that expands or limits what can be said?
- Does the speaker possess any unique assets or liabilities when speaking on this topic?

- *Is there textual evidence that the speaker considered these factors when framing the message in question?*

These questions deal with how social role, personal ideology, and public image constrain, sometimes dictate, what a speaker says. On occasion, for example, a college teacher must struggle mightily to keep a lecture free of personal bias in order to keep students from questioning everything the lecturer has to say (about this, and all other, topics). In such cases, Personal Ideology wages a ferocious war with Social Role in the presence of Public Image. The message produced—the lecture itself—often carries the battle scars.

In other instances, the mere fact of speaking can carry the most important message. Logue and Miller [1995], for example, tell the story of a rural Georgia mayor who began to lose his power in the community when he chose to debate, rather than to reason with, two elderly women who protested their water bill. After many months and much publicity, the mayor very much regretted his decision. He severely underestimated the staying power of his two angry constituents as they constantly made him look the fool, eventually even appearing on the *Tonight Show.*

Rhetoric changes audiences but it can change speakers as well. Jamieson [1988b] notes, for example, that the real advantage of modern presidential debating lies not in the political information provided the citizenry but in the debates' abilities to ensure that the candidates themselves become informed on the issues of the day! Speakers may create messages but, often, messages recreate speakers as well.

AUDIENCE VARIABLES

- Regardless of the practical outcome of the interaction, has the audience made any significant *social statement* by coming to listen?
- To what extent is this audience a "rhetorical audience," that is, one that can directly implement the change the speaker is requesting?
- Can the speaker capitalize on existing common ties with the audience when speaking to them?
- What previous personal or philosophical commitments (e.g., group memberships) has the audience made that may affect their responses to the speaker?
- What contrary information or attitudes does the audience have that can inhibit the speaker's success?
- What recent experiences has the audience had that may affect their responsiveness?
- *Is there textual evidence that the speaker considered these factors when framing the message in question?*

Simply agreeing to become part of an audience can constitute a major social statement. As Meyer [1995] notes, when the Establishment begins to listen to the strident cries of social movement activists, change is surely in the wind. Meyer found that "elite" speakers even began to reproduce movement refrains themselves, dramatic evidence of their having listened to their opponents. On another front, Campbell [1983:105] observes that the rhetorical technique known as consciousness-raising (a form of communication in which speaking and listening roles are exchanged frequently) was particularly well-suited to the early women's movement, then made up largely of at-home women who were used to conversational, rather than public, modes of interaction.

We do not normally think of listening as a form of commitment, but many professional speakers do, which is why they work so hard to match audience with message. Thus, when Harry Truman rode across the United States in a Pullman car during the 1948 election, giving some four-hundred-odd speeches in some four-hundred-odd places, Truman produced a rhetoric-in-search-of-an-audience. He knew that there were people who shared his real-life experiences (as a non-urbanite) but who did not know that his administration was being hamstrung by a Republican-controlled Congress. Truman also knew that most of the really influential newspapers of the day favored his opponent, Thomas Dewey, so the president brought his rhetoric directly to people who were less affected by the opinions of the elite press: rural and small-town voters. In so doing, Truman capitalized on what was "built into" his audiences via their demography.

TOPIC VARIABLES
- Is this topic socially acceptable? Is the fact that it is being discussed a significant *social statement?*
- Is the topic either volatile or innocuous? Is public opinion highly polarized on this matter?
- How complex is the topic? Can it be reasonably discussed with this audience in this setting?
- Because of how this topic has been discussed before, must the speaker deal with it in a certain way?
- Does the topic have any special features that make its discussion via this medium advantageous or risky?
- *Is there textual evidence that the speaker considered these factors when framing the message in question?*

Pity Bob Packwood. The senator from Oregon can discourse confidently about tax reform, oil import fees, Third World relief measures, and military base closings. About such matters he is smooth, often profound. But should some reporter mention the phrase "sexual harassment," the good senator turns pale and inarticulate. Introducing such a wild card into a Packwood speech situation throws his entire rhetorical system out of kilter. This subject matter—no matter what the setting and no matter what the medium or audience—brings to mind the many charges filed against him by women staffers in the early 1990s, making him one whose political influence has been sharply curtailed by a single speech topic.

Each speech topic has a "range of discussability." Some topics (e.g., the Golden Gate Bridge) let a speaker roam freely when discussing it while others tightly rein one in (e.g., sexual harassment). It is difficult for many Americans to talk about such indelicate matters as hemorrhoid treatments or funeral arrangements, products and services requiring advertisers to be especially inventive rhetorically. The range of discussability for a topic may also be constricted by that topic's complexity. For example, some years ago the Mathematical Association of America opened its annual meetings to the press in order to gain wider public understanding of the important work that mathematicians do. Alas, the experiment failed: Only four of the eighty invited reporters bothered to attend [Kolata, 1975:732].

At other times, linking a speaker (say, an actor) to a topic (say, casual sex) within a specialized medium (say, the *National Inquirer*) can create enormous rhetorical difficulties—if you are British actor Hugh Grant and have been caught off-guard in a parked car with a prostitute in Los Angeles. In short, any one element in the configuration of elements can create topical difficulties. Several operating at the same time can create rhetorical nightmares.

PERSUASIVE FIELD
- Taken as a whole, can the speech situation be seen as a *counterstatement* to some other set of messages?
- Have the speaker's previous remarks to this audience expanded or limited current persuasive possibilities?
- What statements have other people made in the past that constrain what can be said now?
- To what sort of immediate "verbal competition" (e.g., heckling) is the speaker being subjected?
- Can any future rhetorical messages be envisioned that require anticipatory strategies now?
- *Is there textual evidence that the speaker considered these factors when framing the message in question?*

The persuasive field consists of all those other messages impinging on an audience in a given speech situation. These messages could have been authored by the speaker previously, by other members of the audience, or by persons not present. During a news conference, for example, a president often must cope with rumors that have been circulating for days in the newspapers, with recent Congressional attacks on his administration, or with the complaints of protestors massed outside the White House. All these forces are added to the mix when the president approaches the microphone for the first question.

At times, the persuasive field will be unusually message-filled as, for example, during a presidential campaign. During 1992, for example, Ross Perot eventually abandoned the traditional press conference for the much less competitive format of shows like *Larry King Live* and *Good Morning America* where "softball" questions and personality profiles can be expected. When forced into more traditional speaking formats, Perot (as well as his 1992 opponents) knew that they would be subjected to "instant analysis" immediately after they spoke. This required that they anticipate and counteract messages that did not yet exist, thereby making their messages highly intertextual.

For these and other reasons, politicians often begin their press conferences with formal statements, trying to establish a base of rhetorical operations before receiving flak from the press corps. In other words, with so many intertextual forces now at work in an age of mass media, all messages contain the ghosts of other messages. Thus, it was not surprising when Gilberg et al. [1980] found that a presidential speech given today will often track last week's newspaper. Like all other public persuaders, presidents must be responsive to an ever-changing persuasive field.

SETTING VARIABLES
- Is any *social statement* being made by the speaker by speaking at this time in this place?
- Is there a special kind of "history" attached to where the speech is being given? Does that place affect what can be said?
- Do any nonverbal events (e.g., aspects of sight, sound, feeling, etc.) affect the speaker's game plan?
- Is an event likely to occur in the future that will affect what can be said now by this speaker?
- *Is there textual evidence that the speaker considered these factors when framing the message in question?*

Over time, some physical locations take on special social (and rhetorical) significance. When announcing his bid for the 1996 presidential campaign, for example, Senator Phil Gramm stood in front of the Texas A&M University military cadets, thereby declaring himself, both verbally and nonverbally, a man of conservative values. Other settings permit other options. The poor acoustics and raucous overcrowding of a rock concert, for example, add excitement to the music played there. In sharp contrast is the ornate quietude of a great cathedral that permits, and denies, still other rhetorical possibilities.

As Edelman [1964:96] says, many physical settings have a contrived character and are "unabashedly built up to emphasize a departure from men's daily routine, a special heroic quality to the proceedings they are to frame." A good example of such contrivances occurs in courtrooms, says Edelman [p. 99], who notes that "The judicial bench and chambers, formal, ornate, permanent and solid, lined with thick tomes, 'prove' the deliberateness, scholarliness, and judiciousness of the acts that take place in them, even though careful study of these acts in a university or newspaper office (different settings) may indicate they were highly arbitrary, prejudiced, or casual."

Aspects of time (the hour of the day) and timing (when an event occurs relative to other events) are also important factors. As Gronbeck [1974:86] says, a persuasive message may fail because the speaker is the wrong person for the moment, because the audience is not yet "primed" to take the appeal seriously, or because the message is otherwise presented too soon or too late. So, for example, Bill Clinton got some political mileage out of the terrible bombing in Oklahoma City in 1995 when he responded to the tragedy with forcefulness and compassion. But when it came to proposing a tax cut, he was beaten to the punch by Newt Gingrich and his allies in Congress. Timing is also important in the business world, where product-messages are carefully adapted to the entertainment schedule. This is why beer is advertised during football telecasts and why soap is advertised during, well, soap operas.

MEDIA VARIABLES

- Is the speaker making any important *social statement* by delivering his or her message via this medium?
- Does the method chosen (i.e., spoken or written) enhance or detract from the speaker's message?
- Does the size of the audience the medium can reach present or deny any important rhetorical possibilities?
- Are there any important "sponsorship effects" associated with messages presented via this medium?
- Does the medium chosen permit the speaker's personality to become an important force of persuasion?
- Do sub-audiences exist because of the medium chosen for the message?
- *Is there textual evidence that the speaker considered these factors when framing the message in question?*

A medium is that which "carries" a message. At the simplest level, for example, we are aware of the very different rhetorical possibilities of speaking versus writing. Normally, marriage is proposed in person—while speaking— rather than by telegram because speech is personal and intimate while telegrams are both too cold and too terse for something as complicated as love. On the other hand, "Dear John" is more likely to receive a letter than a phone call from "Love, Sue" because writing helps one focus one's thoughts, craft one's arguments and, above all, circumvent the emotionalism of the moment.

The Dear John letter, of course, is one of the most hated messages ever devised because its sender makes such a powerful social statement by choosing a distanced medium for a former intimate. It is highly likely, therefore, that most such letters are destroyed before they are read through. No matter how carefully the words may be phrased, the rhetorical *act* is a fundamentally alienating one.

As we will see in Chapter 9, persuasion has been changed in dramatic ways with the advent of the mass media. Before, when speakers addressed throngs of listeners in a live setting, the speaker's message could not be dispersed widely but the speaker could reach out and touch the immediate audience. With radio and television, many more listeners can be solicited simultaneously but they are now presented with "images" rather than with flesh and blood speakers in close proximity.

Scholars are only beginning to sort out the complexities of the mass media. But some things we already know. For example, the mass media create "sponsorship effects," with listeners now having built-in expectations for *any* televised message. That is, TV viewers have come to expect informality rather than formality, personalized rather than impersonal arguments, visual rather than bland supporting materials, interactive rather than monologic formats, and much else. Also, because so many persons can now be reached at the same time via television, rhetorical messages are becoming increasingly complex, as speakers adjust different parts of the same message to the different sub-audiences they face simultaneously.

So, for example, Rosteck [1994] found that the Democrat's 1992 convention film, "The Man from Hope," succeeded because it somehow managed (by using a variety of mythic appeals) to appeal to both the partisan convention-goers as well as to the less partisan, more easily distracted viewers at home. On another front, Wander [1984] has shown that any presidential foreign policy address must now speak directly to the voters, as well as to their journalistic overhearers, and to friendly and unfriendly members of Congress as well. It gets even more complicated: At that very same time, the president must send careful signals to the Russians and the Chinese without missending signals to his European allies. No doubt, this overlapping of audiences makes politics sound as strange as it does at time.

RHETORICAL CONVENTIONS

- Has this configuration of elements ever come together before?
- If so, are there rules of interaction that must be followed by the speaker?
- If this speech situation is a new one, are there any general rhetorical guidelines that must be honored here?
- Does any *one* element (speaker, audience, topic, etc.) have special weight on this occasion?
- *Is there textual evidence that the speaker considered these factors when framing the message in question?*

Without question, people are efficient. Rather than invent a completely new message for each new social event, they formulate rhetorical guidelines to deal with stock situations. The first moment or two of the ordinary street-corner conversation, for example, is highly predictable. We discuss health, the weather, the local ballclub, and little else.

Although seemingly insignificant at first, such standardized locutions tell a good deal about cultural assumptions. For example, it is noteworthy that even on a comparatively bawdy TV show like *Martin,* indiscriminate adultery, personal arrogance, and corporate rapaciousness are—in virtually every instance—ultimately punished. Admittedly, compared to the television dramas of the 1950s, it now takes longer for the transgressions to be discovered and the transgressors disciplined. But it has long been part of the American Code that such behaviors are deserving of censure, and so we have developed formulas for discussing such things. Colonial values are still powerful in the United States and so, were he to return, Puritan preacher Jonathan Edwards might well be able to guest-direct an episode or two of *Martin,* so well does he know the story line of American morality.

At times, configurational elements go together so often that rituals of interaction develop. In such instances, speakers become tightly constrained in what they can say and listeners learn to appreciate the sameness of rhetorical exchange. So, for example, eighty percent of the content of any Roman Catholic mass is predetermined, with worshippers being comforted by the emotional predictability of a powerful ritual. Marriage ceremonies, eulogies, graduation exercises, bar mitzvahs—all these are heavily constrained by rhetorical conventions too, signaling that standard problems (i.e., transitional moments) persist and that these problems are so important that public solutions must be found for dealing with them.

Even when full-blown rituals are not present, one can spot conventions at work. There are, for example, strong sanctions against quietly talking to oneself in the corner of a room. Equally, however, raising one's voice in public is often not permitted. One can discuss athletics in mixed company but one cannot discuss athletic supporters. The term "black" is now acceptable but the term "negro" is not. The careful critic will spot such rhetorical rules and then ask *why* they exist, largely because these verbal habits so often point up a society's special preferences as well as its special vulnerabilities.

CONCLUSION

This chapter has emphasized two things: (1) the very *decision* to speak can be an important kind of social action, and (2) the various elements of a rhetorical situation often become *imprinted* on the message, thereby becoming a valuable source of insight for the critic. Let us conclude our discussion with an example. The case-in-point is an interesting piece of rhetoric portrayed in the movie *Patton* but based on a real speech given in July of 1944 by General George S. Patton [1946] prior to crossing the English Channel for an assault on the German armies in France. Even a brief excerpt from Patton's speech reveals its distinctive tones:

> Men, this stuff you hear about Americans wanting to stay out of this war is a lot of b_____s_____! Americans love to fight, traditionally. All real Americans love the sting of battle. When you were kids, you all admired the champion marble player, the fastest runner, the big league ball player, the toughest boxer. The Americans love a winner, and cannot tolerate a loser. Americans despise cowards. Americans play to win; all the time. I wouldn't give a hoot for a man who lost and laughed.

That's why Americans have never lost, and will never lose a war. The very thought of losing is hateful to an American. . . .

You are not all going to die. Only two percent of you here would die in major battle. Death must not be feared. Every man is frightened at first in battle. If he says he isn't he's a goddam liar. Some men are cowards, yes. But they will fight just the same, or get the hell scared out of them watching men who do fight, who are as scared as they. The real hero is the man who fights even though he is scared. Some get over their fright in a few minutes under fire; some take hours; for some it takes days. The real man never lets fear of death overpower his honor, his duty to his country, and his innate manhood. . . .

An Army is a team: It lives, sleeps, eats, fights as a team. This individual heroic stuff is a lot of crap. The bilious bastards who wrote that kind of stuff for the *Saturday Evening Post* don't know any more about real battle than they do about f_____!. . . We have the finest food, the best equipment, the finest spirit and men in the world. . . . Why, by God, I actually pity those sonsofbitches we are going up against: by God, I do! . . .

My men don't surrender. I don't want to hear of a soldier under my command getting captured unless he is hit. Even if you are, you can still fight back. This is not b_____s_____, either. The kind of man I want is like the lieutenant in Libya who, with a Luger against his chest, jerked his helmet off, swept the gun aside with the other hand, and busted hell out of the Boche with his Helmet. Then he jumped on the Hun and went out and killed another German. By this time, the lieutenant had a bullet through his chest. Now, that is a MAN for you. . . .

Even a cursory look at Patton's remarks will reveal some of the major **social statements** being made in this situation: a great general taking the time to talk to raw recruits; the soldiers seated together, building esprit de corps prior to an important battle; the candor of Patton dealing directly with such topics as courage, self-image, mortality, and immortality, signaling with this choice of topics that the moment was important to him. The clear sense of counterstatement is also obvious, with Patton using the speech-act to argue that the rumor-mongers, Tokyo Roses, and *Saturday Evening Post*s were wrong in every detail. By meeting with the men (on their turf) so soon before battle, Patton no doubt sent them an important message of solidarity, as he did by giving a live speech rather than a radio address.

The imprints of the various situational elements are also unmistakable. The speech is Pattonesque: coarse, crude, unyielding, defiant, a clear indication of a **speaker variable** at work. In some senses, Patton's reputation was so much larger than life that he even may have had to overstate his positions in order to meet the men's exalted expectations of him, which may be why the text combines both superpatriotism with a faint sort of anarchism. Evident here too is the everyday talk of the everyday soldier, a hint of the **audience variables** with which Patton had to deal. Patton's images are earthy and his language colorful because earthiness is the constant companion of the foot soldier and colorfulness his only respite.

In some senses, the speech treats the individual **topic variables** in conventional ways but by *combining* deeply philosophical topics (e.g., the purpose of life) with brutishly practical matters (e.g., getting fed), Patton gives his listeners an exhilarating rhetorical ride. In some senses, the structure of the speech is conventional (one is reminded of football coaches at half-time) but the language used—imperative rather than declarative sentences, contrast devices rather than comparison devices—is unmistakably Patton's.

A comparison of Patton's speech with the trimmed-down version printed by George C. Scott in the movie *Patton* (made some thirty years later) shows how **media variables** can change things considerably. In the original speech, for example, Patton spent a good deal of time talking about the importance of the hard training his men had recently experienced, something omitted in the movie speech because the popcorn-eaters had no doubt been otherwise employed in recent weeks. The original speech also spends a great deal of time talking about the reality of death, giving it a kind of authenticity missing in Scott's speech. There is also a great deal of detail in the original speech missing in the movie version (e.g., of a soldier near Tunis fixing a telephone wire in the thick of battle). Comments like these possess a real-world integrity demanded by the **setting variables** impinging on a real general speaking only moments before a real war.

Movie-makers have their own rhetorical challenges, however. For example, they deleted Patton's careful instructions to his men not to mention that they had seen him (a security measure) since the average theater patron would hardly have understood the historical context for these remarks. Also, the movie version is only half the length of the original speech and has none of the internal repetition found in Patton's version.

These patterns are found because there are very tight **rhetorical conventions** affecting movie-making, conventions dictated by the fast pace expected in the war film genre. Whereas George Patton had to reach out to real soldiers experiencing real fears, George C. Scott needed only to make a quick and dramatic impression on his listeners so that they would be set up to enjoy the next two hours in the darkened theatre. In a sense, then, neither George Patton nor George Scott owned their speeches. Their audiences did.

For the student of rhetoric, situational analysis must be the first procedure in any critical operation. Getting a broad-based perspective on the speech-act is important because rhetoric torn away from its context makes no sense or it makes distorted sense. Later chapters in this book will delve deeper into the sinews of messages. These anatomical excursions will be important because in detail lies precision. But the good surgeon reaches for the scalpel only after having done an overall physical workup of the patient. The critic should do likewise by treating rhetorical situations in all of their complexity. To do less would be a kind of critical malpractice.

Chapter 4

ANALYZING IDEAS

A pool table; don't you understand? Friend, either you're closing your eyes to a situation you do not wish to acknowledge, or you are not aware of the calibre of disaster indicated by the presence of a pool table in your community.

Well, you got trouble, my friend. Right here, I say, trouble right here in River City. Why, sure, I'm a billiard player; certainly mighty proud to say, I'm always mighty proud to say it. I consider that the hours I spend with a cue in my hand are golden. Help you cultivate horse-sense, and a cool head, and a keen eye. Did you ever take and try to give an iron-clad leave for yourself from a three-rail billiard shot? But just as I say it takes judgment, brains, and maturity to score in a balk-line game, I say that any boob can take and shove a ball in a pocket.

And I call that sloth, the first big step on the road to the depths of degradation. I say, first, medicinal wine from a teaspoon—then beer from a bottle. And the next thing you know your son is playing for money in a pinched-back suit, and listenin' to some big out of town jasper hearin' him tell about horse-race gamblin'. Not a wholesome trottin' race. No! But a race where they set down right on the horse. Like to see some stuck up jockey-boy settin' on Dan Patch? Make your blood boil? Well, I should say.

Friends let me tell you what I mean: You got one, two, three, four, five, six pockets in a table, pockets that mark the difference between a gentleman and a bum, with a capital "B" and that rhymes with "P" and that stands for "POOL."

And all week long your River City youth will be a fritterin' away; I say your young men will be fritterin'. Fritterin' away their noontime, suppertime, chore-time, too. Get the ball in the pocket—never mind gettin' dandelions pulled or the screen door patched or the beef steak pounded; and never mind pumpin' any water 'til your parents are caught with the cistern empty on a Saturday night. And that's trouble!

> Yes, you've got lots and lots of trouble. I'm thinking of the kids in the knicker-bockers, shirttailed young ones, peekin' in the pool hall window after school. You got trouble, folks, right here in River City. Trouble, with a capital "T" and that rhymes with "P" and that stands for "POOL." [Wilson, 1958]

Professor Harold Hill, that consummate salesman-cum-shyster depicted in the delightful play *The Music Man* is a man of ideas. He is filled with old ideas (like loving hard work and avoiding sin) as well as new ideas (music as salvation), and he is filled with the best idea of all: combining these ideas in order to make a profit. When he spoke, Professor Hill showed that he was a fine student of American culture, which is itself a complex amalgamation of old ideas and new ideas.

In fashioning his sermon/advertisement, Hill focused not so much on the particular ideas the residents of River City, Iowa, favored in the 1930s. Rather, he concentrated on the enduring ideas their forebears had resonated to at the turn of the century and that their great grandchildren would also appreciate toward the turn of the next century. In doing so, Mr. Hill proved himself a fairly decent intellectual historian of the United States and he proved, too, that all good speakers must first become good listeners.

And Harold Hill was a fine listener. His constant sales trips through the Midwest taught him much about the plain-speaking, plain-thinking middle-Americans who were his customers. Even before walking on the sidewalks of River City he knew the people he would pass. He knew, for example, that the clean streets and neatly trimmed lawns were maintained by people who respected Western assumptions of rationality and orderliness, ideas having their presuppositions in the Enlightenment and their implications in getting the dandelions pulled. He knew that country folks at the turn of the century in the United States had been raised on a stern diet of Calvinism (no matter what their religious denomination) and on conceptions of incremental spirituality ("And I call that sloth, the first big step on the road to the depths of degradation.").

For such people, sin was not only progressive but also concrete. Theirs was a Christian worldview, not a Platonic one, and so unpounded beefsteak could stand as a sign of perdition just as surely as the death of Jesus Christ had stood as real-world rejection of pagan philosophizing. Their life was also a life of immediacy, of planting and tending and harvesting, of coping with Nature. Thus, they distrusted foolishness—"boobs" and the like—favoring instead "horse-sense," since animals were so central to their material survival and since material survival was tied up in complicated ways with moral matters.

Also, because rural life makes land and its care the measure of the individual, and because the greater the expanse of one's land the greater one's personal risk, there was also a self-imposed provincialism to Harold Hill's customers that made them instinctively wary of "out of town jaspers." At the same time, River City residents were heirs to American pluralism. Their resulting friendliness made it possible for them to be seduced by an out-of-towner even as they were being warned of same.

In other words, Harold Hill had to be as much a philosopher as a peddler of slide trombones. For him, persuasion involved understanding people's first premises, their base assumptions. The study of philosophy is the study of these first premises and *the study of rhetoric is the study of first premises-in-use*.

Harold Hill was probably not a self-conscious philosopher. He knew what he knew in the way most practical people know things: by imitation and observation. But unlike most, Hill had a special ability to ground persuasion in people's most basic thoughts. The measure of Hill's artfulness is that his rhetoric did not sound "philosophical" at all. It sounded practical, not abstract; it sounded cozy, not antiseptic; it sounded partisan, not neutered. Miss Marian, River City's resident rhetorical critic (and later Hill's inamorata) quickly saw through his rhetoric. She did what the best critics do: She traced the ideas Hill used to their first assumptions and reasoned that these were probably *not* the assumptions held by the average cosmopolitan professor of musicology. Miss Marian tracked Hill's ideas to their roots and found them lying in River City and not in Harold Hill. Smart lady, Miss Marian.

In a sense, Harold Hill made something out of nothing when he contrasted godlessness with euphonic piety. Neither euphony nor piety invited this linkage but Hill linked them anyway. It took considerable rhetorical imagination to do so. But persuaders have always been opportunistic in these ways, a fact that produces horror, admiration, or bemusement in critics. Miss Marian, a librarian and hence a person sensitive to texts and to the cataloging of ideas, reacted in all three ways from time to time. These will be our options as well, and Miss Marian will be our inspiration as we consider how persuaders use ideas and how critics can catch them doing so.

THE STUDY OF IDEAS

In a way, all rhetorical critics study ideas. And, in a way, each chapter in this book focuses on the rhetorical uses of ideas. But this chapter focuses on the basics, on how persuasive appeals come to be. Here, we will emphasize the gathering of elementary rhetorical facts on the assumption that the most scientific thing a scientist does lies not in the use of computers or measuring instruments but in the scientist's ability to describe a phenomenon in detail and with precision. Careful description is especially important in rhetorical criticism since rhetoric is such an emotional thing to study. That is, if the rhetoric being studied is powerful, the natural tendency is to applaud it or decry it. The descriptive impulse arrests this very natural, but critically dangerous, inclination by asking what is known for sure about the message in question.

Good description requires gathering facts before doing interpretation or evaluation. But description itself can be problematic. For instance, for some observers the essential fact about the statue of a Confederate general in a town square is that that person fought for the Confederacy. To others, the statue symbolizes general (not Southern) leadership or loyalty. To a Leftist, the statue is an abomination because it glorifies war; to a Rightist the statue is an abomination because it is covered with pigeon droppings. A teenager tuned into a Sony Walkman may find the statue boring because its inscription is too flowery, while the geologist standing next to him may be fascinated by the volcanic traces in the rock quarried for the statue. Thus, if we can be unsure what a thing (like a statue) is or what its most central feature is (its Southernness? its geological qualities?), then finding the essential nature of anything as dynamic as a rhetorical exchange becomes even more difficult.

Because of the complexity of rhetoric, it makes sense initially (1) to isolate and (2) to list a message's main ideas. This chapter will present two techniques for doing so, each of which has these benefits:

1. *Analyzing ideas tells what is present and what is not.* A strange proposition, at first, but an important one. By examining a persuasive text, after all, we confront the speaker's final set of ideas, the speaker's best guess of what could be said in the rhetorical situation at hand. But the ideas *not* chosen can also be informative, even though this presents something of a dilemma for the critic: Whereas the message itself records what was said, what was not said obviously includes everything else potentially sayable. Harold Hill talked of pool tables, but he did not talk of inflation or virtual reality or plane geometry or cabbages or kings. The solution to the critic's dilemma is obviously to discover what *important* things Harold Hill did not say. Accordingly, this chapter includes a "universal" list of idea types for the critic's use. This is not a perfect solution. After all, no list of anything human can ever be exhaustive and anything that is list-like can become artificial. But the benefits seem to outweigh the liabilities and so I recommend the use of this universal list.

2. *Analyzing ideas alerts us to rhetorical patterns.* Throughout this book, the critic will be urged to pay special attention to patterns of ideas. Even though exceptions to patterns can be important, the concept of exception makes no sense apart from the concept of pattern. As a result, there is a sense in which all critics are mathematicians because, whether they are aware of it or not, they count things when making discriminations. For example, a critic may say, "The speaker's use of language was brilliant" (Translation: "Compared to a group of speakers, this speaker deviated substantially from the mean on a number of language variables.")

The point here is not to make the critic sound like some sort of crazed scientist but to dramatize how much the critic depends on perceptions of rhetorical pattern and how often, knowingly or unknowingly, the critic makes statements of proportion: e.g., "I was surprised that the speaker ignored the budgetary argument." (Translation: "Given the amount of time most people spend talking about money, spending this much time on aesthetics seems out of the norm.") But even though critics depend on rhetorical patterns, they do not always acknowledge this dependence, nor do they always document their claims about matters of proportion. The critical techniques in this chapter can improve on that condition.

3. *Analyzing ideas helps to explain rhetorical "tone."* A word like "tone" almost always appears in quotation marks. Tone is the sort of thing that all persons feel but that few can describe. Tone is like other phrases that also appear in quotation marks, phrases referring to the "feeling state" or "emotional residue" or "psychic power" of a message. Placing such phrases in quotation marks is not so much to disparage them as it is to admit critical defeat: We know tone when we see it but few of us can talk about it intelligently. And yet even though the tone of a message can be hard to describe, it is often not hard to identify. For example, when students of criticism were asked to describe the Hill speech as well as the Prinz and Patton speeches discussed in Chapter 3, they did so with ease and with impressive unanimity. When asked to position these speeches on the scales presented in Figure 4.1, their agreement approached 90%.

As is often the case with tone, the students could not be shaken in their judgments of these speeches but, equally, they were hard pressed to state *explicitly* how they knew what they knew. However, by stepping back a bit, by taking the time to sketch the flow of ideas, by using standard idea lists to describe the messages being examined, and by asking the question constantly "What, specifically, is telling me what I know to be the case?" the students became more precise.

One ancient, simple technique they used was to translate the texts into their own language via outlining, thereby de-rhetoricalizing what the speaker had made rhetorical. This chapter will present more ambitious techniques, thereby giving the critic a **technical language** for discussing the hard to discuss. Such techniques are no cure-all but they can advance the scholarly discussion, and that is the spirit in which they are offered here.

FIGURE 4.1 Scales for Describing Rhetorical Tone

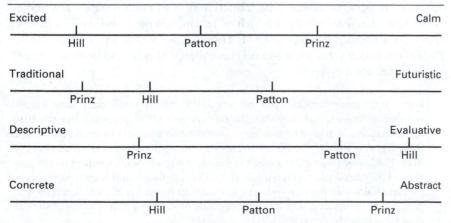

A TOPICAL APPROACH TO IDEAS

Nobody knows precisely where ideas come from or why some ideas bubble to the surface of public discussion more often than others. And yet our daily experiences require us to establish priorities about ideas. The person described as having a "personality problem," for example, is often just a person with an "idea problem"—that is, one who thinks differently from us. Travel to a foreign country can be difficult for the same reason. The impatient American who drums her fingers on the table of the Roman cafe while waiting for service learns that some ideas (like efficiency) are not revered equally in all cultures. Indeed, the very concept of "culture" is a shorthand designation for groups of people who prefer the same kinds of ideas and who go to the same sorts of places to find new ones.

At times, it may seem as if there are as many ideas in the world as there are people. The proof of this is found each day in the pages of the *National Inquirer,* a journal that specializes in the idiosyncratic ("Boy marries great aunt," "Honors student dismembers algebra teacher"). But there is a *predictable* idiosyncrasy to the stories published in the *National Inquirer,* as if the editors rewrote the same stories each week, changing only the names and locations of the aunts and algebra teachers mentioned. Such constancy implies that the millions of individual stories in the world derive from a limited number of "master stories." This chapter assumes that there are sixteen places from which such stories are drawn. This chapter also assumes that knowing about these ideational places increases a critic's sensitivity to rhetorical ideas.

Ever since persuasion has been studied, scholars have been interested in the common themes of public discourse. The ancient Greeks thought of these traditional themes (they called them *topoi*) as the ideas underlying all ideas; similarly, the ancient Romans conceived of a limited set of commonplaces capable of "housing" all conceivable arguments. Two thousand years ago, to be trained in persuasion was to be trained in how to fashion public arguments from these ideas-behind-all-ideas. More recently, Wilson and Arnold [1974] identified a useful list of **Universal Topics** from which most ideas derive. Their claim is that some variation on these topical themes can be found in any public or private message:

> For a good many centuries scholars argued that people talk on a fairly limited number of themes, that they vary the treatments of basic ideas but not the basic ideas themselves. You need not hear or read many speeches or essays to see that these thinkers were right. We all discuss the same general types of ideas over and over. This is not a sign of laziness, it is the natural result of the kinds of things people feel they need talk to each other about. We all discuss and argue chiefly about human affairs, and the ways you can think about human affairs are limited within any culture. The result is that we can actually predict in advance many of the categories of thought any talker will use. . . . [p. 76]

Throughout history, topical systems like Wilson and Arnold's have been used as autosuggestive or cueing devices to help students invent ideas for speaking or writing. Rather than being asked to "just think" about a given subject matter, for example, students have been given a list of topics to help stimulate their imaginations. But systematic use of these universal topics in criticism has not been as common, even though such a system can be helpful to the critic for these reasons:

1. It is a reasonably *complete* way of categorizing persuasive arguments.
2. It is a simple and efficient method of *reducing* a message to its essential rhetorical character.
3. Because it is a fixed system, it is can help reveal *patterns* of argument that might not have been noticed otherwise.
4. It allows the critic to make *proportional* statements about the themes of a given message.

Listed below are the sixteen universal topics Wilson and Arnold have isolated in their studies. Next to each are examples (from Hart et al. [1983: 452–3]) of how the topic might be developed in a hypothetical argument by a hypothetical Surgeon General discussing the not-so-hypothetical problem of hearing disorders:

1. EXISTENCE or nonexistence of things (e.g., "Over 50 percent of the elderly have hearing disorders; workers in a noisy environment are especially prone to hearing problems.").
2. DEGREE or quantity of things, forces, etc. (e.g., "Hearing problems can range from mild ringing in ears to total deafness and even death.").
3. SPATIAL attributes, including adjacency, distribution, place (e.g., "There is an intimate connection between brain and ear; the ear covers only a small area of the body but magnifies sound incredibly.").
4. TEMPORAL attributes, including hour, day, year, era (e.g., "One can lose hearing overnight; many middle-ear infections occur between 4 and 7 years of age.").
5. MOTION or activity (e.g., "Fast movement can cause dizziness because of inner-ear problems; rapidly moving sound waves can cause temporary loss of hearing.").
6. FORM, either physical shape or abstract categories (e.g., "Some hearing losses result from inner ear vs. outer ear problems.").
7. SUBSTANCE: physical or abstract; the fundamental nature of a thing, often signaled by definitions (e.g., "The roots of hearing loss sometimes lie in basic, psychological trauma.").
8. CAPACITY TO CHANGE, including predictability (e.g., "The inner ear can improve itself; surgery can correct middle-ear damage.").
9. POTENCY: power or energy, including capacity to further or hinder something (e.g., "Hearing problems can make us unable to discriminate any sort of speech.").

10. DESIRABILITY, in terms of rewards or punishments (e.g., "Audiological difficulties hinder social interactions and can adversely affect employment opportunities.").
11. FEASIBILITY: workability or practicability (e.g., "Auditory training can be established for those with residual hearing problems; lip reading training is also possible in some cases.").
12. CAUSALITY: the relationship of causes to effects, effect to effects, adequacy of causes, etc. (e.g., "Abnormal growths in the ear cause problems; high fever and infection can also cause damage.").
13. CORRELATION, coexistence or coordination of things, forces, etc. (e.g., "Hearing difficulties can be related to viral diseases.").
14. GENUS-SPECIES relationships (e.g., "Hearing specialists are an important part of the larger medical community.").
15. SIMILARITY or dissimilarity (e.g., "There is sometimes a distinction between the hearing problems of older people and those that affect children.").
16. POSSIBILITY or impossibility (e.g., "The inner ear cannot be corrected by surgery but hearing aids can provide some measure of relief.").

When using this list of Universal Topics for criticism, students have found these guidelines to be helpful: (1) Work with two or three other critics, designating each member of the team a "specialist" on four or five of the universal topics; (2) proceed through the message on a statement-by-statement basis, with relevant members of the critical team making "bids" for "ownership" of individual statements; (3) assign each statement to no more than two of the categories listed; if uncertainties develop (and they will) delay resolving them until the entire message has been inspected; (4) if disagreement persists after thorough discussion of problematic statements, assign the statement to multiple categories on a proportional basis. Classroom exercises using these techniques have shown that these categories can be learned fairly quickly and that after only a few group experiences students can master the system and then use it in their own critical projects. The goal here is surely *not* to develop scientific precision but simply to provide a rough "topical translation" of the message being inspected.

While this approach seems to make sense theoretically, the worth of any critical system lies in its utility. Accordingly, Table 4.1 presents the topical sketches that student critics developed of the Prinz and Patton speeches presented in Chapter 2 and the Hill speech presented earlier in this chapter. When doing their work, the students asked (1) which topics were used? (2) which were not? and (3) why?

Clearly, the three passages present very different profiles. But before discussing the differences, the similarities should be noted, the most dramatic of which is that all three speakers used Correlation quite often. Given the different speech situations they faced, what could such a finding mean? Most likely, it suggests that each speaker felt the need to be something of a bridge-builder,

TABLE 4.1 Comparative Use of Universal Topics

Universal Topics	Rabbi Prinz	Harold Hill	George Patton
Existence	2	14	5
Degree	9	7	6
Spatial	6	9	3
Time	10	11	2
Motion	5	11	5
Form	0	0	2
Substance	18	0	13
Capacity to change	5	2	4
Potency	8	7	6
Desirability	7	28	7
Feasibility	0	1	9
Causality	4	7	13
Correlation	9	8	13
Genus-species	5	0	0
Similarity/dissimilarity	8	1	4
Possibility/impossibility	4	1	9

perhaps because each was in some sense an outsider. Harold Hill's case is an obvious one. He spends much of his time linking pool halls and sin in the first part of his speech and, later, linking musical instruments with virtue. It is probably the obviousness of these strained linkages that makes us smile as we easily uncover Hill's deviousness. *We* can see that Hill is "using" these good Iowans by appropriating their values and anxieties for his mercantile purposes. But it is also true that Hill's status as a geographical outsider left him with little choice other than to be a builder of bridges. Sloth and degradation, frittering and corruption, medicinal wine and riotous living—disingenuous correlations for a seller of band instruments, but not unlike those used weekly at a Billy Graham Crusade.

Rabbi Prinz was not so much a geographical outsider as he was a cultural outsider, and so he too offered equations: of Jewish and black ghettos, of Jewish and Christian morality, of Old World and New World dreams. His correlations are more uplifting than Hill's but in some ways they are remarkably similar. Both took the "high road" morally, Prinz because he was a cleric, Hill because he was a conniver.

And George Patton's exalted status made him an outsider of sorts as well, one presumably removed from the life of the everyday soldier. As a general among generals, Patton had to demonstrate clear relationships between the war he was fighting and the war he expected his men to fight. His equations were graphic in their simplicity: the Army life and the sporting life; dehumanization and German militarization; American virtue and all virtue.

To a lesser extent, all three speakers made use of Potency, Motion, Degree, and Desirability. They did so because each in their own way was a highly energized persuader with a message to share and a grand new world to describe.

Harold Hill's world included a powerful army of young people striding splendidly down Main Street, virtuous and energetic young people marching toward the Good (and carrying his band instruments). General Patton, too, paints a vibrant picture—of strong, active soldiers doing strong, active things, overcoming a feckless and morally bankrupt enemy. Although he is less histrionic than either Hill or Patton, Rabbi Prinz takes pains to link Degree ("the most urgent, the most disgraceful, the most shameful, and the most tragic problem") with Potency ("a glorious, unshakable reality in a morally united America") in order to pound home his themes of justice and equality for all.

All three speakers were therefore activists, and their rhetoric reflects that fact. But none was a college lecturer and hence none spent time detailing abstract, structural relationships (e.g., Form or Genus-species relationships). Also, because each speaker meant to begin dialogue on the matters they treated rather than to nail down practical policies, they generally avoided discussion of such sticky issues as how change would be implemented, at what price, with what difficulties, and how soon. Other speakers on other occasions would tackle these detailed issues, they seemed to reason.

In this sense, Harold Hill was the classic salesperson: long on promises and short on application. Notice that he develops a 28:1 ratio of Desirability to Feasibility, not at all unlike the sales pitch for the power mower delivered weekly in the Sears Garden Shop. In the rousing conclusion to his speech, for example, Hill links the soon-to-be River City Boys Band (which his instrument sales will help to create) to Maine, Plymouth Rock, and the Golden Rule, but he never mentions the price of a piccolo.

Hill also spends considerably more time on the topic of Existence than the other speakers, perhaps because he had a problem: He had no problem. That is, there was no good, compelling reason for the quiet folks in River City, Iowa, to have their collective ears assaulted by the screeches of adolescent music-making (and to pay good money for the privilege of doing so). Harold Hill knew this, and he also knew that the motivating "problem" had to be a major one. So he used what he had—a pool hall—and he willed that shameful instance to a universal sin. His speech is thus really two speeches, with Existence dominating the first and Desirability the second.

Rabbi Prinz made the bravest attempt of all three speakers at Capacity to Change ("America must speak up and act from the President down to the humblest of us") but his attempt is still modest, perhaps because his primary rhetorical purpose was to set up the magnificent oration of Martin Luther King, Jr., immediately following, an address that would amply discuss such themes. It is also noteworthy that the Rabbi completely eschewed Feasibility, perhaps because to raise such matters would take more time than he was allotted, perhaps because a discussion of pragmatics would have been inappropriate in a ceremonial setting, or perhaps because the civil rights movement was then in its infancy and nobody knew exactly *how* human justice could be achieved.

Given such limitations, the Rabbi was wise to stick with Substance. He spent most of his time defining key concepts like dignity, the American idea, neighborliness, silence, hatred, and morality. Such a scholarly (Talmudic?) approach cost the Rabbi Harold Hill's energy and George Patton's assuredness but it no doubt helped him play the part he was intended to play at the March on Washington.

A somewhat different tone emerges in the Patton speech. Patton used some amount of Feasibility and Possibility, no doubt because a Desirable but Unfeasible or Impossible speech would hardly have been motivating to men about to enter battle. More subtly, however, he also stressed Causality, explicitly telling his men which actions would produce which effects (e.g., "Every man in the mess hall, even the one who heats the water to keep us from getting diarrhea, has a job to do."). A causally driven speech like Patton's is indeed heartening. It is clean, clear, linear, pragmatic, and thoroughly Western in its philosophical orientation. Such a speech raises no question (e.g., cowardice, defeat) that it does not also answer. Patton begins his speech with causal patterns (hard work produces athletic success) and he ends it in the same way (bravery under fire ensures immortality in the eyes of one's grandson).

Equally interesting is Patton's use of Substance. It is this topic that distinguishes Patton's remarks from messages heralding sure-fire success or a money-back guarantee. The substance of which Patton speaks is bravery and patriotism. Placed alone in a speech, such matters could have produced empty abstractions. And, indeed, there is a real sermonic quality to Patton's statement, with only Rabbi Prinz (at 18%) surpassing him on Substance. The thing that makes Patton's speech so interesting is that he manages to run both theoretical *and* practical themes against one another, with the former whetting listeners' appetites and the latter ensuring them sustenance. The result is a great amount of rhetorical energy, perhaps explaining why students were so ambivalent when describing the tone of Patton's speech (see Figure 4.1).

As mentioned earlier, the statements in a verbal text indicate where a speaker *ended* thought about the subject at hand. But that is only part of the story. It is also important to know where a speaker *began* looking for thoughts. Topical analysis lets the critic look "beneath" words to find the essential places from which those words emanated. Because it focuses on such basic matters, topical analysis is particularly useful for examining public controversies, arenas in which people often talk past one another precisely because they have *begun* their arguments in different places.

Imagine, for example, how rancorous discussion could become between a speaker who operated from Feasibility ("let's do it this way because it will work") and another who operated from Substance ("let's do it this way because people must be protected from their baser natures"). According to Einhorn [1981], that is precisely the situation in which John Madison and Patrick Henry found themselves during the Virginia Ratification Debates, with Madison arguing on the basis of practicality and Henry arguing philosophically.

Jasinski [1992] found a similar kind of tension in his study of the Colonial era, with the Federalists often using Spatial imagery to broaden the vision of their fellow colonists, while the Antifederalists used more concrete arguments (Correlation, Causality, etc.) to keep their audiences grounded in practicality and turned away from the "preposterous" notion of a broad and cohesive nation.

On a very different front, Parry-Giles [1994] studied the development of post–World War II propaganda strategies and found a decided shift in tone from the Truman to the Eisenhower administration. During these years, American propaganda moved away from an emphasis on the essential Similarity of all democratic citizens to more psychologically based appeals (Potency, Desirability, Possibility) that stressed the fears and uncertainties of nuclear conflagration. In another study, Medhurst [1985] discovered that the public argument between conservatives and the rest of society often hinges on different rhetorical treatments of Desirability and Feasibility, while Mackin [1991] warns that an attempt to build esprit de corps on the basis of people's Dissimilarity from their rivals may work in the short run but that it will ultimately destroy the "ecology" of the human community at large.

Several studies have used ideational analysis to explain the success or failure of individual speakers or movements. Daughton [1993], for example, found that Franklin Roosevelt's ability to combine militaristic arguments based on Potency with more theological arguments based on Existence gave him an unusual ability to sway the masses. But not all rhetoric succeeds in fostering a sense of community. Solomon [1983b] discovered, for example, that the rhetoric of antifeminists often cut off dialogue because it spent so much time on Impossibility and Dissimilarity. By basing so much of its rhetoric on the supposed differences between men and women, the movement painted itself into a very small corner. As a result, the movement could not secure the cooperation of nonideologues, people concerned with more practical matters like Desirability (of guaranteed rights) and Feasibility (of employment opportunities). As Zyskind [1968] has shown, Desirability and Feasibility are the hardiest rhetorical topics in American cultural history. Any movement that cannot deploy such arguments must probably resign itself to marginal status.

An interesting study by Kaufer [1980] showed how some speakers habitually operate from the same topical premises no matter what the rhetorical situation. Kaufer studied Clarence Darrow's famed defense of Loeb and Leopold during their trial in the early 1920s (they were accused of having wantonly killed a fourteen-year-old). According to Kaufer, Darrow was remarkably consistent in his use of Causality, arguing that mercy should be shown to Loeb and Leopold because their cultural and psychological upbringing (the Cause) left them no choice but to commit the crime they did (the Effect). As with the famed 1990s Menendez brothers' trial (young men who killed their parents), Darrow asked for a guilty verdict against society and mercy for the defendants (who, as it turns out, were both wealthy and well educated, also not unlike the Menendezes). Kaufer notes that Darrow's persistent use of Causality even in such a preposterous situation revealed the depths of Darrow's commitment to what is now known as Behaviorism, a philosophy that still undergirds much political and judicial decision-making in the United States today.

The topical approach is only one of many ways of examining ideas. Also, such a general approach only begins the process of criticism. But being somewhat systematic when first approaching a text has its uses. After all, one of the most perplexing things about doing criticism is knowing where to start. The suggestion made here is that critics should start their criticism where persuaders start their persuasion.

A JUDGMENTAL APPROACH TO IDEAS

The topical approach for describing ideas tends to be speaker-oriented. A second approach is Arnold's [1974], which focuses on the judgments *listeners* are asked to make during persuasion. Arnold's approach is based on these assumptions: (1) when speakers speak, they assume that listeners will make judgments about their remarks; (2) a verbal text is a record of the kinds of judgments audiences are being asked to make; (3) a text records only the *potential,* not the actual, judgments listeners make; (4) because rhetorical occasions are often standardized, there are a limited number of *classic* judgmental requests.

In building his system, Arnold catalogued these standard rhetorical occasions and concluded that four arguments predominate in the social world: What is empirically true? What is morally correct? What makes us happy? How should we proceed? Arnold reasoned further that most rhetorical statements reflect one or more of these "stock issues" and thus that all statements radiate from one of four classic judgmental requests. Modified a bit, they are:

1. Factual: Statements that expect listeners to consult the world around them when judging the speaker's remarks. Such consultations can be focused on the past ("the O. J. Simpson trial was one of the most expensive in U.S. history."), the present ("Nobody beats the prices at Acme Landscaping."), or the future ("Let's meet for dinner in Boston next Tuesday."). Because these statements occur in rhetorical texts, they often do not meet a scientist's rigorous standards of factuality. Rather, they are treated as commonsense facts. Thus, even a controversial statement like "The United States is second to Japan in technological know-how" is treated as a Factual request because the listener is being encouraged to consult real-world conditions when judging the speaker's assertion.

2. Optative: Statements that expect listeners to consult their own general wishes and preferences or those of their social grouping when judging the speaker's remarks. Unlike factual statements, optative requests have a clearly valuative flavor. The values undergirding them include taste ("New Yorkers are too pushy for me."), efficiency ("Georgians take too long to get things done."), beauty ("Ohioans let themselves get too heavy."), or practicality

("Californians are completely unrealistic."). The obviousness of these evaluations often differs sharply ("She seems nice." vs. "What a great person!"), but
Arnold's system does not require making subtle distinctions about such
matters.

   3. *Adjudicative:* Statements that expect listeners to consult some sort of
formally proclaimed code of behavior when judging the speaker's remarks.
Adjudicatives are judgmental neighbors to Optatives since both are valuative.
But when a speaker makes Adjudicative requests the speaker asks that formal,
institutional (often written) standards be consulted mentally before passing
judgment. Such codes are normally more specific and rigid than the more general Optative standards. The specifications they make can include law ("The
accused has committed a heinous crime, your Honor."), religion ("The Bible
fully endorses tithing, my children."), etiquette ("One should never kiss on
the first date."), or political ideology ("the true spirit of communism
denounces this practice, my comrades.").

   Over time, subgroups of people often transform general, Optative standards into Adjudicative ones so that some sort of dogma results. For example,
the "Miss America Code" replaces for beauty contestants what normally serves
as general standards of propriety for the rest of us. The "I.B.M. Doctrine"
replaces general notions of efficiency for Big Blue's new employees. The "Scientific Procedure" is ingrained in young chemists, replacing their earlier standards of ordinary carefulness. To become indoctrinated is to learn to use such
codes when making decisions. Knowing such things, and knowing that code-
based judgments are often more reliable than more general wishes and preferences, persuaders are strongly attracted to Adjudicative statements.

   4. *Promissory:* Statements that expect listeners to consult their hopes and
dreams when judging the remarks of the speaker. Promissory statements (or,
as Arnold calls them, Predictive of Desirability statements) explicitly or implicitly detail the positive consequences of adopting a new attitude or standard of
behavior. Rhetorical messages often differ dramatically in how clearly they
explicate the good that will result from speaker/listener agreement. In some
persuasion, for example, the promises are bold and unmistakable but fairly
sketchy ("7.8% home loans at Bank of America. They've never been lower.")
while other forms of persuasion (e.g., a brochure for a resort hotel) detail the
wonders that await the tourist. The promises in yet other rhetoric is all too
clear: "Miller Lite: less filling, tastes great." In still other cases (e.g., perfume
advertising), Factuals and Optatives fill the verbal text while pictures (e.g., a
wind-swept beach in Bermuda) are used to hint at promises. Normally, then,
"hard-sell" and "soft-sell" can be measured by calculating the (1) frequency,
(2) explicitness, and (3) detail of the *verbal* promises made.

   A helpful way of employing the judgmental approach is to catalog the
individual statements making up a text, using the definitions and examples
above as a guide. The experience of critics who have used this system suggests
that in addition to the four "pure" types of judgments, most rhetorical

messages will contain a good number of mixed statements as well. Often, it is the critic's ability to account for these mixed perceptions that makes Arnold's system especially useful. That is, while a statement like "I joined Nate's Health Spa" clearly makes a Factual request of the listener ("you believe me, don't you?"), a statement from a commercial like "I joined Nate's Health Spa and lost 75 pounds in only one month" operates very differently. In the second (Factual/Promissory) statement, the speaker clearly implies "And you can too!" even though this statement never appears in the text itself. Intuitively, we "know" that the second statement differs markedly from the first but it is initially hard to say exactly how the two statements differ. Arnold's system gives us a technical language for talking about such subtle, but undeniably important, differences in rhetorical texture.

Table 4.2 presents the eight most common types of judgmental requests along with brief commentary on their likely uses in persuasion. While the individual critic may find still other judgmental combinations, this list should be sufficient for most purposes. As with the topical system, the critic might proceed through a message statement by statement, noting which judgmental

TABLE 4.2 Some Common Types of Judgmental Requests

Judgment Type	Example	Use
1. Factual	"You can't get to Boise by airplane."	A workhorse strategy in persuasion. Used to establish substantiveness.
2. Operative	"It's not worth the paper it's written on."	Used to establish the desirability or undesirability of a claim.
3. Adjudicative	"Anyone would say that is not a real American."	A "high-profile" strategy often used when the audience subscribes to a clear-cut code of right and wrong.
4. Promissory	"With Smith in our camp, we can't help but win the election."	A very obvious "pitch" in which a speaker delineates the forthcoming benefits of a proposal.
5. Factual/optative	"Mr. Jones told me that your work has been unsatisfactory lately."	Usually appears as (formal or informal) testimony. Used to substantiate evaluations offered.
6. Factual/adjudicative	"If you pursue this course of action, the Church will roundly condemn you."	A strategy that borrows the credibility of another code or institution in order to heighten the acceptability or unacceptability of a policy.
7. Optative/promissory	"Anyone as sweet as you will go places in this world."	Often used in "hard-sell" persuasion. Shows that the evaluation given means something (that is, it has observable consequences).
8. Factual/promissory	"Fred's high IQ will make him a great deal of money later in life."	A narrative approach that hopes that the listener will make a subtle transference to his or her life. Hints that if good things happened in Case A, they will also happen in Case B.

clusters develop, where in the message they are found, and which judgments are conspicuously absent or underrepresented. Especially when first trying out this system, it is useful to work in teams with other critics. However, the ideal methodology is for the critic to make these judgmental discriminations alone and only *later* compare notes with others. In that way, the perceptiveness of the individual analyst is buttressed by the breadth of group vision.

Students of criticism using the judgmental system have made several interesting points about the three speeches mentioned earlier. For example, they noted that the "military code" produced a number of Adjudicative requests from Patton (e.g., "This individuality stuff is a bunch of crap.") but that he warmed up his audience first by making a number of culturally sanctioned, Optative requests (e.g., "Americans traditionally love to fight."). Students who compared the real Patton speech to the movie version found 50% fewer Factual requests in the latter, indicating that real soldiers need hard data but that movie audiences are primarily interested in "color" (i.e., in Patton's undeniably valuative language).

Uses of Promissory judgments differed radically from speech to speech, with virtually all of the latter half of the Patton speech being Promissory but virtually none of the statements in the Prinz speech being of this sort. Indeed, roughly 90% of Prinz's speech contained nothing but Factuals and Adjudicatives. Apparently, the Rabbi saw his job as one of (factually) establishing the similarity between Jewish and black experience and then Adjudicatively aligning the goals of the civil rights movement with appropriate religious and Constitutional mandates. The result is a somber tone (no Optatives) as well as a sober tone (no Promissories), both of which contrast sharply with Harold Hill's message.

The first third of Hill's speech (the portion presented here earlier) is a salad of Optative judgments based on simple pleasure ("the hours I spent with a cue in my hand are golden") or modes of relaxation ("Not a wholesome trottin' race. No!"). Warming to his subject, Hill piles in an equal assortment of Adjudicative judgments in the second third of his speech (e.g., "We've . . . got to figure out a way to keep the young ones moral after school") and closes this segment with a stark Adjudicative admonition: "That game with fifteen numbered balls is the Devil's tool." The final third of Hill's speech (the famous "Seventy-Six Trombones") is heavily Promissory, as Hill marches his now-duped, soon-to-be customers all around the town square. The irony of the speech, of course, lies in the riotous *mixing* of Optatives and Adjudicatives as well as in Hill's presumptuous use of sacred codes for the selling of band instruments.

Having made these observations, however, can we say that the judgmental system is truly helpful? Does it promise more than critical jargon? There seem to be at least six major advantages to this approach:

1. The system highlights speaker/audience relationships. One of the first studies to use this system, Douglass and Arnold, [1970] found it to be much less sterile than other critical procedures because it forces the critic to pay attention to *social* realities and not just to the verbal eccentricities of a given message. By conceiving of a speaker as one who constantly makes requests of listeners, the critic is reminded again and again how cooperative communication must be if it is to succeed. Hart [1970] found, for example, that True Believers (e.g., American Communists or the right-wing John Birch Society) both began and ended their messages with Adjudicative arguments, sandwiching between them whatever facts of the day they were discussing. Because this pattern was so consistent, Hart concluded that all such speeches were designed to celebrate the truths these speakers and audience shared.

In contrast, speakers facing unfamiliar audiences made almost half of their requests on Optative bases since they could depend only on audiences' general wishes and preferences. Intriguingly, speakers facing hostile listeners made twice as many Promissory requests as most speakers, ostensibly because they were trying to "buy off" the hostility with hints of things to come.

2. *The system exposes patterns of rhetoric.* In Chapter 6, we will discuss generic studies of rhetoric, studies focusing on how certain messages can be grouped together in distinctive classes. Most of us are aware of these classes. Using such information, we sort each day's mail: personal letters, bills, charitable solicitations, and a large assortment of junk mail. But what rhetorical markers help us do the sorting? How, exactly, does a letter from Uncle Joshua differ from a letter from Uncle Sam? Most likely, Uncle Joshua loads his letter with Factuals and Optatives ("had a lovely day at the lake last week with your cousin, Ben") whereas Uncle Sam tends more toward the Adjudicative ("the penalty for not replying to this notice within 30 days is . . . ").

The coupon sent to us by Aunt Jemima, in contrast, is filled with Promissories ("ten cents off on your next purchase," "best-tasting syrup you've ever put on a pancake"). Often, clever persuaders try to transport the tone of one rhetorical class (e.g., a revival meeting) to another situation (e.g., a pitch for band instruments) so as to disguise their persuasive intentions. Using the judgmental system, the critic can become sensitive to the tonal features of these different rhetorical classes.

3. *The system identifies influential situational factors.* Most people know that the mass media have changed how persuasion operates, but what do those changes look like? What adaptations must a reporter make, for example, when relating a story to a television audience rather than writing it for the local paper? (More detailed Factuals in the latter?) What is the essential rhetorical difference between a legal drama on television and an actual trial in the county courthouse? (Fewer dull Adjudicatives in the former?) How have members of Congress changed their styles now that C-Span carries their spoken remarks live to every home in the United States? (More lively Optatives?) Now that even out-of-the-way speeches by a presidential barnstormer can be videotaped and replayed for a national audience, how will campaign speeches change? (Less obvious Promissories?) Because the judgmental system is so sensitive to

changes in rhetorical tone, the system holds real promise for monitoring situational influences.

   4. The system increases sensitivity to ideology. A real advantage of the Arnold system is that it distinguishes between Optatives and Adjudicatives, that is, between informal and institutionalized beliefs. As Hart [1971] and Clark [1977] found, religious and secular discourse often differs sharply, with the former depending on Adjudicatives and the latter having to settle for Optatives. Along a different line, Jablonski [1979a] discovered that even though many sociological changes swept through the Roman Catholic church in the 1960s, the judgmental patterns in its rhetoric did not change, suggesting that *rhetorical* conservatism may inhibit philosophical radicalism.

   Campbell [1996] made a parallel discovery. He found that in order to escape theological censure for his new theory of evolution, Charles Darwin dramatically abandoned the scientific code (Factuals + Adjudicatives) at crucial points in his writing, often going off on highly personalized, moralistic, and sometimes even frankly nationalistic tangents in order to disguise the rather startling implications of his new theory. A reverse situation presented itself in a Jehovah Witnesses tract entitled "Are They Harmless Observances?" [1974] wherein the author attempted to prove (Adjudicatively) that celebrations of Valentine's Day, May Day, and Mother's Day must be decried because the Bible enjoins its readers to "quit touching the unclean thing." By comparing the use of formal and informal evaluations, then, the critic can often make uncommon discoveries about public discourse.

   5. The system helps explain rhetorical momentum. Some messages seem to trudge along slowly, making their cases with deadly precision, while others fly by, dazzling the eye with rhetorical fireworks. Often, this latter effect is generated by linking one Promissory statement after another, as we see in the following rather breathless piece of advertising:

> Ski. Mix. Meet. Vail is tall and tan and single and every night's like Friday. It's a swift track down an alpine bowl in tandem with that Austrian accent who rode up in the gondola with you. And helped with your bindings and gave you goose bumps.
>   Vail is wineskins at noon at a romantic level called timberline. It's gaslight, fondue, and accordions. Discovery in a boutique. Youth. And experience that ages well. There's even a trail called Swingsville. . . . [Vail Resort, n.d.]

This excerpt might serve as a baseline against which all messages could be judged for momentum! Most texts do not contain such energy. According to the studies done thus far, Promissory statements comprise about 10% of the average public speech; normally, such statements are found in conclusions. The proportion in advertising is probably much higher; the ad from which the passage above was extracted approached 80% Promissory statements. Often, the proportion of Promissory statements in a message will be a good indicator of rhetorical subtlety, so the critic should be especially attentive to both the number and placement of these judgments. Developing sensitivity to rhetorical momentum can be the best ally of the critic interested in consumer protection.

6. *The system can be used to index cultural change.* Because the judgmental system is simple and yet suitably comprehensive, it helps detect alterations in rhetorical fashion. As we shall see in Chapter 11, changing cultural values are often reflected in popular rhetoric. The judgmental critic can sometimes detect these changes ahead of time. For example, some time ago McDonald's ran a national advertisement extolling its virtues. Standard enough. But the virtues it described were not its traditional ones (cheap and tasty food served quickly), nor did the advertisement contain the usual visual claptrap (smiling faces; colorful logos; lots of red, white and blue). Rather, the advertisement was densely written and visually simple. Its arguments were particularly interesting:

- "At McDonald's, we serve you beef that's leaner than the kind of ground beef most people buy in the supermarket. . . .
- "No fillers. No additives. 100% pure American beef. . . .
- "Grade A milk in our milk shakes, sundaes and cones. . . .
- "Buns from top-quality enriched American wheat—baked locally."
- "We believe you can't turn out the best meals unless you have good nutritious food to start with. So that's where we start." [McDonald's, 1987]

The ad went on to make reference to the U.S. Department of Agriculture, to dietary guidelines, to the basic food groups, to saturated fat and cholesterol, to balanced meals, and it ended by offering free information from its "Nutrition Information Center." Heady stuff for a fast-food operation.

With the exception of its sign-off ("It's a good time for the great taste"), the ad contained very few Optative statements. Virtually all of the evaluations it offered (and there were some forty, rather long statements in the message) emerged from the "Dietary Code" now being promulgated by physicians, nutritionists, health clubs, and school nurses. Naturally, the ad—because it was an ad—was heavily Promissory as well. But the really impressive piece of cultural news lay in *what* it promised (Adjudicative allegiance), indicating the great popularity of the new nutritional consensus in the United States. When a fry-'em-up operation like McDonald's feels the need to bow at the altar of the U.S. Department of Agriculture, cultural change must surely be in the wind.

CONCLUSION

In this chapter we have explored two major ways of examining ideational content. Clearly, the topical and judgmental approaches are only two among many. But both are good places for a critic to start. Both systems take some getting used to but they give the critic a fairly precise way of talking about an art—the art of rhetoric—that is so often imprecise. Both systems urge the critic to "violate" the natural structure of a message by reducing it to its most basic ideational units. In so doing, the critic runs the risk of somewhat distorting the rhetorical experience listeners themselves underwent. But this seems to be a risk worth running, especially if it helps the critic discuss the listening experience in ways that listeners themselves might find strange but which they could not disavow.

Persuaders, of course, do not encourage such dismantling of their arguments. That is why the critic must attempt it. In many ways, the simple act of recategorizing a speaker's ideas is a fundamentally revolutionary act for it means that *the critic's system,* not the speaker's system, will guide the critic's perceptions. In this sense, rhetorical criticism is a game of cat-and-mouse played by critic and speaker. The topical and judgmental systems of analysis give the critic an extra advantage in this continually fascinating game.

Chapter 5

ANALYZING ARGUMENT

My fellow Americans: I come before you tonight as a candidate for the vice-presidency and as a man whose honesty and integrity has been questioned. Now, the usual political thing to do when charges are made against you is either ignore them or to deny them without giving details. I believe we have had enough of that in the United States, particularly with the present administration in Washington, D.C. To me the office of the vice-presidency is a great office, and I feel that the people have got to have confidence in the integrity of the men who run for that office and who might attain them. I have a theory, too, that the best and only answer to a smear or to an honest misunderstanding of the facts is to tell the truth. And that is why I am here tonight. I want to tell you my side of the case.

I am sure that you have read the charge, and you have heard it, that I, Senator Nixon, took $18,000 from a group of my supporters. Now, was that wrong? And let me say that it was wrong . . . I am saying it, incidentally, that it was wrong, not just illegal, because it isn't a question of whether it was legal or illegal: that isn't enough. The question is, was it morally wrong? . . . I say that it was morally wrong—if any of that $18,000 went to Senator Nixon, for my personal use, I say that it was morally wrong if it was secretly given and secretly handled. And I say that it was morally wrong if any of the contributors got special favors for the contributions they made.

And now, to answer those questions, let me say this: Not one cent of the $18,000 or any other money of that type ever went to me for my personal use. Every penny of it was used to pay for political expenses that I did not think should be charged to the taxpayers of the United States.

It was not a secret fund. As a matter of fact, when I was on "Meet the Press"—some of you may have seen it, last Sunday—Peter Edson came up to me, after the program, and he said, "Dick, what about this fund we hear about?" And I said, "Well, there is no secret about it. Go out and see Dana Smith, who was the administrator of the fund," and I gave him his address. And I said, "You will find that the purpose of the fund simply was to defray political expenses that I did not feel should be charged to the government."

And, third, let me point out, and I want to make this particularly clear, that no contributor to this fund, no contributor to any of my campaigns, has ever received any consideration that he would not have received as an ordinary constituent. I just don't believe in that, and I can say that never, while I have been in the Senate of the United States, as far as the people that contributed to this fund are concerned, have I made a telephone call for them to an agency, nor have I gone down to an agency in their behalf. And the records will show that, the records which are in the hands of the administration.

Well, then, some of you will say, and rightly, "Well, what did you use the fund for, Senator? Why did you have to have it?" Let me tell you in just a word how a Senate office operates. First of all . . . .

*****

And now, finally, I know that you wonder whether or not I am going to stay on the Republican ticket or resign. Let me say this: I don't believe that I ought to quit, because I am not a quitter. And, incidentally, Pat is not a quitter. After all, her name was Patricia Ryan and she was born on St. Patrick's Day, and you know the Irish never quit.

But the decision, my friends, is not mine, I would do nothing that would harm the possibilities of Dwight Eisenhower to become President of the United States. And for that reason I am submitting to the Republican National Committee tonight through this television broadcast the decision which is theirs to make. Let them decide whether my position on the ticket will help or hurt. And I am going to ask you to help them decide. Wire and write the Republican National Committee whether you think I should stay on or whether I should get off. And whatever their decision is, I will abide by it.

But just let me say this last word. Regardless of what happens, I am going to continue this fight. I am going to campaign up and down America until we drive the crooks and the Communists and those that defend them out of Washington, and remember, folks, Eisenhower is a great man, and a vote for Eisenhower is a vote for what is good for America. [Nixon, 1952]

This is the introduction and conclusion to what may well be the most famous speech in American political history. Given in September of 1952 by Richard M. Nixon, the vice-presidential candidate on the Republican ticket headed by Dwight Eisenhower, the speech was remarkable in several ways. For one thing, it was unprecedented: Never before had an American politician used the then-young mass media to combine personal appeals with political appeals. Never before had an American politician given an itemized accounting of every penny he owned, as Richard Nixon does in the body of this speech. Never before had an American politician used the visual power of television to conduct a public conversation, with the candidate himself moving freely across a homey set and his wife sitting demurely across from him on a couch. Never before had an American politician directly asked U.S. voters to contact party leaders on his behalf, many of whom were then urging Nixon to resign from the ticket. And never before was an American politician exonerated so speedily—less than twenty-four hours after delivering his address. In the speech, Nixon used his parents and their home mortgage, his wife and her Irish ancestry, his children and their dog, Checkers, but he did so so disarmingly that his speech became a rhetorical classic and Mr. Nixon himself something of a political classic.

There are many interesting features of Nixon's "Checkers Speech." Mr. Nixon saw rhetorical opportunities with television that nobody had seen before. A master strategist, Nixon understood that the best defense (he had been accused of using secret monies illegally) was a good offense and that a TV appearance at the eleventh hour would take his detractors completely by surprise. (It did.) Mr. Nixon succeeds because he denies his rhetorical essence, framing his speech as a response to an attack on an honest man who only incidentally happens to be a politician.

In the language of Chapter 3, Mr. Nixon's speech-act was itself fascinating. The message stood as bravery incarnate: an embattled man unfairly attacked by left-leaning ideologues, a man who had been compelled "to come up here and bare his soul." Indeed, Nixon intersperses themes of anticommunism throughout his speech, making frequent allusions to Alger Hiss, a person who was successfully prosecuted by Nixon for his alleged Communistic leanings in the 1950s. The conclusion to Nixon's speech even goes so far as to link the standard-bearer of the Democratic Party, Adlai Stevenson, to communistic infiltration ("any man who called the Alger Hiss case a red herring isn't fit to be President of the United States"). Such appeals encouraged the audience to view the speech as Action rather than Reaction, as statesmanship rather than electioneering. These framing strategies were critical to Nixon's success: If his audience had remembered his timid introduction rather than his fire-breathing conclusion, he never would have regained the momentum the fund scandal cost him. His speech-act provided just such momentum.

In the language of Chapter 4, the Checkers Speech is a salad of ideas, with Nixon combining all four judgmental types: a Factual listing of his credits and debits; Optative appeals to middle-American values (he says at one point that his wife is without a mink but has "a respectable Republican cloth coat"); Adjudicative flag-waving when he rides forth to slay the communist dragon; and even a good deal of Promissory campaigning ("remember, folks, Eisenhower is a great man, and a vote for Eisenhower is a vote for what is good for America"). There is a remarkable boldness to Nixon's speech, a weaving together of seemingly disparate themes (humility and patriotism, money and morality, family values and warfare, domestic can-do and international communism).

Only Mr. Nixon's emotional intensity ties the pieces together and prevented people from viewing his remarks as political parody.

In this chapter, we will examine argument—the linking of ideas in support of identifiable propositions. We will track how speakers move their listeners from one assertion to the next and, ultimately, to some overriding assertion. In analyzing argument and reasoning, we must rethink what we know about them, for the logic of persuasion is a *human logic* in which reasoners are able to build bridges between ideas that professional logicians would find flimsy. Because the logic of persuasion is also an *informal logic,* the critic must be reminded that listeners' reasoning standards are looser than those used by scientists in the laboratory or by judges in court. It is a logic based as much on feeling as on thinking, or more accurately, it is a logic that presumes that all feelers think and that all thinkers feel. Thus, Richard Nixon's emotional speech "made sense" to a great many of his listeners even though it was filled with pandering and irrelevancies. Here, we will try to discover what sort of sense Mr. Nixon made and for whom he made it.

And it is important to view "sense" as something that is indeed *made.* In persuasion, sense is negotiated by people who use their beliefs, hopes, fears, and experiences to guide them. When listening, listeners never start from scratch. They hear each message in the context of everything they have heard previously. Clever speakers like Richard Nixon understand this and hence build "reasoning aids" into their messages. In this chapter, we will use three different tools to examine how people like Mr. Nixon reason and we will see that each model tells us something different about the Nixon speech.

But perhaps the most important thing that can be learned about reasoning is taught by Mr. Nixon himself. When he asks the rhetorical questions, "Why can't we have prosperity built on peace, rather than prosperity built on war? Why can't we have prosperity and an honest government in Washington, D.C., at the same time?", he responds with classic rhetorical reasoning: "*Believe me,* we can." In persuasion, audiences never separate a speaker's reasoning from his or her credibility. Critics may wish it otherwise, but it is never otherwise. It is this fact that will begin our discussion of argument.

THE LOGIC OF PERSUASION

Many people become frustrated by what passes for logic in the practical world. Heavyweight fighter Mike Tyson, a convicted rapist, becomes a born-again Muslim upon being released from prison and his old popularity resurfaces almost immediately. Jane Fonda, a radical critic of the Vietnam war during the 1960s, becomes a health guru thirty years later. Oliver North, who lied under oath to a Senate investigating committee during the 1980s, almost wins a Virginia Senate seat in 1994. One of Mr. North's neighbors, Gordon Liddy, a convicted felon because of the 1970's Watergate affair, is given a Freedom of

Speech Award by an association of talk show hosts even though he had used his show to instruct his listeners patiently on where to aim when trying to shoot federal drug agents (the groin area, he decided).

This makes sense? Has the public gone mad? Is nothing constant? Are people without memory? Has logic lost its logic? Questions like these can be maddening, but the rhetorical critic cannot indulge them. To understand persuasion is to understand a new kind of logic.

Traditional logic—the logic of the scientist, the judge, and the philosopher—has always stood as Grade A, approved logic, as well it should. Traditional logic, or technical logic, posits certain rigid rules of reasoning (e.g., syllogistic forms), emphasizes certain modes of fact-gathering (e.g., the scientific method), promotes certain modes of inference (e.g., arguing from legal precedent), and preaches the gospel of exhaustive research and rigorous testing of propositions. These intellectual tendencies are said best to distinguish humankind from lower animals and to undergird the most important human discoveries. When the *Challenger* disaster occurred in the late 1980s, for example, evidence indicated that scientists had reasoned poorly when designing the crucial O-rings for the rocket boosters. The postdisaster hearings conducted by the military and Congressional bodies often were models of traditional logic, as computer printouts, weather charts, and laboratory reports were examined in microscopic detail.

But the public hearings were often something else as well. With the astronauts blaming the scientists and the scientists blaming the military and the military blaming the manufacturers and the manufacturers blaming the politicians and the politicians blaming the gods, the hearings were a field day for name-calling, flag-waving, excuse-making, question-begging, back-stabbing, rank-pulling, grandstanding, obfuscating, and every other brand of argument known to civilization.

But the astronauts and the scientists and the military and the manufacturers and the politicians could not be blamed entirely for reasoning in these ways for they all shared one damnable trait: They were human. As humans, they were imperfect logicians. As humans, they had fears, anxieties, memory lapses, biases, and worries about job security that clouded their thinking. As humans, they could reason like machines only so long before reaching for more shameless rhetorical materials. And those charged with deciding the truth in the case—the American people—had to fight through their own prejudices to make sense of a sense-less tragedy.

So the logic of persuasion is neither tidy nor pretty. What passes for sense-making in everyday rhetoric stretches the boundaries of traditional logic. In persuasion, the guidebooks of technical or scientific reasoning must be set aside and a new, more indulgent, standard employed, a standard that looks more generously on people and their curious ways of reasoning. Admittedly, the critic can forsake these standards and use the dictates of traditional logic to censure informal arguers. But the critic who wishes to understand how *people* reason will make assumptions like those we discuss below.

1. In persuasion, everything is rational to the behaver at the time of behavior. This means that people always have "good reasons" for doing what they do. Even though these reasons will often not meet the critic's personal standards of goodness, this proposition suggests that any message that becomes popular will have a powerful logic to it. The consumer who responds to an advertisement featuring a scantily clad model standing next to a new Chrysler should perhaps be censured for sexism, not to mention stupidity. But the critic's job is to discover why this message works: What unspoken needs does it meet for consumers? What fantasies does it trip off? What values does it herald? Rhetorical criticism is the study of *other people's* sense-makings; it is the critic's job to represent such sense-makings faithfully. To do less would be to miss an important part of the human story.

2. The logic of persuasion is always credibility-driven. Persuasion comes to us embodied: Most people cannot separate the substance of a message from its author. This is especially true in spoken persuasion, in which the speaker's attitudes, voice, and personal appearance interact constantly with what the speaker says. While the examples of reasoning found in formal logic books are often unattributed (i.e., *Who* was it exactly who first claimed, "All men are mortal. Socrates is a man. Therefore . . . ?"), examples in rhetoric books almost always have a name attached. Thus, the genetic research of a neo-Nazi scientist has no chance of being taken seriously by the scholarly community, no matter what its inherent scientific worth. In persuasion, inherency lies *within people,* not within ideas.

This is why small children are constantly in danger of accepting rides from strangers since they have long been taught that adults are authoritative and well-intentioned. Speakers with high credibility are thus allowed to ramble, to become patently unclear, or to present distressing evidence and yet retain their appeal. Under such conditions, listeners themselves seem somehow willing to fill in the logical gaps. Thus, as Maranhão [1990] reports, the very possibility of achieving health via the psychoanalytic method rests on the kind of *authority* the analyst has for the client. Maranhão adds that it is the psychiatrist's job to work to increase such credibility during therapy sessions. In persuasion, speaker and message are always wed, as are reasoning and feeling states.

3. The logic of persuasion is always saliency-driven. Saliency is the other great law of persuasion. It states: The listener will virtually always find the *important* and the *immediate* to be most reasonable. In a technical logic designed to test universal facts and establish enduring truths, this proposition would make no sense at all. But in the world of people, logic is a sometimes thing. Needs and experience, not abstract truths, guide human decision-making. It is one thing to discuss the clinical utility of euthanasia and quite another to remove the life support system from one's own mother. During such moments, medical charts and sociological abstractions become dry as dust as the immediacy and importance of such a decision overwhelms one. On a less momentous front, the old advice not to grocery shop while hungry is good advice since the law of saliency decrees that people never decide in the abstract even when they think they do.

4. *The logic of persuasion is audience-dependent.* The logic of persuasion is a "weak" rather than a "strong" logic. Its standards of reasonability vary sharply from audience to audience. This is what makes criticism such a fascinating enterprise: It opens up for inspection an endless variety of reasonings. The rhetoric of skin color, for example, will sound different at a conference of dermatologists than it will at the annual meetings of the National Basketball Association, different still at a gathering of the Ku Klux Klan. Each group will reason about skin color differently; thus it becomes the critic's job to understand the "local logics" at work in each instance. So, for example, after Black [1970] found an excessive number of cancer metaphors in the rhetoric of the radical right, he traced these metaphors to the group's central reasoning process: (1) that they felt on the brink of ruin, (2) that they felt deceived from within, but also (3) that they were willing to fight to the death. In other words, the good critic finds logic wherever rhetoric is found.

5. *The logic of persuasion is a logic of association.* While technical logic focuses on causality, rhetoric is guided by the weaker dictates of association. In a court of law, for example, even though an indictment establishes no necessary (causal) link between a crime and its perpetrator, juries are often swayed by the very fact of indictment ("Innocent people don't wear handcuffs in court, do they?"). Similarly, a smear campaign in politics often is fueled by associations. Although it makes no causal sense to launch a federal investigation merely because of one's work history or ethnicity, it can make *associative* sense to do so. So when a Congressional committee looked into his former business dealings, one-time U.S. Labor Secretary Raymond Donovan charged that former building contractors (like himself) always seem worthy of federal investigation, that former building contractors from New Jersey seem automatically indictable, and that former New Jersey building contractors who also happen to be Italian seem automatically guilty.

Because determining true causality is so rare in human affairs, ordinary arguments rarely prove things with scientific certainty. Rather, they trade on the logically weaker but psychologically attractive standards of plausibility, rationalization, and current biases. So, for example, Mechling and Mechling [1992] report that contemporary Quaker rhetoric came to endorse peace on psychological rather than religious grounds. This happened, the authors argue, because potential converts to the peace movement were increasingly becoming part of a "New Class" (they were more affluent, more worldly, and more middle-class than their forebears) and, hence, the Quakers began to frame their arguments in more bourgeois, less theological, ways.

6. *The logic of persuasion is often a logic of emotion.* The old Western dichotomy between the heart and the head makes little sense in the world of rhetoric. Most students of persuasion now agree that to contrast people's "logical" and "emotional" tendencies is wrongheaded. When they react to

persuasion people react with all of themselves. To describe some rhetorical appeals as logical in nature (e.g., monetary arguments) and others as emotional (e.g., patriotic arguments) is therefore to deal artificially with a complex process of thinking/feeling. During each moment of each day, people think/feel. Speakers think/feel when they speak and listeners think/feel when they listen. The plain fact of the matter is that some people get quite emotional about their tax returns while still others become rather cold-blooded when defending the Persian Gulf war on the basis of keeping world oil supplies intact.

When studying persuasion, therefore, the critic must be primarily concerned with the **emotional authenticity** of a speaker (i.e., Is the speaker really experiencing the emotion she seems to be experiencing?), with the **emotional integrity** of a performance (i.e., Does the speaker's background give him the "right" to be this emotional on this matter?), or the **emotional register** of an argument (i.e., Is the speaker's state of arousal too high or too low for the matters being discussed?). And it must be remembered that questions of this sort are questions about *reasoning,* about how packages of emotions and ideas serve as arguments in the ordinary world.

Given the six features above, the logic of persuasion may seem a completely dishonorable logic: Advertisers convince us that we need clothing we do not need, lawyers encourage clients to cry on the witness stand to win jurors' sympathies, preachers claim they will die if church donations don't increase by 200%. In persuasion, these claims stand as argument. Shame on persuasion.

In light of these features, the critic has two choices: (1) to honor traditional logic by ignoring persuasion completely or (2) to study how and why such appeals work and then to warn others about the logic of everyday rhetoric. This second option seems most sensible. After all, the first is defeatist, not to mention faintly elitist. But the second option encourages closer study of people, a fundamentally humane act indeed.

EVIDENCE AND REASONING

The success of a persuasive argument is often determined not by notions of formal validity but by questions of *sufficiency:* Is there enough to go on here? Will more support be required? Is the case overstated? A good approach for the critic, then, is to examine the weight of the arguments offered in a given message. By contrasting heavily documented propositions to those mentioned in passing, the critic can detect the speaker's areas of confidence and also the rhetorical trouble spots. Naturally, the evidence used in public arguments rarely meets rigorous standards of empirical testing. Although Richard Nixon presented a great many financial facts in his Checkers speech, they were hardly the sorts of facts that would stand up in a court of law. Rather, his factual disclosures gave listeners the sense that Mr. Nixon was a man of probity, that he took the charges against him seriously, that he had emotional and intellectual resources in the heat of battle, that he was in command of his life. On many occasions for many listeners, some evidence is enough evidence.

When inspecting arguments, the critic asks questions like these:

1. Generally speaking, does the message make heavy use of supporting material, or is it flatly assertive?
2. Does the speaker use a large number of sketchy arguments or build a tighter case with few propositions but more evidence?
3. Which arguments have ample supporting materials, which are given short shrift, and why?
4. What *kinds* of evidence does the speaker use and do they change from point to point in the message?

Table 5.1 presents some standard kinds of rhetorical evidence. Also included are a variety of Critical Probes to see how a given message functioned and how its author perceived the rhetorical circumstances. Because evidence forms the foundation and supporting walls of discourse, the critic who uses these Critical Probes becomes something of a building inspector, prowling around in the basement and walking amidst the scaffolding to see if the rhetorical architecture is as good as it should be and, if not, why nobody noticed.

Table 5.2 presents a rough estimation of how frequently the various clarification devices have been used in the Nixon speech and in some of the speeches examined previously. A quick inspection shows that each speech presents a different picture, with some messages resembling others on some dimensions but none being duplicates. This makes sense, since one of the speeches was purely fictional (Harold Hill) while another was quite real (Patton). One was religious with a political tone (Rabbi Prinz) while another was political yet confessional (Nixon). It is little wonder, then, that the evidentiary profiles are distinctive.

These clarification devices can be thought of as reasoning aids, as argumentative promises to listeners: "If you don't like my comparative argument, here's one with contrast." "If these serial examples make an idea clear for you, this extended example will make it even clearer." "If you're having trouble moving from Proposition A to Proposition B, listen to how a respected source made that same intellectual movement." Some speakers choose poorly when selecting evidence: The wrong device may be chosen for the wrong argument; the right device may be chosen but then developed poorly; an argument needing support may be overlooked while a self-evident argument receives unneeded attention. Making the right choices about such matters is what rhetorical excellence is all about.

The evidentiary choices made by our four speakers seem sensible. General Patton saw his job as one of giving his men a clear sense of purpose. His heavy use of Definition shows that. In his speech, he explains the real-life meanings of teamwork and patriotism and does little else. Since his time before battle

TABLE 5.1 Analyzing Clarification Devices

Type	Functions	Example*	Critical Probes
Serial examples	Adds totality to a speaker's remarks by presenting, in scattered fashion, numerous instances of the same phenomenon.	"Parents can act as our reference groups, as can friends, political groups, religious organizations, social fraternities, and so on."	How frequently are groups of examples found in the message? Is there any overall logic to the types of illustrations chosen? Which arguments are devoid of examples? Why?
Extended example	Adds vivacity to a speaker's remarks by presenting a detailed picture of a single event or concept.	"Let's consider what happened to John Jones, a college undergraduate who has had trouble 'sorting out' his reference groups. John started school like most people, and soon. . . ."	How many different extended examples are used? How much detail is provided within them? Are "story qualities" clearly apparent in the examples? Are the examples real or hypothetical? Is the narrative interrupted at any point? Why?
Quantification	Adds a feeling of substantiveness to a speaker's remarks by concrete enumerations.	"Some experts estimate 70 percent of our decisions are affected by our reference groups, and that one out of every three people experiences tensions in relation to reference group choice."	How often are dates, sums, and quantities provided in the message? When are they used? What sorts of arguments do they support? Which arguments that could be quantified are not quantified? Why?
Isolated comparisons	Adds realism to a speaker's remarks by drawing analogically on a listener's past experiences	"Reference groups are like spouses—you can't live without them, but sometimes it's darn hard to live with them!"	What sorts of "equations" are set up by the speaker? Do the two elements of an equation "naturally" go together or is the equation novel? In offering the comparisons offered, what assumptions about the audience does the speaker seem to be making? Are the assumptions justified?
Extended comparison	Adds psychological reference points to a speaker's remarks by successively structuring his or her perceptions along familiar lines.	"A reference group is similar to a mother—it nurtures our feelings when we are hurt; it disciplines us for violating its norms; it helps us mature by. . . . "	Are extended comparisons extensively or infrequently used? What sorts of arguments are developed with this device? Is the "known" half of the comparison well adapted to the audience so that they can appreciate the "unknown" half?

(continued)

*Example: A sociology lecture on the topic of "reference groups."

TABLE 5.1 (*continued*)

Type	Functions	Example	Critical Probes
Testimony	Adds to the inclusiveness of a speaker's remarks by quoting appreciatively from known or respected sources or depreciatively from sources of ill-regard.	"Sociologist Carolyn Sherif has said that none of us can really escape the influence of the groups we identify with—our reference groups."	What sorts of persons/sources does the speaker depend on? How often is this dependency manifested? Is there an obvious logic to the persons/sources chosen for support? How careful is the speaker's documentation of the sources quoted? What types of persons/sources are never quoted?
Definition	Adds to the specificity of a speaker's remarks by depicting opposed elements.	"Let's consider what is not meant by a reference group. It is not just any group we belong to, nor is it always identifiable. Rather it is . . ."	Is any major attempt made here to define important concepts? Which terms/ideas are defined fully? Which key terms/ideas are presented without definition? At what point in the message are definitions offered?
Contrast	Adds a dramatic quality to a speaker's remarks by depicting opposed elements.	"Those who identify with many groups have very different attitudes from those who are more individualistic."	What sort of "reverse equations" are presented by the speaker? Are both elements of the contrasts drawn from listeners' experiences? Is dependence on contrasts heavy, moderate, or light? Do contrasts overshadow comparisons and is it significant that they do?

TABLE 5.2 Comparative Use of Clarification Devices*

Clarification Services	Rabbi Prinz	Harold Hill	George Patton	Richard Nixon
Serial examples	0	11	18	14
Extended examples	14	50	30	31
Quantification	0	11	2	10
Isolated comparisons	17	15	14	12
Extended comparisons	37	0	0	7
Testimony	8	0	4	14
Definition	6	7	17	5
Contrast	17	6	16	17

*Numbers indicate percentages of message using the devices listed was short, Patton chose a streamlined argument, hoping that his men would at least take away a fresh understanding of these two concepts. Patton also uses a good deal of Contrast, distinguishing the fighting ability and moral superiority of the American troops from their German counterparts. Fairly heavy use of Contrast creates "division"—sharp distinctions, opposed viewpoints, observable differences—the kind of black-and-white thinking that keeps confusion to a minimum during battle. All in all, then, a good day's work for Patton or, more precisely, a good five-minutes' work.

Harold Hill's speech could not be more different. He defines very little, makes no Extended Comparisons, offers no Testimony. Such devices would have slowed his speech to a crawl. The producers of *The Music Man* wanted something snappy and hence wrote only a patina of support into Hill's script. They have Hill trying primarily to generate shock and concern in his listeners and, then, a grand enthusiasm for band instruments. Hill bases most of his speech on the Extended Example of the pool table, figuring that this speech would be but the first in an extended campaign to separate the good folks of River City from their currency.

Like Patton, Hill sought simplicity. But unlike Patton, Hill hoped to build intensity of motivation, motivation that might have been dissipated if spread over a wide range of arguments on behalf of tuba-playing. Hill's Extended Example thus became what professional debaters call a need case, a kind of problem-stating that ultimately invites a "plan," which Harold Hill just happened to have handy.

Rabbi Prinz's speech resembled Hill's, in part, because he too needed a streamlined performance. Rather than use examples, however, the Rabbi made dramatic use of the Extended Comparison, showing how the experiences of Jews in Nazi Germany paralleled those witnessed daily by blacks in the United States. This heavy use of comparison springs directly from the very speech-act in which Prinz participated: His physical presence at the March on Washington said "We Jews stand with you Blacks on this matter." So the social action of the *event* neatly parallels the rhetorical action of the *text*.

Comparisons, however, have their rhetorical costs. They tend to be list-like and, when used in great profusion, better suited to lectures or scientific reports than to half-time speeches or advertising copy. Moreover, unlike examples (which the Rabbi almost never uses), comparisons can put audiences to sleep. But given the Rabbi's role—that of rhetorical helpmate to Dr. King—he apparently felt it was enough to take his stand on the right side of the issue, make a simple, unembellished statement, and then quit the scene. He did so movingly.

Compared to the other speakers, Richard Nixon's heavy use of Testimony is significant. No doubt because he was an object of suspicion at the time, Mr. Nixon quotes Republicans, Democrats, reporters, several imaginary citizens, and a real one. At one point in the speech, he even quotes from accountants and lawyers:

I am proud to report to you tonight that this audit and this legal opinion is being forwarded to General Eisenhower, and I would like to read to you the opinion that was prepared by Gibson, Dunn and Crutcher [a law firm in Los Angeles], based on all the pertinent laws and statutes, together with the audit report prepared by the certified public accountants:

"It is our conclusion that Senator Nixon did not obtain any financial gain from the collection and disbursement of the funds by Dana Smith [a Nixon aide]; that Senator Nixon did not violate any federal or state law by reason of the operation of the fund; and that neither the portion of the fund paid by Dana Smith directly to third persons, nor the portion paid to Senator Nixon, to reimburse him for office expenses, constituted income in a sense which was either reportable or taxable as income under income tax laws."

No politician wants to be placed in a position of having to use Testimony extensively. Quoting others puts them on stage rather than oneself, a despised prospect for any elected official. Also, using direct quotations signals rhetorical trouble, as if the speaker had neither the wisdom nor the authority to carry the day. Quotations also often slow down an oral message for listeners who, unlike readers, cannot skim the text. But Mr. Nixon's back was against the wall, so he had no choice but to find credibility where he could find it.

The Checkers Speech is interesting because it is two speeches rolled into one: a speech of moral exoneration and a political stump speech. Because he had so many different jobs to do in his speech, Nixon found himself using all the evidentiary devices available. Fully a tenth of his speech presented quantitative evidence of his innocence. Almost half of his speech relates examples (of his early life, of his wife's devotion, of communistic evil). A fifth of his speech uses comparisons. Here, he compares his early life to the lives of all young marrieds; his service record with the service records of all heroes; his children with all of America's children; his view of the world with Abraham Lincoln's view (they both loved common people, said Mr. Nixon). This persistent string of Comparisons helps to give the Checkers Speech a heavily sentimental tone as Nixon searches under every emotional rock to show what a regular fellow he is. Some forty years later, such devices seem overly obvious, almost a caricature. But Richard Nixon had a way of offering such Comparisons without batting an eye, as if they were the most natural comparisons in the world.

Roughly another fifth of Nixon's speech uses Contrasts, a Nixon favorite. Perhaps because he always saw himself as the odd-man-out in society or perhaps because he had such a dialectical cast of mind (the kind that finds fundamental opposition rather than fundamental synchrony in the world), Nixon reveled in Contrasts. In his 1952 speech, he distinguished himself from Democrats (who put their wives on the political payroll), from other lawyers (who were richer than he), and from other politicians (they could be bought). He also contrasted his wife with other wives, his party with the opposition party, his political gifts with other political gifts (all he got was Checkers). The sharpness of Nixon's Contrasts increase as he draws to the end of his speech and lambastes the Democrats. Always the ex-debater, always the person who never quite fit in, Richard Nixon's gift for Contrast lay not in elegance but in the sharpness of the distinctions he drew and in the emotional intensity with which he drew them.

Although it is a humble type of analysis, examining argumentative support reveals how speakers work their minds rhetorically. For example, Dow and Tonn [1993] found that a key difference between Texas governor Ann Richards' style and that of traditional politicians is that she used far more Extended Examples and Serial Examples than her male counterparts, thereby bringing a new kind of "humanity" to public discourse. On a very different front, Katriel [1994] studied the rhetoric used by tour guides in Israeli settlement museums. She found that Zionist ideology was being subtly woven into these presentations by a preponderance of Isolated Comparisons that favored Jewish, not Arab, readings of history as well as by pieces of biblical Testimony used to explain contemporary phenomena. In other words, Katriel found propagandistic elements by examining some of the most elementary, and most often overlooked, rhetorical devices available.

In another study, Ritter [1985] tracked the patterns of evidence used in the first Alger Hiss trial in 1949 (Hiss was a writer accused of being a communist), a trial that ended in a deadlocked jury, and compared them to those used during the retrial one year later (which succeeded in convicting Hiss of perjury). According to Ritter, the rhetorical approaches used by the prosecution in the two trials differed sharply. The first trial featured a "courtroom drama" (i.e., a parade of larger-than-life personalities and much showmanship) while the second featured a "crime drama" (i.e., one that focused on past activities and on forty-seven different pieces of typewritten evidence). Not only did the reasoning patterns differ sharply, says Ritter, but so too did the resulting rhetorical tones of both the prosecution and the defense.

Naturally, examining evidence patterns of this sort cannot tell us everything that needs to be known about persuasion. But these patterns can often point up what is *at issue* in discourse. Reasoning is more than the marshalling of evidence, but it is no less than that as well.

NARRATIVE AND REASONING

At first, narrative and reasoning seem antithetical. "Poets tell stories" is our initial response, "scientists reason." But a growing number of scholars feel that there is a logic to storytelling, a logic the rhetorical critic must understand. According to such thinkers much public policy is determined by the stories persuaders tell. Sometimes, these stories are complex, springing from deep cultural roots; often, stories told today are but updated versions of century-old tales. Because they are practical people, persuaders do not tell these stories with the novelist's richness of detail or sense of abandon.

And persuaders normally tell only snippets of stories, an anecdote here, an abbreviated fable there, always moving listeners forward to some propositional conclusion. But narratives do advance persuasion because (1) they disarm listeners by enchanting them, (2) they awaken within listeners dormant experiences and feelings, and (3) they thereby expose, subtly, some sort of propositional argument. Recent scholars have shown that people reason differently in the presence of narrative. Its native features suggest why:

1. Narrative occurs in a natural time-line. There are beginnings, middles, and endings to narrative. Once we start on a narrative, we feel compelled to follow it through to its conclusion. All stories, even bad stories, inspire the need to see how it turns out. Narratives always tempt us with closure.

2. Narrative includes characterization. People are interested in people. Narratives are the stories of what people do. Often, narratives introduce interesting people, sometimes grand people, to an audience. When we read or hear such narratives, our natural sense of identification makes us want to find out more about the lives of the people described.

3. Narrative presents detail. A good story, such as a fine novel, transports us to another time or place by offering fine-grained treatments. When the narrator describes the clothes people wear or the customs they follow or the dialect they speak, we come to know that time and place as if it were our own. Details captivate.

4. Narrative is primitive. No culture exists without narrative. Most cultures celebrate their sacred narratives on a regular basis (e.g., a Fourth of July celebration) and most cultures indoctrinate their young by means of narrative (e.g., fairy tales). Narrative appeals to the child in us because, unlike life, it contains a complete story with certain consequences.

5. Narrative does not argue . . . obviously. If a narrator tries to make a point too forcefully, we feel cheated. Good narrative holds open the illusion that we—as listeners and readers—help to determine its meaning. Narrative is depropositionalized argument, argument with a hidden bottom line. Narrators charm audiences because they promise only a story well told.

These propositions apply to all narratives, but rhetorical narratives have special features, special obligations, in addition. For example, because rhetorical narrative is *narrative,* opponents find it hard to attack ("it's only a story, after all"). But because rhetorical narrative is also *rhetorical,* because it is storytelling with a purpose, it must also abide by certain rules of purposiveness. Thus, rhetorical narratives are (1) normally brief, (2) often repetitious, (3) sketchy in characterization, (4) frequently interrupted, and (5) rarely exotic.

In the middle of his Checkers Speech, for example, Richard Nixon launched into just such a narrative. He did not produce great poetry at that time but he did produce passably good rhetoric, especially for the white, Protestant, middle-income voter that he especially wanted to reach:

> I was born in 1913. Our family was one of modest circumstances, and most of my early life was spent in a store, out in East Whittier. It was a grocery store, one of those family enterprises. The only reason we were able to make it go was because my Mother and Dad had five boys, and we all worked in the store. I worked my way through college and, to a great extent, through law school. And then, in 1940, probably the best thing that ever happened to me happened. I married Pat, who is sitting over here.
>
> We had a rather difficult time, after we were married, like so many of the young couples who might be listening to us. I practiced law. She continued to teach school.
>
> Then, in 1942, I went into the service. Let me say that my service record was not a particularly unusual one. I went to the South Pacific. I guess I'm entitled to a couple of battle stars. I got a couple of letters of commendation. But I was just there when the bombs were falling. And then I returned. I returned to the United States, and in 1946, I ran for Congress. When we came out of the war, Pat and I— Pat during the war had worked as a stenographer, and in a bank, and as an economist for a government agency—and when we came out, the total of our savings, from both my law practice, her teaching, and all the time that I was in the war, the total for that entire period was just a little less than $10,000. Every cent of that, incidentally, was in government bonds. Well, that's where we start, when I go into politics.
>
> Now, whatever I earned since I went into politics—well, here it is. I jotted it down. Let me read the notes. First of all, I have had my salary as a congressman and as a senator. Second, I have received a total in this past six years of $1600 from estates which were in my law firm at the time that I severed my connection with it. And, incidentally, as I said before, I have not engaged in any legal practice, and have not accepted any fees from business that came into the firm after I went into politics. I have made an average of approximately $1500 a year, from nonpolitical speaking engagements and lectures. And then, fortunately, we have inherited a little money. Pat sold her interest in her father's estate for $3000, and I inherited $1500 from my grandfather. We lived rather modestly.
>
> For four years we lived in an apartment in Parkfairfax, Alexandria, Virginia. The rent was $80 a month. And we saved for the time that we could buy a house. Now, that was what we took in.
>
> What did we do with this money? What do we have today to show for it? This will surprise you, because it is so little, I suppose, as standards generally go of people in public life. First of all, we've got a house in Washington, which cost $41,000 and on which we owe $20,000. We have a house in Whittier, California, which cost $13,000, and on which we owe $3,000. My folks are living there at the present time. I have just $4,000 in life insurance, plus my GI policy, which I have never been able to convert, and which will run out in two years. I have no life insurance whatever on Pat. I have no life insurance on our two youngsters, Patricia and Julie. I own a 1950 Oldsmobile car. We have our furniture. We have no stocks and bonds of any type. We have no interest of any kind, direct or indirect, in any business. Now, that is what we have. What do we owe?

Well, in addition to the mortgage, the $20,000 mortgage on the house in Washington, a $10,000 one on the house in Whittier, I owe $4500 to Riggs Bank, in Washington, D.C., with interest at 4 percent. I owe $3500 to my parents, and the interest on that loan, which I pay regularly because it is a part of the savings they made through the years they were working so hard—I pay regularly 4 percent interest. And then I have a $500 loan, which I have on my life insurance.

Well, that's about it. That's what we have. And that's what we owe. It isn't very much. But Pat and I have the satisfaction that every dime that we have got is honestly ours.

I should say this, that Pat doesn't have a mink coat. But she does have a respectable Republican cloth coat, and I always tell her that she would look good in anything.

One other thing I probably should tell you, because if I don't they will probably be saying this about me, too. We did get something, a gift, after the election. A man down in Texas heard Pat on the radio mention the fact that our two youngsters would like to have a dog, and, believe it or not, the day before we left on this campaign trip we got a message from Union Station in Baltimore, saying they had a package for us. We went down to get it. You know what it was?

It was little cocker spaniel dog, in a crate that he had sent all the way from Texas, black and white, spotted, and our little girl, Tricia, the six-year-old, named it Checkers. And, you know, the kids, like all kids, loved the dog, and I just want to say this, right now, that regardless of what they say about it, we are going to keep it.

There are many attractive aspects of Mr. Nixon's narrative. For one thing, Nixon displays himself as a **reluctant narrator,** reminding us that "this is unprecedented in the history of American politics," giving us the sense that the story is being pried out of him and therefore especially worthy of attention. It is also an **uncontrived narrative.** That is, Nixon discounts his own heroism ("I was just there when the bombs were falling") and interrupts himself several times ("incidentally, as I have said before, I have not engaged in any legal practice . . ."), establishing that the story has not been preinvented, that it is pouring out of his soul, not out of his head. The **familiar characters** contained in the story are also comforting: a hard-working young man, a selfless wife, sacrificing parents, dog-loving children. Characters like these can be found nightly in almost any television drama and they serve to humanize the protagonist as only storytelling can.

According to Mader [1973], a narrative must also have **rhetorical presence,** a vividness of detail that brings to life the ideas advanced. Mr. Nixon achieves this by nicely weaving in specific places (the South Pacific, Alexandria, Whittier), sums and dates ("we've got a house in Washington, which cost $41,000 and on which we own $20,000"), particular buildings (the Riggs Bank, Union Station), and, most important, people (Patricia and Julie). Nixon also uses some amount of **dramatic variety,** weaving the serious (his wartime experiences) with the whimsical (the beloved Checkers), as well as displaying a nice touch for **dramatic understatement** by suddenly introducing facts that have no obvious argumentative burden (e.g., he could not convert his GI policy; his folks are living in a home he owns; he has a 1950 Oldsmobile).

Finally, Mr. Nixon is careful to establish **narrative authenticity** by never commenting explicitly on the principle guiding his narrative or the generalization he hopes listeners will draw from his story. Rather, he presents the story as just a story, asking only that the audience permit him to tell his humble tale. In 1952, this tale left many a moist cheek.

Scholars who have investigated the rhetorical uses of narratives seem both fascinated and alarmed by what they find. Black [1992:147–70], for example, explains that the narrator's role is an extraordinarily powerful one, a role whose innocence inhibits listeners from thinking about the arguments embedded in the tales being told them. Black concludes, therefore, that narratives often tell the simplest and most comforting story possible, which is ample reason enough to keep an eye on them since life itself is normally not simple and far too often, not comforting either.

For a number of reasons, then, it is useful for the critic to scrutinize narratives carefully. The following critical probes seem especially suited to doing so:

1. *Does the narrative spring from a Master Narrative?* Hillbruner [1960] notes that many contemporary narratives have their roots in older narratives and that the critic who is sensitive to such parentage can discover the new implications of these old stories. He found, for example, that the ancient Greek notion of a Great Chain of Being, wherein all life forms occupied a different rung on some mystical ladder with God at the top, was still being used by U.S. segregationists twenty centuries later to justify their treatment of blacks (blacks supposedly being a rung down from whites on the Great Chain).

In a more recent study, Olson and Goodnight [1994] found a fascinating shift in the overall storyline used by those who wish to continue to wear fur. In earlier times, fur was justified on the basis of fashion alone. More recently, fur fanciers have attached themselves to the old cultural narratives of capitalism (in this case, the subnarrative of consumers' rights). In doing so, they have given their cause *political* weight and thereby circumvented the more constraining, self-serving, and ephemeral narratives of "moving up" or "getting a piece of the dream."

2. *What propositional content is the narrative designed to reveal?* Although narratives do not argue explicitly, they do indeed argue. Their style of argument is devastatingly natural because it uses a realistic time line to tell who did what when. But behind any narrative lie primitive rhetorical decisions for the speaker: Which facts should be stressed and which ignored? Which characters should be mentioned and which amplified? When should the story be started and when stopped? By making each of these decisions and dozens more like them, the persuader/narrator is also deciding which *ideas* to amplify and which to thrust into the background.

Perry [1983], for example, notes that one of the most popular narratives in Nazi Germany conceived of the Jew-as-parasite, an organism that had infiltrated German society and later undermined it. Perry argues that the power of such a story lies in its "figurative logic," in the way it encouraged audiences to think of Jews as "evil, unnatural, and destructive" [p. 234] and hence not worthy of concern. By "bracketing" the Jews in this way, by removing their human status, the parasite story licensed new conclusions about their cultural and political status as well. To accept such a metaphor, says Perry, was to accept a whole new way of thinking as well.

3. *What propositional content is the narrative designed to mask?* This probe encourages the critic to inquire into the underlying purpose of the narrative at hand. When telling a story, after all, the persuader operates preemptively by *not* doing something else. Instead of telling his tale, for example, Richard Nixon could have straightforwardly detailed (1) whose idea it was to have an expense fund, (2) how many dollars were given to how many persons for what purposes, and (3) when the last expenditure was made and why. Dealing directly with these matters would have been uncomfortable for Mr. Nixon. So he told a story.

Kirkwood [1983] comments on the mood-changing power of narrative (it comforts us; it relaxes us) and observes how fiction or a shocking tale suspends "ordinary rationality" and places it in the service of escapist visions. He notes that the humble parable, for example, is really a very powerful form of argument because it (1) shifts the discussion from actual fact to imagined or recreated fact, (2) subsumes the discussion of principle to the discussion of narrative detail, and (3) reduces the listener to childlike (i.e., story-loving) status. Because the narrator takes on a "mantle of spiritual parenthood" [p. 72], says Kirkwood, narrative is not a small matter. When narrative is on-stage, then, the critic is wise to look off-stage.

Some critics would have us add a fourth, less descriptive, question about narrative: *How effectively and how faithfully does the narrative deal with its subject matter?* This, of course, is the valuative question and it is important to ask because storytelling seems so innocent. Fisher [1987] argues that any narrative will have varying amounts of both **narrative probability** (i.e., good story qualities: followability, completeness, believability) and **narrative fidelity** (reliability and truthfulness) and that the critic should inspect narrative closely for both features. General guidelines for effective rhetoric can help the critic judge narrative probability but we do not yet have clear standards for measuring either truthfulness or reliability. As for fidelity—the extent to which the narrative matches the reality it purports to describe—individual critics will have to use their own good judgment by determining (1) what was knowable in a given case, (2) what was knowable by the speaker in particular, and (3) how faithfully the resulting narrative captures what was known.

Ultimately, of course, there can be no final determination on such matters, for accuracy and goodness often exist in the eye of the beholder. But it seems clear that narrative must be inspected carefully. Alone, narrative can be diverting. When combined with rhetoric and introduced into discussions of public policy, however, its diversions must be studied for a basic reason: Rhetorical stories have entailments; they imply consequences. Narrative demands vigilance because the reasoning it encourages is often as facile as the stories themselves are compelling.

TOULMIN AND REASONING

A useful method for understanding reasoning is based on the work of Stephen Toulmin [1958] who many years ago outlined a new way of thinking about informal human argument. Toulmin's approach was a reaction to the models of formal logic then popular in philosophical circles. He felt that such models were too static to deal with something as dynamic as human thought and so he proposed a system better adapted to the actual logic used by actual people. Toulmin did not prescribe how people ought to reason; instead, he tried to describe how they actually behaved. Toulmin's approach was quickly seized on by rhetorical scholars. One such application was that of Hart [1973] who inspected some fifty-four different messages using a modified version of Toulmin's approach. It is this modified version that will be considered here.

Toulmin's system reduces arguments to a kind of outline so as to establish their overall logical movement. By collapsing a text to its skeletal structure, the critic becomes less encumbered by the great amounts of diversionary or supporting material normally contained in a message. Used in this rough fashion, the Toulmin system is more robust than it is precise but it does provide an economical way of talking about large quantities of discourse.

At the simplest level, the critic using the Toulmin system "translates" a message into Toulminian terminology. At a more ambitious level, the system allows the critic to (1) make patterned sense out of discourse by focusing on its most essential logical movements; (2) use the Toulmin layout of a message as a general starting point for later, more fine-grained, analyses; and (3) employ a standard system so that many different kinds of discourse can be compared on the same basis.

In modified form, the Toulmin system asks the critic to isolate in a given message three key features:

1. *Major Claims* (a) are the broadest, most encompassing, statements made by the speaker, (b) lie at a level of abstraction higher than all other statements the speaker makes, (c) represent what the speaker hopes will become the "residual message" in listeners' minds (i.e., the main thoughts remembered when the details of a message have been forgotten), and (d) are frequently repeated or restated in the message.
2. *Major Data* lie at a level of abstraction immediately beneath that of the Major Claim. Major Data are the supporting structures of discourse, statements answering the listener's questions: What makes you say that? What do you have to go on? Major data themselves subsume what might

be thought of as Sub-Data: facts, illustrations, bits of evidence, and other clarifying devices used to ground the speaker's assertions.

3. *Warrants* are the keys to the Toulminian approach. They make the "movement" from Major Data to Major Claim possible. Toulmin [1958: 98] described warrants as "general, hypothetical statements which can act as bridges and authorize the sort of step to which our particular argument commits us." So, for example, if a speaker makes the assertion that "Ransom money should never be paid to free U.S. hostages seized abroad" (Major Claim) because "you can't deal with terrorists" (Major Data), the "missing" part of the argument is something of the sort: "Only terrorists would seize an airplane" (Warrant).

Ehninger and Brockriede [1963] describe three types of warrants commonly found in public argument: (1) **Substantive warrants**—ideas based on what is thought to be actual fact (such as the terrorists-are-irresponsible notion used above); (2) **Motivational warrants**—ideas suggesting that some desirable end must be achieved or that some desirable condition is being endangered (e.g., The argument "We must pay the ransom money" [Major Claims] because "the people will crucify us in the upcoming elections if we don't" [Major Data] somehow depends for its reasonability on the notion that "getting re-elected is a good thing" [Warrant]; (3) **Authoritative warrants**—ideas based on the credibility of the speaker or on the source of testimony offered by the speaker (e.g., To warrant the argument "We can't pay the ransom" [Major Claims] because "I've told the people in the past I wouldn't do so" [Major Data], a speaker would be depending on some such notion as "inconsistent people are crucified in politics" or "this ransom issue isn't worth my political scalp" [Warrant].

In laying out a given message, the critic follows some fairly simple steps:

1. Isolate the Major Claims being offered by the speaker, keying particularly on repeated or reparaphrased statements.
2. Isolate the Major Data presented, many of which (but not all of which) will be found contiguous to the Major Claims made.
3. Without consulting the message directly, isolate the range of warrants that could reasonably authorize such Data-Claim movements.
4. Categorize these potential warrants, using the tripartite system described above.
5. Determine which of these warrants were **explicitly supplied** by the speaker and which were left unspoken.

Step 5 is especially crucial in criticism. Most discourse, if not all, depends heavily on the cooperation of listeners to complete the reasoning circuit begun by the speaker. A streetcorner shout to "get out of the street [Major Claims], a bus is coming [Major Data]" hardly needs to be attended by the warrant "buses can make mincemeat out of you." Our reactions to such a cry of warning are instinctual: We quickly help the argument along by supplying from our knowledge (e.g., of physics) and our biases (e.g., self-preservation) the missing pieces and parts needed to make sense out of the warner's "argument."

Thus, most persuaders rarely say everything that could be said, trusting that if the correct data are chosen for the correct claim that the audience will allow the argumentative movement, if not propel it. From such a perspective, the persuader becomes a solicitor, one who uses language to entice listeners to participate silently in an argumentative exchange. The Toulmin system encourages us to search for such "missing" elements since examining the *unstated* in discourse provides the most subtle understanding of speaker-audience relationships.

To understand the value of the Toulmin system, let us consider a simple example, a letter to the editor in a small town, Midwestern newspaper that is neither subtle nor argumentatively complex:

> On the Democratic ticket you see Ben Anderson's name. He is a good Christian man. He is an honest man, and you can trust him.
>
> Let us all go to the polls and vote for Mr. Anderson. I've known him for a long time.
>
> We need good men in our offices and more like him. Let's you and I go and vote for Mr. Anderson.

Figure 5.1 lays out the letter's argument. Several things are striking: (1) three of the claims are simply asserted. No data are supplied to establish their validity. This gives the message its choppy, telegraphic feeling; (2) the central argument—that Anderson should be elected— is supported by four different pieces of data, none of which has subdata. This gives the message its confident and businesslike tone; (3) none of the data-claim movements is explicitly warranted.

The three needed motivational warrants (i.e., that Christianity, honesty, and trustworthiness are desirable) are omitted, as is the one authoritative warrant (i.e., that the letter-writer is credible). These missing warrants give the message its homey, emotional touches. Neighbors speaking over the back fence do not need to supply warrants, and people who are sounding off often do not supply them either.

As a result, this message is "presumptuous." The argument demands a good deal from the newspaper reader because of its sketchiness, a feature somewhat required by the enforced brevity of these letters but also expected from anybody letting off steam. These distinctive, often charming, qualities make letters to the editor the most popular feature in almost any local newspaper.

The Toulmin approach can also describe more complex discourse— like that of Richard Nixon—and so Figure 5.2 presents a Toulmin layout of the early portion of the Checkers Speech. One of the real advantages of the Toulmin system is that by outlining a message skeletally, it emphasizes a message's

FIGURE 5.1 Toulmin Layout of Letter to the Editor

Major claims	Warrants	Major Data
	A = authoritative M = motivational S = substantive 0 = suppressed ** = supplied	† = subdata provided 0 = subdata omitted

1. Anderson is a ◄——————— (None) ◄——————— (None)
   Democrat.

2. He's running for ◄——————— (None) ◄——————— (None)
   office.

3. Let's vote for him. ◄———┐   3-1. Christians make ◄——— He's a Christian. (0)
                          │   good officials.
                          │   (M/0)
                          │
                          ├— 3-2. Honesty is ◄——— He's honest. (0)
                          │   important in
                          │   government. (M/0)
                          │
                          ├— 3-3. Trust is important ◄——— You can trust him.(0)
                          │   in government.
                          │   (M/0)
                          │
                          └— 3-4. You can rely on my ◄——— I've known him for
                                   judgement. (A/0)   a long time. (0)

4. We need good men. ◄——————— (None) ◄——————— (None)

5. Let's vote for ◄——————— (None) ◄——————— (None)
   Anderson

value appeals and deemphasizes its beguiling use of language. A Toulmin sketch tells us, for example, that Nixon began his speech defensively. Unlike our midwestern letter-writer, Nixon densely packs his arguments: Most Major Claims are attended by two or three different pieces of data, with Data-Claim movement #5 being the densest of all (ten identifiable pieces of Major Data). This is a lawyerly Nixon, one who makes his case by trying to overwhelm his listener, offering them a variety of data but (as in Data-Claim movement #5) never letting them forget the Major Claim—that he is innocent.

The Toulmin system is useful for several reasons. For one thing, it helps explain tone. For example, the boldness of the Patton speech mentioned earlier probably resulted from his rapid transition from Major Data to Major Data, all of which are placed in the service of one Major Claim ("We will be victorious.") but none of which is developed via Sub-Data. In contrast, the frivolous tone of Harold Hill's speech results from his dependence on sacred warrants (the wages of sin, the importance of industry, communal obligations, etc.) for profane purposes (the selling of band instruments).

FIGURE 5.2   Toulmin Layout of Nixon's Checkers Speech

Major claims	Warrants	Major Data
	A = authoritative M = motivational S = substantive 0 = suppressed ** = supplied	† = subdata provided 0 = subdata omitted
1. I'm innocent of ◄──── wrongdoing.	1-1. Personal gain is ◄──── wrong in politics. (M/**)	I used no money for personal gain. (0)
	1-2. Secrecy is wrong ◄──── in politics. (M/0)	The fund wasn't a secret fund. (†)
	1-3. Bias is wrong ◄──── in politics. (M/**)	I was not biased toward the fund's contributors. (0)
2. Private expense ◄──── funds are necessary in politics.	2-1. Constituent work ◄──── is important. (M/0)	Senate offices are not funded sufficiently for constituent work. (†)
3. I had no choice ◄──── but to use an expense fund.	3-1. Poor people have ◄──── fewer choices. (S/0)	I'm not a rich man. (0)
	3-2. Funding one's wife ◄──── isn't an honorable choice. (M/**)	My wife wasn't on the payroll. (†)
	3-3. Continuing legal ◄──── practice morally compromises a politician. (M/**)	I couldn't practice law. (†)
4. I used the fund in ◄──── honorable ways.	4-1. Communism is a ◄──── great evil. (M/0)	I'm in the business of rooting out communism. (0)
	4-2. Doing special ◄──── favors is wrong. (M/**)	I don't do special favors as a politician. (0)

(continued)

Tone is also an important factor at the end of the semester when college professors get to hear The Student Lament—"I simply must have an 'A' in this course." Many professors regard this as a presumptuous argument, perhaps because it depends so heavily on certain highly questionable warrants needed to legitimize the movement from data to claim. These warrants include: *The Puritan Ethic* ("I've worked really hard in here."), *Ego Unbounded* ("I've really liked your course."), *In Loco Parentis* ("I'll flunk out of school unless

FIGURE 5.2 *(continued)*

Major claims	Warrants	Major Data
	A = authoritative M = motivational S = substantive 0 = suppressed ** = supplied	† = subdata provided 0 = subdata omitted
5. There is ample evidence that I am innocent.	5-1. Price Waterhouse can be trusted. (A/0)	A Price Waterhouse audit has said so. (0)
	5-2. Gibson, et al. can be trusted. (A/**)	Gibson, Dunn, and Crutcher have affirmed it. (†)
	5-3. Private records are indisputable. (A/0)	My private financial records prove it. (0)
	5-4. Modest people are guileless. (M/0)	I was born in modest circumstances. (†)
	5-5. Those who serve their country like me are honorable. (A/**)	I could make no money during the war. (†)
	5-6. It would be wrong to make money as a politician. (M/0)	As a politician, I had no chance of making money. (†)
	5-7. Modest people are guileless. (M/0)	Our personal assets are modest. (†)
	5-8. It would be wrong not to pay one's debts. (M/**)	We have debts to pay. (†)
	5-9 Assets honorably gained can be kept. (M/0)	All of our assets are honorably ours. (†)
	5-10 The gift of a dog doesn't compromise one. (S/0)	Our only extra asset was Checkers. (†)

you help me out."), or *Capitalism Incorporated* ("A lesser grade will hurt me on the job market."). Because these values are so deeply ingrained in U.S. culture, students using them are bewildered (not to mention irritated) when instructors call attention to these warranting structures. The professor who responds to such a request with the faintly European assertion, "Only excellence, not character, is rewarded in here," comes across as a cultural alien.

The critic using the Toulmin approach is equipped, finally, with a system that may explain why a given message failed to persuade. Like other critical tools, the Toulmin approach provides the critic with a technical language for describing rhetorical trends that cannot easily be described in lay language. So, for example, a message may be said to fail because its Major Claims are too disparate (e.g., the speaker rambles), because claims are offered without data (e.g., a speaker who rants), because Major Data are offered but not linked to any obvious claim (e.g., the speaker becomes anecdotal), because there are no culturally available warrants for the data chosen (e.g., the speaker seems irrelevant), or because the speaker explicates warrants too insistently (e.g., the speaker becomes pontifical). Thus, the Toulmin system seems the best method developed thus far for explaining that curious brand of thinking/feeling known as human reasoning.

CONCLUSION

For many years, the study of reasoning was the sole province of the philosopher. Later, the children of philosophers, psychologists, began to explore the workings of the human mind. Whereas the philosopher treated ideas in their pure forms (which is to say, in their most abstract forms), the psychologist investigated what people felt when thinking about ideas. More recently, rhetorical critics have set out to discover how persuasive messages mediate human reasoning. Such critics have not become as abstract as the philosopher or as individualistic as the psychologist. Instead, they have searched for evidence of *social reasoning* by looking "through" messages to the human beings producing and receiving them. In that sense, the study of public argument is the study of how minds meet.

This chapter has championed a psychological model of argument, taking the position that reasoning is more than ciphering. This model purposively abandons the thinking/feeling dualism so often found in Western culture and the elitism found in technical or idealist models. It urges the critic to study the rules of *ordinary* reasoning, even if those rules spring from the humble advice found in everyday proverbs and folk tales. It urges the critic to study the rhetoric of "peculiar" people because learning about strangers so often translates into genuine self-knowledge. It urges the critic to study the "intuitive validity" a message has for listeners, even if the listeners' standards for validity are not the critic's. Finally, it reminds the critic that reasoning is something that people do in their own marvelously complicated ways. May that ever be the case.

Chapter 6

ANALYZING FORM

Lear: Attend the lords of France and Burgundy, Gloucester.
Gloucester: I shall, my liege. [Exeunt Gloucester and Edmund.]
Lear: Meantime we shall express our darker purpose.
Give me the map there. Know that we have divided
In three our kingdom: and 'tis our fast intent
To shake all cares and business from our age;
Conferring them on younger strengths, while we
Unburthen'd crawl toward death. Our son of Cornwall,
And you, our no less loving son of Albany,
We have this hour a constant will to publish
Our daughters' several dowers, that future strife
May be prevented now. The princes, France and Burgundy,
Great rivals in our youngest daughter's love,
Long in our court have made their amorous sojourn,
And here are to be answer'd. Tell me, my daughters,
Since now we will divest us, both of rule,
Interest of territory, cares of state, Which of you shall we say
doth love us most?
That we our largest bounty may extend
Where nature doth merit challenge. Goneril,
Our eldest-born, speak first.
Goneril: Sir, I love you more than words can wield the matter;
Dearer than eye-sight, space, and liberty;
Beyond what can be valued, rich or rare;
No less than life, with grace, health, beauty, honour;
As much as child e'er loved, or father found;

               A love that makes breath poor, and speech unable;
               Beyond all manner of so much I love you.
Cordelia: [Aside] What shall Cordelia do? Love, and be silent.
   Lear: Of all these bounds, even from this line to this,
               With shadowy forests and with champains rich'd,
               With plenteous rivers and wide-skirted meads,
               We make thee lady: to thine and Albany's issue
               Be this perpetual. What says our second daughter,
               Our dearest Regan, wife to Cornwall? Speak.
  Regan: Sir, I am made
               Of the self-same metal that my sister is,
               And prize me at her worth. In my true heart
               I find she names my very deed of love;
               Only she comes too short: that I profess
               Myself as enemy to all other joys,
               Which the most precious square of sense possesses;
               And find I am alone felicitate
               In your dear highness' love.
Cordelia: [Aside] Then poor Cordelia! And yet not so; since, I am
                  sure, my love's
               More richer than my tongue.
   Lear: To thee and thine hereditary ever
               Remain this ample third of our fair kingdom;
               No less in space, validity, and pleasure,
               Than that conferr'd on Goneril. Now, our joy,
               Although the last, not least; to whose young love
               The vines of France and milk of Burgundy
               Strive to be interess'd; what can you say to draw
               A third more opulent than your sisters? Speak.
Cordelia: Nothing, my lord.
   Lear: Nothing.
Cordelia: Nothing.
   Lear: Nothing will come of nothing: speak again.
Cordelia: Unhappy that I am, I cannot heave
               My heart into my mouth: I love your majesty
               According to my bond; nor more nor less.
   Lear: How, how, Cordelia! mend your speech a little,
               Lest it may mar your fortunes.
Cordelia: Good my lord,
               You have begot me, bred me, loved me:
               I Return those duties back as are right fit,
               Obey you, love you, and most honour you.
               Why have my sisters husbands, if they say
               They love you all? Haply, when I shall wed,
               That lord whose hand must take my plight shall carry
               Half my love with him, half my care and duty:
               Sure, I shall never marry like my sisters,
               To love my father all.

>   Lear: But goest thy heart with this?
> Cordelia: Ay, good my lord.
>   Lear: So young, and so untender?
> Cordelia: So young, my lord, and true.
>   Lear: Let it be so; thy truth, then, be thy dower. . . .
>   [Shakespeare, 1603:35]

"Thy truth, then, be thy dower." Not a happy epitaph for a would-be heiress. And not a very rhetorical epitaph either. Young Cordelia, faithful daughter of her aging and self-indulgent father, need only have uttered sweet nothings to inherit a kingdom. Cordelia's sisters, Goneril and Regan, surely had no trouble meeting Lear's challenge. They understood the speech-act implicitly: Tell him you love him and make him forget that he forced you to say such things. When in human history have such riches hung on the mere saying of a speech?

And Lear was hardly choosy here. Were he our contemporary, the lyrics to any Top Forty love ballad would have sufficed. So what's wrong, Cordelia? Why not "mend your speech" for a moment or two? Why let your audience confuse your integrity with a lack of tenderness on your part? Why get philosophical when the situation so clearly invites you to be mercenary?

Cordelia's defense of her actions is hardly compelling. She pleads lack of rhetorical competence: a love "richer than her tongue." She stands on personal principle: an unwillingness to "heave her heart into her mouth." But Cordelia's outrage seems even more basic: She resents using a standard rhetorical form to show unstandard love of a parent. She resents being trooped across Lear's stage, the third in a line of singing princesses, forced to mimic speech that is neither exalted nor subtle. Cordelia was not unloving nor was she unwilling to discuss her love. Rather, she felt that love has its own timetable and that it is diminished when employed suddenly and unfeelingly. Above all, Cordelia resents the formulas of love, formulas repeated daily to her father by courtiers, formulas her sisters have turned into rites of devotion. In rejecting these formulas, Cordelia became less a persuader than a critic. Sadly, critics almost never please kings.

This chapter discusses forms and formulas. It is concerned with three things. First is **structure**—the apportionment and sequencing of message elements. Structural decisions are decisions about which ideas should be given what amount of attention and how ideas should be arranged for maximum impact. So, for example, an important structural feature of Cordelia's speech is the balance struck between discussions of her love for her father and the love she someday expects to have for a husband. This equivalence made little sense: Lear was clearly not interested in sharing the rhetorical spotlight, especially not with a nonexistent son-in-law. Cordelia's sisters, on the other hand, were highly conventional. Their rhetoric placed Lear on stage by himself, dominating all with his several fascinations. They did not confuse their father, covering less ground in their speeches but with greater impact. Cordelia's rhetorical ambition, in contrast, prompted only scorn.

This chapter is also concerned with **form**—the patterns of meaning listeners generate when they take in a message. Form refers to the "shape" of meaning, how ideas are linked together by listeners. Some ideas (e.g., inflationary spirals) sit in a listener's mind alone and unloved, associated only with abstruse economic principles, boring political editorials, and a vague sense of unpleasantness. Other ideas (say, a circus) instantly generate a host of associations: hot dogs, clowns, elephants, calliopes, popcorn, colorful tents, earthy smells, fancy costumes, and memories of innocence. Thinking of a circus fills up the mind in ways that inflationary spirals cannot. If it has been a long time since our last circus, the booming welcome of the ringmaster will immediately help to "fill out" the mental form of the circus, making us properly anticipatory as circus-goers.

Implicitly knowing such things, Goneril tells Lear that her love surpasses those things her father already prizes ("eye-sight, space, and liberty"). Her speech asks Lear to think of life's most precious qualities ("grace, health, beauty, honour") and then to round out this mental picture by adding her love to the concoction. Cordelia, in contrast, runs competition with herself, asking her father to ponder her affection in the company of such unpleasant things as contracts ("I return those duties back as are right fit") and jealousy ("that lord whose hand must take my plight"). Law, envy, and love—hardly a comfortable mixture of ideas for a defensive old man.

Finally, this chapter treats **genre**—a class of messages sharing important structural and content features and which, as a class, creates special expectations in listeners. Genre exist because speakers are imitative, borrowing from yesterday when deciding what to say today. A genre like the religious invocation at a sporting event, the political commercial on television, and the gold-watch speech at the retirement dinner develop because people's life experiences are so similar: They are born, they grow up, they fall in love, and they die. They always have, and they always have needed to speak of these experiences, resulting in pink and blue birth announcements, bar mitzvah addresses, marriage proposals under the stars, and moving funeral orations. Each of these messages echoes its forebears, at least in part.

Naturally, history can be a tyranny. Utilizing the formulas of speech requires a Faustian bargain: guaranteed social acceptability in exchange for independence of thought. Lear's daughter, Regan, opted for this deal, drawing on a rich tradition of courtly love ("I profess myself an enemy to all other joys."), thereby anticipating her father's anticipations. Cordelia, in contrast, intentionally violated the generic rules. She combined biology ("you begot me") with sociology ([you] bred me") and delivered herself of a dispassionate, intellectually balanced college lecture. Good genre. Wrong audience.

This chapter probes how message structure interacts with expected patterns of meaning (form) to produce persuasion. Structure and form are a complex business, but examining rule-following and rule-violating is almost always profitable. This chapter's thesis is that by knowing who follows rhetorical rules and who does not, the critic can learn much about the whys and wherefores of these rules. Perhaps this is why Shakespeare opened his great tragedy with the generic struggle presented above. Perhaps he sensed that an important moral lesson could be taught by depicting who used rhetoric and who was used by it. With Shakespeare as our first teacher, then, let us become better students of structure and form.

STRUCTURE AND FORM IN RHETORIC

The key distinction between structure and form is this: Structure is something that speakers do and form is something that listeners and readers do. Structures are identifiable in texts, forms emerge in audience's minds. Figure 6.1 provides a clear, albeit elementary, example of this distinction. If asked the question, "Which picture has the *clearest* meaning?" most people would pick Figure 6.1A. If then asked "Which picture has *special* meaning?" the same answer would be given. Figure 6.1A symbolizes the United States of America. Versions of it have been planted on the moon, on the hills of Iwo Jima, on Kuwaiti oil tankers in the Persian Gulf, on Olympic team jackets, on the lapels of conservative bankers, and on the coffins of heroes in Arlington National

FIGURE 6.1 Relationships between Content and Structure

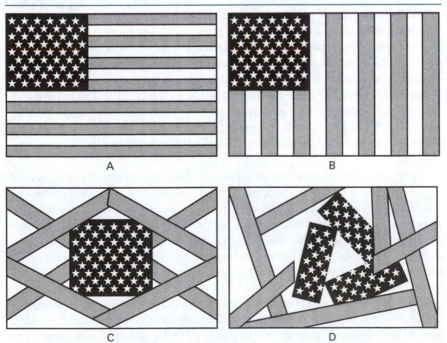

Cemetery. Figure 6.1A has also been worn on the backsides of student protestors in the 1970s, burned in the streets of Baghdad in the 1980s, and displayed during Fourth of July automobile sales in the 1990s. Figure 6.1A
inspires many, infuriates others. It is drenched in meaning.

But Figures 6.1B, C, and D show that Figure 6.1A's content is not exceptional. Figure 6.1A is merely a special arrangement of iconic characters: stars,
bars, and backgrounds. Its meaning, the form it takes in the perceiver's mind,
is heavily dependent upon its basic *structural* elements. Even a slight
rearrangement of these elements (Figure 6.1B) changes the evocative power
of the symbol completely. A more ambitious rearrangement (Figure 6.1C)
removes virtually all of its "Americanicity." While Figure 6.1C possesses a certain raciness not present in Old Glory, it is still unlikely to draw a salute.

Figure 6.1D seems so distorted as to be sacrilegious. It takes perceptual
gymnastics to see that its content is identical to that of Figure 6.1A. On viewing it, schoolchildren would wonder and patriots would quake, both assuming
that there is only one "right" way to assemble such elements. They would
resist *any* arbitrary arrangement of these features, sensing that even the slightest variation on the "true" optical theme would steal its "form-al" meaning.
When it comes to Figure 6.1A, most Americans are visual fundamentalists.

Figure 6.1 teaches an important lesson: Structure and content cannot be
separated easily. As we moved from Figure 6.1A to 6.1D, the contents of the
messages became increasingly radical. *Only* Figure 6.1A is acceptable if conventional meanings are to be shared. Figure 6.1D therefore meant nothing to
us. We were incapable of forming its elements into something sensible, never
mind into something important, never mind into something motivating. That
is, certain message structures arouse particular expectations within perceivers,
who are often unwilling to change those expectations— or forms—once they
have been aroused (e.g., once stars and bars have been presented in the same
visual field). Thus, formulating rhetoric involves selecting and arranging message elements and predicting how listeners will react to these elements additively. As Arnold [1974:137] notes, listeners *will* generate forms in their
heads constantly. The speaker uses structural devices to guide this process of
forming.

The centrality of structure to content is best seen when structure is missing (as in Figure 6.1D) or misappropriated. For example, if a preacher somehow forgot to ask the bride and groom to exchange vows during a wedding,
the event would not be "formed" as a proper ceremony by those in the church
pews. On first noticing the omission, the wedding guests might well treat the
experience as a novelty, as a preacher's ritualistic experiment. As the ceremony
progressed, they would try to re-form this newly evolving reality into traditional meanings ("perhaps the vows will be exchanged just before the reces-
sional"). Normally, a speaker would help relieve such ambiguities by giving the
audience clues on how to interpret these unexpected and discordant darta.
Should the speaker fail to do so, listeners will take over the task themselves:

"Poor Pastor Johnson has become addle-brained" or "maybe John and Sue are putting us all on."

Critics have often treated structure formalistically by applying a set of pre-scriptive laws to message organization. Research by Douglass and Arnold [1970], however, shows that few real-life messages fit these standard patterns. A more promising line of inquiry, they suggest, is to treat structure as a psychological, not as a linguistic, process, and to examine a message not as a set of self-contained statements but as a *stimulus to reasoning* for listeners. They warn critics that while structure can be found in messages, the more important element, form, is found in listeners' reactions to these structures.

So, for example, Douglass and Arnold urge critics to search for the kinds of "organizational help" a speaker provides and for the inferences audiences are likely to draw as a result. By asking which ideas were emphasized and which were not, which came first and which last, which were interrupted and which were not, a critic begins to learn what audiences "did" with the rhetorical materials they were asked to process. Thus, a speaker who tells a long-winded story without a point or who relates facts in reverse chronological order is likely to frustrate listeners' forming instincts. Ideally, then, a critic looks through message to listener, through structure to form, to find rhetorical effect.

A useful way of examining message structure is to ask a set of questions about how rhetorical materials have been arranged in a given case. These probes deal with **message design** (the use of standard structural devices), **message emphasis** (the comparative treatment of individual ideas), **message density** (the depth of coverage of individual ideas), and **message pacing** (the distribution of ideas through time). In each case, the critic is urged to look for the effects message patterns have within listeners. The first of these questions has to do with message design:

- Does the speaker use an *identifiable* traditional message structure? Is this approach used throughout or only from time to time?

Here, the critic inspects a text's overall architecture to see if it conforms to any of the classic patterns of message structure. Table 6.1 presents those patterns, although it must be emphasized that only rarely will textbook examples of these patterns be found in real-life persuasion (since speakers often take shortcuts). Also, merely identifying these patterns is of little use unless they can also shed light on the overall rhetorical situation being studied. Since message structure relates so closely to how people think, it can tell much about a speaker's mental habits or an audience's operating hierarchy of beliefs.

These structural cues are suggestive because people often do not think about *how* they will present ideas but only about what they will say. Thus, asking why a speaker's first argument came first and not last forces the critic to explain what nonarbitrary logic the speaker used when making the always-arbitrary decisions of firstness and lastness. And the fact that these decisions

TABLE 6.1 Common Structural Techniques in Persuasion*

Structural Type	Rhetorical Function	Example (State Legislative Debate)	Main Advantages	Main Disadvantages	Critical Probe
Chronological sequence	Places time relationships in the foreground so that narrative becomes clear	"In the 1970s, we tried a sales tax and that proved inadequate. We moved to sin taxes in the '80s. The '90s require something new: a tax on professional services."	Builds suspense as the past unfolds into the present (or future)	Propositions the speaker is advocating can become subordinated to the telling of the "story"	What appears to be the speaker's rationale for discussing the particular points in time chosen for discussion?
Spatial sequence	Shows relationships between parts and parts or between parts and wholes	"The opportunities in this state are enormous. The lake area has tourist development. The tri-city area is luring high-tech industry. And the plateau region has the new Space Command Center."	Makes ideas "visual" for listeners	Too much detail may cloud the ideas being advanced	What devices did the speaker use to demonstrate the "adjacency" of the elements described?
Ascending/ descending sequence	Ideas are arranged according to their relative importance, familiarity, or complexity	"I agree with Senator Davenport that cable regulation must be at least considered this session. And I agree with Senator Foley that the open-meeting law is important. But we can't even think about those things until we agree on funding basic state services."	Gives a sense of precision by emphasizing the relationship of one concept to another	Once begun, the sequence must be completed, with all necessary stages being discussed	What specific strategic advantage is the speaker hoping for by emphasizing climaxes or anticlimaxes?
Causal sequence	Links observable effects to underlying factors allegedly responsible for those effects	"Ladies and gentlemen of the legislature, I ask you to reflect on industrial development in this state. What's responsible for our growth in that area? I'll tell you what: a superior educational system. Let's never forget that."	Western listeners particularly appreciate causal structures	Listeners have been taught to distrust *simple* cause-effect linkages	What steps did the speaker take to guard the *credibility* of the causal attributions made?

Sequence	Description	Example	Advantage	Disadvantage	Question
Problem-solution sequence	Appropriate courses of action are endorsed on the basis of their capacity to remedy problems	"You and I both know that we need a revenue bill that's at least three things: timely, fair, and adequate. That's what my plan is about."	Builds on the common psychological need within people to overcome difficulties	If listeners are unconvinced of the seriousness of the problem, boredom results	Did the speaker spend the most time emphasizing problems or were solutions primarily stressed?
Withheld-proposal sequence	Favorable materials are piled up and the speaker's solution mentioned only briefly at the end	"Let's reflect for a moment on what the park system has done for this state. It's the best run system in the nation and it adds four hundred million dollars a year in tourist revenue to our budget each year. Let's keep all of that in mind when we discuss funding for the parks this year."	An ostensibly "innocent" approach and therefore especially useful for a hostile audience	Highly dependent for effectiveness on the speaker's knowledge of what the audience currently knows and feels	Does the speaker make the *transition* from general to "preferred" material gracefully and nonmanipulatively?
Open-proposal sequence	Direct, deductive presentation of a proposal followed by support for that proposal	"You people have already heard the conservative approach to doing things. Tonight I'm going to give you another perspective: We need to raise taxes immediately. Here's why."	A simple and clear sequence that appears "forthright" as a result	Can be boring for listeners if they feel that they have "heard it all before"	How does the speaker compensate for the lack of suspense such an approach entails?
Reflective sequence	A variation on the problem-solution sequence in which the speaker professes no particular preference for a solution	"Quite frankly, I'm not sure how to proceed at this point in the debate. State revenues have never been lower and welfare needs have never been higher. The problems are obvious. But what are the solutions?"	Sets up an "exploratory" mood by involving listeners directly in problem-solving	Can be seen as manipulative if the speaker suddenly opts for a particular solution	Does the speaker maintain a sense of *mutual* problem-solving by actively considering all possible alternatives?

(continued)

*Adapted from Arnold [1974].

TABLE 6.1 (continued)

Structural Type	Rhetorical Function	Example (State Legislative Debate)	Main Advantages	Main Disadvantages	Critical Probe
Elimination sequence	A solution-oriented approach in which all but one remedy is successively eliminated by the speaker	"So we've looked at five different options this morning and found each of them wanting. What choice do we have other than to adopt the Harris plan forthwith?"	Highly useful when the audience readily acknowledges the relevance and importance of the problem	Can be seen as manipulative of the speaker seems to be using a strawman argument	What does the speaker do to guard against listeners' *impatience* with such a lockstep structure?
Motivational sequence	Speaker follows a fixed pattern of attention, need, satisfaction, visualization, and action	"Ten thousand. That's the number of state-funded abortions performed last year. Without more money, pretty soon only rich women will be able to afford abortions and the welfare rolls will swell. We simply must pass H.B. 21 and we must do it *today*."	Parallels what is thought to be a universally attractive and psychologically "whole" sequence of thought	A fairly vague series of steps that are not always easily distinguished from one another	How much time does the speaker spend on each "stage" of the sequence, and were such allocations of time justified?
Topical sequence	Breaks a subject matter into several equivalent subparts and then treats them in somewhat arbitrary order	"This has been a really productive legislative session. We've solved the budget crisis; we've tackled deregulation; and we've begun the Industrial Development Commission. I congratulate each and every one of you on a job well done."	Perhaps the simplest method available of organizing a message	Speakers are often seduced into giving equivalent treatment to subtopics that do not merit equivalent treatment	Is there a strategically sound *ordering* to the subtopics selected for treatment by the speaker?

never *seem* arbitrary to a speaker adds to their capacity to shed light on unstated intellectual and cultural premises.

Some of our earlier messages show the importance of message design. Harold Hill, for example, used a Causal Sequence to prove that all versions of local sin could be attributed to the goings-on in the pool hall. After making this case, Hill returned to the high school gymnasium and presented a second speech ("Seventy-six Trombones") that functioned as the conclusion to his overarching Problem-Solution strategy.

Perhaps the most interesting thing about Hill's structure is its purity. His speeches emerge in the play as set-pieces, unadulterated examples of classic rhetorical design. The unerring way in which they unfold seems to be the playwright's tip that Hill is up to no good. These structures are so pure, so self-propelling, that the theatre audience becomes enthralled with Hill-the-strategist and, at the same time, begins to feel slightly superior to him. This sense of superiority is important since if Hill's manipulativeness cannot be readily seen by the audience, they will be unable to appreciate his eventual reconstruction. Thus, Hill uses the sin-then-salvation motif to perfection which, in turn, stands as evidence of his imperfection.

Things are more disorderly in real life. George Patton, for example, rambled when speaking, moving from discussion of a winning spirit, to the availability of superior equipment, to the psychology of combat, to the need for toughness, and finally to the immortality of bravery. Such a Topical structure is not without its advantages. Rambling gives the audience the sense that they are being let in on the speaker's unconscious; it allows Patton to become human, even though he almost never refers to himself in the speech. Similarly, his transitions are no more elaborate than the word "now." These brief punctuations signal to the audience that something else has just occurred to Patton and that he might as well get that off his chest too. This sort of lazy structure also signals the novelty of Patton's situation: a hastily called speech delivered by a busy general who just happened to be in the area and who had no time to prepare a formal message.

This was hardly Rabbi Prinz's case, whose brief remarks were well scripted and carefully choreographed to fit into the overall scene of the March on Washington. Prinz generally followed a Chronological pattern (yesterday's Jewish ghettos, today's black ghettos, tomorrow's ghettoless America), although he is not compulsive about it. Ceremonial situations normally demand a conventional structure, which is perhaps why so many have cursed so mightily when watching the Academy Awards show each year. (Gushing nonsequiturs are occasionally charming but more often irritating.) Prinz's use of the past in service of the future was therefore sensible given his role (as a teacher) and his status (as an elder). Anything more experimental on his part would perhaps have seemed out of character.

Richard Nixon was hardly ceremonial. He was an arguer. Portions of his Checkers Speech establish how carefully he linked evidence with conclusions. He used the Elimination sequence to show why his only choice was to use a campaign fund, Causality to point up the Communist threat to the nation, and the Withheld-Proposal technique as well ("I leave the decision up to you. Write and call now."). But the Open-Proposal approach can also be found in his speech ("I'm innocent and here's the evidence.") as can Chronology (his life and times).

Nixon's speech was therefore a complex speech: Its early structure differs from its later structure and its substructures contain substructures. This complexity points up the complexity of Richard Nixon himself, a man who was never reducible to an easy gloss. It also shows the complexity of his political circumstances: How exactly does one combine a jury summation with a solicitation for votes? And it reveals the complexity of reaching a TV audience, some of whom love you, some of whom hate you, and many of whom would rather be watching something else. It is little wonder, then, that Mr. Nixon's speech was as complex in design as it was obvious in content.

A general inspection of a message's design features is useful for the overall questions it raises. More specific questions can also be asked, some of which have to deal with message emphasis:

- How rigidly does the speaker adhere to the *topic-proper*? Does the speaker roam widely from subject matter to subject matter or is the message highly constricted in content? Why?
- Are a great many arguments presented in scattergun fashion or are just a few arguments *developed* (but developed in depth)? Are the interconnections of evidence and arguments made clear via previews, transitions, and internal and concluding summaries? Why?
- Does an idea's *context* give it special importance or attractiveness? Do the statements made just before or just after an idea make it less likely or more likely that that that idea will be received well (understood and accepted)?

The first two sets of questions urge the critic to examine how tightly, or formally, the speaker developed his or her case. Such inquiries help the critic examine the crucial matter of rhetorical tone. We know, for example, that an attractive thing about informal conversations is that they proceed at their own pace, with each new topic having only a marginal relationship to the foregoing topic. At times, we are attracted to structureless dialogue, which is perhaps why "talk radio" is so attractive to so many people. At other times—in a legal contract, in a newspaper editorial, in a performance appraisal—only clear, and clearly coordinated, arguments are tolerated.

Naturally one ought not take a purist's approach to message structure since much real-life discourse does not slavishly utilize standard organizational patterns. Jamieson [1988a] extends this argument when documenting the growing disuse of formal argument during political exchanges on television. She claims that the structural rules of everyday conversation (be interesting, be relevant, be anecdotal) best match the structural patterns of televised speechmaking. Jamieson further claims that because of television, traditionally "masculine" speech patterns (patterns emphasizing classic structures) are giving way to the traditionally "feminine" qualities of personalization, ornamentation, and casual organization.

Ronald Reagan, a person who constantly substituted narrative structures for propositional structures, frequently proved Jamieson's point. An interesting example occurred in Mr. Reagan's summation during his third debate with Walter Mondale in 1984. After arguing that the meaning of the election lay in the future and that economic growth was important, Mr. Reagan suddenly made the following observations:

> Several years ago, I was given an assignment to write a letter. It was to go into a time capsule and would be read in a hundred years, when that time capsule was opened. I remember driving down the California coast one day. My mind was full of what I was going to put into that letter about the problems and the issues that confront us in our time and what we did about them.
>
> But I couldn't completely neglect the beauty around me: the Pacific out there on one side of the highway, shining in the sunlight, the mountains of the coast range rising on the other side. And I found myself wondering what it would be like for someone . . . wondering if someone, a hundred years from now, would be driving down that highway, and if they would see the same thing.
>
> With that thought, I realized what a job I had with that letter. I would be writing a letter to people who know everything there is to know about us. We would know nothing about them. . . . [Reagan, 1984:1609]

It is hard to know what Mr. Reagan had on his mind here. The story has nothing to do with the economy (his immediately preceding statement) or with the remarks that followed (nuclear weapons, preserving freedom, and George Bush), topics that were themselves disconnected. The argument of his story is unclear and even its narrative plot line is off kilter. Mr. Reagan appears to be free-associating, moving his mouth while his brain searches for a conclusion to the debate. There are no previews, transitions, or internal summaries; his speech is a digression within a digression.

But Mr. Reagan's supporters hardly seemed bothered by his closing remarks. For them, his informality had a mystical warmth, the stamp of a person willing to share even his moments of reverie with his audience. His remarks had "conversational structure," therefore signaling his trust in them as listeners. That is why they were charmed by it.

Reagan's critics, in contrast, used this example to describe a mind unable to structure thought, to connect evidence with conclusions, or to process information consecutively. His critics argued that his digressive speech signaled a digressive mind and that the *context* within which his remarks were found—during a national debate on foreign policy—was especially damning. How could such an undisciplined mind be trusted, they asked, to cope with the complexity of a nuclear age? (A few years after his retirement, Mr. Reagan was indeed diagnosed with Alheizmer's disease, a destructive kind of mental deterioration, although one cannot be sure if this particular speech event previewed that sad outcome.)

In a sense, both Reagan's admirers and his critics were making the point made earlier: Structure argues. They differed as to what Mr. Reagan's structure said (A man who retained his humanity even when discussing nuclear war? A man out of touch with the dangers of his times?), but in both cases they showed the effects produced when an argument appears in one context rather than another.

- Which points are *emphasized* and which given short shrift by the speaker? Does the speaker cover the waterfront of ideas or home in on just a few? Do these decisions expose the persuasive obstacles being faced?
- How much time is spent on the introduction of *novel* information? How much time is spent recasting the familiar? Does this known/unknown ratio reveal anything important about the rhetorical situation?

These two questions relate to message density, the extent to which individual ideas are allowed to predominate in a given text. As mentioned in Chapter 1, rhetoric is often an attempt to spotlight certain ideas or to push other ideas backstage. So, for example, when a young couple begins house-hunting, they become locked in an ideational struggle with the realtor (whether they know it or not). The realtor's job is to highlight the built-in curio cabinet, the mauve carpeting, and the easy-care lawn and at the same time to deflect attention from the price of the home, the windowless family room, or the cracks in the sheetrock.

Naturally, the realtor will continually justify this rhetorical coverage during the home tour, so wary consumers must know not only their price but their topic as well. As long as the purchasing decision hinges on mauve versus persimmon carpeting, the realtor is equally advantaged. And so an important rhetorical principle suggests itself: *Whoever controls the shape of the discussion controls its consequence as well.*

In confrontational situations, topical emphasis becomes especially important as the disputants try to elbow aside their rivals' topics. This is true in court where the lawyer for the defense uses the grounds of direct relevance to keep the toxicologist from testifying. It is also true in political affairs, as, for example, during the Watergate era of the Nixon administration. One fabled press conference, that of August 22, 1973, was especially interesting. Until this point, Mr. Nixon had been avoiding press conferences for over five months, but he ultimately had to face the press. But he did not come unarmed. After being badgered with one Watergate question after another, Nixon made a bald attempt to shift the topical direction of the discussion:

> Question: Mr. President.
> The President: Just a moment. We have had 30 minutes of this press conference. I have yet to have, for example, one question on the business of the people, which shows how consumed

we are with this [Watergate]. I am not criticizing the members of the press, because you are very interested in this issue, but let me tell you, years from now people are going to perhaps be interested in what happened in terms of the efforts of the United States to build a structure of peace in the world. They are perhaps going to be interested in the efforts of this Administration to have a kind of prosperity that we have not had since 1955—that is, prosperity without war and without inflation—because throughout the Kennedy and throughout the Johnson years, whatever prosperity we had was at the cost of either inflation or war or both. I don't say that critically of them. I am simply saying we have got to do better than that. [Nixon, 1973a:719]

Mr. Nixon's ploy did not entirely change the direction of that day's discussion, but it did reinforce those who felt that he was being hounded out of office by the press. Particularly interesting was how Mr. Nixon justified the topical alteration: He reached for transcendent goals, painting himself as a statesman and the press as small-minded. Throughout his career, Richard Nixon was a hard-charger. He never let anyone else set his rhetorical agenda.

- What is newsworthy about the *sequence* of arguments? Do first-saids and last-saids reveal anything important about the speaker's rhetorical circumstances? What would have happened if the arguments had been reversed?
- Does the speaker alternate the *mood* of the message? Is narration or verbal intensity or itemized lists or rhetorical questions dominant in certain portions of the message and absent in others, thereby creating peaks and valleys of rhetorical pressure on the audience?
- Does the *beginning* of the message anchor later ideas and arguments? Does the speaker begin as if listeners already possessed common feelings on the subject, or does the speaker try to disabuse listeners of currently held values and beliefs?
- When, if at all, are unusually *controversial* or *complex* ideas introduced in the message? Early, middle, late, or not at all? What sort of material precedes or follows such potentially troublesome segments?

Message pacing is another important structural matter. It is concerned with *when* in time ideas are presented. Because listeners (unlike readers) cannot "turn back the pages" when they miss something, order effects are especially important in oral persuasion. For many years, researchers tried to determine which sequence of arguments was most influential. By using the same arguments in each case but by varying the ordering of appeals from experimental audience to experimental audience, these researchers determined that familiar ideas should be placed before unfamiliar ideas, that an attention/stress/solution pattern is especially effective, that first ideas and last ideas are remembered better than those in the middle, that a Withheld-Proposal sequence may backfire with hostile listeners, etc. [See, for example, Bettinghaus and Cody, 1994].

But such studies are limited in generalizability and rarely help the critic understand the nuances of a particular message. Typically, it is more useful to examine a given sequence of arguments, tracing how that speaker approached that unique set of rhetorical problems.

An example of the importance of message pacing was the U.S. Army's pamphlet, "Eleven Point Checklist for Job Hunters". The checklist began with the statement "If you are a young man about to graduate from high school, you certainly want the best possible job you can find. To help you in accomplishing this task, we have prepared a checklist for your use. We sincerely wish you the best of luck." Having thus offered its services as a guidance counselor, the Army proceeds through its checklist as follows:

1. Pay
2. Vacations
3. Education
4. Allowances
5. Leisure time
6. Medical care
7. Marketing [i.e., shopping]
8. Retirement
9. Travel
10. Bonuses
11. Training

Each point on the checklist had specific advice for the job-hunter (e.g., "Travel—Your employer should agree to relocate you at your request anywhere in the U.S. or Free World at his expense. If married, this includes your family.") At the bottom of the page the audience was invited to use the checklist when weighing other job offers and then was left with the preferred suggestion: "Better yet, don't waste your time, see your Army Representative today."

Several items are of structural interest here. For one thing, no item on the checklist asked the job-hunter to consider the *kind of work* they would be doing. Apparently, soldiers' day-to-day activities were not attractive enough to merit even a twelfth position on the hierarchy. And the checklist is indeed a hierarchy, with four of the first five elements relating to either money or time off. While Education is placed in third position, no details are given. In contrast, the benefits associated with most other items are amply provided: 30 days PAID vacation, a $10,000 bonus to stay more than three years, etc.

Given the age of the target audience, the authors were wise to drop Retirement to the bottom of the list with Training. Two other items at the bottom, Travel and Bonuses, are essentially restatements of Vacations and Pay at the top of the list and are thus filler material. Also, at no point in the sequence is the reader more than one item away from a monetary argument.

The organizational pattern is thus carefully adapted to the Army's perpetual target audience: America's underprivileged. Financial opportunity reaches out from beginning to end in this message.

A number of critics have examined the effects of structual devices on persuasion. Gerland [1994], for example, did an interesting study of the first Rodney King trial in Los Angeles, the trial that resulted in the acquittal of the policemen who beat Mr. King (a decision that was later overturned by another jury). The extraordinary thing about the first trial, according to Gerland, was that the acquittals were granted even though the jury was provided with *irrevocable visual evidence* of the beatings (via videotape). Rather brilliantly, however, the lawyers for the defense showed the jury the videotape (1) endlessly and (2) interruptedly. The former technique ultimately dulled jurors to its sensationalistic nature (we stimulus-seeking humans bore easily) while the latter technique prevented jurors from "forming" the beating as a single, coherent *statement*. In other words, the King beating became—visually—both boring and confusing. Neither quality argues well.

Pacing and emphasis are especially important in social movement rhetoric, which, by definition, proceeds sequentially through time so as to alter beliefs and attitudes. Darsey [1991], for example, compared the rhetoric of the early gay rights movement (1948–1977) to that of its more recent manifestations (1978–1990). One of his most interesting findings was that the early rhetoric focused on building the self-identity of gay members ("we're gay and we're o.k.") while the latter phase abandoned that emphasis entirely, presumably because self-esteem issues were no longer as prominent for this by-now-powerful minority group. In its place, however, came arguments focusing on personal security. Because they *had* been successful in commanding public attention and securing important political gains, gays now had a kind of visibility in society that often endangered them. Clearly, political success can exact a price. Estimating that price was Darsey's job and it was his *structural* perceptions of the movement that ultimately informed him most usefully.

GENERIC STUDIES OF FORM

As defined earlier, *a genre is a class of messages having important structural and content similarities and which, as a class, creates special expectations in listeners.* Inaugural addresses, then, constitute a genre because they share textual features and are delivered in similar circumstances every four years. Thus, when he first spoke as president, Bill Clinton did not sound exactly like John Kennedy or Abraham Lincoln, but he did not sound completely unlike them either. Mr. Clinton spoke in a 1992 sort of way because he spoke to 1992 sorts of people. But 1992 Americans were still Americans; while they were curious about new possibilities they were also attracted to old realities. So, when writing his inaugural address, Bill Clinton had help—the help of the ages—

whether he wanted it or not. Because he was part of a historical process, he labored under generic constraints.

Generic study is the study of such constraints. It describes patterns of discourse and explains their recurrence. It asks questions like these: Why does this text seem more rule-governed than another? Why are these rules operating here rather than other rules? What happens if these rules are violated? Why do people care about rules at all? The generic critic intentionally looks for structural and content similarities and then tries to explain them. The generic critic is therefore something like the entomologist who traces the regularities, and interesting irregularities, found in the natural world. But tucking all of life's speeches into their own generic beds is hardly worthwhile if it results in nothing more than taxonomical fascination. Rather, it is *the story behind the taxonomies,* the general ideas about the natural condition, that intrigue both the entomologist and the generic critic.

Thus, when doing criticism, the generic critic operates on the following assumptions:

1. Generic patterns necessarily develop. Black [1992:97 ff.] demonstrates that there are a limited number of situations in which a speaker can be found and a limited number of ways of responding to these standard situations. As a result, messages form identifiable clusters over time. So, for example, when he invented the first inaugural address, George Washington could not know that subsequent inaugurals would resemble his. But he might have guessed such a thing, because the thoughts and feelings of a culture, if it is a culture, will be similar from age to age. Whoever addresses such people—in any era—must reckon with such constancy.

2. Generic patterns reveal societal truths. The generic critic examines message patterns in order to comment on the universal as manifested in the particular. The generic critic therefore looks for basic truths about people by examining the sometimes modest, often indistinct, trends that develop when they talk to one another. Thus, the "odd case," the text that breaks the pattern, will be of particular interest because it highlights the *rationale* behind the generic formula thereby exposed. So, if a new president fails to mention God in an inaugural address (something that has never been done), the resulting furor would call attention to the persistence of the special bond between religion and government in the United States.

3. Knowledge of generic forces is largely implicit. People can distinguish between a sincere and an insincere apology because they somehow understand the pure form known as "apology." Thus, when an unexpected text suddenly intrudes into a prime time show—"We interrupt this program for a special report from ABC News. . . ."—viewers instinctively become alarmed even though it is hard to say precisely *why* they are alarmed or *how they know* it is time to be alarmed. The implicitness of such rules is important to the critic because the Not-noticed throws light on people's first premises, beliefs so fundamental they are rarely called to conscious attention. The bulletin-within-the-show alarms viewers because it means their community has somehow been threatened and so they sit up straighter in their chairs when hearing it. In doing so, they thereby honor their community in thought as well as action.

4. Generic patterns stabilize social life. Genres are conservative. They keep things in place. To speak in established ways by following the rules is to tip one's hat to the forces-that-be. Thus, the two-year-old expresses displeasure by wailing, and the adolescent by sulking, but the teenager slowly learns to disagree without being disagreeable. Parents take delight in observing such maturity, in the child's growing ability to express emotion in generically sanctioned ways. Should that teenager someday become a U.S. Representative, he or she would learn how to express contempt even more elegantly: "The honorable gentleman from Missouri must surely be mistaken." Formulas like this develop because society has decreed that talking is superior to fighting. So, even though generic formulas sometimes seem silly, careful inspection finds them perpetuating important, agreed-on truths.

5. Generic perceptions affect subsequent perceptions. All critics are generic critics, whether they know it or not. That is, when approaching a text, critics bring preconceptions of generic types and compare that text to the data bank of texts they have studied previously. Because there is no "semantic autonomy of texts," says Hirsch [1967:94], a critic's initial, categorizing judgment will color all subsequent judgments of that message. So a statement like "John, I'd like to talk to you" immediately starts the categorical search: Is this going to be a reprimand? Until that generic question is satisfactorily answered, John is unlikely to rest easy.

According to Rosenfield [1968], any message will look different alongside another message. A rap song's X-rated lyrics may seem shocking until it is examined in the context of its genre, whereby it might be concluded "that's how it is with New Black Funk." It is also true that when viewed in isolation, any message can seem distinctive. But a careful dissection often shows that that text has borrowed some features from Category A and others from Category B when creating itself (for example, rap owes a great debt to both street slang as well as the blues). Finding such generic tracings in no way detracts from the brilliance of a given text. Nor does it detract from its individuality, which properly lies in the creativity of its borrowing, in the uniqueness of the rhetorical assemblage.

An interesting example of Rosenfield's observation occurred upon the death of former president Lyndon Johnson. Columnist Nicholas von Hoffman [1973:B1] penned a statement about the late president, a portion of which went like this:

> Ah, Lyndon, you're not cold yet and they're calling you great. That's what happens when one politician dies: The rest of them call him great, but, Lyndon, you deserve better than patriotic hagiography. You were better than the eulogistic junk they're saying at the memorial services.
>
> Lyndon, you got your teeth into us and we got our teeth into you. Those five years of you in the White House were a barroom brawl, and, just four years ago almost to the day, when we staggered out of the saloon, dusty and bloody, we didn't hate you anymore. We understood better how you got us into Vietnam

than how Nixon got us out and we liked you more, you cussed, cussing bull-headed, impossible, roaring, wild coot.

You had your credibility gaps and your silent sullennesses, but we read you. Oh, man, Lyndon, did we know you! You were the best and the worst of ourselves, the personification of our national deliriums. You were always so completely, so absolutely you. Kennedy had Pablo Casals to play for him, Nixon's got Pat Boone to pray for him, but you, Lyndon, you had Country Joe and the Fish singing songs soaked in four-letter words at you. . . .

On first reading von Hoffman's column, most will notice its irreverence. A more careful analysis shows that, despite its color, the editorial is also a fairly standard eulogy. Naturally, von Hoffman operates on the fringes of that genre here but he is still well within its bounds. Eulogies place one person on stage exclusively. von Hoffman does that. Eulogies isolate the distinctive features of the deceased. von Hoffman clearly does that. Eulogies make the dearly departed seem more dear by reframing his deficiencies and less departed by recalling his personality. von Hoffman does both. And eulogies tell a selective history and project a diminished future because of the dead person's passing. von Hoffman does those things as well.

Naturally, this is not a pure eulogy. Had he been asked to speak at the graveside service in the presence of President Johnson's widow, von Hoffman would have been more restrained. Equally, however, von Hoffman shows us that the eulogy and the editorial are not uncordial to one another and that his column cannot be appreciated without understanding both of its generic parents.

Rhetorical studies show that genres perform a number of important functions. For one thing, genres are *preservative;* they keep established social patterns viable. von Hoffman, for example, did not have total license when he wrote since Lyndon Johnson was a president (and hence part of an institution) and because Johnson was dead (and hence defenseless). Similarly, Jamieson [1973] has shown that the papal encyclical's regal phrasing, doctrinal allusions, and use of the Latin language help to slow the introduction of radical ideas into church governance. Asante and Atwater [1986] also advance this conserving theme by arguing that some genres (e.g., lecturing, sermonizing, formal criticism, etc.) require the speaker to "stand above" the audience and hence preserve existing hierarchies of power. As they say [p. 171], "the rhetorical condition is established as soon as the form is chosen." Lucas [1986] indicates that Washington's first inaugural address took the form it did because it borrowed liberally from British monarchial history and Protestant religious heritage. America's first president therefore spoke like a priestly colonial king. This rhetorical complexity perfectly reflects the political complexity built into the American form of government and it also shows how the new always carries tracings of the old.

Other studies show that generic alterations often proceed slowly. Finkelstein [1981] found that inaugural texts have become shorter over time, more figurative in language, and less linguistically complex. Finkelstein attributes these changes to the increases in size and diversity of the American audience and to the difficulty of finding nonpolarizing words for a diverse populace. In another study, Medhurst [1993] examined Oliver Stone's film *JFK* and found that it owed a great deal to certain ancient mythic stories even though it was very much a modern docudrama as well.

Another important feature is that genres suggest verbal *possibilities*. Because he had heard many eulogies before writing his, Nick von Hoffman did not have to start from scratch. His generic knowledge let him benefit from established patterns that had worked well previously. Analogously, Snow [1985] found that Martin Luther King, Jr.'s, "Letter from Birmingham Jail" used an epistle to turn the tables on clergymen who had decried his civil disobedience. By directly addressing a letter to his fellow preachers (in the manner of the biblical Paul), King turned a political matter into a religious matter, thereby making it hard for his opponents to use political quibbles to stall racial integration.

A different study is that of Cherwitz and Zagacki [1986] who noted a rise in "consummatory" discourse, discourse designed to "give form to public anger" [p. 321] about international affairs without starting a nuclear holocaust. They note that when American hostages are captured or when American soldiers are attacked in the Middle East, an American president can either fight or not fight. Consummatory rhetoric provides a third alternative: fighting with words. That is, the president can sharply denounce the incidents and place America's enemies on warning, thereby establishing "a therapeutic 'buffer' between the desire for revenge and the necessity of rational deliberation." [p. 321]

Other studies also show the power of generic forms. Olson [1995] examined the *New York Times'* coverage of the Bitburg Controversy of 1985 in which President Ronald Reagan agreed to visit a German cemetery that contained Nazi graves (a fact initially unknown to Reagan). Olson shows how the very form of the news story—its continual, day-by-day, dramatic plots—kept the story alive and gave the President no end of headaches as a result.

Jamieson and Campbell [1982] show that the **generic hybrid,** a message borrowed from two or more generic traditions, also alters standard social arrangements. So, for example, a ceremonial speaker can sometimes issue a call for political action in memory of certain age-old beliefs, thereby adding a policy-related bottom line to an otherwise solemn piece of ritual. Similarly, Jablonski [1979b] notes the creativity of **generic transference,** the substitution of one *kind* of message for another. She cites the example of Richard Nixon who, rather than hold a standard press conference to announce his replacement for the just-disgraced Spiro Agnew (Nixon's first vice-president), actually conducted a formal ceremony in the East Room of the White House. Apparently reasoning that people behave better during ceremonies than during press conferences, Nixon pulled the generic rug from beneath his detractors. Jablonski [p. 171] describes his rhetorical wisdom thusly:

> . . . the East Room provided a vivid counterpoint to Nixon's earlier Watergate speeches delivered from the Oval Office. The East Room, which typically accommodates formal state affairs, was filled on this occasion with a formally attired audience of Washington dignitaries. As television cameras panned the elaborate

chandeliers of the East Room, viewers at home could hear the invited guests chatting amiably, their laughter rising occasionally above the soft music played by the Marine Corps Band. Then, like bridesmaids, the majority and minority leaders of the Congress, the Cabinet, and Nixon's family filed in, processional-style. After a heightened pause, trumpets sounded the familiar "Ruffles and Flourishes" and the President and Mrs. Nixon were announced.

In a grand setting like this, it was easy indeed for listeners to forget that Mr. Nixon's first vice-president was under indictment and that the president himself was currently being charged with high crimes and misdemeanors (later known as the Watergate affair).

A third function of genre is that they facilitate *listening and reading*. As Burke [1968] notes, recurring forms create "appetites" in audiences by promising, and then meeting, rhetorical expectations. People can therefore miss several days of a soap opera because its predictability (who slept with whom when and where) lets them catch up easily. But just as genre can help audiences, its misapplication can be a problem. So, for example, Jamieson [1973] notes that when the existential tragedy/farce, *Waiting for Godot,* first played in Miami, the audience rioted because they expected to see a Broadway comedy! This is why speakers often provide generic clues for proper listening: "I come before you tonight with a heavy heart. . . ."

Some genres have become especially useful. One of these, the jeremiad, is a religiously tinged oration calling people back to their solemn duties under God. Johannesen [1985] reports that the jeremiad has been popular in the United States since colonial times because it gives an ultimate rationale for less-than-ultimate political activities. The jeremiad describes sin, threatens punishment, demands repentance, and promises heavenly reward for a heavenly elect. During 1992, for example, Ross Perot used this genre extensively, constantly equating his campaign—a lower national deficit, worldwide trade, a computer in every home—with the Second Coming. George Bush used this same approach to justify America's role during the war in the Persian Gulf, as had John Kennedy when forming the Peace Corps and as had Jimmy Carter when sanctioning other nations for human rights' abuses. In the United States, at least, the Chosen People have always been very busy.

Research on genre recommends this approach to the critic for a variety of additional reasons:

1. *Generic study exposes cultural tastes.* Huspek and Kendall [1991] note, for example, that the streetcorner conversations of blue-collar workers continually reflect the essential contentiousness of the American people and their unwillingness to submit to a single, consistent ideology.

2. *Generic study explains rhetorical power.* Jamieson [1975a] argues that one cannot understand why some rhetoric (e.g., the papal encyclical) has the influence it has unless one also understands its "chromosomal imprints," the rhetorical features it retains from its historical roots (in this case, the speeches of Roman emperors).

3. Generic study reveals psychological style. Vartabedian [1985] argues that some speakers are "generically blind," excessively committed to one style of speech. He notes, for instance, that Richard Nixon tried to justify himself rather than his policies in Vietnam largely because self-justification had served him so well earlier in his career (e.g., the Checkers Speech).

4. Generic study uncovers latent trends. O'Leary [1994] has tracked the increasing use of apocalyptic rhetoric (i.e., talk of imminent doom and gloom) and found it to have been popular in the United States throughout the years. Despite this popularity, one wonders if the genre's attractions may eventually cause people to despair of peaceful solutions to the world's problems and make them susceptible to defeatism: "Things are so bad that we might as well try anything."

5. Generic study provides evaluative standards. Griffin [1990] has studied the rhetoric of autobiographies, particularly those written by former criminals. He notes that such a work cannot be judged by the standards applied to the general biography (e.g., Did all of this really happen?) but must be evaluated by a different set of standards entirely (i.e., Does the author seem genuinely remorseful?). Only then, says Griffin, will the critic be dealing with the text on the same basis as its intended readers.

When doing generic research, the critic uses critical probes to explain textually distinctive trends. Among the most useful of these questions are the following:

1. Do verbal *patterns* give unity to the ideas, values, language or methods of organization employed in the text?
2. Have these patterns been observed so often that they have become *standard*?
3. Do these patterns dominate the message? That is, how *idiosyncratic* is the speaker?
4. What *generic* label best fits this text? Is the message characterized merely by topic (e.g., a sermon) or situation (e.g., a televised sermon) or can it be described with more conceptually ambitious labels (e.g., a religious diatribe)?
5. How *tight* are the generic constraints and what accounts for their rigidity or looseness?
6. If the rhetorical situation is partly *traditional* (e.g., a western movie), does it also have *novel* rhetorical features (e.g., a Chinese cowboy in the lead)?
7. If the rhetorical situation is comparatively *unprecedented* (e.g., a televised advertisement for condoms), is any generic borrowing being done (e.g., a scientist's testimonial for the product)?
8. Does the speaker provide generic *clues* to help listeners (e.g., "I'm your psychiatrist, not your mate. We can be candid but not lovers"). Is the specter of previous rhetorical events invoked (e.g., "Speak to me as if I were an old friend")?

9. Does the speaker offset generic *interference* by distinguishing this message from its ancestors (e.g., "Dear Friend, this is not just another piece of junk mail. . . .")?

10. Given the generic constraints in place, was the speaker *successful* (on strategic, psychological, moral, etc. grounds)?

While generic study can be highly useful, it can also be misapplied or used excessively. There is no particular merit in classifying discourse for its own sake. Its value lies, rather, in its utility: Does it identify a rhetorical trend that might have been missed? Does it explain why a given speaker failed or succeeded? Does it highlight an interesting rhetorical problem that might have been missed? In other words, the most creative generic research asks and answers important questions.

CONCLUSION

As King Lear painfully discovered, he had raised a radical for a daughter. She refused to honor the rhetorical conventions established for receiving a piece of his kingdom. Cordelia was not offended by the content of the speech Lear wanted her to give. The woman did love her father. But she could not separate the What of Lear's love from the How of her own. She knew that for love to be love it had to be her kind of love, that it had to meet her generic expectations. She, not Lear, had to find the time and the place of love as well as its language. She understood that to use the formulas of love would be to lose love. She knew that love by generic proxy was a cheat.

Cordelia's message is thus the message of this chapter: structure and content are siblings, form a cousin. They cannot be treated separately without fundamentally destroying the natural complexity of human communication. If it is content that gives speech its substance, it is structure that gives it its variety. People become wedded to their ways of doing things (a cup of coffee with the morning paper, another while opening the mail). They come to believe that it is these patterns that make them distinctive as individuals and, in a grander sense, that make life worth living.

People also feel special about their ways of saying things. At some level, they may sense that everything worth saying has already been said at least once. But they sense that it has not yet been said *in their way* and that feeling, too, gives life meaning. Because they are social creatures, people will imitate one another. That is where genre come in. Because they are individuals, people will give speech its color by exploring its variations. That is where rhetoric comes in. And because they are complex, they will sometimes say more than they realize they are saying. That is where critics come in.

Chapter 7

ANALYZING SYNTAX AND IMAGERY

[T]he scene amidst which we stand does not permit us to confine our thoughts or our sympathies to those fearless spirits who hazarded or lost their lives on this consecrated spot. We have the happiness to rejoice here in the presence of a most worthy representation of the survivors of the whole Revolutionary army.

Veterans! You are the remnant of many a well-fought field. You bring with you marks of honor from Trenton and Monmouth, from Yorktown, Camden, Bennington, and Saratoga. Veterans of half a century! When in your youthful days you put everything at hazard in your country's cause, good as that cause was, and sanguine as youth is, still your fondest hopes did not stretch onward to an hour like this! At a period to which you could not reasonably have expected to arrive, at a moment of national prosperity such as you could never have foreseen, you are now met here to enjoy the fellowship of old soldiers, and to receive the overflowings of a universal gratitude.

But your agitated countenances and your heaving breasts inform me that even this is not an unmixed joy. I perceive that a tumult of contending feelings rushes upon you. The images of the dead, as well as the persons of the living, present themselves to you. The scene overwhelms you, and I turn from it. May the Father of all mercies smile upon your declining years, and bless them! And when you shall here have exchanged your embraces, when you shall once more have pressed the hands which have been so often extended to give succor in adversity, or grasped in the exultation of victory, then look abroad upon this lovely land which your young valor defended, and mark the happiness with which it is filled: yea, look abroad upon the whole earth, and see what a name you have contributed to give to your country, and what a praise you have added to freedom, and then rejoice in the sympathy and gratitude which beam upon your last days from the improved condition of mankind! [Webster, 1825]

*****

Throw [these enclosures] away within 24 hours. The sexual abuse of children is so ugly, so unbelievable, so Satanic that no one wants to think about it.

But someone's *got to rescue kids from incest, beatings, and rape.* "Momma, Momma, make him stop hurting me!!" they cry.

That someone's you . . . and me . . . we are the ONLY ones who can stop the incest, beatings, and rape.

An eight-month-old baby rushed to the hospital with gonorrhea of the throat! How does an eight-month-old baby get gonorrhea of the throat? You can figure it out. A booklet, "How to Have Sex with Kids" telling a man (1) how to penetrate the vagina of a four-year old, (2) how to keep it hush-hush so that she does not tell her parents, and (3) that, "hey . . . you're doing the kid a favor by de-flowering her."

Please send a check for 1,000 dollars or 1500, or 2,000 or 20 or 100 or 50 . . . whatever.

You want to sacrifice hard and tough for this one. Sell a car, land, borrow (I did), or go to your savings account. I challenge YOU to be the one to send the $10,000 or 5,000 check.

An Ivy-League philosopher, I abandoned university teaching to work at this full time.

And I'm not alone. You're with me. We—*you and me*—stop the sexual abuse of kids.

Read the enclosed. Cry. Rage. Tell others. And rescue.

I'll send to anyone (including you) a free copy of my tape, "How to STOP the Sexual Abuse of Children." Send me names. The other side of the tape is "How to Protect You and Your Family from Attack." *Please help me to send this tape out to thousands and thousands of people.* . . . [Gallagher, 1984]

These passages were authored by different persons. No surprise. In different time periods. Again no surprise. To different audiences. Obvious as well. Their genres are also different: The first passage bears the marks of the commemorative oration and the latter that of junk mail. The texts are so different that even placing them next to one another is an ironic exercise. Indeed, an admirer of the first author (Daniel Webster) might be offended by even a remote comparison between Webster's intellect and that of the second author, one W. Neil Gallagher of Tupelo, Mississippi, whose greatest distinction seems his access to a photocopier and an ample supply of stamps. So the passages are predictably different. Any fool could tell that. But it takes a special kind of fool, a stylistic critic, to tell why.

This chapter focuses on **style,** *the sum total of language habits distinguishing one text from another.* Here, we will examine language microscopically, noting which words a speaker chooses and how they collectively produce special effects. We will investigate tone and nuance, features that audiences sense but cannot describe. We will discover why some words provoke more intense reactions than their synonyms and why language sometimes hides meaning rather than reveals it. Mostly, we will try to become precise about imprecise things: Why does one word sound stronger than another? Why does some rhetoric seem sacred and other rhetoric profane? How does language contribute to passion? To majesty? To mystery? To boredom? What makes a lawyer's language tedious when written in contracts but gripping when presented to a jury? How must the language of advertising change when new Cadillacs are being sold rather than used Yugos? Why do physicians' words insulate them from public scrutiny, and why is this almost never the case with politicians?

But the most basic thing we will do in this chapter is to look closely at language. Most people do not do so. Most people pay attention to the Big Picture in persuasion: ideas, arguments, themes, examples, stories. So by looking carefully at language, the critic has a natural advantage over the casual listener. Most contemporary Americans, for example, could quickly tell that Daniel Webster's Bunker Hill Oration was alien to their era and culture. "But why?" the stylistic critic asks. To ask such a basic question is all too rare, but to ask it is to begin to find its answer.

For example, Black [1978], a preeminent stylistic critic, explains that Webster's sentimental style is now unfashionable because people no longer respect absolute values and are therefore unwilling to surrender to Great Persons espousing Great Ideas. But for the right people, says Black, Webster's style permits an emotional "recreation under sanctioned auspices" [p. 78], a way of being shielded from unpleasant realities. To describe war veterans as the "remnant of a well-fought field" is to indulge language and thereby to indulge oneself.

This is the language of melodrama, language that elevates ordinary soldiers to "fearless spirits," that turns a battlefield into a "consecrated spot," and that transforms helpfulness into "succor in adversity." This is grand language and hence distasteful to modern Americans. A statement like "We have the happiness to rejoice here in the presence of a most worthy representation . . . " cries out for the journalist's editorial pen. Raised on a diet of glib advertising phrases, modern Americans would be asleep by the time Webster got past the dependent clauses in the sixth sentence: "At a period to which you could not reasonably have expected to arrive, at a moment of national prosperity such as you could never have foreseen. . . ."

Perhaps because they read few books and watch much television, modern Americans hate language that calls attention to itself: "May the Father of all mercies smile upon your declining years." Modern Americans also like verbs rather than adjectives, action rather than embellishment. In their scientific detachment, they are suspicious of "heaving" breasts, "contending" feelings, or "agitated" countenances and they are embarrassed by excessive emotionality: "The scene overwhelms you, and I turn from it." While modern Americans still remember their dead and recognize their military heroes, they are more businesslike about it. Modern Americans might therefore feel an ideological kinship with Daniel Webster but, stylistically, he alienates them.

Neil Gallagher's style alienates many of them too but for different reasons. Unlike Webster, Gallagher has plenty of verbs: "read," "cry," "tell," "rescue." Unlike Webster, Gallagher's adjectives are short, pungent: "ugly," "Satanic," "hard and tough." Unlike Webster, Gallagher does not shield his readers from reality. He pours fact upon fact ("incest, beatings, rape"), trying to impress his audience with quantitative rather than qualitative experience: "hundreds and hundreds of . . . workshops," "thousands and thousands of people." Because he is writing rather than speaking, Gallagher tries hard to address his listeners personally, seeking in one brief message to both commence and consummate a relationship: "Sell a car, land, borrow—I did—or go to your savings account." While Webster's promises to his audience are philosophical, Gallagher's are concrete: "I'll send to anyone . . . a free copy of my tape." While Webster invites his listeners to reach up to him, Gallagher reaches down to his.

Despite his verbal energy, Gallagher misses the mark. His words demand too much too soon ("throw this away within 24 hours") and his emotionality seems excessive for a person we hardly know. While his streamlined sentence structure is simpler than Webster's, Gallagher piles too many disjointed thoughts into too little space and hence they become a tumult: four-year-olds, money, gonorrhea, the Ivy League, land sales, free tapes. While his language is informal ("kids," "hush-hush," "Momma"), its staccato-like pace is inelegant and emotionally abrupt. Gallagher's too-rapid treatment of the victims he claims to care for (one brief paragraph) and the speed with which he repairs to his own bottom line ("send the $10,000 or 5,000 check") make him seem a hit-and-run artist. At times, Gallagher's gracelessness makes us yearn for Webster.

To say that a 19th-century commemorative speech differs from a contemporary mass mailing on child abuse is hardly profound. But even our brief examination of them has exposed *two different worlds;* it is these worlds of meaning that the stylistic critic tries to understand. In making their language choices, Webster and Gallagher revealed—wittingly and unwittingly—a bit about themselves and their audiences. Webster wanted to make the world slow down in order to better savor the past; Gallagher sought a faster rotation in order to better salvage the future.

All persuaders, many unconsciously, develop a style. They do so, according to Gibson [1966:24], partly as "a matter of sheer individual will, a desire for a particular kind of self-definition." If Daniel Webster and Neil Gallagher were somehow placed in the midst of a modern cocktail party, they could be found because of their styles: Webster would hold court, Gallagher would buttonhole. But there is more to style than personality. Style is also imposed on speakers by time (the nineteenth century versus the twentieth century), by occasion (known versus unknown audiences), and by genre (eulogies, mass mailings, cocktail party chatter). As Klaus [1969:61] notes, style is important because it often "does not originate within the man; it exists apart from him, as an inheritance, a legacy, that shapes his conceptual ends as surely as he does."

Although it is intellectually promising, studying style is often a humble business. Noting that Daniel Webster habitually used the passive voice while Neil Gallagher used the active voice may seem trivial. But it is less trivial to say that Daniel Webster's world was a world in which audiences felt dominated by great ideas (like freedom), great myths (like heroism), great beliefs (like Christianity), great events (like Yorktown), and great people (like himself). This entire system of beliefs, this worldview, may have resulted in Webster's use of the passive since, as Milic [1971:87] says: "even some of the greatest [writers] knew very little about what they were doing when they wrote."

Gallagher's breathy use of the active voice may, in contrast, have signaled the onrushing events of his times and a confusing world in which children must become warriors to protect themselves. Gallagher's language may reflect a whole way of seeing the world, a take-charge way. When choosing their verbs, then, Webster and Gallagher may have been reaffirming the times in which they lived. Equally, they may have been doing nothing more than choosing verbs.

The good critic knows that to emphasize a single stylistic feature in a text is to risk getting a hasty impression of that text. Thus, in Chapters 7 and 8 we will urge the critic to use as many tools as possible when studying language. Approaching the same message from numerous perspectives builds in safeguards against foolishness. To appreciate the subtlety of language, one must get beyond impressionism by cataloging and counting, by gathering different kinds of linguistic data, by sorting them out in complex ways, and then by thinking some more. Language is wonderful. It charms and delights. All of us love it. But like any lover, it must not be taken for granted. The good stylistic critic never does.

EXAMINING SYNTAX

Despite centuries of interest in rhetorical style, it remains elusive. Turner [1973] notes that some would do away with the concept completely, treating it like the physicist's ether, a seemingly important but impossible-to-find phenomenon. But few have followed this lead, primarily because daily life documents the importance of style. How, for example, would historians have treated the first moon landing if Neil Armstrong had not said the perfect thing: "That's one small step for man, one giant leap for mankind"? Neil Armstrong was no stylist, but his statement does have a pleasing parallelism and a dash of imagery.

The remarks of other ordinary stylists are also remembered. We remember the World War II general who, when asked to surrender, replied to the enemy in an exceedingly economical way: "Nuts." We remember the head coach of the Philadelphia Seventy-sixers who, when asked if his team had a chance to win, drew on his Italian heritage and replied operatically: "It's never really over 'til the fat lady sings." We remember the embattled Secretary of the Interior who, when asked to defend his hiring practices, responded with the statement: "We have every kind of mix you can have. I have a black, I have a woman, two Jews and a cripple." And we remember the baseball slugger who, when asked what his role on the team was, replied "I'm the straw that stirs the drink."

In their ordinary ways, all of these speakers were stylists. While few scientists speak in balanced couplets, ambassadors often do so and, in July of 1969, Neil Armstrong was an entire planet's ambassador. Similarly, in his one-word statement, Anthony McAuliffe captured the no-nonsense, tough-it-out style of his fellow soldiers and hence inspired them. Dick Motta's comparison between basketball and opera was so bizarre that it quickly put a smile on the nation's face. In contrast, James Watt turned the nation's stomach with his tasteless aside and it eventually cost him his job. Reggie Jackson's metaphor was rather high-style for a baseball player but had the pungency fans expected from Mister October.

When the individual words of such memorable phrases are viewed in isolation, they are often not impressive. As Blankenship [1968:53] notes, 195 of the 265 words spoken in Abraham Lincoln's Gettysburg Address were one-syllable words, indicating that style emerges from *word patterns*. That is, words that seem weak on their own gain strength when they come together. The genius of style is therefore the genius of architecture, not of brick-making.

Pascal's [1660:7] famous comment on style is therefore as apt today as it was in the seventeenth century: "Words differently arranged have a different meaning, and meanings differently arranged have different effects." In other words, stylistic excellence lies in **syntax,** in how words are arranged. The truth of this proposition can be seen by looking at the components of style. Although the diagramming of sentences has lost favor recently, it can still be useful. Arnold [1974], for example, urges the critic to separate the grammar of a message into its (1) primary and (2) secondary structures. **Primary structures** often consist of an initial noun phrase, a verb phrase, and a final noun phrase (containing either a prepositional phrase or what was formerly called the direct object.) All other words found in a given sentence can be assigned to its **secondary structure,** including predicate modifiers, dependent clauses, adverbial phrases, etc. By segmenting a text in this way, its natural linguistic intricacy is disrupted, but doing so can help the critic better appreciate its style.

Consider, for example, the humble chain letter. Rhetorically, it is completely predictable: It promises that good fortune results from a conspiracy of letter-writing. All participate, all win. Although nominally illegal in most states, chain letters will not die. Often, the impulse behind them is financial, a pyramid scheme based on people's willingness to become pests to their friends. The rhetoric of such letters mixes threats for breaking the chain with rewards for maintaining it. "Everyone an entrepreneur" goes the appeal, and the letters clog the mail.

Given the rhetorical circumstances of chain letters—an unknown author, a questionable product, and an uncertain recipient—one might expect basic rhetoric from them. Figure 7.1 justifies those expectations. The letter examined [Kiss, 1985] could hardly be simpler, with 13 of the 34 sentences consisting of *nothing but* primary structures (the Figure's boldface elements). The remaining sentences are only slightly less pure: Almost none begin with a dependent clause; only a few sentences are compound; there are virtually no imbedded constructions.

This is Dick-and-Jane language. An avalanche of simple sentences cascades on the reader, as if the slightest violations of its primary structure would ruin its persuasion. Nouns and verbs predominate, transitions are omitted, and even paragraph breaks are eschewed in the original typescript. The basic conceptual appeal of the letter is only slightly more subtle than its grammar: "Keep the letter going or you, too, might die like Helen Fairchild."

Over 59 percent of the words in the chain letter are contained in its primary structure. In contrast, Figure 7.2 presents a letter from General John Pershing [1919] whose primary structure accommodates only 23 percent of

FIGURE 7.1 Grammatical Structure of the Chain Letter

(1) **This paper® has been sent® to you**
                                              for good luck.

(2) **The original copy® is® in New England.**

(3) **It® has been® around the world**
                                    nine times.

(4) **The luck® has   been sent® to you.**
                  now

(5) **You® will receive® good luck® within four days**
                                              of receiving this letter, provided you, in
                                              turn, send it back out.

(6) **This® is® no joke.**

(7) **You® will receive® it® by mail.**

(8) **Send® copies® to people.**

(9) **Do not send® money,**
                            it has no price.

(10) **Do not keep® this letter.**

(11) **It® must leave® your hands® within ninety-six hours.**

(12) **An R.A.F. officer® received® $70,000.**

(continued)

FIGURE 7.1 (continued)

(13) **Joe Elliott® received® $40,000**
and lost it because he broke the chain.

(14) **Gene Welch® lost® his wife® after receiving this letter.**
While in the Phillipines

(15) **He® failed to circulate® the letter.**

(16) **he® received® $7,755.**
However, before his death

(17) **send® copies® of this letter**
Please   and see what happens in four days.

(18) **The chain® comes® from Venezuela**
and was wriiten by Saul Anthony deCroof,
a missionary from South America.

(19) **you® must make® 20 copies**
Since the copy must make   and send them to your
a tour of the world,   friends and acquaintances.

(20) **you® will get® a surprise.**
After a few days

(21) **This® is® true**
even if you are not superstitious.

(22) **Do note® the following.**

(23) **Constantina Dias® received® the chain® in 1983.**

(24) **He® asked® his secretary® to make 20 copies**
and send them out.

25) **he® won® a lottery® of two million dollars.**
A few days later

(26) **Eric Deddit,   ® received® the letter**
an office employee,   and forgot it had to leave his hands
within ninety-six hours.

(27) **He® lost® his job.**

(28) **he® mailed out® the twenty copies.**
Later, after finding the letter again,

(29) **he® got® a better job.**
A few days later

(30) **Helen Fairchild® received® the letter**
and not believing, threw the letter away.

(31) **she® died**
Nine days later

(32) **send® no money.**
Remember,

(33) **don't ignore® this.**
Please

(34) **It® works.**

FIGURE 7.2 Grammatical Structure of the Pershing Letter

(1) Now that your service with the American Expeditionary Forces is about to terminate, I® cannot let you go® without a personal word.

(2) At the call to arms, the patriotic young manhood ® responded of America eagerly

(3) With the support of the nation firmly united to defend the cause of liberty, our army® has executed® the will® of the people with resolute purpose.

and became the formidable army whose decisive victories testify to its efficiency and its valor.

(4) **Our democracy® has been tested** and the forces of autocracy have been defeated.

(5) To the glory of the citizen-soldier, our troops® have fulfilled® their trust faithfully and in a succession of brilliant offensives have overcome the menace to our civilization.

(6) As an individual, your part ® has been® an important one® in the sum total played® his part. each® has of our achievements. in the world war

(7) Whether keeping lonely vigil in the trenches, or gallantly storming the enemy's stronghold; whether enduring monotonous drudgery at the rear, or sustaining the fighting line at the front, bravely and efficiently

(8) By willing sacrifice of personal rights; by cheerful endurance of hardship you® inspired® the war-torn Allies® with new life and privation; by vigor, strength and indomitable will, made effective and turned the tide of by thorough organization and coordial cooperation, threatened defeat into overwhelming victory.

(9) With a consecrated devotion to duty and a will to conquer, you® have served® your country. loyally

(10) By your exemplary conduct a standard® has been established and maintained never before attained by any army.

(11) With mind and body as clean and strong as the decisive blows you delivered against the foe, you® are to return® to the pursuits soon of peace.

(12) In leaving the scenes of your victories, may I® ask that you carry home your high ideals and continue to live as you have served—an honor to the princi- ples for which you have fought and to the fallen comrades you leave behind.

(13) It is with pride in our success that I® extend® to you my sincere thanks for your splendid service to the army and to the nation.

137

his remarks. *All* thirteen of his sentences are burdened by secondary structures. His primary segments are weighted down in front by dependent clauses and in the rear by a compound structure or a series of prepositional phrases. Also, adverbs frequently peek between Pershing's verb phrases, further slowing down the message. It is as if the General could not leap into a sentence without first doing calisthenics.

Statements 7 and 8 are particularly noteworthy, as Pershing gets a long running start only to step across two short primary segments. Balanced constructions ("whether keeping lonely vigil in the trenches, or . . . "), unneeded adjectives ("monotonous drudgery," "overwhelming victory"), and double nouns ("with mind and body," "its efficiency and its valor") abound in the message. Indeed, the chain letter managed to pack thirty-four sentences into less space than it took Pershing to lumber through his thirteen sentences (there are 316 total words in the former and 357 words in the latter). Where the author of the chain letter envisioned an impatient reader, Pershing seemed to anticipate the opposite.

Pershing's expectations were sensible. His letter was distributed on February 28, 1919, to all GI's returning from World War I. This was a time for reflection since, for the first time in a long time, General Pershing's men had time. So the General paused and thought of grand things—valor, achievement, dedication, sacrifice, and mortality—sensing that the significance of his ideas justified the grand style. The ideas he treated were timeless, ideas that would help fill the unhurried, reflective moments as his men aged. The chain letter, in contrast, blows away with the first wind or when the next piece of junk mail is opened. Its very style invites, even demands, such treatment. But the Pershing letter issues a different invitation, which may explain why it was found, lovingly preserved, in the attic of a World War I veteran sixty-five years later.

By uncovering the grammatical structure of these two messages, we discover what Lanham [1983] calls the **Periodic** (or Paratactic) **Style** and the **Running** (or Hypotactic) **Style.** Each style has a special rhetorical purpose and each responds to a different human psychology. Lanham urges the critic to make an early determination of these features since they so often reveal the author's voice. The Periodic style, exemplified by Pershing, and the Running style, exemplified by the chain letter, make different commentaries about the texts that embody them. Lanham urges the critic to listen for this inner, fainter voice to truly understand the subtlety of rhetoric.

The Running style is a "verb" style, not a "noun" style. It is also the most natural style because it is simplest. In a Running style, the author tells who did what to whom when, where, and how. The chain letter uses this laundry-list type of development, as fact pours upon fact, event upon event, emotion upon emotion, until the author finally screeches to a halt. Neil Gallagher's diatribe on child abuse is similar. In neither case is the reader given time to reflect.

Immediate responses are the order of the day and clean, Primary structures ensure that that order will be carried out.

Lanham points up another feature of the Running style when offering Julius Caesar's "I came; I saw; I conquered" as its prototype. Lanham notes that this style typically suppresses information by not ordering phenomena, thereby placing responsibilities on the audience's shoulders. When Caesar put coming, seeing, and conquering on the same syntactic level, says Lanham [p. 33], he left it up to the reader to determine their relative priority: "If Caesar had written instead 'Since it was I who arrived, and I who saw how the land lay, the victory followed as a matter of course,' he would have said outright what the tight-lipped 'came-saw-conquered' formula only invites us to say about him."

Similarly, because the chain letter has so few orienting devices (e.g., dependent clauses), the reader is not invited to distinguish between the plight of Joe Elliot (who lost $40,000) and Gene Welch (who won $7,755 but who also lost his life). Such facts merely shoot forth, propelled by the noun-verb-noun-verb syntax its excited author has chosen.

The Periodic style—that of Daniel Webster and John Pershing—operates quite differently. If the Running style is loose, the Periodic style is tight: reasoned, intricate, connected. Here, Secondary structures constantly tell the audience what they should do with the Primary structures. Lanham [p. 77] notes that the Periodic style, "with its internal parentheses, balanced phrasing, and climactic resolution, stops time to let a reader take in the complete pattern." The Periodic style does more of the audience's work—categorizing, weighing, proportioning, and qualifying.

Periodic speakers trade (1) authority for interest and (2) spontaneous responses for delayed, but more emotionally complex, responses. Webster and Pershing willingly made such trades. Use of a more telegraphic style at such sacred moments would have seemed to them a cultural mockery. If human sacrifice did not warrant a complex style, nothing did, they may have reasoned. On the other hand, because their purposes were so practical, Neil Gallagher and the author of the chain letter also chose the right style. Given the enormity of the child abuse problem, Gallagher's simple, direct language stood as a stylistic signal that a solution was possible, if not imminent. Like other direct-mailers, Gallagher did not know his audience; he thus became plain in order to avoid being ignored.

Running and Periodic motifs deal solely with the structural features of language. *How* these structures are used by individuals is a very different matter. That is, not all Running styles need be tacky and not all Periodic styles produce poetry (they can as easily result in obfuscation). Dwight Eisenhower was an interesting example in this context. As a writer, Ike had a nice, sprightly, Running style and his memoirs are a pleasure to read as a result. But as a speaker, he often lost his compass amid secondary structures. This was true even during

TABLE 7.1 Eisenhower's Actual versus Potential Style

Delivered Version	Potential Version
It is a privilege to welcome you once more to the annual egg-rolling contest on the White House grounds.	Welcome to our annual egg-rolling contest.
I surely hope that the weather cooperates with you properly and that you do not have the discomfort of a shower.	Let's hope it doesn't rain.
Moreover, I just learned this morning that many of the schoolchildren had to go to school on this Easter Monday . . .	I've just learned that some children had to go to school today . . .
and so to them I extend my sympathies for missing the fun of the day . . .	and I'm sorry they're going to miss the fun . . .
that I hope the rest of you will have.	that the rest of you will have.
Mrs. Eisenhower joins me in saying Happy Easter to all of you. Goodbye.	Mrs. Eisenhower joins me in saying Happy Easter to all of you. Goodbye.

simple ceremonial occasions as, for example, when he welcomed children to an Easter Egg roll at the White House.

This point is dramatized in Table 7.1 by contrasting what Eisenhower [1958:65] said (Hypotactically) with what he might have said (Paratactically). Clearly, Ike used twice the number of words he needed and, unlike Webster or Pershing, got no extra mileage from them. His prepositional phrases are unnecessary since his audience already knew they were standing "on the White House grounds" and joined together "on this Easter Monday." The dependent clauses in the second and third statements add neither information nor grace to his remarks, and his bloated syntax ("and so to them I extend my sympathies for . . . ") robs the message of elegance. Thus, it is not enough to determine a text's basic stylistic structure. The critic must also reckon with the *effects* achieved, or lost, by them as well.

Gibson [1966] offers a useful way of getting at these stylistic effects. He would describe Eisenhower as a **Stuffy** talker because of the length of his clauses, his avoidance of simple words, and his use of the passive voice. In his system, Gibson argues that the combination of more than a dozen language variables creates distinctive styles like Eisenhower's. In addition to the Stuffy style, Gibson posits a **Tough** style (monosyllabic words, many "to be" verbs, few adjectives) and a **Sweet** style (a you-orientation, a good number of contractions, use of the active voice). Gibson worked out the exact stylistic ingredients for each style and his recipe is presented in Table 7.2.

The Gibson system is useful not because it is precise (it is only a rough guide) but because it helps explain rhetorical voice. "Voice" is a difficult thing to describe, but it is hardly a difficult thing to hear. For example, General Pershing's measured voice is different from Daniel Webster's grand voice and both differ substantially from the frenetic voice of Neil Gallagher. Gibson's

TABLE 7.2 Criteria for Measuring Style

Variables	Tough	Sweet	Stuffy
1. Monosyllables	> 70%	61–70%	< 60%
2. Words of 3 syllables or more	< 10%	10–19%	> 20%
3. 1st & 2nd person pronouns	One "I" or "we"/100 words	Two "you" per 100 words	No 1st or 2nd person pronouns
4. Subjects (neuters versus people)	1/2 or more people	1/2 or more people	2/3 or more neuters
5. Finite verbs	> 10%	> 10%	< 10%
6. To be forms as finite verbs	> 1/3 of verbs	< 1/4	< 1/4
7. Passive verbs	< 1/20 verbs	None	> 1 in 5
8. True adjectives	< 10%	> 10%	> 8%
9. Adjectives modified	< 1 per 100 words	> 1/100	< 1/100
10. Noun adjuncts	< 2%	> 2%	> 4%
11. Average length of clauses	< 10 words	< 10 words	> 10 words
12. Clauses (percent of total words)	< 25%	< 33%	> 40%
13. "Embedded" words	< 1/2 S/V combinations	< half	> twice
14. Uses of "the"	8% or more	under 6%	6–7%
15. Contractions and fragments	> 1 per 100 words	> 2/100	None
16. Parentheses & other punctuation	None	> 2 per 100 words	None

From Gibson [1966]

system helps us discuss such felt-but-not-explained phenomena. The example Gibson [p. 29–30] gives of the Tough style is especially vivid:

> In the late summer of that year we lived in a house in a village that looked across the river and the plain to the mountains. In the bed of the river there were pebbles and boulders, dry and white in the sun, and the water was clear and swiftly moving and blue in the channels. Troops went by the house and down the road and the dust they raised powdered the leaves of the trees. The trunks of the trees too were dusty and the leaves fell early that year and we saw the troops marching along the road and the dust rising and leaves, stirred by the breeze, falling and the soldiers marching and afterward the road bare and white except for the leaves.
>
> The plain was rich with crops; there were many orchards of fruit trees and beyond the plains the mountains were brown and bare. There was fighting in the mountains and at night we could see the flashes from the artillery. In the dark it was like summer lightning, but the nights were cool and there was not the feeling of a storm coming. [1929:37]

These are the words of Ernest Hemingway, a tough-talker if there ever was one. Gibson describes the tough-talker as an experienced, close-lipped, first-hand reporter who knows what he knows and who is unafraid to share it. The tough-talker is self-absorbed, sure of his footing: Hemingway sees things from *his* house, reports *his* sightings of the artillery flashes.

Gibson says there is a flatness to the speaker's voice here, a self-limiting but unquestionable sense of authority. "You would not call this man genial," says Gibson [p. 31], since "[h]e behaves rather as if he had known us, the reader, a long time and therefore doesn't have to pay us very much attention." Instead, the "voice" concentrates on facts, describing things as they are, not as they seem to be. The phrases are short, the sentences compound rather than complex, and adjectives and adverbs are kept under control by nouns and predicates. This is the spare language of a clear-headed speaker.

A second style is what Gibson calls Sweet talk. It could hardly be more different from Stuffy talk, as the language of advertising so often shows:

> Have you ever tried **Kathy's Kitchen Products** before? You'd be amazed at how quick and easy they are—and how incredibly tasty as well. Wait 'til you smell the scrumptious smells of **Kathy's** *new* frozen dinners, made as always with only the finest of **Kathy's** ingredients.
>
> Tomorrow, help yourself to **Kathy's** new Taco Delight. Loads of lettuce and cheese, extra helpings of perfectly seasoned beef, the crispiest taco shells you can buy, and all the hot sauce you'll ever need. Even a little guacamole on the side. Everything you need for a stay-at-home fiesta. Ole!

This voice is unquestionably more social: You and your life experiences, your tastes, and your kitchen routines are emphasized. Gibson notes that Sweet talk is filled with cliches ("the finest ingredients," "everything you need"), no doubt because cliches are the language of us all. There is also a more informal (Running) style here because the speaker seeks action, not rumination, from the audience. Unstated, but very much present, is the speaker's assumption that he or she has the *right* to counsel the audience. The "voice" knows that you need something quick, something easy, something tasty, even though this voice has never met you before. This claim of unearned familiarity is the hallmark of the Sweet style, says Gibson, as is the lavish use of adjectives. The Sweet talker is a solicitor par excellence.

Gibson calls the third of his styles Stuffy because it removes the Tough talker's sense of self and the Sweet talker's sense of other. In their place hovers a disembodied assemblage of words. Gibson [p. 93] uses a government report on smoking as his paradigm example of the Stuffy style:

> Cigarette smoking is causally related to lung cancer in men; the magnitude of the effect of cigarette smoking far outweighs all other factors. The data for women, though less extensive, point in the same direction.
>
> The risk of developing lung cancer increases with duration of smoking and the number of cigarettes smoked per day, and is diminished by discontinuing smoking.

> The risk of developing cancer of the lung for the combined group of pipe smokers, cigar smokers, and pipe and cigar smokers is greater than for nonsmokers, but much less than for cigarette smokers.
>
> The data are insufficient to warrant a conclusion for each group individually. [U.S. Government, 1964:5]

This is the language of the corporation, of the bureaucrat so fearful of personal exposure or, more charitably, so diligent about not misstating the truth, that he or she hides behind qualifications: "the data for women, though less extensive. . . ." Stuffy talk removes passion from discourse, substituting for it a sense of detachment in which all variables (in this case, gender and smoking habits) cancel each other out. Gibson [p. 107] notes that the Stuffy talker is in some senses scared: "If this is an age of anxiety, one way we react to our anxiety is to withdraw into omniscient and multisyllabic detachment where nobody can get us." The passive voice also helps to confuse ownership of the speaker's ideas. Thus, "smoking" and not "smokers" become the culprit of the report and "the data," not the researcher, become responsible for the bad news about lighting up.

Gibson's system is limited but nevertheless useful. It roughs out the stylistic terrain fairly efficiently and it gives the critic a *base point* against which to compare individual messages. Naturally, there is more to style than syntax. The statistics of grammar cannot alone explain why the Webster address seems somehow dated or why the chain-letter seems somewhat slippery. It takes other, richer forms of analysis to see why some discourse registers high notes and why other discourse sounds so flat. It takes more than a woodwind to make a melody. It also takes human genius to play the oboe properly. It is to such aesthetic matters that we will now turn.

EXAMINING IMAGERY

Both the rhetorical critic and the literary critic study imagery. But unlike poetic imagery, the imagery found in rhetoric is often pedestrian. If poetic images invite tarrying, rhetorical images invite movement. Passion, not nuance, is their hallmark:

> This is God's blazing message to America in this hour—and it is without question its very last chance.
>
> This is the time to energize these spiritual weapons for the salvation of our land. It must be done immediately, fervently, with faith, and with tears!
>
> If this is done by the Christian people with all of their heart immediately, and with perseverance, this land shall not only be saved, but there shall also explode from this united prayer-power the most astounding revival in all history.
>
> MORE POWERFUL THAN
TEN THOUSAND HYDROGEN BOMBS
>
> We have declared spiritual war on God's enemies and our enemies. NOW LET'S WAGE IT! [Boone, et. al., 1970:30]

This passage is from a pamphlet entitled *The Solution to Crisis—America,* authored by teen-idol-turned-evangelist Pat Boone and two colleagues. The booklet is a 1970s forerunner of the Far Right rhetoric still in evidence today. Its imagery is neither subtle nor novel. It combines temporal metaphors ("this hour," "this is the time"), thermal metaphors ("blazing message"), and kinetic metaphors ("energize," "explode," "prayer power") to produce a sense of urgency. Also included are metaphors of conflict ("hydrogen bomb," "spiritual war," "God's enemies"), which add an oppositional force against which the rhetoric can struggle. The physical metaphors ("with tears," "revival," "with all of their heart") humanize the conflict and, by relating it to bodily processes, make the struggle lifelike.

Bombs falling, hearts palpitating, fires blazing—a good deal of action for a short passage. Should a literalist ask how bodily fluids ("tears") could serve as weapons, or how cerebral processes ("prayer-power") could rival atomic chain reactions ("ten thousand hydrogen bombs"), the passage would reduce to silliness. But for Pat Boone's readers, the pamphlet makes sense despite its nonsense. For them, its cacophony of images produces an integrated, emotional whole. Many of them would be willing to share their quite literal money with Mr. Boone's movement because of the factually untrue truths embedded in his imagery. Throughout history, people have marched off to literal wars because of the metaphoric battles they have already fought—and won.

Not all rhetoric is this rich with imagery. Thus, two important questions for the critic are these:

- To what extent does a message employ nonliteral language?
- What specific purposes does such language serve?

Most people cannot speak without imagery because imagery increases the range of things that can be said and, more fundamentally, the range of things that can be thought. That is, despite his oppositional images, Pat Boone was hardly ready to kiss his family goodbye and march off to trench warfare. If his family had questioned his use of language, he probably would have told them that the sacrifices he was willing to make for his cause *felt like* the sacrifices made by the footsoldier during battle. Such martial ways of thinking perhaps freed Boone to take on challenges he would have been unwilling to take on if he had thought of his duties in less exalted terms. Even though he was, literally, only writing a cheap pamphlet for mass distribution, and even though he was, literally, intending to go home and not to war after putting his printing press to bed, his wartime imagery made his job seem all the more grand that day. Pat Boone really meant what he unreally said.

When he wrote to thank Mr. Boone for having sent him a copy of his remarks, then-president Richard Nixon used language that was as literal as Boone's was figurative. Even though the President seemed to appreciate Boone's bequest, his rhetorical style suggested something else entirely:

THE WHITE HOUSE
WASHINGTON

Dear Pat:

I want you to know how much I appreciate your thoughtfulness in let-ting me have a copy of your recording, "The Solution to Crisis—America," which you gave to Secretary Romney for me at the Religious Heritage Dinner on June 18. It was especially kind of you to remember me with this meaningful and timely message, and may be sure I am pleased to have this evidence of faith and patriotism brought to my attention.

With my best wishes,

Sincerely,

Richard Nixon [1970b]

This is how presidents talk. Carefully. There are no wild flights of fancy, no embroidered stories, no riotous mixing of images here. Nixon's language is spare, precise, businesslike. While his salutation is suitably informal ("Dear Pat"), the remainder of the message is distanced: Nixon appreciates Boone's "thoughtfulness," not Boone himself; the recording was given to Romney, not to Nixon personally; Nixon is pleased to see such "evidence of faith" but he is not going to *do* anything about it. Boone's gift is described as "mean-ingful and timely," a phrase that could describe either the Holy Bible or *Newsweek* magazine. The passive voice ("I am pleased to have this . . . brought to my attention") places the rhetorical action in Boone's arena, not in Nixon's. Thus, while Nixon's reply is cordial on the ideational level, on the stylistic level it repudiates Boone's entire message.

By exercising stylistic restraint Nixon says, in effect, I have heard you but I am not listening to you. Because the use of imagery often signals a speaker's heightened state of sentiment, an attempt by Nixon to match Boone's style ("You really socked it to 'em in that one, Pat"), would have joined them *emotionally* as well as argumentatively. Thus, by sending a formal, literalistic letter, Nixon's speech-act signaled he was unwilling to travel down the slippery slope of Far Right politics.

The word "imagery" derives from the same root as "imagination," a tran-scendence of the normal. Thus, a speaker's relative use of imagery maps that speaker's comfort with life-as-given. Clearly, Pat Boone is ready for a trip somewhere, while Richard Nixon is committed to staying where he is: in the middle of the political road. Of course, establishment politicians often use imagery when they speak. But they rarely do so with the sense of wild aban-don displayed by Pat Boone.

Also, politicians' imagery typically throws light on specific pieces of policy ("a chicken in every pot," "a New Deal," "the war on poverty") and their pragmatism makes them abandon failed imagery quickly (e.g., Bill Clinton's "New Covenant" in 1995). Politicians are afraid of the world-yet-to-be; movement activists, on the other hand, embrace it willingly since it, and it alone, fully substantiates their values: "re-engineering" the corporation, saving "unborn" babies, advancing "green" politics, etc. Thus, to track the use of imagery is to track the length of a speaker's wish list.

One standard category of imagery, the metaphor, has been the object of much scholarly inquiry. Metaphor has been variously defined but here it will be treated as a kind of depiction equating one thing with another: For example, builders of earthen dams in Kenya are likened to destroyers of dams along the Rhine in World War II and hence dubbed a Peace "Corps." Lakoff and Johnson [1980] have written perceptively about metaphor and feel that everyday talkers would become mute without it. They also argue that (1) *metaphor results from thought* (e.g., if one's beliefs are unpopular, one will feel besieged and hence reflect such feelings when one speaks—Pat Boone's fate), but also that (2) *metaphor stimulates thought* (e.g., if one lives on a diet of warlike rhetoric, one begins to look only for martial solutions to life's problems, the fate of many contemporary Bosnians.) In their book, Lakoff and Johnson describe a number of functions served by metaphor, among which are the following:

1. Metaphors selectively highlight ideas. If an idea is important to a person or a culture, it will find its way to imagery. So, for example, Lakoff and Johnson observe that martial imagery like "I demolished his argument" or "his claims were indefensible" [p. 4] is used because some cultures treat communication as a contestable, rather than a sharable, activity. Communication can be talked about in other ways, of course, such as argument-as-journey: "We've covered a lot of ground," or "You're off in the wrong direction." Thus, the critic tracks the facts of metaphorical usage, looking for the meanings behind the meanings.

2. Metaphors are often generative. That is, they help people see things in a new light. So, for example, if a client thinks of love as madness ("It just happens; you can't control it."), a marriage counselor might introduce the new metaphor of love-as-labor ("A marriage is something you really have to work at."), thereby calling attention to relational possibilities previously hidden by the madness metaphor. In a sense, to use metaphor is to admit a kind of defeat, to acknowledge that literal language cannot always make complex ideas and feelings clear. Imagery often helps to approximate what literal language cannot even estimate.

3. Metaphors often mask ideas and values. As metaphors become routinely used in a given language community, their implied meanings become less and less noticeable. Knowing this, the perceptive critic traces these "forgotten" meanings carefully. So, for example, Lakoff and Johnson [p. 236–7] observe that when corporate leaders treat labor as a business "resource" (for example, by placing it on a par with cheap oil), they become blind to the exploitation of workers such a metaphor encourages. As Lakoff and Johnson say [p. 237], "The blind acceptance of [this] metaphor can hide degrading realities, whether meaningless blue-collar and white-collar industrial jobs in 'advanced' societies or virtual slavery around the world."

4. *Metaphors have entailments.* That is, metaphors mean certain things but imply other things too. So, for example, a metaphor may bespeak one's personality (e.g., *sharing as a commodity:* a person who believes that "time is money"), one's intellectual worldview (e.g., *friendship as a journey:* "our relationship isn't going anywhere"), or one's cultural assumptions (e.g., *up and down:* "I'm on top of the situation" vs. "he's low man on the totem pole.").

Entailments are the policy implications of metaphor. That is, if one believes that argument-is-war ("she shot down my case"), one may make certain *offensive* assumptions when speaking: (1) that people are naturally competitive, (2) that truth is less important than strategy, and (3) that short-term triumph is most important. In contrast, one who sees argument-as-a-container ("his case won't hold water") may argue *protectively,* focusing on the issue's substance rather than its personal dynamics. While people are usually unaware of their preferred images, their preferred images often expose their premises for action.

Given the rhetorical functions of metaphor, how can they best be studied? Most critics look for what Lakoff and Johnson call metaphor's **systematicity.** That is, they urge the critic to look for patterns of metaphorical usage since, while "complete consistency across metaphors is rare; coherence, on the other hand, is typical" [p. 96]. By proceeding carefully through a message, the critic can often find an underlying thematic unity to the metaphors chosen. Thus, an important critical probe becomes the following:

- What families of *metaphors* reside in the text? Are they internally consistent? What is their cumulative effect?

A helpful system for examining metaphor is Osborn's [1976] who inspected a large number of public messages from ancient Greece to the present and grouped the metaphors he found into eleven metaphorical families. Osborn says that these patterns "endure in power and popularity despite time and cultural change" [p. 16] because of the almost primordial pictures they paint. While Osborn's categories are hardly exhaustive, they are a good critical starting place since they touch on basic human experiences. Modified slightly, his categories include:

1. *Water and the Sea* (e.g., "the ship of state," "I'm going down for the third time.").
2. *Light and Dark* (e.g., "He's a bright fellow." "I'm in the dark on this issue.").
3. *The Human Body* (e.g., "She's my right arm." "Just turn the other cheek.").

4. *War* (e.g., "a battle for the mind," "Our team was blitzed yesterday.").
5. *Structures* (e.g., "That argument won't hold up." "We're operating in different frameworks.").
6. *Animals* (e.g., "He's a bit too foxy for me." "They really wolfed down that dessert.").
7. *The Family* (e.g., "Necessity is the mother of invention." "Defeat is always an orphan.").
8. *Above and Below* (e.g., "Let's go over the top in this campaign." "She's really in the depths of depression.").
9. *Forward and Backward* (e.g., "Let's get this country moving again." "We're falling behind our quota for the month.").
10. *Natural Phenomena* (e.g., "That was a peak experience for me." "I'm between a rock and a hard place.").
11. *Sexuality* (e.g., "Those policies will rape this nation." "That is a genuinely seminal idea.").

The good critic will branch out beyond Osborn's general categories since so much rhetoric is specific to a culture or a subculture. A more narrowly Western supplement to his list, for example, might include *mechanistic* metaphors (e.g., "I'm already wired in on this deal."), *monetary* images (e.g., "I'm going for broke in my relationship with Jane."), *athletic* metaphors (e.g., "I'll knock this exam out of the park."), and others. But using Osborn's list is a good first step because it identifies the speaker's general mental habits and the audience's perceived motivational bases.

Although it is somewhat barbarous to dissect Dr. Martin Luther King, Jr.'s, lyrical style, it does give us the intellectual distance needed to see how a powerful rhetoric works its magic. Even the most casual analysis of his famous "I Have a Dream" speech shows that he used metaphor compellingly:

> And as we walk, we must make the pledge that we shall always march ahead. We cannot turn back. There are those who are asking the devotees of civil rights, "When will you be satisfied?" We can never be satisfied as long as the Negro is the victim of the unspeakable horrors of police brutality.
>
> We can never be satisfied as long as our bodies, heavy with the fatigue of travel, cannot gain lodging in the motels of the highways and the hotels of the cities. We cannot be satisfied as long as the Negro's mobility is from a smaller ghetto to a larger one.
>
> We can never be satisfied as long as our children are stripped of their selfhood and robbed of their dignity by signs stating "for whites only." We cannot be satisfied as long as a Negro in Mississippi cannot vote and a Negro in New York believes he has nothing for which to vote. No, we are not satisfied, and we will not be satisfied until justice rolls down like waters and righteousness like a mighty stream.
>
> I am not unmindful that some of you have come here out of excessive trials and tribulation. Some of you have come fresh from narrow jail cells. Some of you have come from areas where your quest for freedom left you battered by the storms of

persecution and staggered by the winds of police brutality. You have been the veterans of creative suffering. Continue to work with the faith that unearned suffering is redemptive.

Go back to Mississippi; go back to Alabama; go back to South Carolina; go back to Georgia; go back to Louisiana; go back to the slums and ghettos of the Northern cities, knowing that somehow this situation can, and will be changed. Let us not wallow in the valley of despair.

So I say to you, my friends, that even though we must face the difficulties of today and tomorrow, I still have a dream. It is a dream deeply rooted in the American dream that one day this nation will rise up and live out the true meaning of its creed—we hold these truths to be self evident, that all men are created equal.

I have a dream that one day on the red hills of Georgia, sons of former slaves and sons of former slave-owners will be able to sit down together at the table of brotherhood.

I have a dream that one day, even the state of Mississippi, a state sweltering with the heat of injustice, sweltering with the heat of oppression, will be transformed into an oasis of freedom and justice.

I have a dream my four little children will one day live in a nation where they will not be judged by the color of their skin but by content of their character. I have a dream today!

I have a dream that one day, down in Alabama, with its vicious racists, with its governor having his lips dripping with the words of interposition and nullification, that one day, right there in Alabama, little black boys and black girls will be able to join hands with little white boys and white girls as sisters and brothers. I have a dream today!

I have a dream that one day every valley shall be exalted, every hill and mountain shall be made low, the rough places shall be made plane, and the crooked places shall be made straight and the glory of the Lord will be revealed and all flesh shall see it together. [King, 1964: 373–4]

King's artistry derives more from human sensitivity than from stylistic trickery. His naturalistic imagery, for example, carries a kind of primitive power: "storms of persecution," "winds of brutality," "valleys of despair," "sweltering injustice," "an oasis of freedom." Bodily processes ("all flesh shall see it") and basic social units ("sisters and brothers") also emphasize how emotionally and politically *fundamental* his argument for freedom was.

Some of King's metaphors are almost offensive in their roughness: blacks "wallowing," lips "dripping," people "stripped." Perhaps King reasoned that more urbane language would have made him seem effete in the eyes of the underprivileged and a potential object of manipulation in the eyes of the overprivileged. Hence, he proposed no banquets of grandeur but just a "table of brotherhood," no stairways to the stars but just "rough places made plane," no captains of destiny but just "veterans of creative suffering."

King also established a sense of *forward movement* for his people by transmuting the literal march on Washington into a symbolic march in which people "come here out of excessive trials and tribulations." He launched them on a "quest for freedom," forbidding their "turning back," commanding that they "march ahead," "facing" the difficulties of tomorrow, and moving with the swiftness of a "mighty stream." Forward motion was coupled with *ascendent movement* so that King's people could "rise up" to climb mountains "made low" by their efforts. Metaphorically, the only thing that King left standing was justice itself, which was to "roll down" on his people like a cascade.

Virtually all of King's metaphors can be accommodated by the Osborn schema. This fact establishes how "primitive" King's speech was and why, as a result, it had such political and psychological power. The black members of his audience were, after all, historically *landed* people who worked the nation's farms, cooked the nation's meals, built the nation's buildings, and fought more than their share of the nation's wars. King concentrated on these basic images because the people he loved were so often relegated to basic pleasures. His metaphors of wind and sea and fire remind us of how central the natural world is to human experience and why, since the beginning of time, people have turned their eyes skyward, looking for explanations.

King broke this naturalistic pattern only once in his speech but it was a significant departure. Fairly early, he produced a small yet captivating cluster of **monetary** metaphors that were curiously juxtaposed to his organic images. This section of his speech is not elegant: Blacks have been issued a "bad check" from the nation, a check returned with "insufficient funds" stamped on it. The "vaults" of opportunity have been closed to blacks and an important "promissory note" has been "defaulted" on by the nation. Just as quickly as King introduces this line he abandons it, returning immediately to traditional imagery.

But King's monetary images made his speech genuinely American. Virtually everything else he said could have been said anywhere anytime. But in mimicking the language of capitalism, King staked a claim to the land on which he stood and also made an ironic commentary on his age. By allotting his audience one economic metaphor for every seven naturalistic images, King approximated the comparative economic ratio between the Blacks and whites of his day. In other words, only one seventh of King's speech was fully "American," perhaps because King's people had not at that point been enfranchised in the most traditionally American way: economically. In a sense, then, Dr. King spoke in August of 1963 as something of a stranger in a strange land.

As the King speech makes clear, imagery can propel rhetoric like nothing else can. It becomes a kaleidoscope for the mind's eye, allowing audiences to see ideas that otherwise would be inert and lifeless. Table 7.3 goes beyond metaphor to present a more complete catalogue of images. It can be used by the critic to answer such questions as the following:

- How experimental is the text being examined (as measured by the *types* of stylistic devices used)? What factors explain such liberal/conservative uses of language?

Unless we are especially careful, stylistic analysis can become a mere exercise, cataloging for the sake of cataloging. To learn that a speaker used three

TABLE 7.3 Some Common Stylistic Devices*

Device	Definition	Function	Example
Anaphora	Exactly repeating a word or phrase at the beginnings of successive clauses	Highlights the speaker's mental grasp of a concept by displaying the *completeness* (and hence determination) of his or her thinking	"We shall not flag or fail. We shall go on to the end. We shall fight in France. . . . " (Winston Churchill)
Antithesis	Juxtaposing contrasting ideas in balanced phrases	An "argumentative" piece of imagery that *sharpens* differences significantly	"Naked came I out of my mother's womb, and naked shall I return thither." (Job, 1,21)
Hyperbole	An extravagant statement used as a figure of speech	A conscious distortion used to *describe* something that would otherwise be beyond description	"Publishing a volume of verse is like dropping a rose-petal down the Grand Canyon and waiting for an echo." (Don Marquis)
Metonymy	Using the name of one thing as the name for something else to which it has a logical relationship	Creates a new association among ideas or exploits an old association in order to add *freshness* to thought	"Agonies are one of my changes of garments. . . . I am the mashed fireman with breastbone broken." (Walt Whitman)
Oxymoron	A phrase that seems to have an internal contradiction	A contrastive device designed to, first, confuse and, then, *intrigue* listeners	"That building is a little bit big and pretty ugly." (James Thurber)
Synecdoche	Identifying something whose "real" meaning is (recognizably) opposite of what is literally said	A kind of rhetorical shorthand that provides a more *interesting* view of commonly understood objects or ideas	"Wherever wood [a ship] can swim, there I am sure to find this flag of England [the British fleet]." (Napoleon)
Irony	A statement whose "real" meaning is (recognizably) opposite of what is literally said	In-group humor used to *certify* that speaker and listener share the same evaluative code (accomplished by either overstatement or understatement)	"Your well-known integrity has cleared you of all blame, your modesty has saved you, your past life has been your salvation." (Cicero, when attacking Clodius)
Rhetorical question	Declarative statements taking a (falsely) interrogative form	Generates a sense of *commonality* between speaker and listener via imagined dialogue	"Are you better off now than you were four years ago?" (Ronald Reagan [Franklin Roosevelt])
Parallelism	Groupings of similarly phrased ideas presented in rapid succession	*Quickens* the rhetorical pace and therefore generates psychological momentum in listeners	"We shall pay any price, bear any burden, meet any hardship, support any friend, oppose any foe in order to assure the survival and success of liberty." (John Kennedy)

*Based in part on Espy [1983], Arnold [1974], and Kaufer [1981].

rhetorical questions and eleven hyperboles hardly advances knowledge. All speakers use imagery and they do so all the time. The really important questions about style relate to the pattern of devices used and what the speaker gains or loses by such stylizing. The examples in Table 7.3 adequately establish what these forms of imagery are like. There is little need to do criticism solely to find new examples of same. Instead, the good critic concentrates on the *intellectual operations* signaled by the use of these stylistic tokens.

For example, Campbell [1972] studied the speaking of former Vice-president Spiro Agnew and noted his heavy use of antithesis. Rather than leave the matter there, however, Campbell went on to explain how Agnew's style revealed his Manichaean worldview, an us-versus-them mindset that constantly divided the world into two and only two categories. This black-and-white thinking, warned Campbell, pointed up Agnew's inability to cope with the grayness of political compromise (a dangerous characteristic for an American politician, says Campbell.) In a similar vein, Kaufer [1981] urges the critic to monitor persistent use of irony because it points up the existence of a **shared code** between speaker and listener. He asserts that irony always has evaluation built into it and that a statement like "Nice weather, huh?" made by (drenched) Person A to (drenched) Person B is an attempt to reestablish that A and B still agree on standards for evaluating weather. Irony is thus an in-joke often used by in-crowds when the pressure is off. It tends to fall flat when used in other contexts (e.g., among strangers at a funeral).

In a similar vein, Lakoff and Johnson [1980:39] have examined metonymy and note that it serves as a kind of argumentative spotlight, calling attention to one feature rather than many features. So, for example, a metonymic statement like "Saddam Hussein marched into Kuwait" is a rhetorically powerful way of isolating who was responsible for a given set of actions and, consequently, who should be singled out for praise or blame. Metonymy can therefore help to determine the **intellectual focus** of a message.

But what if a text contains little imagery or "dead" imagery? Even here the critic can learn something. Arendt [1963] notes, for example, that the remarks of Adolph Eichmann, the notorious Nazi leader, typically contained only cliches, unoriginal figures of speech (e.g., "a bolt from the blue") that stand out because of their banality. Arendt argues that a mind so incapable of stylistic inventiveness was also a mind ideally suited to the dulling themes of Nazi orthodoxy. In Eichmann's own rhetoric, then, Arendt found traces of the rhetoric to which Eichmann himself had become addicted.

Some of the most interesting criticism has focused on metaphor. Daughton [1988], for example, tracked Lyndon Johnson's metaphors from his early years as a congressman to his final days in the Oval Office and found an increasing complexity in Johnson's metaphors as he matured. While LBJ used familiar images as a young politician (e.g., "We have shortchanged our youth."), his presidential metaphors became more ambitious (e.g., "Education is the guardian and steward of democracy."). Daughton chalks up this effect to the increasing complexity and institutionalization of the political jobs Johnson took upon himself during his latter years in office.

Another study is Jamieson's [1980] novel comparison of Pope Paul VI and former California Governor Jerry Brown. What could such different speakers have in common? Very little. That is precisely what Jamieson found, but her point was more subtle. She discovered that the Pope often used metaphors to increase his authority, a tendency built into the hierarchy he oversaw. So, for example, Paul used bodily metaphors because bodies have only *one* head; he used dark-light metaphors and placed the light on *his* position; he used familial images because traditional families are headed by a *male* parent.

Jerry Brown, in contrast, used powerless metaphors. He depicted himself as a Sisyphus pushing boulders up a hill or as an incidental member of a Greek chorus or as a little Dutch boy holding his finger in a political dike. These sharp metaphorical differences explain the contrasting **worldviews** of the Pope and the Governor: One, a dominant, perhaps domineering, religious leader and the other a practical, perhaps pessimistic, politician. Metaphorical patterns like these, says Jamieson, carry the undertones of rhetoric, and it is to these undertones that listeners often respond unconsciously.

Metaphor is also a good device for embodying changing **cultural trends.** Osborn [1977:359, 362–3] notes, for example, that certain metaphors died off in popularity over time as people domesticated the sea. Thus, whereas Edmund Burke in the eighteenth century could describe a rival as being "on a wide sea, without chart or compass . . . whirled about, the sport of every gust," such metaphors were eventually replaced by space imagery (e.g., Adlai Stevenson's "We travel together, passengers on a little space ship, dependent on its vulnerable reserves of air and soil. . . ."). These alterations, says Osborn, signal more than changing rhetorical fashion. To switch from one metaphorical system to another is also to switch from one style of thinking to another. After all, a nation that finds imminent danger lapping at the edge of its own continent may well operate with greater military caution than one brazen enough to see itself as the master of the stars and beyond.

Imagery can change in the short run as well. Hughey et al. [1987] studied alterations in the AIDS metaphors found in popular newstories, keying particularly on when AIDS was used as the tenor, or subject, of the metaphor (e.g., "AIDS is the holocaust revisited.") and when AIDS was the vehicle, or object, of the metaphor (e.g., "She treats me like I've got AIDS."). Hughey and his associates note that as the AIDS story saturated American culture, there was a dramatic increase in AIDS-as-vehicle metaphors. That is, in an astonishingly short period of time, AIDS moved from the thing clarified to the thing so well understood that it explained yet other concepts. In other words, metaphor can become something of a cultural timepiece for the enterprising critic.

Imagery is important. It is important because it tells us about what motivates people, what mystifies them, what frightens them. Animals, oceans, mountains, birth—these things mystify. Money, inventions, voyages, salvation—these things motivate. War, whirlwinds, torture, disease—these things frighten. Rhetoric uses them all, for good and for ill. Edelman [1964] urges us to take metaphor seriously because it is so sensitive to social changes. Thus, he warns, while a phrase like "an American presence in the Middle East" sounds exceedingly friendly, the sort of visit one cousin might pay another, this is imagery that masks policy and should therefore be treated with deadly seriousness by the discerning rhetorical critic.

CONCLUSION

Analyzing style is a complex business. For whatever reason, language will not reveal its mysteries to the casual observer. Stylistic analysis takes patience: noting metaphorical clusters, being sensitive to a special use of anaphora, remembering who employs the passive voice and who does not. Often, making such discrimination is a tedious business, yielding a handful of message facts but no obvious explanations. Even for non-Catholics, the special friend of the stylistic critic is St. Jude, patron saint of the hopeless.

But this is hyperbole. Stylistic criticism can be done and it can be done well. The critic begins as all worthwhile projects are begun: slowly, patiently, sensibly. The critic notices an isolated phrase structure here, a strange colloquialism there, and sets to wondering what it all means. These thoughts percolate awhile as adjectives are counted and found to be more plentiful than expected. Then, an odd set of repetitions is noticed, repetitions missed when the passage was first read. Later, it is discovered that a rather old-fashioned sort of maternal imagery both begins and ends the message. These isolated observations tumble about in the critic's head as the passage is read again and again.

In some cases, the critic will suddenly shout "Eureka," but more often a vague sense of the rhetor's strategy will gradually, fitfully, develop. At about this time, the critic might become aware that the text is interestingly different from another text just studied, and so the message begins to take on new meaning as it is viewed comparatively. Lanham [1983:155] likens stylistic analysis to pulling first one thread and then another until a pattern begins to unravel for the critic. This thread-pulling eventually helps the critic recognize the speaker's distinctive voice. It is at this special moment of familiarity that the critic's task takes on steam.

Perhaps this makes it seem that stylistic criticism is somewhat mystical. It is. Somewhat. And it will remain somewhat mystical until people become less complicated and until language exposes its several mysteries to one and all. Such a day may arrive, but it is not here yet. And so the critic goes to work.

Chapter 8

ANALYZING
WORD CHOICE

Give rest, O Christ, to thy servant(s) with thy saints, where sorrow and pain are no more, neither sighing, but life everlasting.

Thou only art immortal, the creator and maker of mankind; and we are mortal, formed of the earth, and unto earth shall we return. For so thou didst ordain when thou createdst me, saying, "Dust thou art, and unto dust shalt thou return." All we do down to the dust; yet even at the grave we make our song: Alleluia, alleluia, alleluia.

Into thy hands, O merciful Savior, we commend thy servant [Name]. Acknowledge, we humbly beseech thee, a sheep of thine own fold, a lamb of thine own flock, a sinner of thine own redeeming. Receive him/her into the arms of thy mercy, into the blessed rest of everlasting peace, and into the glorious company of the saints in light. . . .

Christ is risen from the dead, trampling down death by death, and giving life to those in the tomb.

The Sun of Righteousness is gloriously risen, giving light to those who sat in darkness and in the shadow of death.

The Lord will guide our feet into the way of peace, having taken away the world.

Christ will open the kingdom of heaven to all who believe in his Name, saying, Come, O blessed of my Father; inherit the kingdom prepared for you.

Into paradise may the angels lead thee; and at thy coming may the martyrs receive thee, and bring thee into the holy city Jerusalem. [Prayer, 1979:484–5]

These are the familiar words spoken at the traditional Christian funeral. They were taken from *The Book of Common Prayer*, an Episcopalian document, but any modern Christian—Baptist, Methodist, Lutheran, probably even Mormon or Roman Catholic—could recognize and approve of them. Even though the edition cited here was dated 1979 with a first printing in 1789, few changes have been made over the years, making its style old yet ageless. While ordinary Americans do not offer formal salutations ("Come here, O Steve") or use antiquated tenses ("didst ordain," "createdst"), they can understand what is being said here. Also, while they now "request" rather than "beseech," "sing" a song rather than "make" one, and refer to each other as "you" instead of "thee," they can still appreciate the prayer. Its imagery is either naturalistic ("formed of the earth," "Sun of Righteousness") or corporeal ("arms of thy mercy," "guide our feet") and hence reaches across the generations. The prayer's themes—human sinfulness; the divinity of Jesus; salvation for all believers—are so well wrought and so familiar that even their archaic language cannot sap them of vitality.

No doubt, *The Book of Common Prayer* could be rewritten to take advantage of modern language habits. Some denominations have done so. But for many believers, these words will do just fine, even if they are very old words. For modern believers, this prayer's language is precious, in part because it is old and in part because it has brought comfort over the years to so many loved ones standing at so many gravesides. Words like these can be counted on. Their never-changingness connects modern Christians to the first Christians and thence to not-yet-born Christians. "This is *our* language," says the Christian, "it marks us as special. People who cannot love our language probably cannot love our beliefs."

This chapter focuses on **lexicon,** *words that are unique to a group or individual and that have special rhetorical power.* Lexicons are important to study because they set people apart. For example, even if one had never read the above prayer and was presented with a disconnected list of its constituent words, one could learn something. Even in isolation, words like "martyrs," "humbly," "sheep," "dust," and "guide" warn a prospective group member that *submission* to something or someone is expected in the text. On the other hand, words like "redeem," "mercy," "risen," "glorious," and "kingdom" imply that personal *improvement* can be expected in return for submission. Finally, words uncommon to everyday speech like "paradise," "alleluia," "immortal," "righteousness," and "Jerusalem" add a dimension of *mystery* to the message. In effect, the very lexicon of Christianity tells its story: Repentance for sin will be rewarded eternally by God in paradise.

Lexicons make for efficiency. By using preferred words, a speaker can establish the right to address an audience. But what happens when a speaker does not have access to such a lexicon? What kinds of *ideas* are possible when certain kinds of words are unavailable? This was the situation confronting Mr. F. J. Gould [n.d.:26–8] some years ago when writing *Funeral Services Without*

Theology for atheists. Knowing that atheists' loved ones also need to hear comforting words, Gould offered sample messages for the nonbeliever's funeral service. One of his remembrances was this:

We assemble in this place to say a kind and solemn farewell to the remains of _____.

We come as mourners. But the act of mourning is no strange event in human life. Not only do we grieve at the passing of friends. We may often have occasion to grieve over lost opportunities, or lost wealth, or lost health. And whenever a loss brings sorrow, it is our part not simply to mourn, but also to turn the affliction to some wise purpose in our life's experience. In death, therefore, we seek to find a meaning that shall bring consolation, and enable us to draw a hidden joy from the depth of sorrow. And this joy we discover in the thought that the living and the dead make up one vast family. Memory and love unite us to the departed in sacred ties. A household may be divided among various chambers, and the members, though parted by walls, may yet dwell in real union and sympathy. And so, also, we who live in the light of the sun and stars are yet comrades of the dead, bearing their image in our thought, their names on our lips, or their influences in our very blood and ideas and habits. . . .

Life is but the latest note in a music that began with the birth of humanity itself. The music is a song of households knit in the bonds of mutual love; of cities and states built up by courage and self-devotion; of benefits bestowed by wit and labor for the aid of the weak and helpless; of knowledge won from nature; of precious thoughts and teachings imparted by the sages. How immense and how deep is our debt to the past! How much of thankfulness we owe to the goodness, the intelligence, and the energy of men and women who are now dead, and who toiled in faith and patience for the children of their day, and for us remoter children whom they were never to look upon! How few of these forefathers and foremothers can we know as we knew the dead to whom we here offer our parting words! Yet we derive from them our health, our stores of sustenance, our learning, our all. It is one of our profoundest joys to know that we are united to this great past. "To live with the dead is one of the most precious privileges of humanity. . . ."

Each one of us can help in the glorious task of rendering some service to the family which numbers more members dead than living. Each can offer an impulse of pity, of mercy, of justice. Each can add a useful thought, a cheerful and sensible word, a happy song, an effort to express something beautiful. Each can contribute a little bravery, a little wisdom, a little aim accomplished. And, by reason of that little tribute to the general wealth, we may enroll ourselves among the influences that will pass from age to age in fruitfulness and blessing. . . .

Clearly, Gould has been creative here. Denied use of the religious lexicon, he canvases human sentiments ("joy," "grief," "courage"), human challenges ("opportunity," "affliction," "labor"), and human virtues ("bravery," "intelligence," "goodness"). These are fine words, these human words, but they are hardly special in the way that "Dust thou are and unto dust shalt thou return" is special. The metaphors Gould uses are adequate (a "family" of humankind, living in the "light" of the stars, parted at times by "walls" of separation but ultimately heartened by "stores" of sustenance), but they do not have real rhetorical punch.

Also, while the Episcopalian memorial is spare and direct, the atheists' remarks are too self-consciously embellished. Each purpose is a "wise" purpose, each joy "hidden," each family "vast." Sometimes it takes double adjectives to make the point ("how immense and deep is our debt") and the use of the superlative degree ("profoundest joys," "most precious privileges") makes the passage sound almost like advertising copy. Where one noun would have sufficed, the author uses two ("precious thoughts and teachings") or even three ("the goodness, the intelligence, the energy . . . ").

In short, Gould was not short. He overfills his thoughts with words. It is as if he were constantly afraid of offending some constituency and so he includes them all ("forefathers and foremothers," "cities and states," "the living and the dead"). Deprived of Biblical images of hellfire and damnation, denied the stories of saints and sinners, robbed of textured depictions of an afterlife, Gould resigned himself to abstractions. He asked his audience to enroll itself "among the influences that will pass from age to age" without specifying what such influences actually *do*. He says that in death "we seek to find a meaning that shall bring consolation" but the consolation he offers—turning the affliction "to some wise purpose"—is as gray and lifeless as death itself. Gould's abstractions are so intellectualized that at one point he even speaks of the "*impulse*" of pity, not the felt emotion itself.

In a Judeo-Christian culture, it is hard to be an atheist. It is even harder to talk like one. This is not to say that Mr. Gould has done poorly. After all, he was writing a generic eulogy, a fill-in-the-blanks address for no one in particular and hence was almost necessarily driven to the heights of abstraction. But the *Book of Common Prayer* is equally generic and its words seem timely as well as timeless. At least in part, this effect is produced by a lexicon whose history authorizes and whose familiarity comforts. As Chapter 7 demonstrated, effective style emerges from words well arranged, both functionally and creatively. But effective style also depends on the *types* of words a speaker chooses. That is the topic of this chapter.

EXAMINING GROUP LEXICONS

Like people, words have histories. That is why even synonyms come to mean (and feel) differently. Blankenship [1968:59] makes this point when commenting on variations like "I am thrifty; you are stingy; he's a miser" or "I agree; you must admit; he's forced to confess." Rhetoric requires the speaker to wander through these lexical thickets when deciding what to say. In 1995, for example, the lead singer of Blood, Sweat & Tears declared to a sweltering summertime audience that it was "as hot as the last train to Auschwitz." What is the real problem here? No doubt it was hot in that Detroit suburb on that late July afternoon. No doubt it is a good idea for a performer to try to identify with his audience, people who had been baking in the sun for many hours before the group began to play. And no doubt talking about the weather is normally a safe thing to do. But then there is that word . . . Auschwitz.

Words like "Auschwitz" are part of a disapproved lexicon, as are "fag," "deficit spending," and "sexism." These words can be unnerving, whether they appear alone or in context. Other words tell a happier story, words like "patriot," "integrity," "commitment," "family," etc. In the world of politics, "safe" words like these, often accompanied by a blizzard of short, pictorial clips, now fill the televised air, often disconnected from genuine argument. It is as if the words themselves had magical power, as if by intoning words like "strong defense," "human rights," and "high technology" a candidate could be assured of political worthiness. Similarly, attacking one's opponent with such words as "Japanese imperialism," "nuclear waste," or "welfare state" makes it seem as if *the saying* of these words can alone end discussion.

Words having special evocative power for a society have been dubbed **Ultimate Terms** by Weaver [1953]. Phrases like "true Americanism," "equal justice for all," and "scientific advancement" are, according to Weaver, modern God Terms that make us mentally genuflect when hearing them. Weaver notes that much public oratory is little more than a clever interspersing of such words at appropriate times, which often turns genuine communication into mere word-saying. Weaver also noted that Devil Terms, terms like "racism," "drugs," and "illiteracy," give us a clear picture of malevolence and are therefore also rhetorically useful.

Weaver urged critics to track uses of such language to get an early reading on emerging societal values. In the 1950s, for example, Senator Joe McCarthy could have called his detractors misfits, scoundrels, or ingrates but instead he called them Communists, and therein lay the story of his decade. In the 1980s, Ronald Reagan could have labeled his pet armaments intercontinental ballistic missiles but instead he called them Peacekeepers, and that told volumes about Mr. Reagan's international vision. Using such words allows speakers to suspend the rules of reasoning and to shift the agenda for discussion, especially if its users are specially licensed keepers of the nation's sacred terminology (as Reagan and McCarthy were). Weaver himself was deeply disturbed by the potential for unscrupulous use of Ultimate Terms. Even a brief listing of their rhetorical capacities shows why:

1. Ultimate Terms are abstract. They normally refer to ideas (like democracy) rather than to objects (like hot dogs). They normally refer to the deceased (George Washington) rather than the living (Michael Jordan). Because they are abstract, their meanings can be twisted: e.g., "Buy Magic Cola, an all-American drink." They can also be made to encompass more than they were intended to encompass: e.g., "A good Christian should vote conservatively." And they can be used in situations for which they were never intended (e.g., when "right to work" became a synonym for union-bashing).

2. Ultimate Terms are efficient. Although it only has three letters, a word like "pig" can trigger powerful emotions. Thus, when the police were called pigs in the 1960s by radical activists, this Devil Term evoked images of "filthy" individuals doing the bidding of corrupt politicians, of the police's unabated "appetite" for power, and of the monstrous "breeding" practices of the police who, in the eyes of the Left, always appeared on the scene in excessive numbers.

3. *Ultimate Terms are hierarchial.* That is why they are called ultimate. They lie at the top of society's pantheon of values and subsume all lesser terms. For this reason, they are used to pull rank, to make an opponent's case seem small and expedient. So, for example, the teenager who argues that going to the lake with friends sounds like more fun than staying at home for the evening barbecue can quickly be disadvantaged. The parent who responds "You don't want to spoil *the family's* plans, do you?" knows full well where "fun" and "family" rank on the value hierarchy.

4. *Ultimate terms are preemptory.* They let a speaker carve out rhetorical territory and then seal it off from others. By calling his bomb a Peacekeeper, for example, Ronald Reagan challenged his opponents mightily: "All *real* Americans are in favor of Peace," implied the president. Similarly, Joe McCarthy threatened his opponents with the rhetorical question: "Only the Communists want me to fail. You're not one *them,* are you?" In persuasion, whoever scrambles to the high ground first can set the parameters for the debate and, often, its necessary conclusion as well.

5. *Ultimate terms have unstable meanings.* This is a particularly important, and dangerous, feature. Being abstract, Ultimate Terms can change in meaning from age to age and from topic to topic but their *form* never does. That is, "freedom" is spelled the same way today as it was in 1776 but it no longer just means an absence of British troops on New England shores. For that matter, in an age of Russian entrepeneurism, Chinese capitalism, and Cuban baseball leagues, "Communism" no longer just means Stalinist purges either.

But persuaders try to make us forget this distinction between form and content. They operate as if a word is a word is a word and that a term's final meaning is determined at its christening. Thus, when a campaigner contrasts the "economic freedom" built into the Republican platform to the "collectivist tyranny" of the Democrats, the campaigner is inviting the triangulation of colonial Boston in the 1770s, Leninist Russia in the 1920s, and contemporary conditions. Even though times change, meanings change, and policies change, language sometimes does not change.

At other times it does. In a fascinating book entitled *Crafting Equality,* Condit and Lucaites [1993] present what is essentially the history of a word, the word "equality." They argue that equality has meant different things to different people at different times in the U.S. Sometimes it has meant "separate but equal." Sometimes it has meant legal but not economic equality. Sometimes it has meant recompense for previous inequalities. Condit and Lucaites show that the word equality is an odd one because it has always had "ultimate" meaning even though it has never meant a *single* thing. Equality, they conclude, is not a black-and-white term, precisely because it has meant one thing to blacks and another thing to whites throughout American history.

It is easy to think of Ultimate Terms as mere semantics, as an idle game with no consequence. Nothing could be more dangerous. The lives lost and careers destroyed by Joe McCarthy's rampage in the 1950s remind us how deadly a game labeling can be. But if language is a game, Weaver would observe, the critic must become its referee. After all, God Terms like truth, justice, peace, freedom and love really *are* worth defending from their corrupters. Racism, sexism, poverty, oppression, and ignorance really *are* worth attacking. A sacred lexicon remains sacred only as long as it is revered in practice, and so the critic must help determine who has the ultimate right to use Ultimate Terms.

A second approach to lexicon is to analyze **Code Words,** specialized terms that designate uncommon phenomena (or that designate common phenomena in uncommon ways) and that are unique to a subgroup. Typically, the more precise a word is, the more remote it becomes (e.g., "ribonucleic acid"). This remoteness makes for efficiency. The surgeon who asks a nurse for a trephine, for example, gets what is needed and gets it quickly. To have asked for "that saw-type thing over there" might have produced the same result but more likely would have produced an array of potential cutting instruments. Such inefficiency can be costly in surgery: A word lost can mean time lost and time lost can mean a patient lost.

For similar reasons, Code Words are used by scientists (they speak of an "angle of trajectory" instead of its tilt), by bureaucrats ("vehicular traffic" rather than cars and trucks), by lawyers ("indemnify" for protect), by athletes ("reddogging," "sky hook," "double-up"), and by other specialists ("downloading," "psychotic disorder," "G-clef," "occlusion," etc.). As tastes become more refined, as people become more segregated, as ideas become more technical, Code Words become more common.

Code Words have an unsavory reputation because they are inherently discriminatory: They set their users apart from the larger society. As a result, many people react to Code Words defensively, as if such terms constituted a silent rhetorical conspiracy against them. Sometimes, Code Words are just that but equally often they result from normal socialization. We use linguistic shortcuts because grunting "torque!" is easier than orating: "Seeing as how I am lying on my back fixing the transmission linkage and hence cannot extricate myself to reach that curious, wrench-like implement at your feet, would you be so kind as to. . . ."

Others' Code Words keep us out of the picture and hence we resent them. *Their* Code Words are arcane, obtuse, an affront to civility. *Our* Code Words are "the language of our fathers" or our "distinctive linguistic heritage." Our Code Words are our semantic birthright while theirs become legalese, scientism, or bureaucratic gobbledygook. Especially when it comes to nursery rhymes, their Code Words make us twitter: "A triumvirate of murine rodents totally devoid of ophthalmic acuity was observed in a state of rapid locomotion in pursuit of an agriculturalist's uxorial adjunct. Said adjunct then performed a triple caudectomy utilizing an acutely honed bladed instrument generally used for subdivision of edible tissue." [Youngquist, 1983:153]

Code Words are standard rhetorical tools that perform a number of functions, among which are the following:

1. *Code Words insulate.* Code Words are a way of hiding in public, of sending messages to select persons without risk of interruption or interference from the unselected. Hayes [1976] documents this in a study of "gayspeak" where he describes two distinct cultures within the gay community, one that uses Code Words openly (including such terms as "nelly number," "S/M," and "Chippendale queen") and another that uses ordinary language in jargonized ways (e.g., "liberal-minded," "artistic," "tendencies"). This latter group, says Hayes, is seeking to maximize its rhetorical range and to guard against the social isolation the former group reluctantly accepts.

2. *Code Words unify.* Turner [1973] makes the point that slang (informal Code Words) is a token that can be shared with new members of a group to make them feel included. By using slang, the neophyte participates in the group rhetorically but not financially, organizationally, behaviorally, etc. As Turner says [p. 189], "Slang may even have its usefulness among children as a protection, so that they can begin to learn social behavior without staking too much of themselves at once." He also notes that the very act of learning Code Words is an important ritual for new members: "The student of geometry is never to *draw* anything; he may *describe* circles, *construct* a triangle, *produce* its sides and *drop* a perpendicular, so that geometry is in part the learning of new collocations of words special to the subject" [p. 172].

3. *Code Words neutralize.* Code Words often drain emotion from social or political events. In the language of Chapter 7, Code Words are frequently found in the Periodic (or noun-filled) style that hides the essential action that verb-styles reveal. Thus, Code Words help us deal with unpleasantness, a point made some years ago by George Orwell [1946:363]:

> Things like the continuance of British rule in India, the Russian purges and deportations, the dropping of the atomic bombs in Japan, can indeed be defended but only by arguments which are too brutal for most people to face and which do not square with the professed aims of political parties. Thus . . . [d]efenseless villages are bombarded from the air, the inhabitants driven out into the countryside, the cattle machine-gunned, the huts set on fire with incendiary bullets; this is called *pacification*. Millions of peasants are robbed of their farms and sent trudging along the roads with no more than they can carry; this is called *transfer of population* or *rectification of frontiers*. People are imprisoned for years without trial, or shot in the back of the neck or sent to die of scurvy in Arctic lumber camps; this is called *elimination of undesirable elements*.

4. *Code Words sanctify.* Code Words make bad things neutral (e.g., a "cardiac event" seems less threatening than a "heart attack"), neutral things good

(e.g., explaining one's religion becomes "witnessing"), and good things magnificent (e.g., cutting off-tackle becomes a "Heisman move"). Himelstein [1983] observes that Code Words can desensitize voters by making political issues seem technical issues. In analyzing racism, for example, Himelstein asked [p. 156] "How does one avoid blatant offense to black voters and at the same time communicate faithfulness to the racist canons of the recent past?" The answer? Code Words. Words like "ward politics," "sectionalism," and "neighborhood representation" filled the campaign rhetoric Himelstein studied, silently giving voters directions without appearing to have done so: "The politicians had winked, and the voters had understood" [p. 165].

5. *Code Words stabilize.* Edelman [1971] observes that Code Words keep people in positions of power. So, for example, those who have not learned the language of the bureaucracy or who cannot use it with authority are denied its riches. That is why there is so little semantic creativity in politics, an arena whose numbing technicalities make ideas technical and audiences numb. It is this numbing, this state of nonfeeling, that makes the voter ripe for political exploitation. For a political figure to avoid Code Words, warns Edelman [p. 73], and "to speak and write in fresh or unconventional terms while jargon swirls all about one in an organization [would be] to state definitively that one is not buying the accepted values and not docilely conforming to authority." Few politicians run such risks, says Edelman.

When examining Code Words, the critic does what critics always do—asks questions: Why are Code Words used here and not there? Why this lexicon and not another? What attitudes and values are the Code Words walling in? Which are they walling out? Whom do they protect? Whom do they disenfranchise? There are many such questions for the critic to ask because there are so many Code Words. So the critic studies them, sorting out in each instance what is being said and what is not. All too often, Code Words make ideas do the bidding of language. It is the critic's job to reverse that process.

EXAMINING INDIVIDUAL LEXICONS

Thus far, we have focused on groups' sacred or secret words. But individuals' language choices are also worthy of study. Indeed, a person's "style" is often judged to be a special way of wearing clothes or shooting a basketball or saying hello. We tune into David Letterman each night, not knowing exactly what he will say but confident that it will be familiar because his style is so distinctive. **Style,** *the sum total of the variations a speaker makes on standard linguistic schemes,* is therefore a basic force in everyday interaction. But how much of this sum total must a critic assess? Which of its variations are really important? This section will try to answer these questions.

An interesting example of the importance of individual style occurred in the case of publishing magnate William Randolph Hearst's granddaughter,

Patricia, who was captured by the radical Symbionese Liberation Army in the 1970s and then became a gun-toting bank-robber by the name of Tania. During her trial, Ms. Hearst's lawyers produced a university examination she had written and compared it to a taped message she sent her father two months after her capture.

Were Tania and Patty the same person? Did Hearst freely author the statement to her father or, as she claimed in court, was she forced to read SLA propaganda into a tape recorder? Is the person who wrote the cool scholarly exposition the same woman who authored the cant-filled diatribe her father received? Can people change their styles so radically and so quickly? Are the differences in the two messages a function of different audiences (a professor versus her father) or of changing modalities (oral versus written communication) rather than of changing ideology? Or did the passages reflect a genuine philosophical conversion on Hearst's part and, as SLA member Emily Harris said in court, did the SLA actually try to *tone down* Hearst's rhetoric?

Patty Hearst's trial hinged on what Bailey [1979] has termed forensic linguistics. In Hearst's case, neither the jury nor the appeal judge was convinced of her innocence and expert testimony on the contrasting rhetorical styles was not permitted in open court. A subsequent study by Bailey, however, argues persuasively that Hearst underwent only a *partial* conversion and that while she may have authored some semiradical statements, she did not author the most damning of them. By examining Hearst's lexical style (e.g., use of nouns, proportion of monosyllables, ratio of auxiliary to main verbs, mean sentence length, etc.) and comparing them to the passages in dispute, Bailey called into question both Hearst's culpability and her gullibility.

Naturally, this sort of lexical analysis is a conjectural business. The evidence available to Bailey was insufficient to establish Hearst's innocence conclusively. But the questions he asked are important: How unique is an individual's lexicon and how can it be reliably determined? To begin to answer these questions, at least two things are required: (1) a sizable sample of a speaker's style, a sample that represents diverse rhetorical conditions and (2) a sample of others' word choices (so that language norms can be used for comparison). As Enkvist [1971] says, the study of style is therefore the study of deviance from known linguistic patterns.

This sort of comparative logic has guided a number of studies. Knapp et al. [1974] compared the spontaneous (truthful) remarks of people to lies they told at the behest of experimenters. Individuals' styles changed dramatically from condition to condition: fewer words spoken when lying, fewer self-disclosures, more caution in their remarks, more repetition of words, and fewer factual citations. It was as if the "liars" were trying to step away from themselves, as if their natural lexicons would not cooperate with the lies being told. Another study by Osgood and Walker [1959] compared real suicide notes to those fabricated in the laboratory. They found that the real statements had a leaner, more efficient style and more verbal energy. They did not supplicate by using adjectives or large words; they did not make preachy, philosophical statements; and, interestingly, they used more positive language than those in the comparison group, presumably because suicide makes one contemplate *both* good and evil.

Another study by Sinclair [1985] looked for a "successful" style among preachers whose congregations were growing and an "unsuccessful" style among those losing church members. After gathering statistical data on church growth, weekly attendance, and financial support by the laity, Sinclair examined the language choices of a large sample of preachers. His findings: The growing churches heard sermons that were more personal, more narrational, more assured, and more detailed than parishioners in the declining churches, while the less successful preachers used more passive constructions, less interesting language, and a less businesslike, more folksy, style.

A more general study by Carbone [1975] compared speakers rated highly credible to those rated unimpressive by a group of dispassionate judges. She found that highly credible speakers used more human interest language, a richer vocabulary, a more concrete style, and less cumbersome sentence structures than those rated low in believability.

In each of these studies, scholars examined what Sedelow and Sedelow [1966:1] call the distributional properties of language use, word patterns varying in some systematic way from speaker to speaker or from condition to condition. Research of this sort has a quantitative bent to it. It assumes that any claim about stylistic distinctiveness is ultimately a mathematical claim: Feature A does or does not appear in this text; Feature B appears more often or less often than Feature C; Feature D appears less frequently than the norm. Turner [1973:25] makes these same points when he says:

> If there are choices in language, there are probabilities. . . . Even such basic concepts as a 'rare word' or a 'common word' are statistical concepts. . . . To take a simple illustration, if I am about to spell an English word, the probability that I will use a particular letter to begin it, say *n* or *g*, can be roughly measured with a ruler and a good dictionary; if I choose *n* to begin with, the probability that the next letter will be *g* becomes zero; if I reach the stage *notwithstandin-*, the probability that the next letter will be *g* becomes certainty.

The stylistic critic need not trade in good sense for a ruler (or a computer). Counting things only takes one so far. But counting the right things at the right times under the right circumstances produces insight, and can guard against a researcher's natural biases as well [see Gastil, 1992]. The rest of this chapter will show why.

Figure 8.1 presents a speech John Kennedy [1961b] gave to the Democratic National Committee the day after his inauguration. The speech is not remarkable: It is a back-slapping piece of political celebration. It is brief, convivial, and spontaneous. It includes teasing and bantering. But it is not John Kennedy. Not really. Although the speech conforms to popular stereotypes of

FIGURE 8.1 Kennedy's Speech as Analyzed by the DICTION Program

I WANT to express my (appreciation) to all of you for your (kind) (welcome), and also to take this occasion to express my (great) appreciation—and I think the (appreciation) of us all—to Senator Jackson who assumed the chairmanship of the Democratic Party at the Convention, who was greatly responsible for our (success) in November and has been an invaluable (aid) during the transition. Whatever has been done that is useful in the party in the last 5 or 6 months he has played a great part in it. And I feel that the party has served a most useful national purpose—and while Senator Jackson is obligated to serve the people of Washington in the Senate, I know that we can continue to count on him in the days to come for counsel and advice and support. So I hope we will all stand and give a good cheer to Scoop Jackson.

Scoop automatically loses his share of the $4-million debt—we are not going to let him in on it. John Bailey has become the proprietor, along with Mac, of this enterprise. I think we are particularly fortunate to have John Bailey. I heard Governor Lawrence in his seconding speech say the trouble with everything is that they don't know enough of what is going on here in Washington; they ought to get out in the field. I agree with him completely. We have got a man from the field who knows what's wrong here in Washington, and I am delighted that John Bailey is going to take over this job. He is more popular today than he will be any time again in his life. I will feel that he is doing a good job when you all say, "Well, Kennedy is all right, but Bailey is the one who is really making the mistakes." That's the way it was in Connecticut. Ribicoff was never wrong, it was always Bailey's fault. So that is what he is going to do down here.

Up beat introduction results from Kennedy's Optimism score of 238, which was one of the highest in the sample.

Heavy use of prepositional phrases and passive voice constructions decrease Kennedy's Activity score.

JFK's realism score of 241 is exceptionally high and derives from a combination of personal, temporal, concrete, and spatial references.

Semantically, humor is often the product of overly assured language devoid of qualification, all of which results in a high Certainty score.

But /I/am/delighted/that/he/is/going/to/do/it./It/is/a/sacrifice/for/him./ But/I/think/we/are/getting/the/services/of/someone/who/works/in/the/party/ year/in/and/year/out.,/understands/what/the/party/can/do,/understands/what/ the/role/of/the/Chairman/is—and/I/must/say/that/I/am/delighted/to/see/ him/assuming/the/position/vacated/by/Senator/Jackson./

Colloquial phrases produce a very high Familiarity score; monosyllabic words result in a low Complexity score; and a paragraph devoid of adjectival constructions accounts for the low Embellishment score.

Lastly, I want to thank all of you for being with us at the inaugural. The party is not an end in itself—it is a means to an end. And you are the people who, in victory and defeat, have maintained the Democratic Party, maintained its traditions and will continue to do so in the future. I hope the relationship between all of us can continue to be as cordial as possible. I believe in strong political organizations in our country. The Republican Party is strong and vigorous today after the election of 1960. I think we are, also. And when we do that, I think we serve great national purposes.

Parallel constructions linked in sequence produce a Kennedyesque flourish as well as a very low Variety score.

The party is the means by which programs can be put into action—the means by which people of talent can come to the service of the country. And in this great free society of ours, both of our parties—the Republican and Democratic Parties—serve the interests of the people. And I am hopeful that the Democratic party will continue to do so in the days to come. It will be in the interest of us all, and I can assure you that I will cooperate in every way possible to make sure that we do serve the public interest.

Kennedy uses hallowed, albeit stock, phrases to generate an uncharacteristically high Symbolism score.

You have done so well in the past. We couldn't possibly have won without your help. I look forward to working with you in the future, and I want you to know that here in Washington, we may not know always what is going on as well as you do, but at least we are trying.

Thank you.

This is traditional political peroration consisting of high Self-Reference and Human Interest scores which, together, build speaker–audience bonds.

the Kennedy Style, this speech was not a normal one for him. Most of his speaking was drier, less personal, and more restrained. Table 8.1 shows how we know this to be true.

The information in Table 8.1 comes from analyzing Kennedy's text with a computer. The program guiding the computer (DICTION) was developed by Hart [1985] and tells the machine which words to look for in a passage. The computer breaks a message into its individual words and then searches for word patterns, thereby determining the speaker's basic lexicon. The program does so by employing **dictionaries,** lists of words the critic specifies ahead of time. So, for example, if the computer were prompted with a dictionary called *Animals,* it might look for dog, cat, sheep, etc. After finding all such usages, the computer would print out how many times these words were employed versus those found in other texts previously searched with the Animal dictionary.

DICTION does not have a category called Animals, but it does employ such word lists as **Activity** (including words like "achieve," "change," "plunge," etc.), **Realism** ("city," "buildings," "farmer"), **Certainty** ("everyone," "shall," "entire"), **Optimism** ("pleased," "generous," "exciting"), **Self-Reference** ("I," "me," "myself"), and **Human Interest** ("boy," "friend," "you"). The program searches for God Terms (here called **Symbolism:** "America," "democracy," "peace") and also calculates how **Embellished** a passage is by comparing its proportion of adjectives and adverbs to its number of nouns and verbs.

Finally, the program studies the richness of the speaker's vocabulary (a high **Variety** score means the text is not repetitious), its use of everyday words (i.e., **Familiarity**), and how complicated it is (a high **Complexity** score means the speaker used large words frequently). Guided by such search tools, the computer proceeds through a message word-by-word, remembering which terms of which type were used when. Figure 8.1 simulates how the computer did its "looking" when examining the Kennedy speech.

TABLE 8.1 Stylistic Features of the Kennedy Speech

Verbal Category	1/21/61 Speech	Kennedy Average	Other Presidents' Averages
Activity (aggressive, planned)	192.0	204.0	200.5
Realism (concrete, specific)	241.0	198.0	91.0
Certainty (assured, totalistic)	196.0	190.0	185.3
Optimism (inspired, praising)	238.0	213.0	220.0
Complexity (large words)	4.70	4.58	5.20
Variety (different words)	.410	.493	.488
Self-reference (I, me, etc.)	18.00	4.68	8.57
Familiarity (everyday words)	135.0	102.0	102.1
Human interest (references to people)	32.0	26.0	27.8
Embellishment (colorizing words)	.042	.070	.066
Symbolism (God terms)	6.00	2.21	5.45

From Hart [1984c:19].

For those interested in doing automated textual analysis, information about DICTION 4.0 (for both Mac and PC-Windows) can be obtained by filling out the card at the end of this book and sending it to Dr. R. P. Hart, College of Communication, Univ. of Texas at Austin, Austin, TX 78712 or by sending e-mail to: diction@mail.utexas.edu

The real value of such a tool is its efficiency. Although computers are dull-witted when compared to a sensitive critic, a program like DICTION has these advantages: (1) It examines every text in exactly the same way; (2) it ignores all words except those it has been instructed to "look" for; (3) it performs its tasks with lightning speed; (4) it never gets tired; (5) it never forgets what it has "learned" about any message; (6) it can track many kinds of words simultaneously (i.e., it can tell which portion of a text is highly Certain and which is *both* Optimistic and Certain).

Another advantage is that a computer cannot be seduced by the rhetoric it examines. Because it rather stupidly looks only for what it has been asked to look for, it is never sidetracked by interesting imagery or a humorous aside or a tear-stained narrative. It looks only for words, words, and more words. But afterward, it can report on verbal *patterns* that the imagery-noting critic was too busy to spot when inspecting the same message.

DICTION therefore operates like the Secret Service personnel who watch the crowd while the crowd (and the president) watch the tennis match. At the end of the day, when the president relaxes with them recounting the excitement of the contest, the Secret Service folks cannot comment on the overhead smash that won the fifth set. But they can tell the president how the crowd's mood changed when Andre Agassi threw his racket in the air. Reporting on crowd behavior can also be a type of tennis criticism.

A computer will never supplant the critic's wisdom, but its comparative information calls attention to features the critic may have missed. Table 8.1 shows this. At first, these findings seem odd since the popular press continually ran newsclips of the John Kennedy displayed in the Democratic National Convention speech. The Kennedy in that speech was witty, almost frisky, the same Kennedy who regaled reporters during press conferences. But DICTION shows that this was a *rare* John Kennedy. While this speech did display his characteristically simple style (see Complexity and Familiarity), in other ways it was singular. He was more concrete here than normal (see Realism) and more disclosive (see Self-Reference); he used many more Ultimate Terms (see Symbolism) and was substantially more upbeat (see Optimism). No matter what this speech implies, then, Mr. Kennedy's *general* style was quite dry and institutional. While a conventional critic might have discovered this same thing eventually, DICTION did so more quickly.

An important limitation of a program like DICTION is that it examines words out of context. By not distinguishing between "The boy hit the ball" and "The ball boy was hit" but only noting that the word "ball" appears in both statements, DICTION violates context. But context is not all there is to rhetoric. For example, the fact that the word "ball" appears in both passages signals a common concern with game-related matters (as opposed to religion-related or fashion-related or ostrich-related matters). The traditional critic might well miss these themes. But these themes may have *additive* effects on audiences who hear game-centered reference after game-centered reference, thereby contributing to their perceptions of rhetorical tone. So, when sweeping across a text quickly and "destroying" its linguistic unity, DICTION may simulate what listeners themselves do when processing messages.

The DICTION analysis of the Kennedy speech largely squares with our intuitions. Even a casual reading of the text reveals its personal, pragmatic tones. Then why use a computer? Because computers capture these tones quickly, reliably, and, most important, comparatively. Consider, for example, Table 8.2, which compares the Kennedy text to others examined previously. Few persons would confuse the Kennedy message with Martin Luther King's "I Have a Dream" speech. DICTION is also not confused. It finds an assuredness in the King speech missing in Kennedy's (see Certainty), perhaps showing that social movements permit more exhortation than do political celebrations. This difference is striking since, *for Kennedy,* this was one of his most assured speeches. But as a practical politician, he could not paint with King's broad brush, nor could he be as precise. On the other hand, Mr. Kennedy could be more upbeat than King (see Optimism) and do what politicians do best: flatter ("give a good cheer to Scoop Jackson") and promise ("I can assure you that I will cooperate in every way. . . .").

All of this is in sharp contrast to Rabbi Prinz's speech, which DICTION profiles as lecturish: heavy use of unfamiliar words, little Human Interest, and

TABLE 8.2 Comparative Use of Rhetorical Style

Verbal Category	Martin Luther King	Rabbi Prinz	John F. Kennedy	Franklin D. Roosevelt
Activity (aggressive, planned)	Low	Low	Medium	High
Realism (concrete, specific)	High	Medium	Very high	Low
Certainty (assured, totalistic)	High	Medium	Medium	Low
Optimism (inspired, praising)	Very low	Medium	High	Medium
Complexity (large words)	Medium	Low	Medium	Very low
Variety (different words)	Low	Low	Low	Low
Self-reference (I, me, my, etc.)	Medium	Medium	High	Low
Familiarity (everyday words)	Medium	Low	Very high	Very low
Human interest (references to people)	Medium	Low	Medium	Medium
Embellishment (colorizing words)	Medium	High	Medium	Medium

*In comparison to a total sample of 861 public messages.

heavy Embellishment (adjectives usually slow down a message). The Activity found in Rabbi Prinz's speech is also the lowest of the five, documenting the philosophical tone of his remarks. It is little wonder, then, that DICTION finds almost no similarity between the Prinz and Kennedy texts.

The main advantage of DICTION is that it remembers the features of thousands of other messages when analyzing a text. By doing so, DICTION does what listeners also do (without knowing it): It uses old texts to interpret new ones. When they listened to President Roosevelt on December 8, 1941, for example, most Americans knew they were hearing something extraordinary, in part because the president had just asked Congress to declare war but also because of the new tone in his remarks.

DICTION also senses this when featuring the Activity in Roosevelt's remarks ("Last night Japanese forces attacked Hong Kong. Last night Japanese forces attacked. . . ."). While F.D.R.'s language is not hard to understand (low scores on Complexity and Variety), he does draw on the special vocabulary of war ("hostilities," "air squadrons," "torpedoed") and of international geography ("Honolulu," "Guam," "Midway Island"), thereby scoring low on Familiarity. No doubt, the *divergence* between his simple words and his strange words told listeners that something unprecedented was afoot and that listening to Roosevelt at that moment would be like nothing they had experienced before.

Another interesting aspect of the Roosevelt message is its midrange score on Optimism. At first, this seems an anomaly since Roosevelt was delivering a war message. But DICTION prompts us to think anew about the President's rhetorical task. He of course had to discuss the war, and words like "infamy," "deceive," "invasion," and "danger" show that he did. But for each negative statement he made, he also included a positive one, thereby creating dialectical tension. Early on, for example, he contrasts the "treachery" of the Japanese ambassadors with the peace-seeking United States. Later, after detailing the evil done the night before, Roosevelt talks of "inevitable triumph," "unbounding determination," and "absolute victory." Naturally, Roosevelt wanted the American people to deal realistically with the new challenges he described, but he also knew that they could not hope to do so unless they had Hope to do so. DICTION shows that he provided it.

DICTION also records low Certainty and Realism scores for Roosevelt, which seems strange since the President needed to inspire the nation and help it deal concretely with the Japanese threat. But his Certainty score is curiously low, resulting from heavy use of the Passive Voice: "Japan has . . . undertaken," "The attack yesterday . . . has caused," "American ships have been reported. . . ." Roosevelt watched his words carefully perhaps because he did not know precisely what was then happening in other parts of the world, what military response the United States could make (or how soon), or what domestic problems he would face in the immediate future.

His low Realism score also signaled tentativeness. Roosevelt spoke of "implications to the very life and safety of our nation" without spelling out these implications. He promised that "always will our whole nation remember the character of the onslaught against us" but did not detail specifics. In short, he seems to have used the speech to buy time, to provide emotional reinforcement but also to preserve his military options. Hence, he opted for strategic ambiguity.

Computerized language programs are valuable not because they provide numerical answers but because they suggest new critical questions. This is the approach Hart [1984c] took when examining the speaking of Presidents Truman through Reagan via DICTION. Although his book tells a good deal about the presidents' styles, it more usefully reveals the factors having major impact on any speaker's lexicon. These factors are presented here as a series of useful critical probes:

1. Does the speaker's social upbringing affect style? Of all the presidents, Harry Truman used the greatest amount of Certainty. His plain-spoken, midwestern assuredness charmed his friends and irritated his enemies. But neither reaction changed him. Today, in contrast, politicians fear accountability. In such an era, Harry Truman's voice is missed: "Business was never so productive, vital and energetic as it is today. All this talk about weakening private enterprise is sheer political bunk." [Truman, 1950:497]

2. Does the speaker's employment history affect style? Dwight Eisenhower's rise to power in the army resulted more from his bureaucratic skills than from his brilliance as a military tactician. These bureaucratic experiences resulted in a wordy (high in Variety) and abstract (low in Realism) style. Ike was therefore less a public speaker than a script-reader, one whose mouth was too filled with words, as he once showed when talking about public service with college students: "In the government, one must obviously have no special end to serve, but citizens should not, invariably, be required to divest themselves of investments accumulated over a lifetime in order to qualify for public service." [Eisenhower, 1960:174]

3. Does the speaker's political vision affect style? John Kennedy scored the lowest of all eight presidents on Optimism. At first this seems surprising since Kennedy motivated a generation of young people to enter politics to do good. Apparently, however, politics for Kennedy was a matter of *righting wrongs,* a sense we get when listening to him on civil rights: "Are we to say to the world—and much more importantly to each other—that this is the land of the free, except for the Negroes; that we have no second class citizens, except for Negroes; that we have no class or caste system, no ghettos, no master race, except with respect to Negroes?" [Kennedy, 1963:547]

4. Does the speech setting affect the speaker's style? Lyndon Johnson could never adapt to television. Out on the stump, he could shake hands with the folks and palaver until dark. But on television he tied himself to his text, causing his Self Reference and Human Interest scores to drop off and his words to become complex and cautious. But in a face-to-face setting, LBJ could be moving indeed:

I'm not 65 yet, but I have known many people in my lifetime who were 65. Some have been mighty close to me. I have seen their eyes when they wondered whether they would be welcome in their old age in their sister-in-law's home, or whether their brother-in-law would be happy when they are all there using the one bath. I have seen them worry about how they were going to pay the doctors or the medical services. I have seen them grateful for the considerations that the preacher and the women of the church had extended to them in times of illness. . . . [Johnson, 1966a:777–8]

5. *Does the speaker's strategic mindset affect style?* Richard Nixon was a rhetorical classic, constantly adjusting his words to whatever situation he faced. Above all, he was controlled; some would call it conniving. The DICTION program shows how unerring his adaptations were. Keying on the Certainty variable, the data show that Nixon was sure of himself at times but quite tentative on other occasions. During Watergate, for example, Nixon watched each word he spoke, gauging what he said and gauging his omissions and indirections as well. When speaking during the Vietnam war, however, Nixon pounded his fist on the national podium. The effect of these two styles is sharply different, suggesting that there were at least two Richard Nixons, if not more.

6. *Does the speaker' social power affect the style?* DICTION found that Gerald Ford's use of Self Reference was the highest of all the presidents. This makes sense. Having entered office without a political vision or a mandate from the voters, Ford sold the only product he was sure of: himself. While this please-trust-me style rarely sounded presidential, it had its human attractions: "I see no reason why the Congress and the President cannot work together. That doesn't mean that all 535 Members of the House and Senate will agree with me. But I can assure you that what I have said on more than one occasion . . . that I will work with the Congress, and I know many, if not all, in the Congress will work with me." [Ford, 1975:389]

7. *Do the speaker's cognitive habits affect the style?* Jimmy Carter saw himself as a problem-solver, not as a politician. Thus, even though he worked hard as his rhetoric, it never worked well for him, largely because of his high Complexity scores (they were far higher than any other president). This professorial lexicon impressed "businesspersons who heard Carter refer knowingly to 'pension fund regulations,' 'small business initiatives,' 'energy pricing policy,' an 'upward spiral,' 'synthetic alternatives,' and 'windfall profits tax'" but no doubt bored educators who once heard him describe a " 'greatly magnified opportunity for the enhancement of better relationships' and who later were promised 'an encapsulation of what they can do in political motivation' when they returned home.' " [Hart, 1984c:162–3]

8. *Does the speaker's communicative history affect style?* Compared to his predecessors, Ronald Reagan had exceptionally low Embellishment ratings. Deprived of adjectives and adverbs, what does one have? Nouns and verbs. With only nouns and verbs, what can one do? Tell stories. A sportscaster in his

youth, an actor in early adulthood, and a pitchman for General Electric later on, Ronald Reagan was always a storyteller. Thus, even with defense budgets, Reagan could humanize ideas via narrative: "I received a letter from a young lad who's a sailor on one of our submarines. He said he was writing . . . on behalf of his 180 shipmates. And he said he just wanted us to know how good it felt to be an American. And he said, 'We may not have the biggest Navy in the world, but we've got the best' " [Reagan, 1981:1258].

More recent work with DICTION focused on the famed Senate hearings during which Supreme Court nominee Clarence Thomas was confronted by one of his former aides, Anita Hill, then a law professor at the University of Oklahoma, with the charge that he had taken sexual liberties with her some years earlier. The resulting furor pitted Hill against Thomas but, as history shows, Hill was unable to keep Thomas from rising to the highest court in the land.

According to Hart [1995], DICTION showed these hearings to be highly distinctive, almost a genre unto themselves. They had legalistic qualities (low on Human Interest and Embellishment, as well as Certainty) but they also had two traits rarely seen in a court of law: High Self-Reference and low Realism. These latter qualities gave the hearings their pyrotechnic quality: Hill and Thomas, as well as their defenders, were locked in a personal *and* ideological battle. And so they pontificated a great deal, far more than would have been permitted by a trial judge. The hearings were therefore part tent-revival and part *L.A. Law.* It was this hybridization, no doubt, that made many Americans stay up until 2:00 o'clock in the mornings to watch the hearings conclude.

Computer programs like DICTION are hardly omniscient. They cannot think; they can only count. They cannot deal with the majesty of style, just its plumbing. They cannot give final answers, just pose initial questions. Ultimately, it takes an intelligent critic to decide what the printouts say about lexicon. But as we have seen in both this chapter and the preceding one, style is so subtle that even an army of critics could not solve its mysteries entirely. If the computer can thereby free the critic from the more mundane work of sorting and counting words, it seems a useful adjunct to criticism. Given the complexity of style, the critic can always find better things to do than to sort and count.

CONCLUSION

Knowing about Ultimate Terms, Code Words, and individual lexicons is important in studying style but the critic's best tool is developing a sensitivity to word choice. It is this sort of sensitivity that Wallman [1981] demonstrated in her study of blue-collar British politics. She traced the ways in which the word "race" was used by a counterestablishment figure named Enoch Powell.

Wallman noted that Powell's discussions of "race" entered into the everyday conversations of British voters, even though the term was *not* used by them to designate skin color. Rather, they used Powell's rhetoric to explain virtually every problem then besetting them. Worries associated with immigration, unemployment, economic scarcity, urban violence, state monopolies, communists, and student demonstrators were all laid at the door of "the race issue." Powell's rhetoric was influential, Wallman observes, because it gave ordinary people a language to talk about their difficulties, even though many of its users had never heard of Enoch Powell.

Wallman's study demonstrates the essential message of this chapter: Words are important. This is true even though speakers often choose their words without thinking about them. Lexical study is therefore interesting because words never exist alone. They are always nestled in the company of other words, each of which produces its own special effect and each of which contributes to the overall impact of the message. These streams of words come tumbling rapidly, forcefully, sometimes chaotically, at listeners. At their most powerful, these words become a torrent, sweeping the audience into a sea of persuasion.

The critic stops all of this. By examining word choice carefully, often minutely, the critic becomes a spoil-sport, refusing to be carried off by an unexamined rhetoric. This is upsetting to persuaders, who prefer that listeners appreciate, rather than study, their words. That is why critics study them.

Chapter 9

ANALYZING MEDIA

Figure 9.1, a cover from *Newsweek* magazine, may contain all we need to know about persuasion in an age of media. After all, the mass media made Saddam Hussein a household name in the U.S. almost instantly and then caused him to be reviled as well. The *Newsweek* photo gives us the leering dictator and the pristine lad, perfect malevolence and perfect innocence—a fitting dialectic for a nation raised on Grimm's fairytales.

By reducing the War in the Gulf to a single image, *Newsweek* writes another chapter in the nation's visual history. Saddam-and-child are now nestled in our political memories with pictures of children burned by napalm in Vietnam, the Challenger shuttle bursting into flames, Rodney King being beaten senseless in Los Angeles, Cal Ripken trotting out on the field to begin his 2,131st consecutive baseball game. With an entire generation having been raised on these images, it is entirely possible that the American people can no longer think past their eyes.

The complexity of our very visual age is significant. In the case of *Newsweek*, for example, we have one medium (a magazine) reproducing an image from another medium (Iraqi TV), but only after it had been uplinked, downlinked, and then repackaged by CNN. And then there is the labeling of the image. *Newsweek* describes it as Saddam's "Horror Show," thereby asserting that the interchange is both horrible and contrived, a made-for-TV image. In its quick, efficient way, *Newsweek*'s labeling undoes Saddam's rhetoric of kindliness even while creating a counterrhetoric of its own.

FIGURE 9.1 *Newsweek* Cover of September 3, 1990

During the past forty years, the mass media have changed how we live. Because of television, we now eat differently (TV dinners), go to school differently (distance learning), buy clothes differently (The Home Shopping Channel), and entertain ourselves differently (*America's Funniest Home Videos*). The songs we sing are now visual (MTV), the athletes we revere are now beautiful (Michael Jordan), and the preachers we heed are now political (Pat Robertson). All of this happens with lightning speed, as satellites feed thousands of images across the globe and as huge computers search through them, discarding some and forwarding others to an editor's desk. Because these changes are so new, critics are only now beginning to ask the right questions about them. But even a cursory examination of the *Newsweek* cover shows that there are important—thoroughly rhetorical—questions to be answered:

- **Historical backdrop**—Did Americans look at *Newsweek*'s cover photo with eyes trained by other wars (Vietnam, for example), by other locales (Iran, for example), or by other Arabs (Muammar Qadhafi, for example)?

In other words, did the American people see this picture before they actually saw it?

- **Immediate context**—Why did readers accept the subtitle "Prisoners of War" when, at the time the photo was taken, no state of war existed between the U.S. and Iraq and no Western families were idling away in Iraqi jails? Is it possible that the narrative of the Gulf War was being subtly fashioned out of materials made available by Hollywood U.S.A.?

- **Linguistic set**—If *Newsweek* had titled the photo "Searching for Peace: Saddam Courts Western Guests," would readers have "seen" the picture differently, perhaps regarding it as a guileless, maybe even diplomatic, exchange between an Iraqi and a Westerner? Or does the picture have an "inherent" meaning regardless of how it is captioned?

- **Medium's credibility**—If the picture had been found on the cover of *The National Inquirer* would it have been less believable than it seemed in *Newsweek*? Would it have been more credible, or less credible, if it appeared in the *U.S. State Department Bulletin*? In *Mad* magazine? In *Photography Today*?

- **Viewer's perspective**—What might Iraqi citizens have seen in this picture? Would they have regarded the look in the lad's eye as an apprehensive one (as Americans did) or would they have seen a look of admiration? What might a Jordanian have seen? A Brazilian?

This chapter will examine the media through a rhetorical lens, studying how "policy options" are made available or denied by the pictures television creates. That lens is especially needed when it comes to the Gulf War. As historian Robert Dallek [1991:3] observes, "what makes war interesting for Americans is that we don't fight wars on our soil, we don't have direct experience of it, so there's an openness about the meanings we give to it. War for us is a tabula rasa, a blank slate, which we can turn into a moral crusade." Via television, journalists and politicians now artfully etch on that slate.

Consider, for example, the Gulf War's etchings [*Newsweek*, 1990–91]: (1) one press poll gave Americans five options for dealing with Saddam (including killing him), but none of the options involved diplomacy; (2) entrepreneurs used the mass media to market Saddam Hussein voodoo dolls and Halloween masks, causing one ad executive to say "everybody's trying to piggyback on Saddam's notoriety;" (3) a major newsweekly reported the possibility that Saddam was really Joseph Stalin's grandson (the report included side-by-side pictures of the two); (4) an ethics professor affirmed on *Larry King Live* that "we should wipe [Saddam] out without question," while another professor examined a CNN interview between Peter Arnett and Saddam Hussein and noted that Saddam blinked 113 times per minute, a rate the professor declared to be "frantic"; (5) England's Margaret Thatcher stated in one press conference that Saddam hid "behind the skirts of women and children," while George Bush declared in another that Saddam "plays with human beings as if they were pawns."

In other words, both the United States and its media establishment declared war on Iraq in 1991. Local TV news gorged itself on yellow ribbons tied to maple trees and Norman Schwartzkopf became an instant celebrity via his deftly managed briefings. Humorists like Steve Martin joined in ("if the press would keep talking about [Saddam's] mistress, his wife would kill him"), and the network news anchors showed endless footage of laser-guided missiles zeroing in on enemy bunkers. The Washington public relations firm, Hill and Knowlton, sold the war in the U.S. for the people of Saudi Arabia and, while some media personnel chafed under the wartime restraints imposed by the U.S. military, they passed on to the American people the military's carefully supplied visuals nonetheless.

The Gulf experience, in short, brought us the First Great Media War. President Bush knew that the nation had little stomach for a protracted conflict so he feverishly sold the war and the nation's media joined him. Thus, the *Newsweek* cover is part of a larger story of how war now requires a new delivery system—the mass media. As this chapter will show, almost everyone now requires the mass media. Advertisers and teamsters, preachers and senators, lawyers and fund-raisers, soldiers and comics—all now dance television's dance or they do not dance at all.

RHETORIC AND MEDIA

Because the study of visual persuasion is new, we do not yet have a standard way of discussing it. Some scholars (we might call them **Synthesizers**) argue that we simply need to modify existing models of rhetoric when examining media products. So, for example, they might urge us to catalogue the pictures contained in a political advertisement alongside its words and then gauge how these different forces complement one another. Other researchers (they might be called **Iconologists**) demand that we abandon all verbocentric notions when studying mediated texts. They argue that the visual/electronic world is a radically new one and that scholars ought not examine it with language-based assumptions. Iconologists have invented new terms—basic visual elements are called "memes" and missing photographic elements "elisions"—to deal with the "visual grammars" that affect how people perceive film or television.

We will not enter this controversy here. Instead, we will survey some practical ways of dealing with mass media products. Our approach will be a rhetorical one for we will focus on *how the verbal frames the visual in policy-relevant ways*. While rhetorical studies of the media are still in their infancy, some general principles are becoming clear:

1. *The mass media are changing people's mental habits.* The evidence for this proposition abounds: Modern political campaigns are skyrocketing in costs, largely because candidates feel they cannot "crack through" to the voter unless they have a large media budget. In addition, via the kind of publicity

only television can provide, criminals are now being caught (*America's Most Wanted*), third parties are being formed (Ross Perot), and national celebrities are being created overnight (Stephen Baldwin, Kato Kaelin, Shaquille O'Neal), largely because the media prize contemporary information over all other information.

In other words, people are beginning to learn differently as a result of the media, a notion that Georges Dukomel [Benjamin, 1969:238] predicted when he said that, with film, "I can no longer think what I want to think. My thoughts have been replaced by moving images." Overstatement, no doubt, but the hyperrealism and dramatic movement of the mediated image surely has a special kind of authority over us.

Robert Pittman [1990:19], creator of MTV, agrees with Benjamin when arguing that modern teenagers differ from their parents in the most fundamental way possible—in how they process information: "TV babies . . . seem to be processing information from different sources simultaneously. They can do homework, watch TV, talk on the phone and listen to the radio all at the same time. It's as if information from each source finds its way into a different cluster of thoughts. And at the end of the evening, it all makes sense."

Perhaps. But as Abraham and his colleagues [1995] found, MTV makes a *particular* kind of sense. They tested young people's reactions to public service announcements done in MTV style and found that while teenagers found the PSAs "more relevant" than traditional announcements, they actually learned less from them. As Abraham and company argue, the "positive effects of targeting young viewers [via MTV] may be achieved at the price of some loss of comprehension of the message, with possibly negative implications for education and public awareness campaigns on political and health issues."

2. *The mass media have a distinctive mode of authority.* Todd Gitlin [1980] has made a strong case for the following claim: It was television, primarily, that fueled the antiwar movement in the 1960s and it was television, primarily, that undid the movement as well. The media did so, says Gitlin, because they are unmoored by political principle. What moors them is omniscience, the need to become viewers' earliest and best source of information. This makes television a reliable delivery agent of the grand event but it also makes it an agent for the bizarre and the colorful. Viewers come to depend on these things, endlessly searching for the novel scene, the emerging voice. And so the media did to the antiwar movement what any fickle lover does: They treated the movement as a means (for increased ratings) rather than an end (for a particular political reality).

The issue of terrorism also raises questions about television's authority. The popular view is that of Britain's Margaret Thatcher [Picard, 1986:386], who noted the media's eagerness to cover the myriad explosions in Northern Ireland's pubs. The civilized world needs a way, Thatcher declared, "to starve the terrorists and hijackers of the oxygen of publicity on which they depend." As if to document her claim, the U.S.'s own Unabomber, a malign character who maimed dozens of people via letter bombs, paid homage to the media when demanding in 1995 that the *Washington Post* print his magnum opus in exchange for an end to the bombing. The *Post* complied and so did the Unabomber.

Two recent pieces of research also show the media's authority. An interesting study by Donsbach and his colleagues [1992] asked people to attend a political rally in person and then compared their reactions to those who had watched the same rally on television. They found that less than twenty percent of those who saw the event in person were negatively disposed to the speaker compared to almost 60% of those in the TV news audience. A different, but parallel, study compared the economic outlooks of watchers and nonwatchers. The result, says Hetherington [1996], were stark: Television viewers were much more pessimistic about the economy in 1992 than were the nonwatchers *even though there was no appreciable difference between their real-life economic circumstances*. In other words, when asked about the economy, viewers gave back the media's messages rather than reporting the contents of their wallets.

3. The mass media appear to be unmediated. According to Hart [1994: 60], television creates an "arrogance of the eye," a feeling that anything seen is, in fact, fact. Television constantly genuflects in front of us, making it seem stupid not to "believe what we have seen with our own eyes." We watch the O. J. Simpson trial and gauge his innocence or guilt with ease. We see Harry Connick, Jr., on *Entertainment Tonight* and feel we know him truly. Television appears to give us all of the Simpson and Connick that can be known.

But television is a *medium,* a coming-between. We were not there to ask O. J. our own questions but saw only the parts of him deemed seeable by the networks. Too, the on-stage Connick politely shielded the off-stage Connick from our prying eyes, thereby giving us the sense-of-Connick but not the all-of-Connick. Perhaps this is what Henry Fairlie [1980:E1] means when he says that "if you see it on television, it did not happen."

How can Fairlie say such a thing? When we watch a football game on television, after all, do we not watch real people playing a real game in real space and time? Yes and no. Television does not give us *all* of the game, after all. It shows us more of the players than the spectators, more of the quarterback than the linesmen, more of the sideline announcers than the popcorn vendor, more of the running backs than the blocking backs, more of the good teams than the sorry teams. When watching a TV game we see only what we have been allowed to see.

Television's power comes from two things: (1) it edits what it receives and (2) it hides the effects of that editing. So, for example, research by Adams [1986] shows that television is rarely a window on the world but is carefully adapted to its local audience. Adams found that coverage of natural disasters bore little relationship to the severity of the disaster. Rather, such coverage was heavily determined by the political importance of the affected country to the United States. In other words, viewers seem to get a complete view of the world when, in fact, they only get the news that is fit to see.

4. *The mass media produce multidimensional texts.* The power of pictures is undeniably important but as Gumpert and Cathcart [1985:28] point out, pictures are "influenced by other factors such as genre, context, and the other sensory modalities" (like sound and texture). That is, a picture rarely means one thing since it is composed of sometimes rival subelements and because language gives it a context (that is, a con-text). Nowhere was this truer than in the famed Rodney King case, in which, despite a videotaped record of the beating, a jury acquitted the Los Angeles police of all wrongdoing (the verdict was later overturned). Political cartoonist Paul Conrad captured the irony of this result in Figure 9.2.

FIGURE 9.2 Paul Conrad on the Rodney King Incident

ONE PICTURE IS WORTH ZERO

Courtesy of Paul Conrad; reprinted by permission, Los Angeles Times Syndicate

During the first King trial, the videotape was played again and again—in slow-motion, in stop-action, at full speed, in reverse, frame-by-frame—until overuse drained it of meaning. In addition, the defense constantly told the jury how to view the video. Eventually, a sufficient number of jurors "saw" things the defense's way. As Roland Barthes [1985:29] explains, in such cases language is used to direct the viewer "among the various signifieds of the image, causing him to avoid some and to accept others; through an often subtle dispatching, it teleguides him toward a meaning selected in advance." Rather amazingly in the King case, the defense's interpretations were offered *after* the videos had been seen by the jurors, and still the defense was able to dislodge their powerful first impressions.

Language can also *pre-exist* a visual as "latent registers of phantasy, memory, and knowledge" [Burgin, 1983:235] tell a viewer how to view a stimulus. These registers instruct a news photographer, for example, which pictures to take for the morning newspaper (a traffic accident, for example, rather than a bowling match), thereby revealing the lurid agenda favored by today's media. In a similar vein, Davies and Walton [1983] discovered that newsworkers in Germany treated an Italian assassination as a *political* event, while their U.S. counterparts ran it as a *criminal* story, thus shedding light on the different ideologies guiding the two nations.

5. *The mass media carry their own, compelling logic.* In a media-saturated age, people think and act differently. A famous example of this occurred in 1984 when CBS commentator Lesley Stahl sharply denounced the Reagan administration's manipulation of the American people. Stahl showed a series of lush photo opportunities in which President Reagan pressed the flesh and mouthed sweet nothings to the assembled crowds, all of whom were trapped in a sea of red, white, and blue balloons. Stahl decried the emptiness of the scene, upbraiding the President for pandering to the American people and avoiding the important issues of the day.

While Stahl fully expected to incur the wrath of the White House for her documentary, she was shocked to receive a pleasant thank-you instead for depicting the President in warm, patriotic scenes, wrapped in the embrace of appreciative crowds. Stahl learned that, despite her negative commentary, pictures count a great deal in television, with viewers often discounting what they hear while remembering what they see.

It is for this reason, says Hart [1987], that presidents now spend so much time speaking in ceremonial settings (see Figure 9.3). Because political ceremonies televise so well, presidents are using them instead of more contentious formats like press conferences and briefings. "If you want us on the nightly news," presidents are telling reporters, "do it on our terms, not yours." To ensure such coverage, White House handlers are now attuned to media deadlines, carefully arranging the president's schedule so that he is seen in crowd-receptive formats just in time for the nightly news.

Without question, then, the mass media place new demands on the rhetorical critic. They require a new language of description as well as a new

FIGURE 9.3 Presidential Use of Speech Settings

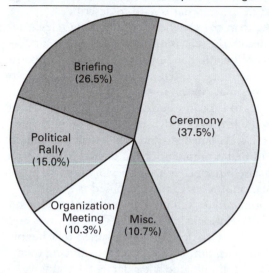

language of critique. Visual images do not sit placidly waiting for the critic to discover them. Instead, they are folded into a dynamic and complex matrix of stimuli, parts of which—or all of which—may affect an audience. As a result, new questions arise each day: How are children affected by the tens of thousands of commercials they watch before becoming adults? Do situation comedies like *Seinfeld* makes us more convivial? Does a show like *Roseanne* make us more cynical? Is international reporting bringing the world closer together, or is it merely providing new data for old prejudices? These are new questions and they require new moves from the rhetorical critic.

PERCEIVING TELEVISION

In *Seducing America: How Television Charms the American Voter,* Hart [1994] argues that to understand fully the power of television, a critic must look at it **phenomenologically.** Phenomenology is the study of how people perceive the world around them. It begins with the artist Cezanne's assumption that "nature is on the inside" [Spurling, 1977:46], that the most important stuff in life is easy to feel but difficult to explain because it is buried so deeply within us.

Phenomenology assumes, for example, that a child will instinctively experience an almost tactile thrill when a brass band comes marching down the street. But why? What is it, specifically, that creates the tingling down the child's back? Is it sight or sound, motion or color, massed humanity or brass instrumentation, anticipation or actuality, the general or the particular, or all of these things together? A good phenomenologist tries to answer such questions by giving language to the emotions the child feels, by digging "up what is buried in our everyday, unthinking and prereflective experience" [Spurling, 1977:50]. The phenomenologist describes what is hard to describe.

Nothing is harder to describe than the experience of watching television. That may sound odd. Perhaps watching television seems eminently understandable—body slumped, shoes off, beer in hand, brain on hold. This is complex? But what seems simple and sedentary is often neither. If nature is indeed on the inside, our sedentary watcher may not be so sedentary after all.

In *Seducing America*, Hart tries to explain some of the deeper pleasures of television, the deepest of which is the **intimacy** it delivers. Television puts viewers in touch with rock stars, athletes, and comedians and then lets viewers plumb their depths. Television informs us that a president of the United States wears boxer shorts (or was it briefs?), that a Supreme Court Justice did not like pubic hairs in his soft drink, that each star on *Melrose Place* was abused as a child.

There is nothing that television will not tell us. This builds what Horton and Wohl [1986] call "para-social" relationships between TV characters and their viewers. So, for example, Johnny Carson often complained that people would begin sidewalk conversations with him without ever introducing themselves. Because the *Tonight* show had illuminated their darkened boudoirs so regularly over the years, Carson's viewers felt they knew him personally. Johnny Carson seemed to be their neighbor, but who among them had ever borrowed his lawnmower?

Brummett and Duncan [1992:229] argue that television is powerful because (1) it is voyeuristic (I see others without being seen in return), (2) it is fetishistic (being knowledgeable about television shows gives me social power), and (3) it is narcissistic (TV's messages are directed at "my" personal life.). Because of these features, television now affects how politicians and voters make decisions. The 1992 presidential debate in Richmond provides an example. During the debate, a citizen asked the candidates the following question: "How has the national debt personally affected each of your lives? And if it hasn't, how can you honestly find a cure for the economic problems of the common people if you have no experience in what's ailing them?"

In response, Ross Perot launched into a discussion of his grandchildren, Bill Clinton talked about his experience in rural America, and George Bush fell flat on his face:

> Moderator: Thank you, Mr. Perot. Mr. President.
> Bush: Well, I think the national debt affects everybody.
> Moderator: You personally.
> Bush: Obviously it has a lot to do with interest rates—
> Moderator: She's saying, "you personally." You, on a personal basis. How has it affected you? Has it affected you personally? [Bush, 1992:35–6]

Poor George Bush. He ultimately made three or four more false starts but ultimately flummoxed the assignment entirely.

Why? Because he was brought up in a pretelevision era and hence knew not the language of intimacy. His uptight, cerebral rhetoric was off the mark, as was his awkward body posture (he tried to half-sit on a tall stool during the debate) and his inability to make personal contact with his questioners. In general, he forgot, or had never learned, the iron law of television: Be intimate or begone.

This law is a law, says Schmuhl [1990:99], because people are increasingly "cocooning" themselves at home, alone except for a gaggle of electronic devices. As a result, they begin to think in private ways about public officials. Instead of asking themselves "What is the candidate's platform on the environment?" they talk to themselves this way: "The candidate is almost in tears when she talks about the environment. She must really care. Or maybe she can't handle the pressure of the debate. I wonder if all this talk about her pending divorce is true. And why is she wearing that particular dress? It's wrong with her hair coloring. But I'm glad she's still jogging regularly. . . ."

In other words, television is a mass medium that presents itself as a coffee klatch. According to Gumpert and Drucker [1992:195], electronic home shopping is a case in point. When the host interacts with a call-in viewer, the researchers argue, "fragments of personal discourse punctuate the air: 'Hi, how are you today, good to hear from you. . . . Who are you buying this for? . . . Your 14-year-old niece will love this." Only occasionally does the host suggest "Why don't you tell everybody why you ordered more of these so they will know what they would be missing." Being this bold would call attention to the public nature of the interaction, thereby piercing the veil of intimacy disguising the show's mercantile purposes.

Rawlence [1979:63] argues that the television audience "never has a sense of itself as an audience—only as individuals." Why is this important? Because it gives the viewer a sense of empowerment, a feeling of control over the interaction. The emblem of that empowerment is the remote control device, which says, in effect, "I and I alone will decide which message is granted access to my cranium."

Television also achieves intimacy by fitting in neatly with our everyday worlds. A morning newscast blends into a soap opera into an half-hour infomercial into a British documentary into late night comedy into Brazilian soccer at 3:00 a.m. As a result, says Langer [1981:356], "television's 'flow' is contemporaneous with the flow of life. So, not only is television 'always already available, there will be something to watch immediately, as soon as the set warms up." In other words, television never announces itself. It becomes our unassuming friend from morning to night.

Genuine intimacy implies informality. An intimate relationship is one in which the rules of engagement are relaxed, in which people can speak to one another spontaneously and without fear of censure. Television adheres to these rules, too, giving viewers a sense of control even as it seeks to wrest control away from them. Carpignano and his colleagues [1990:117] argue that this explains why "talk television" is so popular. These shows inevitably trivialize discourse and pander to viewers' most basic instincts as, for example, when Morton Downey, Jr., "physically threatens his guests, the women sexually, the men with 'wiping the floor up' with them." Such crude displays, say Carpignano et al., rule out all elite notions like expertise. Television puts everyone—performers and viewers alike—on the same level. In so doing it tells viewers that they are in charge of their lives and that nobody—nobody—stands above them.

What is the effect of television's intimacy? To addict us. Television's power comes from its constant willingness to keep us company and, also, because it refuses to treat itself as powerful. Its informality gives us freedom and its remote control devices give us creativity. A free, creative viewer, however, can also become cocky. The critic tries to warn people about that.

EXPLORING VISUAL SYMBOLS

Because we live in a visual age, pictures count as never before. Documenting that claim is Lester [1994] who surveyed fifty years of magazine coverage, recording the number of times African Americans had been depicted in such outlets as *Time, Newsweek,* and *Life.* He discovered that blacks dramatically increased their presence, ranging from an invisible 1.1% of the pictures in the 1930s to almost 9% fifty years later. Moreover, blacks were increasingly depicted in advertisements as well as sports photos, in public forums and also in everyday scenes.

Lester found that the *quality* of minority coverage escalated too, with the early, stereotypical pictures of blacks giving way in the 1950s and 1960s to civil rights scenes and, later, to images of African Americans working within The System. Transformations like these are important, since the media's pictures are often precursors to larger societal changes. So, for example, unless an activist group can deliver stirring visuals in time for the nightly news (oil-soaked beaches for environmentalists, bruised bodies for gay rights advocates) or unless a rally can be held in eminently photographable locations (outside a medical clinic for antiabortionists, in front of the White House for a rainbow of other groups), persuasion suffers.

Out-of-sight, in other words, has become out-of-mind. But how do pictures persuade? And why are some more powerful than others? Do visuals follow the same rules guiding verbal rhetoric? Does language inevitably "frame" visuals, making them meaningless until captioned by an enterprising persuader?

The great modernist painter Pablo Picasso had a clear answer to the latter question: NO! "I don't want there to be three or four thousand possibilities of interpreting my canvass," said Picasso [Worth, 1981:172], "I want there to be only one." Picasso expanded on this position:

Otherwise a painting is just an old grab bag for everyone to reach into and *pull out what he himself has put in*. I want my paintings to be able to defend themselves, to resist the invader, just as though there were razor blades on all the surfaces so no one could touch them without cutting his hands. A painting isn't a market basket or a woman's handbag, full of combs, hairpins, lipstick, old love letters and keys to the garage.

Picasso's notion of "visual inherency" is obviously debatable. At times, no doubt, pictures force a single meaning on us. A snapshot of a department store Santa Claus with a youngster astride his knee will probably not be interpreted as a Satanic ritual or as some sort of bizarre, athletic event. That picture means good cheer, youthful exuberance, fanciful expectations, and little more.

But pictures like this are also rare. Most visuals are replete with several meanings, unprotected by Picasso's razor blades. The picture of a drought-afflicted Biafran child, for example, could represent (1) the luck of the geographical draw, (2) the divine will of an inscrutable God, (3) the evils of agrarian communism, or (4) the moral bankruptcy of an uncaring West. That same picture could also be found (5) in a medical textbook on malnutrition, (6) in an anthropological study of tribal kinship, (7) in a U.N.E.S.C.O. brochure on political realignment, or (8) clutched in the hand of a dying Biafran father.

Because pictures are "rivalrous" in this way, critics must ask complicated questions of visual texts. It is not enough to ask *what* a picture means. One must also ask *how* a picture means. There are countless such trajectories but here we will focus on four basic ones:

1. Does the visual image carry ideological force? That is, does it grow out of a systematically articulated belief system? Ideological images surround us. Pictures of the pope in his priestly garments, for example, signal a person set apart from the world of business suits, a person who deals with matters more mysterious than those addressed at Citibank. A photo of men walking down Wall Street in their business suits, on the other hand, suggests a uniformity to the world of commerce, a place where people dress alike because they honor the same bottom line. Pictures of the pope in swimming togs can be unnerving, as can pictures of women wearing ties and sports coats. The first image implies ideological slippage: Can a pope remain infallible on the beach at St. Tropez? The second image can promote ideological antagonism: Isn't it enough that they are taking "our" jobs? Must they also appropriate "our" uniform?

All cultures achieve distinctiveness through their icons. Pictures of the Arc de Triomphe tells Parisians they are cultured and subtle; Australia's kangaroo paraphernalia characterize it as an outdoors, muscular society; one cannot think of England without thinking of Westminister Abbey—traditional, stolid, hierarchial, remote. The United States, too, is known by its icons: the Statue of Liberty for democratic governance, Trump Tower for free-market entrepeneurism, Yankee Stadium for boisterous plebianism.

According to Olson [1987], however, the early United States was much less sure of itself. Its icons reflected that. His study focuses on two images that vied for popularity in the early colonies, each of which contained significant ideological freight.

In Figure 9.4 we see one of the earliest political icons in the United States. Benjamin Franklin's "Join or Die," an image first published in the *Pennsylvania Gazette* on May 9, 1754, clearly sought to whip the colonies into a new kind of confederation. This is a bold and unrelenting image, its animalistic aspect suggesting a nation of rugged pioneers but its disjointed aspect suggesting the need for a new kind of political fraternity. But according to Olson, Franklin created "Join or Die" to bring the colonies together for economic reasons, not to defy Mother England. As is so often true with visual rhetoric, however, "Join or Die" quickly took on a life of its own and came to symbolize the need for true separation from Great Britain.

Knowing that, Franklin produced a second icon, "Magna Britannia," in 1765 (Figure 9.5). Like its forerunner, this image exhorts the colonies to pull together. But note that England herself is the focal point here, with the colonies serving as her appendages. Franklin is warning his fellow colonists

FIGURE 9.4 Benjamin Franklin's "Join or Die" (*Pennsylvania Gazette*. May 9, 1754, p. 2, col. 2, designer: Benjamin Franklin, publisher: Benjamin Franklin and David Hall, media: newspaper, size: 2" x 2⅞", photograph courtesy of the Library of Congress.)

FIGURE 9.5 Benjamin Franklin's "Magna Britannia" ("MAGNA Britannia: her colonies REDUC'D." circa January 1766, designer: Benjamin Franklin, media: single sheet, size: $4^1/8$" x $5^7/8$", photograph courtesy of the Library Company of Philadelphia.)

(and the Lords back in London) that if certain economic and political matters remain unaddressed, all will be lost. Franklin is peddling both subordination and interdependence here, trying to blunt the radicalism of "Join or Die," which, by this time, had taken on strident ideological overtones as it circulated among the early colonists.

Like so many nations, the United States began in political turmoil, as well as in political iconography. As Franklin's experience shows, a persuader can easily lose control over an image as secondary persuaders respond to, and then reappropriate, its elements. Even ostensibly innocent images can become embroiled in such ideological give-and-take. In the early 1990s, for example, underground murmurings had it that Proctor and Gamble's rather enigmatic logo—a bearded man-in-the-moon amidst a cluster of stars—proved that the company was sponsoring devil worship. The rumors persisted for so long and became so feverish that the company eventually spent several million dollars to have its logo shorn of the offending associations. In a rhetorical world, it seems, there is no such thing as visual innocence.

2. *What condensations can be found in the visual image? Does the image act as a synecdoche for a particular set of ideas?* In her book *Eloquence in an Electronic Age*, Jamieson [1988a] argues that television's pictures are now the central carriers of political information. Media events like pouring blood on draft cards during the Vietnam War or burning bras during the early women's'

movement became synecdoches for a rebellious generation. Traditionalists use visuals too. No one was better at doing so than Ronald Reagan, who used horse-riding to signal youthful energy, the beaches of Normandy to signal his political vision, football games at Notre Dame to signal basic American values. Reagan had an eye for what others liked to see and so he used the world around him to tell his stories.

A captivating visual is captivating in two senses: (1) it "contains" an idea or ideology, eliminating its extraneous or complicating aspects to make it more compelling; (2) it reduces the interpretations an audience can make, filling their eyes with a single, dominant meaning. Political cartoonists are particularly adept in this regard. In *Doonesbury*, for example, Gary Trudeau represented George Bush as a feather, implying that the President could not think weighty thoughts. Trudeau reduced Bush's successor, Bill Clinton, to a waffle because he continually shifted political positions. Like all gifted reductionists, Trudeau zeroed in on exactly the right vulnerability. The deftness of his touch is proven by the anguished outcries of those he skewered.

According to Bostdorff [1987:52], synecdoche is naturally attractive to cartoonists because they operate in "the limited space and complexity of a one panel drawing." Quite often, says Bostdorff, cartoonists bring incongruous elements together in the same frame, as when Dwane Powell of the *Los Angeles Times* depicted former Interior Secretary James Watt as a troop leader escorting a group of Boy Scouts through a "forest" composed of oil derricks (Watt was pro-business). Combining youthful naivete and calamitous devastation produced **counterpoint** for Powell, making Secretary Watt one-dimensional. The best cartoons, that is, do not work us very hard.

A fine study along these same lines was undertaken by Goldman and colleagues [1991], who showed how corporate America has tapped into what they call "commodity feminism," a quality on display in a Vanity Fair ad for "the high performance fitness bra." At first it appears to be a flattering portrayal of the modern woman: healthy, athletic, professional, only slightly indulgent. Goldman and his colleagues note that certain signs (the athletic-looking model holds a towel and a water bottle) stand for *feminist* goals of independence and professional success while other signs (a demure smile) connote a more traditional *femininity*. "The mass media signify femininity," argue the authors, by visually emphasizing the line and curve of the female body along with a code of poses, gestures, body cants, and gazes.

This visual lexicon has become so familiar that we "now accept the signifier, e.g., the close up curve of a calf or the hip or an ear lobe, to stand for the feminine." [p. 337] The authors also note that, in the ad, "the male world of commerce and status forms a silent, but present, party" to the dialogue between the feminine and the feminist. Rather than being a slave to the male world, the ad implies, the feminine feminist balances her work life with "privileged access to her own sensual body."

In a radically different study, Kaplan [1990] found a similar relationship between the old and the new. Kaplan surveyed advertisements for home computers and found them blending traditional values like workmanship and enduring quality with newer bounties like speed, efficiency, and complexity. In both studies, advertising served as a synthetic force, reducing people to their elemental needs even though some of these needs turn out to be oppositional when examined carefully.

3. *What significant tensions can be found in the visual image? Are these tensions easily resolved or are they deep and abiding?* Jamieson [1984:449–50] argues that some images are "promiscuous" in that they contain many, often contrary, submeanings. Even the American flag can be read in this way, with the bars representing the original colonies and the fifty stars representing the modern states. This flag-image is so familiar by now that we rarely attend to the problems it hides—thirteen of the states (Massachusetts, Pennsylvania, Virginia, etc.) receive "double-billing" by being given both stars and bars. The remaining thirty-seven are short-changed. In addition, six of the colonies receive *long* bars while the other seven get *short* ones (intercepted as they are by the field of stars). Worse yet, some of the colonies are assigned a white bar (purity, innocence) while the rest are blood red. In other words, even though the flag was designed to soothe intracolonial tensions, it still retains those tensions.

Are we overreading the flag here? After all, no modern American notices such tensions. Precisely. The flag works its magic by "containing" its tensions. Over time we have come to see the flag holistically, as a testament to the *United* States. But are interstate tensions a thing of the past? In an era of welfare cost-shifting, Medicare fund-matching, and differential immigration pressures, does not each state still have forty-nine rivals? In short, the United States may have one flag but that flag still contains its diversity, even though its rhetoric hides that fact from us.

An interesting study by Gallagher [1995] extends this line of thinking. Her study reminds us that, unlike the American flag, some icons cannot hide their tensions successfully. Her exemplar is the Martin Luther King, Jr., Memorial in Atlanta. Architecturally, says Gallagher, the Memorial is part mausoleum, part church, part library, part office building, and part school. The Memorial's complexity derives from the tensions in African-American life itself: It cannot "afford" to be just a burial place or a church since it sits in a neighborhood hit hard by economic calamity. It must be an office building as well as a school since commerce and education are the keys to success in the United States. These conflicting needs cost the icon rhetorical integration, says Gallagher, but it also represents the complexity of the task King faced. Rhetorical integration can wait, King might have said, until racial integration becomes a reality.

A similar kind of analysis is that of Foss [1986] who examined the "statements" made by the Vietnam Veterans Memorial in Washington, D.C. The key thing about this Memorial, says Foss, is that it violates "conventional form." As we see in Figure 9.6, the much-heralded (and maligned) black granite wall is low, not high; black, not white; personal, not abstract. People approach it intimately—touching its engraved names, leaving personal notes and poems, walking along its parabola of names to retrace the war's death count. "No heroic action is depicted to suggest bravery and nobility and to generate a sense of patriotism," says Foss [p. 332], "and no inscription quotes a general or a president on the goals or benefits of war to remind us of American values." Instead, the wall is pure wall—opaque, steadfast, inscrutable.

The wall's inscrutability is fitting since, twenty-five years after the war ended, Americans are still trying to discern its meaning. The Wall is a testament to the people who fought and died but not to the uncertain cause for which they fought. Given the turmoil of that war, it is not surprising that the Vietnam Memorial has grown over the years. The trio of soldiers in Figure 9.7 was added to appease American traditionalists. Later, the nurses in Figure 9.8 joined them to represent the sacrifices of the nation's women.

And so in a curious way the Vietnam Memorial represents its era. Its three components now "argue" with one another each day, just as the nation argued passionately during the war. This fractiousness may make it a postmodern

FIGURE 9.6 The Original Vietnam War Memorial

FIGURE 9.7 First Supplement to the Vietnam War Memorial

memorial, as Blair and her colleagues [1991] have declared. But that makes sense too, since the war had so many different meanings for so many different persons that it ultimately lost its meaning altogether.

As Savage [1994:135] has said, "public monuments do not arise as if by natural law to celebrate the deserving; they are built by people with sufficient power to marshal (or impose) public consent for their erection." Icons and monuments are created because time is fleeting, memories short, and life confusing. We resort to public displays to settle things down, to make one last argument about that which has gone before. Because the past is often conflict-ridden it produces symbolic tensions. The critic seeks out those tensions, treating them as guides to a complex world the visual has tried to make simple.

FIGURE 9.8 Second Supplement to the Vietnam War Memorial

ANALYZING MEDIA CONTENT

Judging by the proliferation of scholarship in the area, mass media content has never been more heavily scrutinized. Many of these studies have taken a rhetorical approach, examining the policy-endorsing or policy-undermining aspect of the media. Often, they have focused on politicians and social movement leaders (i.e., traditional rhetors), but here we will concentrate on less obvious kinds of influence—advertising, the news, and popular entertainment—and see how these powerful forces insinuate themselves into our lives.

The Rhetoric of Advertising

Halliday and his colleagues [1990] have made an important observation about modern advertising: it subsumes almost all other discourse within it. On any given night in any American home a viewer can see—in thirty seconds or less—turmoil and pity, pathos and impossibility, love and honor, as well as talking cats, dancing toilet bowls, and the Fifth Cavalry on the march. Each societal discourse, each human emotion, submits to the lash of the modern advertiser. Advertisers "graze" over the cultural landscape, grabbing each relevant emotion, each common experience, and then retrofitting them for a product pitch. Advertising begins within us and ends within us. It knows what we know and feels what we feel. It absorbs our most sacred historical moments and connects them to a magical future time, a place where all is perfect (and cheaper, and slimmer, and newer, and less toxic).

Figure 9.9 is an ordinary advertisement for an ordinary product—a device for making business graphics. But it is also an *extra*ordinary advertisement. It places its product on a literal pedestal, a pancultural sign of power and authority, and surrounds it with an ancient piece of alabaster. It gives us a human Athena and a cybernetic Athena, even though Athena herself was neither. If Athena had taken human form, it would seem, she surely would have resembled a Greek woman rather than the light-skinned blonde posed here.

But these are quibbles, and advertising brooks no quibbles. Advertising carves out its own territory and then becomes voracious, reducing ancient folklore to the pragmatic: "Simple, yet brilliant. Like the lady herself." Advertising creates its own rhetorical space, disorienting the reader in order to reorient the reader. It blends the human (Athena) with the nonhuman (the computer) and also the aesthetic (her form, her flower) with the prosaic (comparative statistics, price break-points, etc.). It promises an unlikely thing—a relationship with a goddess—and does so in a typically American way—speedily, efficiently ("just use the reader service card").

As Chapman and Eggar [1983] suggest, critics need to examine an advertisement's **referent systems,** those desirable values and moods enjoyed by Group A that become the envy of Group B. Our ad collects a host of these jealousies: Ideal people are practical (a MicroVAX II product is only $565) but also whimsical ("something for framing. A poster calendar of the lovely ATHENA"). They are resolute and competent ("Forecasts, trends, shares, budgets, demographics") but they can also be intimidated by group opinion ("ATHENA has been critically acclaimed in all leading journals"). And ideal people are at home in the heavenly hierarchy even while they embrace the democratic mandate ("anyone in the office can understand and work with ATHENA"). Advertising is a pluralistic discourse, enticing all, refusing none.

According to Leiss and his colleagues [1990], Figure 9.9 is a fairly typical modern advertisement. Surveying the research, they note the following trends: (1) "status ads" (a heavenly goddess, for example) have increased over

FIGURE 9.9 The Goddess and the Machine

time, as have (2) lifestyle ads (e.g., the white-on-white elegance of the ATHENA ad suggests a bourgeois culture). In addition, (3) compared to earlier times, products themselves are rarely the focus of today's advertisements, having been replaced by "poetic distractions" suggesting escape or luxury. Also, like our ATHENA example, (4) modern ads emphasize themes of self-transformation—they do not reflect what people are *doing* but what they are *dreaming*. And, curiously enough, (5) actual product users are depicted less-and-less often these days (no bespectacled nerds in our ATHENA ad, for example).

Advertising guru Tony Schwartz [Leiss, 1990:301] has observed that, in a highly litigious and accident-prone world, advertisers get into trouble when making claims about their products. So they don't. They make claims about other things. The Maytag Corporation, for example, refuses to guarantee a fault-free washing machine but does produce heart-rending vignettes about its lonely repairman. As we see in Figure 9.10, "utility appeals" have dropped off in advertising over time while "sensual appeals" have steadily risen. Why is this important? Because it means advertising has become a **cultural discourse,** not just a mercantile one. And why is that important? Because cultural discourses affect policy preferences in the most basic of all ways.

In other words, there is a politics of advertising. According to Christopher Lasch [Leiss, 1990:26], advertising does not sell specific products as much as it promotes consuming as a way of life. Advertising keeps us in a constant state of dissatisfaction so the nation's economic engine can run at top speed. After World War II, say Leiss and his colleagues [1990:52], advertising took on an "anxiety format" in which the fear of social mortification (keeping up with the Joneses, etc.) became a dominant theme. As a result, despite *real changes* in economic growth during the postwar years, the number of people who rate themselves as "very happy" has not changed.

The ultimate effect of advertising, according to Gitlin [1987], is to make us politically docile. After all, a society that sees consumption as its raison d'être has precious little time to throw itself into political causes, thus leaving affairs of state in traditional hands. Advertising does so via its escapist, antiestablishment appeals. The modern jeans ad featuring the "loner" with a "blank and cynical" look, says Gitlin, sends out a series of clear political

FIGURE 9.10 Changing Emphases in Advertising over Time

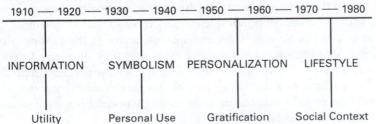

messages: Power has already corrupted society; do not get involved; consume instead; that will teach them.

There is another sense in which advertising is escapist. Politics deals with the concrete and the tangible—What is the best route for the new highway? Should the United States intervene in Bosnia?—while the world of advertising is decidedly abstract. It deals in essences, not forms; feelings, not practices. According to Geis [1982], it accomplishes much of this work through language. For example, advertising uses **abstract nouns** rather than concrete nouns (e.g., "more tomato for your money" vs. "more tomatoes for your money") and also **weak verbs** rather than strong ones (e.g., "Dawn *helps* keep grease away" or "AC filters *help* protect your engine"). In addition, we find in advertising an abundance of **elliptical comparatives** in which the product being advertised is compared to an unmentioned norm (e.g., "Carlton—the lighter 100" or "Super Plenium—the higher-potency vitamin."). Finally, **mysterious modals** imply a large world (e.g., "many people say it relieves their pain" or "most folks swear by it") but specify a much smaller one.

Scholars are only beginning to discover advertising's effects, but there seems little doubt that advertising has become part of the modern consciousness. We sing the jingles absent-mindedly, our politicians quote ad copy more often than the Constitution, we stay fixed in our seats during halftime of the Super Bowl waiting for the blockbuster ads. But what is advertising saying about us as a nation? After all, advertisers are often the first to spot emerging trends in society and then to exploit those trends. Thus, the critic is wise to look over the shoulders of the advertiser and to see how they go about making us believers of a certain sort.

THE RHETORIC OF NEWS

It took a fairly long time for critics to look at the news rhetorically. Traditional reporters, after all, had surrounded themselves with the trappings of objectivity, declaring to the world "Nothing but the facts here; look elsewhere for persuasion." A news documentary for example, does not have the "scars of mediation and transformation" [Silverstone, 1986:81] to signal it has been manufactured from odds and ends. And so there has been a tendency to trust documentarists implicitly and to discount the often arbitrary decisions they make.

Scholars have been rethinking this approach to the news. Patterson [1993], for example, found the news producing an **alternative authority structure** in recent years, with the voices of political leaders increasingly being de-emphasized in favor of news personnel. Hart and his colleagues [1984d] report a similar finding. Focusing on televised news coverage, they discovered that U.S. presidents were directly quoted in only 8 of the 45 broadcasts sampled *even though the newscasts dealt exclusively with the president's most recent speech!* In other words, the news establishment is increasingly positioning itself as an independent source of political authority.

Griffin [1992] investigated how this is done. Focusing on television's visual conventions, he observes that the mass media use "symbols of access" (e.g., stand-up footage in front of the White House, the Capitol, or the Pentagon) to suggest that they and they alone can enter the corridors of power. Similarly, they use "signs of information"—on-location photos in far-flung places, for example—to give viewers the sense that television is omniscient. So, for example, one plane crash story carried less than 30 seconds of on-site video in its 3-minute lead story. But the footage was sufficiently spread out during the report so that it seemed both authentic and comprehensive. Griffin says these few shots were used to

> metonymically represent the drama of rescue. Most of the report is taken up with interviews filmed away from the crash. The use of a few selected images to represent a much larger story and more complex series of events is especially evident in the way this story centers on the shot of the little girl crying from the top of the plane's tail section. This shot is longer than the rest, includes a camera zoom for emphasis, and is paired with interview footage of a rescue worker identifying this as his most-vivid memory. The editing and placement of this shot have made it a central dramatic symbol for the rescue story. [pp. 135–6]

The rhetoric of the news, then, is a rhetoric of authority, with news institutions constantly making bids for preeminence. One such bid can be seen in how the press covers politics. Hart and his colleagues [1990] inspected some four hundred news stories in *Time* magazine between 1945 and 1985. As seen in Figure 9.11, the presidency has been described as increasingly besieged over the years: (1) international crisis, material want, lapses of character, etc. (as summarized in an overall Difficulty Score) have steadily climbed, as has (2) Behavioral Disagreement between the president and Congress, the president and the electorate, the president and the press, etc.

Have presidential traumas *fundamentally* increased over the years, or have only *descriptions* of that institution changed? That is a complex question and perhaps an unanswerable one. But one thing seems clear: The press has found it convenient to feature political turmoil. Institutionally, this is a useful choice because it allows the press to portray itself as a politically neutral, and therefore slightly superior, profession. Rhetorically, it has allowed the media to tell a suspenseful story. As all dramatists know, conflict sells. As political dramatists know, conflict at the highest echelons sells especially well. Notions like these now seem to guide political reporting in the United States.

But these approaches come at a cost: Milburn and McGrail [1992] found that overly vivid reporting actually *decreases* an audience's ability to learn from the news or to think in complex ways about public affairs. Worse, Kerbel [1994] discovered that strategically oriented, conflict-ridden coverage makes the electorate cynical, causing them to lose faith in democratic governance. Most dangerous of all are the findings of Jamieson and Cappella [1996], who found that such coverage can actually decrease the likelihood of voting.

FIGURE 9.11 Changes in Political Coverage over Time

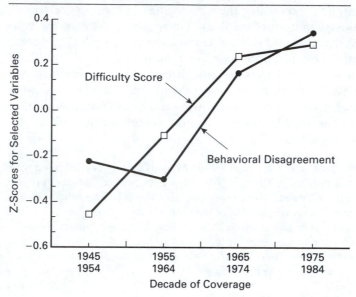

Our discussion thus far suggests a jealous relationship between journalism and the political mainstream. But this is not to say the American media offer a fundamental critique of the western, capitalistic mandate. In fact, numerous scholars have shown how the rhetoric of news is a **source of system maintenance.** For example, Miller [1987] notes that while newscasters often smirk at the *individuals* holding office, they rarely call into question basic aspects of the American creed. Instead, they criticize politicians' techniques (e.g., their shortsightedness, their manipulativeness), which leaves the democratic/technocratic commitment quite safe.

A variety of studies demonstrates this. Entman [1991] compared news coverage of two airplane disasters, one involving the downing of an Iranian airliner by a U.S. Navy ship and one in which the Soviet Union shot down a Korean jet. On the surface the events seemed similar, but the rhetoric surrounding them was quite different. The Soviets were described in mainstream papers as acting with "deliberate cruelty," of committing a "barbaric atrocity." Instead of referring to "passengers" the press described "victims" and "loved ones," using the Korean jet incident to offer global commentaries about the Soviet Union, almost all of which were negative. In contrast, the Iranian airline situation was described as a "tragic accident." Later research showed that that same description applied equally well to both affairs.

Other studies found similar biases. Steuter [1990] notes that coverage of political "terrorism" in newsmagazines normally reflects the victim's viewpoint rather than complex economic and political forces. "The analysis revealed a picture of terrorism that was volatile and sensational," says Steuter, "the product of Communist and left-wing conspirators whose aim is the destabilization of Western democratic society." No doubt that is part of the story. But the critic must scrutinize any narrative told this consistently. "Terrorism," after all, is a value-laden word. It implies a set of evil motivations (i.e., political anarchy) and a set of cowardly behaviors (i.e., the terrorist's anonymity). By this definition, those who dumped tea into the Boston Harbor in 1773 were terrorists, as were those who rioted in Tienanmen Square in 1989. But it is uncomfortable for Americans to think of such persons as terrorists. That is why they like the rhetoric their newspapers make.

The news, then, is a rich source of persuasion. Critics are beginning to learn more about this discourse, discourse characterized by certain odd, often conflicting, features. Here are some of them:

1. *The news is presentistic.* When we watch the news we watch the moment. Rarely does the news give us a sense of history. That can cause us to lose a sense of perspective as well as to lurch about from solution to solution. Reflecting on such presentism, some scholars worry that it will cause us to act precipitously and to abandon historic compacts in favor of untried, potentially dangerous, solutions.

2. *The news is undertheorized.* That is, the news appears to have no encompassing worldview; it seems innocent of overarching prejudice. It reports only "the facts" and thus seems more trustworthy than does partisan rhetoric with its hortatory style and overly dramatic warnings. But no rhetoric is devoid of a worldview. The critic's job is to find the story behind the media's stories.

3. *The news is calibrated.* Newswriters are not fools. They adjust their texts to the marketplace. Whether they do so consciously or unconsciously is unclear but there seems little doubt that reporters adapt their stories to audience tastes. So, for example, Hart and his colleagues [1980] found that *Time* magazine's religion sections were carefully pegged to its Eastern, Episcopalian (vs. Southern, Baptist) subscription base, even though there are far more of the latter in the United States than the former and even though *Time* is, ostensibly, a national newsmagazine.

4. *The news is fantastic.* Much of what we read in the news does not exist. There is no such thing as "public opinion," for example, until a writer *labels* a particular set of attitudes as popular. Similarly, as Meyers and her colleagues [1978] discovered, newswriters often argue that a political candidate has a great deal of "political momentum" even though no human being has ever seen or touched such a quality.

The essence of rhetoric is selectivity. To make a rhetorical decision is to choose this image rather than that one, to frame an argument for this audience rather than another. Because so much happens in the world each day, and because reporters operate under such tight constraints (e.g., what they know about a topic, what their budget will let them find out), they tell only part of the world's story. That makes them selectors of the first order and hence makes what they write a vital source of insight for the rhetorical critic.

THE RHETORIC OF ENTERTAINMENT

Some argue it is silly to criticize unserious texts. After all, is deconstructing *Home Improvement* really worth it? Should we waste time teasing out grand insights from today's rap songs? Can a popular film or a baseball broadcast really tell us something important about the world? It is clearly possible to wax philosophical about such matters, but should we?

Many critics say yes for these reasons: (1) rhetoric is most powerful when it is not noticed, and nobody notices popular culture; (2) people are easiest to persuade when they are in a good mood, and entertainment creates such moods; (3) some of our most basic values come to us when we are young, and the young consume entertainment voraciously; and (4) the mass media disseminate entertainment far and wide, thus affecting millions. Perhaps the only thing sillier than studying popular culture, then, is not studying it at all.

Critical studies of mass entertainment have exploded during the past twenty years. We cannot survey that vast literature here but we can feature three of its most suggestive findings. Several critics have noted, for instance, the **radical individuality** found in entertainment texts. Consider Jonathan Crane's [1988] research. He studies what he calls the "slasher movie," the "slice and dice thriller." Amidst the gore he finds one consistent argument: Collective action is doomed. The real power of the horror movie, says Crane, is its ability to reduce the individual to the primordial body, to the endangered unit of protoplasm.

For example, in movies like *The Night of the Living Dead* and *Halloween* we are thrust into Everytown, an amorphous but easily identifiable place that has "no architectural identity or historical specificity" but whose very ordinariness "generates reality effects among the audience members." The real horror in a horror film, says Crane, is that evil has become situated in our most private and unprotected locations. One by one the townspeople are killed, with the hero remaining to battle the Feared Invader. Evil is eventually dispatched but the greatest horror is this: Each of us is alone; community is a myth.

Perhaps this seems absurd. After all, we do not live in horror films. But these themes of radical individuality are now repeated so often that they aggregate within us. Sanchez [1993], for example, found them in a very different venue—in old-time political films like *Mr. Smith Goes to Washington* and in more recent ones like *Bob Roberts* and *Dave*. These films echo the horror films: The political community is corrupt; only the purified individual can be trusted. Sanchez says that such notions contribute to our intense dissatisfaction with modern politics, causing us to search for the Lone Politico who can deliver us from the darkness. In 1995, many Americans sought that individual in Colin Powell.

Rosen [1987] found these themes in soap operas, where all problems were reduced to the psychological and where each transgressor was given a second chance (and a third and a fourth chance) for redemption. Rarely did the soap operas praise group cooperation. Oddly enough, Rasmussen and Downey [1991] discovered these same themes in Vietnam War films, where the politics of war were sidestepped in favor of cameo stories about the boy-in-the-rice-paddy and the girl-back-home. "Therapeutic" films like this, say Rasmussen and Downey, never really let the American people learn anything from the war because they focused so heavily on the individualistic and hence provided no *policy* guidance for the future.

Popular entertainment is also distinguished by its **radical presentism,** an ahistorical understanding of human problems and an antihistorical rejection of old truths. When presentism and individualization are combined, popular culture becomes a somewhat rootless place. But it is also a place for grand experimentation where the individual is set loose to explore the lived moment. We see such themes in MTV videos, where the past becomes a shadow and where life is lived on the edge—thrashing, grasping, groping, and writhing to the beat. If the past does make an appearance in such videos, it is in the guise of a harsh and demanding parent or a discipline-crazed high school principal.

Why is presentism attractive? For one thing, abandoning the past (and bracketing the future) lowers our sense of responsibility. Responsibility can exact a heavy toll, after all, and so hearing the smack of a home run or feeling the energy of a *2 Live Crew* concert both rewards and distracts. But as Tucker and Shah [1992] have shown, presentism can also blind us. They compared Alex Haley's epic slave narrative, *Roots,* to the television miniseries by the same name and found it had been turned into a "classical immigrant story" suitable for modern Americans. In doing so, say Tucker and Shah, the adapters tore the story from its historical moment, diluting "the horror, complexities, and seriousness of slavery as a societal institution" [p. 325]. No doubt, it would have been uncomfortable to watch the horrors of slavery for five nights in a row. Deft rhetorical restructuring allowed for other possibilities.

Armstrong and his colleagues [1992] add a chapter to this story. They noted the increased presence of African Americans in TV dramas and wondered how these portrayals affected viewers. The more people were exposed to such shows, the researchers found, the more they overestimated the socioeconomic positions of blacks in general. That is, by focusing on the unrepresentative lives of Cliff Huxtable or Martin Lawrence each week, television implies they are the norm. Inevitably, viewers respond this way: "Haven't we gotten past this race thing by now? Surely we've done our penance and things have changed. Just look at Bryant Gumbel." Armed only with their statistics, sociologists have a hard time countering such claims.

Two other studies detail the power of presentism. Lowry and Towles [1989] examined portrayals of sexuality in soap operas and found (1) a substantial increase over the years in sexual promiscuity and, more important,

(2) *no attendant consequences* to such actions. These findings parallel those of Greenberg and Atkin [1983], who found that prime time television showed more than 2700 "irregular driving acts" to viewers during the average year but only 15 cases of seat belt usage. Does this imply, as conservatives have argued, that television publicizes licentiousness? Perhaps. But even worse it robs us of consequence. On television, behavior occurs suddenly, often devoid of context. It comes from nowhere and (often) leads to nothing. This makes television a pleasure to watch. But what does it make of us?

A third aspect of popular culture is its **radical ambivalence.** That is, while television delivers exciting and clear-cut characters to viewers, it inevitably leaves them with a sense of incompleteness. This open-endedness is crucial to television's success because it keeps viewers tuning in. But it is also important rhetorically because it lets television deal with complex and divisive issues without losing its audience.

For example, we are told each week on *Murphy Brown* that it is possible to be a working woman, a single mom, and have a sparkling personality. At the same time, Murphy is careful not to alienate stay-at-home mothers. She does so by being down-to-earth and humorous, which is to say, she depoliticizes herself or, better, pluralizes herself. She is contemporary but traditional, hard-headed but soft-hearted, gregarious but thoughtful. Murphy becomes her viewers—all of them.

Television clings to ambivalence because it is a *mass* medium in a *conflicted* society. Its narratives and its heroes therefore become complex. Cloud [1992] describes this complexity in her study of *Spenser for Hire,* where she focuses on Hawk, the detective's controlled-but-tempestuous sidekick. Cloud notes that Spenser treats Hawk with "part fascination, part fear." "Hawk does not decapitate heroines," says Cloud [p. 318], "but his violence is often extreme. He exhibits none of Spenser's reluctance to kill, nor does he wait to attack until attacked himself. . . . He functions as the marker of Spenser's personal and moral boundaries."

Although *Spenser for Hire* takes pains to portray Hawk as a strong-willed and proud man, Cloud is unconvinced. She argues that the Hawk character retains much of the willful and predatory stereotypes long established for African-American males. Hawk is somewhat civilized, but only in part. His complexity derives from television's need to be politically correct but also interesting. Television trades in cliches because they are comforting, but it also feels the need to align itself with changing mores. Marchetti [1989] found this sort of complexity in *Saturday Night Fever,* where the male lead was both sexy and sexist, a polished dancer but also a blue collar roustabout.

No doubt, good fiction requires characterological complexity. But popular culture—because it is popular—has a special need for it. Because popular culture is also cultural, it must sample the full range of person-types within a culture. This means that there is often a shallowness to television's characters since they are ultimately based on attitude surveys—57 percent this, 23 percent that—rather than springing from some deeply rooted, organic reality.

Not surprisingly, Powers and his colleagues [1992:25] found a similar vacillation among Hollywood's female characters. Traditionally, such women were distinguished by their "civility, maternal instinct and devotion to family" the authors observe. But recently they have been cast as "vicious, greedy, and villainous," even while they cling to some of the older images as well. The result is that unique confection of the cinematic 90s: Conflicted Woman, Confused Man.

Critical work in the area of entertainment is in its infancy. But it is becoming increasingly important work, since the American viewer now consumes individuality, presentism, and ambivalence on a nightly basis. *The Simpsons* embodies these strains as does *60 Minutes*. Football announcers deliver these themes when hyping their weekly products, and the Fox Network became a network by deftly following the same formula.

The rhetorical critic is left to ponder this: How do such motifs affect what we think and how we feel about what we think? With television now being watched so heavily, are American consumers destined to become what they consume? Will they grow happy with their individualization and comfortable with their uncertainties? Or are the effects of entertainment being overemphasized? Perhaps the world today is no different than it has always been. Perhaps we all need to relax more, stop taking life so seriously, take a deep breath, watch more TV. Perhaps not.

CONCLUSION

At first glance, the ancient study of rhetoric seems alien to a modern, electronic world. The discipline of rhetoric was invented to deal with the great declarations of individual orators patiently explaining the affairs of the day to a learned citizenry. Things have gotten stranger. In an era of 300+ cable channels the individual orator now swims in a sea of competing hucksters. With network airtime costing hundreds of thousands of dollars a minute, "patience" has gone by the boards as persuaders try to "hit 'em hard and hit 'em fast." The "affairs of the day" also struggle against a tide of distractions: reruns of *Barney Miller,* Australian rules football, the plaintive sounds (and sights) of the Country Music Channel. In such an era the "learned citizenry" seems to have taken a permanent vacation as well.

But just because public discourse has changed does not exempt the critic from showing up for work. Why? Because too many important questions are still unresolved: Do situation comedies increase or decrease racial tolerance in the United States? Can a capitalistic democracy survive without the capital generated from commercial advertising? Are network executives operating as patriots or serfs when representing the Pentagon's press releases? Was justice served or thwarted when the O. J. Simpson trial was telecast live for so many months? Can soap operas be defended by anyone, on any grounds?

The world of persuasion has changed, yes, but that only means the critic must stay on top of things. Late night impresario Larry King [1994:136] explains why when discussing the challenges the Founding Fathers would face today:

> [Just think about] Jefferson, who was shy, kind of introverted: "Who is this woman, Tom? Black woman, mistress," they'd want to know. "Who is this woman?"
>
> Imagine Ben Franklin, with "Hard Copy" following him over to Paris. All over. Film of Ben Franklin in Paris? "Exclusive, tonight, at 5:00, Mrs. Franklin speaks out on 'Inside Edition'. . . ." I mean, they were just as raucous—it's just that they didn't have television.
>
> Today, if we had a July 4th Declaration of Independence, it still would have been signed, let's say, in Philadelphia. But all the signers would have been on all the shows the next three nights, putting a spin on it: "Hancock, how come your name's so big? Are you plugging the insurance company? What do you mean by "When in the course of human events . . . ?"
>
> And try to picture the wacko right-wing talk show host on the Declaration of Independence—he'd have gone berserk: "Who *are* these people? Revolutionaries, mercenaries, violating the king?"

Some may be inclined to shed a tear for the Founding Fathers when reading King's imaginings. But the critic cannot be among them for, today, there is too much work to do. There will be time enough for tears tomorrow.

Chapter 10

ROLE CRITICISM

No subject enrages campus Thought Police more than Holocaust Revisionism. We debate every other great historical issue as a matter of course, but influential pressure groups with private agendas have made the Holocaust an exception. Elitist dogma manipulated by special interest groups corrupts everything in academia. Students should be encouraged to investigate the Holocaust story the same way they are encouraged to investigate every other historical event. This isn't a radical point of view. The premises for it were worked out centuries ago during a little something called the Enlightenment.

Revisionists agree with establishment historians that the German National Socialist State singled out the Jewish people for special and cruel treatment. In addition to viewing Jews in the framework of traditional anti-Semitism, the Nazis also saw them as being an influential force behind international communism. During the Second World War, Jews were considered to be enemies of the State and a potential danger to the war effort, much like the Japanese were viewed in this country. Consequently, Jews were stripped of their rights, forced to live in ghettos, conscripted for labor, deprived of their property, deported from the countries of their birth and otherwise mistreated. Many tragically perished in the maelstrom.

Revisionists part company with establishment historians in that Revisionists deny that the German State had a policy to exterminate the Jewish people (or anyone else) by putting them to death in gas chambers or by killing them through abuse or neglect. Revisionists also maintain that the figure of 6 million Jewish deaths is an irresponsible exaggeration, and that no execution gas chambers existed in any camp in Europe which was under German control. Fumigation gas chambers did exist to delouse clothing and equipment to prevent disease at the camps. It is from this life-saving procedure that the myth of extermination gas chambers emerged. . . .

During the war, and in the postwar era as well, Zionist organizations were deeply involved in creating and promulgating anti-German hate propaganda. There is little doubt that their purpose was to drum up world sympathy and political and financial support for Jewish causes, especially for the formation of the State of Israel. Today, while the political benefits of the Holocaust story have largely dissipated, the story still plays an important role in the ambitions of Zionists and others in the Jewish community. It is the leaders of these political and propaganda organizations who continue to work to sustain the Holocaust legend and the myth of German monstrosity during the Second World War. [Smith, 1990–3]

These are the remarks of Bradley Smith, a self-proclaimed "historical revisionist" who has attempted to popularize the notion that the extermination of 6 million Jews during the second world war in Germany was a cruel exaggeration. Mr. Smith has proclaimed his message aggressively. During the early 1990s, for example, he sent his tract (entitled "The Holocaust Controversy: The Case For Open Debate") to hundreds of college newspapers, daring them to print his views and then challenging their dedication to freedom of speech if they did not. Schools like UCLA, Penn, Texas, Stanford, and the like suffered the agonies of the damned as they wrestled with Smith's challenge.

Not all campus newspapers printed his message but many did, even those in universities with sizable Jewish student bodies. Published or not, however, Mr. Smith milked the controversy for all it was worth. But given what we know about the Second World War, about German mendacity and Jewish suffering, how could such a preposterous case be made? More specifically, how could *Bradley Smith,* a person who had neither academic credentials nor community standing, inspire such a whirlwind of controversy? How could he slink out of the shadows of hate and then gain a piece of the national spotlight?

This chapter focuses on the nature of *rhetorical role, a regularized set of verbal strategies resulting in a distinctive personal image.* That is, we will try to understand how a speaker's words interact with an audience's perceptions to create social change. Mr. Smith was clever in that regard. He knew, for example, that "revisionism" is a popular academic sub-speciality in departments of history these days and so he opted for that same label. The irony, of course, is that many academic revisionists do their work because they feel that the voices of the poor, the disenfranchised, and the unpopular have been excluded from the history books. So, for example, they study diaries kept by colonial housewives and examine the membership lists of black churches to understand life in the nineteenth century better.

Bradley Smith adopts the same approach. He begins by asking for sympathy since tremendous forces have been aligned against him. He points out that "thought police" now survey the scene at every turn but that he has resisted them heroically. "Elitists" have used dogma to manipulate others and yet Smith has clung to his humble truths. "Special interest groups" have consistently pummelled the unprotected and so Smith has joined the downtrodden. Humble, downtrodden, heroic—and all in the first paragraph.

In framing his text, Smith knew that he would be facing **role constraints,** *the communicative rules imposed on a speaker by the rhetorical situation.* Smith knew that blatant anti-Semitism is no longer fashionable and so he tipped his hat to "establishment historians" and then acknowledged, a bit weakly, that Jews have suffered when "stripped of their rights" and "deported from the countries of their birth." The language Smith uses also acknowledges his constraints. He uses the scholarly passive voice, eschews the code words of racism, and opts for qualifying phrases ("potential danger to the war effort"), all in an attempt to avoid looking like a drooling idiot.

And so Smith creates a new and distinctive **rhetorical persona,** *that complex of verbal features that makes one person sound different from another,* and this is why he and his kin are so dangerous. "Holocaust revisionists" are but revised anti-Semites, borrowing liberally from both the discourses of the academy and the discourses of hatred. More perniciously, they draw on the discourses of democracy as well when shielding themselves and their putrefactions from those who would silence them. The resulting amalgamation is powerful. Respecting as they do the life of the mind and the traditions of liberalism, today's college editors are often putty in the hands of people like Smith.

To his credit, Smith maintains his controlled persona throughout. Ever the political scientist, he refers to the "German state" rather than the "Nazis." Ever the proletarian, he describes the "Zionist" overlords who rule the world. Ever the humanitarian, he patiently explains the delousing procedures used during the war. Bradley Smith, a man among men.

It is one thing to decry people like Smith and another to understand how they do what they do. This chapter is devoted to the latter pursuit. We will investigate the impact of social obligations on discourse, on how roles create rhetorical limitations and possibilities, and how speakers work to take on such roles. Our premise will be that selfhood and text collude to produce rhetoric. Here, we will monitor those collusions.

THE EMERGENCE OF ROLE

If role does not come at birth, it arrives soon after. "Infant" becomes "son" or "daughter" and learns to gurgle or smile on cue. "Infant" also becomes "brother" or "sister" and, despairingly, learns to share. Learning to become a "niece" or a "nephew" is trickier because aunts and uncles are around infrequently. But these roles, too, are learned and after them "student," "shortstop," "grocery sacker," "best friend," "lover," "lawyer," "homeowner." Each stage of life brings its jobs, each job a clientele, each clientele a rhetoric.

Rhetorical personae come from many sources. Often, one's **personal rhetorical history** produces a distinctive way of saying things. Being brought up in a particular locale (say, the midwest), learning a particular style of speech (directness), identifying with a particular group of people (the middle class), having distinctive learning experiences (being the daughter of a businessman), and attending a particular kind of college (Wellesley) can produce a modest, conservative young woman like Hillary Clinton.

But **ideological influences** can also shape the social self. Attending a progressive law school (Yale) during a particular era (the 1960s), marrying a distinctive fellow (a handsome young politician on-the-make) with a particular philosophy (high-tech populism) can produce a sharply transitional Hillary Clinton.

And rhetorical role can also be the product of **institutional affiliations.** When making the transition from Little Rock to Washington, D.C., Ms. Clinton increasingly found herself in role difficulty. She was part wife, part mother, part lawyer, part politician, and all First Lady. Each job had its own, long-standing rhetorical roles associated with it. It is small wonder then that as her time in Washington proceeded, Ms. Clinton learned to speak very, very carefully.

Hillary Clinton's story shows that the critic has to be careful when doing any sort of speaker-centered analysis since public people are so tightly role-constrained. This explains the importance of the final vowel in the term *persona*. Person and persona are not the same. The former is hidden within layers of selfhood while the latter is presented for public inspection. The American people knew the persona of Hillary Clinton (e.g., "we should help the least fortunate among us") but perhaps only the President knew her person. Since a public message is made for a unique audience in a unique situation, it will necessarily bear their imprints. Thus, *the good critic never presumes that a text faithfully reflects the unique mind and personality of its author.*

The importance of this notion cannot be overestimated. Too often, critics become amateur psychoanalysts, searching for a speaker's psyche within the metaphors the speaker uses. This is a hazardous and unproductive game. Psychologizing about speakers by looking at their public statements is normally both inaccurate and inconclusive. Instead, the critic must describe a speaker's persona, the person-type the audience is being *invited* to see.

Thus, a research question like "What good or evil lurks inside the Hillary Clinton who uttered these remarks?" equates person with persona and hence is unanswerable. But a question of the sort "What sort of person were audiences invited to notice when hearing Hillary Clinton speak?" is answerable because the critic has Ms. Clinton's explicit and implicit self-descriptions as guideposts. Keeping this biographical fallacy in mind, we can consider several critical probes useful for describing a speaker's persona:

WHAT REASONS FOR SPEAKING ARE OFFERED BY THE SPEAKER?

To study claimed motivations is to study the speaker's self-portrait and, hence, the speaker's understanding of audience values. Earlier in this book, for example, we heard Harold Hill proclaim it was his solemn duty to stave off the corruption of River City, Iowa. Why a duty and not a whim? What is it about "duty" that sells in Iowa? In his speech, Rabbi Prinz said that he spoke not as a Jew and not as an American, but as an American Jew. Why the double motivation? In his speech, George Patton made no mention of his reasons for speaking. What did his audience make of that?

As Kenneth Burke [1962] says, motive is never not at issue in rhetoric, that all such situations prompt the question: What is this person trying to do to me? As Arnold [1968] says, motive is especially crucial in oral persuasion. There, the speaker's physical presence and nonverbal behavior (e.g., shifty eyes, perspiration) provide personalized information unavailable to the reader. This complicated package of cues brings the humanity of the speaker into the picture more directly, both for good and ill. Naturally, the clever rhetor will try to deemphasize this question of motive, often by providing flattering self-characterizations early in a message. In so doing, he or she also provides an understanding of what it takes to do business with this sort of audience in this sort of culture.

HOW SHARPLY DELINEATED IS THE PERSONA OF THE MESSAGE?

According to Harrell et al. [1975], persona gives authority to a text it would otherwise lack. For this reason, says Carlson [1991], lawyers in court sometimes try to "borrow" a persona from the literary realm (e.g., The Tempting Seductress or The Evil Leech) when defending their nonfictional clients in court. On other occasions, argue Erickson and Fleuriet [1991], presidents issue "unattributed" messages shorn of persona so that public reaction can be gauged to a proposal without the proposer risking personal censure. A middle ground between the distinct and indistinct personae was described by Darsey [1995], who found Senator Joseph McCarthy's persuasive power to derive from his ability to create a "fantastic" world so captivating to its audience that they never bothered to inspect McCarthy's own motives.

Hillbruner [1974] suggests that a critic distinguish between the **signature** of a message (verbal tics unique to the speaker) and its use of **archetypes** (cultural stories and traditional language used by all speakers). In these terms, Bradley Smith's holocaust tract was all archetype and no signature. The opposite condition is found in the following variation on a notice that once appeared in a personal column:

> Intelligent guy (38–55) wanted by beautiful woman to love, honor, and obey. Want to leave the hustle and bustle of a superficially glamorous career to raise a family. I'm 35, but can pass for 28. I'm attractive (many say gorgeous, some say cute), sincere, passionate. I like power and settle for nothing less than excellence. I'm also caring, loyal, faithful, monogamous, artistic, spiritual, physically fit, health oriented but indulgent, traditional (I've never written to a personal column before!). Sweet, caring, sexy, bright, demonstrative. Enjoy opera, elegant restaurants,

hayrides on starlit nights, goofy affection, Chinese food, satin sheets, bubble baths, Bach, shopping malls, and playing Monopoly by the fire on winter nights. Write on company letterhead to Box 223, *The Times.*

This passage is a benchmark for clarity of persona! On reading it, the reader can quickly decide whether or not to pursue the possibility. The Self described here is a unity of diversity, all of it well buoyed by perhaps the healthiest ego in human history. Strine and Pacanowsky [1985] describe texts of this sort as having **prominent authorial status,** whereby the author becomes central to the rhetorical action. In sharp contrast is the rhetoric of science, which derives its authority from a distanced, pedantic style containing no self-references or personal reflections. In rhetoric with such **diminished authorial status,** the speaker's faithful adherence to role-constraints, not the speaker's personal flair, provides its suasive force.

Critics such as Waddell [1990] are now studying the question of which style is least dangerous, the egomaniacal (but ultimately honest) rhetoric seen above or the cool, self-effacing (but remote control) rhetoric of the scientist or bureaucrat. Personal passion or aloof control? The difference is not unimportant.

DOES ROLE, NOT SITUATION, DOMINATE THE SPEAKER'S MESSAGE?

This question encourages the critic to track a speaker from situation to situation to find regularities. And it takes a *critic* to do so since most people pay little attention to their social habits. Even the simple act of raising one's hand in class, for example, marks a learner's deference to the instructor and a willingness to be guided by the norms of politeness. If hand-raising is a product of role constraints, then so too are the infinitely more complex patterns of daily discourse.

Hart [1984b] studied these role-related demands by searching for the "natively presidential" features of political language. He tracked the use of ten verbal factors (described in Chapter 8), comparing Presidents Truman through Reagan to a group of nonpresidents that included preachers, corporation executives, social activists, and candidates for political office. Table 10.1 presents samples from the texts studied.

Generally speaking, three features seemed linked to presidential role: (1) **humanity** (presidents used the greatest number of self-references, were most optimistic, and, compared to business executives at least, were more people-centered); (2) **practicality** (presidents used highly concrete language and chose a much simpler style than their counterparts); and (3) **caution** (presidents used less assured language than did those running for office and much less than did the preachers studied). Not only did these factors distinguish the presidents from the nonpresidents but Lyndon Johnson and Richard Nixon also changed their speaking in these ways when moving from the vice-presidency to the presidency.

TABLE 10.1 Presidential and Nonpresidential Speech Contrasted

Presidential	Nonpresidential
"I have tried to base my decisions and my thinking and my actions on what I think is really best for this country. I believe that is what my country expects me to do." [Johnson, 1966b:659]	"The Democratic Party does not believe that we can hold back and go forward at the same time. We do not believe that we can get ahead by standing still. We do not believe that we can be strong abroad and weak at home." [Johnson, 1960:4]
"We have the chance today to do more than ever before in our history to make life better in America, to ensure better education, better health, better housing, better transportation, a cleaner environment, to restore respect for law, to make our communities more livable, and to ensure the God-given right of every American to full and equal opportunity." [Nixon, 1973b:14]	"There are some threats to our existence which are fundamentally environmental. . . . The urbanization problem is so severe over the world today. . . . Here is a single example from outside the United States of how we can make very silly mistakes. . . . These are the people who are looting and polluting the world." [Erlich, 1972:118-9]
"Now as we strive to bring about that [peaceful] wisdom, there is, in this moment of sober satisfaction, one thought that must discipline our emotions and steady our resolution. It is this: we have battleground, not peace in the world." [Eisenhower, 1953:642]	"Mark these words well. This is what the Communists really mean by 'peaceful coexistence.' They do not mean 'peace.' 'Peaceful coexistence' is simply the Communist strategy for world conquest." [Goldwater, 1964:37]

These findings suggest that the *president's job itself* has rhetorical require-ments built into it, dictating that the president humanize highly technical problems and put a happy face on them as well. The president's job also demands language the layperson can identify with and an avoidance of geopo-litical abstractions. Finally, the president must choose words carefully: A Dwight Eisenhower must avoid the formulas of radical politics used by a Barry Goldwater [see Table 10.1], a Richard Nixon cannot be as pessimistic as envi-ronmentalist Paul Erlich, and a President Johnson must personalize issues that a Senator Johnson might have made more general. For several reasons, then, presidents follow a rulebook when they speak, clearly showing how role can dominate person on occasion.

THE MANAGEMENT OF ROLE

Among the most primitive resources in persuasion are the qualities of mind, behavioral habits, and factors of personal appearance that attract people to one another. But like a talented but raw young boxer, one's person must be "man-aged" if it is to have social effect. Generosity of spirit and a twinkle in the eye cannot advance a speaker's goals if they are not noticed by others. And so rhetoric requires the speaker to make choices in self-presentation; criticism demands that the critic track these choices. Two sets of critical probes are use-ful for doing so, as discussed below.

WHAT IS THE SPEAKER'S THEORY OF DISCOURSE?
HOW ARE LISTENERS' AND SPEAKERS' ROLES
DEFINED IN THIS MODEL?

Everyone has a theory of discourse, whether they know it or not. Mary Poppins' classic refrain, "a spoonful of sugar makes the medicine go down," affirmed that common premises can win over hostile audiences. Similarly, when Harold Hill's fellow salesmen in *The Music Man* claimed that "you've got to know the territory," he isolated audience analysis as the key to persuasion. And when Forrest Gump demonstrated an ability to converse amiably, if stupidly, with both the humble and the exalted ("Momma said we're all just alike"), he proved the practical value of innocence. As Johnson [1975] notes, these **implicit communication theories** are just that: implicit. Mary Poppins and Forrest Gump could not discuss their rhetorical theories with precision, for life had taught them such lessons in its taken-for-granted way. More important, however, Poppins and Gump *used* these unspoken assumptions when talking, thereby providing the critic with an important, and accessible, object of scrutiny.

Seven such theories seem particularly useful to the critic. For example, Johnson [1975] studied the rhetoric of cabalists, persons who huddled together for fear of worldwide conspiracies. These persuaders operated on a **Magical** theory of communication, warning that the forces of totalitarianism were using silent propaganda to undermine people's wills, and they colorfully described how their "mindless" neighbors succumbed to these clandestine conspiracies (this is probably Bradley Smith's model).

A related model is more **Mechanical** in nature. In it, listeners are warned that society is being worn down by "implements of propaganda" that "overwhelm" the stalwart but "inept" citizen. Within such rhetoric, Benson [1968] found metaphors of poison used to explain why people succumbed to error (i.e., they were "helpless" to resist it). With the Magical theory, then, the speaker becomes a master wizard who uncovers the vile deceptions of the day. With the Mechanical theory, the speaker becomes a kindly but worried physician of the mind who provides the ideological antidote needed for listeners' attitudinal health.

Lake [1983] discusses a third theory of persuasion—**Experiential.** Here, language is seen as an obstacle to truth. Strains of such thought are found in the rhetoric of the American Indian Movement, which argued that the world of words is the white person's world and therefore corrupt. These rhetors argue that whites' treaties and conferences have subverted Native Americans and, as a result, that only natural and supernatural forces can be trusted. The persona here is defiant and emotional, a rhetoric suited to insiders.

In contrast is the **Rationalistic** theory of economic progress, held by many engineers, which often drives their marketing colleagues crazy in modern corporations. When left to their own devices, these engineers create hopelessly detailed manuals for their customers and, when making product announcements at trade shows, rarely mention their personal experiences with the product. The rhetoric their theory produces is, as a result, bland, spare, and remote.

Another popular theory of communication is **Parental.** Here, the persona of the speaker is clear and unmistakable, a dominating presence. The image is one of a kindly shepherd leading a flock, helping even the weakest among his charges traverse the difficult course. Speakers operating on this model become all-knowing and yet patient, a sage but nonpartisan helpmate to the listener. The leaders of both religious and social movements often opt for this image, especially after their movements have reached maturity. Crable [1977] found that Dwight Eisenhower projected this persona and argues that it was the key to Eisenhower's leadership skills during the postwar years.

Speakers operating on the **Antagonistic** model of persuasion see the audience as an enemy to be assaulted; submission, not cooperation, becomes the end of rhetoric. The college debater, the rapid-fire salesperson, the Nader-trained consumer advocate, and the fact-spewing trial attorney often project this persona when "attacking the fortress of public opinion." Hart's [1978] study of modern atheists shows this theory in action, with the atheists producing pamphlet after pamphlet, most of which were badly written, poorly documented, and terribly edited but which, as a result, had tremendous rhetorical energy ("We *can* turn the tide!"). The idea here is to produce *enough* persuasion so that religion is washed away in a sea of rhetoric. The logic of this approach also holds that atheistic ideas, even when unadorned, are so powerful that the merest contact with them will produce conversion.

A final, **Formulaic,** theory is especially popular today. This model holds that listeners will succeed if they use certain recipes for personal profit. The shelves of bookstores now bend under the weight of these recipes: *Ten Easy Ways to Lose Weight, Dr. Sam's Guide to Instant Health, How to Beat the Stock Market.* The persona here is supremely confident: The formula works for all customers under all circumstances. As a result, people now "dress for success" and "feel better with Herbalife." According to Payne [1989], this rhetoric sharply increased during the 1960s, when scores of capitalistic gurus appeared on the American scene. As with the other implicit theories, these persuaders endorse a policy ("Reach paradise. Follow The Way.") but also peddle a philosophy of listening ("Record this list of tips; don't question them.") and a philosophy of life ("Anything worthwhile comes easily.").

Most people are unaware of their assumptions about discourse and might well deny these assumptions if brought to their attention. Still, the good critic realizes that to speak is to reveal attitudes—about oneself and one's ideas, but also about one's listeners and what is best for them. The good critic is always on the lookout for such attitudes.

How Consistently Does the Speaker Opt for a Particular Role? What Does This Show about the Rhetorical Situation?

Consider the following message:

> People today often ask if I mind whether they smoke. No, I don't mind. Because I like the smell of cigarette smoke. I like the way it triumphantly, insouciantly glides through the air.
>
> I like the look and feel of cigarettes. They're streamlined and look like they're weight conscious. There were times when they felt smooth and sexy between my fingers.
>
> One day, I decided to quit smoking. No reason. I just felt like it. At times, I dearly missed that cylinder of tobacco fashionably wardrobed in white.
>
> Just like a modern woman, who fears she's become too dependent on her man, I was curious to find out whether I was liberated enough to live apart from my carton and my lighter. I've been unattached, so to speak, since then. One day, I'll probably renew the relationship. For now, I'm a loner.
>
> On the other hand, my husband will never end his affair with cigarettes. He's devoted to them as deeply and sincerely as he's committed to me. I don't mind. I'm an understanding wife. I know how it is to want something, to find pleasure in it, to be grateful that it delivers on its promises.
>
> I find the odor of cigarette smoke no less appealing than the aroma of perfume. It reminds me that my husband is nearby. The scent teases his clothing and our bed linens. Confidentially, I think it's a turn-on.
>
> Smokers and nonsmokers think I'm strange because I don't object to entering an office where people are permitted to smoke. To me, the smoke creates an atmosphere of industriousness, of assertiveness, and sometimes of a macho presence.
>
> When I stopped smoking, my friends were uncomfortable. "Will it bother you if I smoke in front of you?" they solicitously inquired. I laughed.
>
> "It would bother me if you **didn't**," I told them. I know what it's like to enjoy smoking yet to feel obligated to deny yourself the pleasure because you're amidst nonsmokers.
>
> When I'm in the passenger seat of our car, I don't order my husband, "Open a window!" When I'm driving, and a friend who smokes is seated alongside me, I immediately put her at ease by pulling open the dashboard ashtray and saying, "Feel free. It doesn't bother me." In those close surroundings, I anticipate the wafts of smoke that will drift my way. Ahhh, yes.
>
> Perhaps I'm merely a temporary ex-smoker. Nevertheless, I continue to be amazed and amused that I offend **other** ex-smokers when I lean toward smokers, inhale deeply, and say with a broad smile, "Could you blow it in my face?" [Sandler, 1987]

Here is a text to make a contrarian's heart glad. It was published in the *Philip Morris Magazine,* perhaps the only available forum for such a set of remarks. Viewed from a strictly argumentative standpoint, the essay says very little. As an "industry" response to the antismoking lobby, it does not comment on health-related matters or on nonsmokers' rights. Although it counters some arguments (e.g., that stale smoke smells awful or that secondary inhaling in small spaces is offensive), it does not genuinely debate the issues. Rather, the real news here is the author's **role appropriation.** She presents herself as a *nonsmoker* and hence can adopt a rhetorical posture otherwise unavailable to her. As a "nonsmoker," she can advance the arguments of fair-mindedness, reasonability, and being a good sport without opening herself up to the full savaging of the antismokers.

The author's persona is carefully managed here. She combines Modern Puritan ("Smoke creates an atmosphere of industriousness.") with New Feminist ("I was curious to find out whether I was liberated enough. . . .") and Femme Fatale ("The scent teases his clothing and our bed linens,") but also The Little Woman ("I'm an understanding wife.").

But perhaps the most interesting feature is that this message was published during a time when the tobacco industry suffered a sharp drop in profits because of national opposition to smoking. So this text is a case study in rhetorical desperation, a casting off of the traditional role of Industry Debater for the hydra-headed persona described above. The rhetoric is so obvious that it probably made even the Philip Morris editors blanch when publishing it. But the bottom line is the bottom line, and desperate people say desperate things. This passage therefore establishes an important proposition: *role signals circumstance.*

Critics have investigated a variety of roles to learn about circumstances. For example, Ware and Linkugel [1973] found that the role adopted above, that of **Apologist,** featured four ways of rebuffing attack: outright denial ("I'm not guilty."), bolstering ("We've got better things to be concerned about."), differentiation ("Here's a new way of thinking about it."), and transcendence ("There's a larger principle at stake here."). Along similar lines, Scott [1987] observed that when Senator Edward Kennedy tried to explain the tragic Chappaquiddick affair (in which one of his aides died by drowning), he directed his remarks to the people of Massachusetts (even though the address was televised nationally), thereby claiming the role privileges of a native son. Another study of the Apologist by King [1976] detailed the strategies of leaders on the brink of losing their influence. King's study presents a catalog of signals (use of ridicule, crying anarchy, claims of betrayal, etc.) useful for predicting when power is beginning to shift.

Another rhetorical character is the **Agent,** who speaks on behalf of some institution. At first, this role seems attractive since it gives the speaker legitimate authority. But what power gives, power can also deny. As Hart [1971] found, spokespersons for groups like the Mormon Church and the American Communist Party often had to sacrifice their individuality by rarely using personal anecdotes and by quoting heavily from agreed-upon dogma. In a related study, Jablonski [1980] found that when Catholics resisted certain liturgical reforms in the 1970s, American bishops tried to strong-arm them by using doctrinal materials, thereby cloaking themselves in the mantle of the Church. Kessler [1981] documents the usefulness of agency in politics. There, surrogates like family members and local officials are often used to try out ideas in a national campaign without the candidate having to take responsibility for those ideas. The downside, of course, is that such Agents can misinterpret the party line, thereby creating more trouble than they are worth.

While Agents filter their words through revealed truth, the **Partisan** strikes out in new directions, speaking the truth powerfully and passionately. For these reasons, Partisans prosper during times of turmoil, using their charisma to galvanize public opinion by goading entrenched forces of power. Gregg [1971] notes that such rhetoric is often autosuggestive: Its strong, negative tone better serves to reinforce in-group feelings than to make new converts. Similarly, Woodward [1979] notes that British prime ministers are typically less populist and less conciliatory than American presidents since British politicians are so tightly tied to their party's apron strings. Even when declaring war, says Ivie [1974], American presidents avoid polarizing language, justifying their decisions on idealistic rather than partisan grounds. The United States' cultural diversity and political complexity, it seems, necessarily removes the color and intensity from institutional discourse.

The role of **Hero** is not easy to play although many try to play it. Ronald Reagan played it better than most. According to Fisher [1982], Reagan's rhetoric combined two key heroic features: a *romantic* quality and a commitment to *action*. One thing a Hero does is rescue fair maidens, which Reagan did by reclaiming America's lost loves: the work ethic, moral sobriety, and fiscal responsibility. In a drug-filled, immoral welfare state, Mr. Reagan implied, only a new vision (consisting of many old visions) would do. Newt Gingrich, Mr. Reagan's legatee, used this same role (and much of the same language) to build his political base five years after Reagan left office.

Whether one attempts to become Apologist, Agent, Partisan, or Hero, however, one must bring to that role **emotional integrity** so that its pieces and parts fit together and **dramatic consistency** so that one does not try to become a Partisan one day and an Agent the next. Role-enactment can therefore fail for many reasons: (1) The role may be played poorly, (2) it may be unsuitable for the times, or (3) different roles may become intertwined. Bill Clinton faced all of these problems during the 1992 campaign when trying to outrun his image as a campus radical, to cope with his rival's political seniority, and to speak for New Democrats without forsaking traditional union support. Tracking the maneuverings of people like Bill Clinton can tell the critic much about the theater of everyday life and about the players who walk its stage.

THE ASSESSMENT OF ROLE

This final section presents two practical ways of analyzing speaker-based rhetorical patterns. Neither approach is especially sophisticated, but together they can round out the critic's analysis of persuasive role. Once again, we will begin our discussion with critical probes:

Does the Speaker Make Overt Use of Credibility Devices? Do These Uses Vary across Time and Circumstance?

In September 1960, John F. Kennedy had a credibility problem: Although his campaign for the presidency was moving apace, he could not shake the charge that his Roman Catholicism would curtail his political independence as a chief executive. Because he was heir to several generations of antipapist sentiment in the United States, Kennedy tried to defuse the issue by speaking to the Greater Houston Ministerial Association, thereby making the Catholic issue a nonissue.

Kennedy's speech was a remarkable success. Some say it won him the presidency. The speech not only charmed the Texas ministers but also moved the religious issue to the backburner throughout the United States (either by convincing or by cowing his critics).

The speech itself was perhaps less remarkable than the speech-act. Kennedy's willingness to face his detractors in a volatile situation impressed people, even though his message had few rhetorical flourishes. Kennedy began by thanking the ministers for the invitation to speak, commented on several international and domestic problems, and then framed the central issue succinctly: "It is apparently necessary for me to state once again—not what kind of church I believe in, for that should be important only to me, but what kind of America I believe in" [Kennedy, 1961a:427]. Kennedy then spoke with unusual directness about the issues: Would he become a political captive of the pope? Would he encourage mindless bloc voting? Would other religious groups suffer at his hands? No, no, no, he replied.

The second half of the speech was more positive, with Kennedy discussing freedom of speech, the history of religious tolerance, and the sacrifices that had been made for both freedoms: "Side by side with Bowie and Crockett [at the Alamo] died Fuentes and McCafferty and Bailey and Bedillio and Carey—but no one knows whether they were Catholics or not. For there was no religious test there" [p. 428]. In the final portion of his statement, Kennedy made a series of highly specific predictions for his intended administration: No aid to parochial schools, no religious litmus tests on abortion, censorship, or gambling, no untoward alliances with Catholic countries. He concluded his speech with a warning: "If this election is decided on the basis that 40,000,000 Americans lost their chance of being President on the day they were baptized, then it is the whole nation that will be the loser . . . in the eyes of history, and in the eyes of our own people" [pp. 429–30].

When speaking, Kennedy used a number of credibility strategies, six of which are presented in Table 10.2 (a seventh dimension, Dynamism, is largely a nonverbal factor signaled by bodily action and vocal activity). While all rhetorical situations involve these dimensions, a speaker's *words* perform only some of the work of image-making. That is, credibility is also determined by such factors as human prejudices, the rhetor's sponsor, media effects, the time of day, audience confusion, etc.

TABLE 10.2 Verbal Dimensions of Credibility

Credibility Dimension	Perceived Capacity	Methods of Demonstration	Example (United Fund Campaign)
Power	Speaker can provide significant rewards and punishments (either actual or psychological) for audience.	(1) Indications of previous victories the speaker has won in behalf of the topic.	"I've had the honor of directing the last three successful campaigns and. . . ."
		(2) Suggestions of how listener can share influence already possessed by the speaker.	"I'd now like to pass out the gold pins to the ten-year volunteers."
		(3) Subtle reminders of status differences between speaker and listener.	"Just last week the mayor said to me, 'John, . . .' "
Competence	Speaker has knowledge and experience the audience does not have.	(1) Association with recognized experts.	"Studies of malnutrition by the federal governments show conclusively that. . . ."
		(2) Unique, personal familiarity with the topic is demonstrated.	"Having worked with the Meals on Wheels Program, I. . . ."
		(3) Mastery of relevant technical vocabulary.	"The hospital's new Epidemiology Lab is now complete, thanks to the last campaign."
Trustworthiness	Speaker can be relied on beyond this one moment in time	(1) Present and past behaviors are consistent.	"The United Fund stands on its record: low overhead, maximum help to the community."
		(2) Verbal and nonverbal behaviors are consistent.	"A full two-percent of annual salary. That's what I give. Here's my canceled check."
		(3) Explicitly address alternative viewpoints.	"Yes, the Harris scandal did set us back. But there are no more skeletons in the closet."
Good will	Speaker had the best interests of the audience in mind.	(1) Benefits of speaker's proposal are dramatized.	"People get sick. Those of you who aren't people needn't bother giving to the Fund."
		(2) Reasons for speaker's concern for audience are specified.	"My family's been in town for three generations. *That's* why I kill myself for the Fund."

(continued)

After Hart et al. [1983].

TABLE 10.2 (continued)

Credibility Dimension	Perceived Capacity	Methods of Demonstration	Example (United Fund Campaign)
Idealism	Speaker possesses qualities to which the audience aspires.	(1) Socially acceptable eccentricities are revealed.	"Yes, a 'Uni Fnd' license plate is strange. So call me strange. Publicity is publicity."
		(2) Speaker's risks in behalf of the proposal are specified.	"I put in thirty hours a week for the Fund in addition to my regular job. How about you making ten phone calls for us?"
Similarity	Speaker is seen as resembling the audience in important ways.	(1) Association with valued beliefs.	"We've got to remember that folks should care for folks. And that's doubly true for folks who have no folks to care for them."
		(2) Disassociation from unattractive beliefs.	"Communism and the United Funds are both collective actions. That's where the similarity ends."

Moreover, credibility bestowed one day is sometimes withdrawn the next, often for reasons having little to do with what the speaker says (for example, the many innocent fund-raisers who suffered financially because of the United Way scandal in the early 1990s). In short, the devices listed in Table 10.2 are available for control by the speaker, but this is not to say that they alone "produce" credibility.

Table 10.3 presents the credibility strategies used by John Kennedy and some of the other speakers discussed earlier. The chart has been produced by using the "Methods of Demonstration" listed in Table 10.2 and searching for sample instances of them in the five messages studied. Nothing like scientific precision is being claimed here, but the results are interesting. Kennedy, for example, tried a bit of everything. He used Competence ("the hungry people I saw in West Virginia"), Good Will ("Today, I may be the victim [of religious prejudice]—but tomorrow it may be you."), Idealism ("This is the kind of America I fought for in the South Pacific."), Similarity ("I am wholly opposed to the state being used by any religious group."), and even Power ("Judge me on the basis of my fourteen years in the Congress.") and Trustworthiness (when he cites his previously "declared stands against an ambassador to the Vatican"). Kennedy's speech is therefore quite experimental since there were no guidelines for handling such an unprecedented situation.

George Patton's situation was obviously more comfortable than Kennedy's so he used Trustworthiness heavily. In a sense, Patton's address was a coun-

TABLE 10.3 Comparative Uses of Credibility Strategies*

Credibility Strategies	Rabbi Prinz	Harold Hill	George Patton	John Kennedy	Richard Nixon
Power	0	9	19	5	1
Competence	44	61	4	22	19
Trustworthiness	0	0	32	8	9
Good will	18	5	26	26	29
Idealism	2	2	9	27	14
Similarity	36	23	18	12	30

*Percent usage in text.

terstatement to the anxieties his men were experiencing on the eve of battle. He therefore used his long-standing relationship with the military to become part of his men's internal dialogue and to become identified with the emotional life of the foot soldier. Patton also used his speech to empower the troops, explaining that they were braver and stronger than any who preceded them. While Patton used Good Will and Similarity also to show concern about GI's daily lives, he spent virtually no time on Competence, no doubt because he already had a legendary reputation. To have dwelt on his previous exploits at this time would have surely been untoward.

Rabbi Prinz and Harold Hill operated in a remarkably similar manner, a finding that would no doubt be disconcerting to the good Rabbi. But their behavior makes sense: Given the time constraints, neither could count on extended interaction with their hearers and, given their status as unknowns, neither could base their case on personal biography. Power, Idealism, and Trustworthiness were thus eliminated as rhetorical options.

So Harold Hill went with what he had—his imagination—and used Competence to demonstrate his authority about the wages of sin. He alluded to corruptions found in the pool hall (with its "three-rail billiard shots"), at the racetrack ("some stuck-up jockey-boy settin' on Dan Patch"), and on life's sidewalks ("libertine men and scarlet women"). Rabbi Prinz also used Competence but did so far differently: He simply told his own story of persecution. This "I've been there" approach is universally compelling and was especially appropriate for a person trying to build bridges in the early civil rights movement.

Similarity also builds bridges. Prinz offers an almost perfect equation between his life in Nazi Germany and his audience's experiences with racial discrimination in the United States. Hill responds in kind, disassociating himself from middle-American evil (e.g., not getting the screen door patched) and associating himself with cherished values and traditions: "Remember the Maine, Plymouth Rock, and the Golden Rule!" As we have seen earlier, Hill's speech is largely a sermonette. The correspondence between its credibility structure and that of a legitimate clergyman like Prinz further attests to Hill's talents at generic transference.

Nobody used Similarity with more bathos than Richard Nixon in his "Checkers Speech." His hard-working parents, his adorable children, and his wife's cloth coat all came to his aid in 1952. So much Similarity produces a syrupy mixture, which may explain why, later in life, Nixon viewed the Checkers speech as his most humiliating experience in public life. A more expectable strategy was the Good Will he emphasized during his long-winded paean to his boss: "and remember, folks, Eisenhower is a great man, and a vote for Eisenhower is a vote for what is good for America."

Although Nixon also used Idealism when reminding listeners of his anti-communism, he did not do so extensively. Instead, he dwelt on Competence by detailing his personal finances. It is this portion of his address that is best remembered, perhaps because it contrasts so sharply with the Similarity and Good Will normally expected in a campaign speech. That Mr. Nixon worked so hard to combine such different appeals surely attests to his moxie, if not his subtlety.

One value of canvassing such strategies is that it shows which aspects of image were *overtly* dealt with by the speaker and which aspects listeners may have supplied on their own. For example, Richard Nixon could have spoken about Trustworthiness directly, but since this was the very issue being questioned publicly, he chose a less frontal approach. Documenting his personal consistency over the years or explicating his opponent's charges more completely would have called undue attention to his weakest suit. So he concentrated his efforts elsewhere, hoping that the aspects of credibility he did cover would make the question of his Trustworthiness moot, prompting listeners to ask "How could such a nice young man have done something like that?" That is precisely the response many listeners made to his remarks.

HOW OFTEN DOES ONE FIND SELF-REFERENCES IN THE TEXT? WHY ARE THEY THERE?

I-statements are important because they are not particularly common and because they index a person's feelings and ambitions in especially prominent ways. Some speakers refer to themselves constantly while others never do. What accounts for such patterns? Personality? Social norms? Situation? Do certain rhetorical tasks (e.g., being a late-night host on television) encourage self-references while others (e.g., being a diplomat) discourage them? Why do speeches typically contain twenty times the number of self-references found in writing? Why do presidential campaigners significantly increase their I-statements once elected, and why have recent chief executives increased this rate dramatically? [See Hart, 1984b]. We have plenty of questions such as these. Answers are less available.

A critic should look with special care at I-statements since they make special claims on listeners' attention. Even in casual chatter this is true. When a speaker suddenly starts to tell a personal anecdote, listeners' ears perk up as they sense a shift in the discussion. Naturally, their expectations can be quickly dashed if the story turns into a boring monologue. But, temporarily at least, they are open to influence because identifying with one another is such a basic human instinct.

A useful critical procedure is to extract from a text any phrase or clause containing an "I" and then to lay out these statements one after another (paraphrased, if necessary). Even this simple procedure gives the critic a fresh perspective on the message, as context is torn away and the Self made more prominent. Table 10.4 shows the results of this procedure for an address given by Ronald Reagan on March 4, 1987. This speech was Mr. Reagan's first response to the Tower Commission's report on the Iran-Contra affair, a scandal in which certain agents of the Reagan administration sold arms to the South American "contras" so they then could trade for American hostages in Iran.

TABLE 10.4 I-Statements in Ronald Reagan's Speech of 3/4/87*

---

(01) I have spoken before (from the Oval Office).
(02) I want to talk (to you).
(03) I have been silent (about Iran-Contra revelations).
(04) I guess you're thinking (I'm hiding).
(05) I haven't spoken before (because of sketchy details).
(06) I felt it was improper (to react precipitously).
(07) I have paid a price (for silence).
(08) I have had to wait (for the whole story).
(09) I appointed (Abshire).
(10) I appointed (the review board).
(11) I am often accused (of optimism).
(12) I have had to hunt (for good news).
(13) I will discuss criticisms.
(14) I was relieved (by the Tower Commission report).
(15) I want to thank (the panel).
(16) I have studied the report.
(17) I accept the Board's findings.
(18) I want to share my thoughts (about the findings).
(19) I am taking action (to implement the findings).
(20) I take responsibility (for my actions).
(21) I am angry (about aides).
(22) I am accountable (for their actions).
(23) I am disappointed.
(24) I must answer (to the people).
(25) I find secrets distasteful.
(26) I told the American people (there'd be no arms trade).
(27) I didn't trade arms for hostages.
(28) I undertook (Iran initiatives).
(29) I let my concern for hostages (spill over).
(30) I asked questions (about the hostages).

(Continued)

---

*Paraphrased.

TABLE 10.4 (*continued*)

(31) I didn't ask about the plan (to swap arms for hostages).
(32) I promise we'll try to free the hostages.
(33) I must caution (Americans in Iran).
(34) I am confident (the truth will come out).
(35) I told the Tower board (I didn't know about diversions).
(36) I didn't know (about diversions of funds).
(37) I cannot escape (responsibility).
(38) I identify (problems before acting).
(39) I have found (delegating to be effective).
(40) I have begun (to correct problems).
(41) I met (with professional staff).
(42) I defined values (that should guide them).
(43) I want values to guide policy.
(44) I told them (integrity was essential).
(45) I want a justifiable policy.
(46) I wanted (an "obedient") policy.
(47) I told them (freelancing was over).
(48) I can tell you (the NSC staff is good).
(49) I approved (an arms shipment).
(50) I did approve (an arms shipment).
(51) I can't say when (approval was given).
(52) I have been studying (the report).
(53) I want people to know (the ordeal has not been in vain).
(54) I endorse (the Board's recommendations).
(55) I am going beyond recommendations.
(56) I am taking action in three areas.
(57) I brought in (a new team).
(58) I am hopeful (that experience will prove valuable).
(59) I am honored (by Baker's acceptance).
(60) I nominated Webster.
(61) I will appoint Tower.
(62) I am considering other changes (in personnel).
(63) I will move "furniture" as necessary.
(64) I see fit (to make staff changes).
(65) I have ordered NSC (to review operations).
(66) I have directed NSC (to comply with correct values).
(67) I expect to have an honorable covert policy.
(68) I have issued directives (about covert operations).
(69) I have asked Bush (to reconvene task force).
(70) I am adopting (Tower report's model).
(71) I am directing Carlucci (to improve staff operations).
(72) I have created a post (of legal advisor).
(73) I am determined (to make new policy work).
(74) I will report to Congress (about new policies).
(75) I have taken steps (to implement Board's recommendations).
(76) I have gotten (the message).
(77) I have heard (the message).
(78) I have a great deal to accomplish (in the future).
(79) I want to accomplish much (in the future).
(80) I intend to accomplish much (in the future).

While not charging Mr. Reagan with high crimes or misdemeanors, the Commission did find that the President had been lax in managing those responsible for the arms-for-hostages deal. Because the Commission was a distinguished one (chaired by a Republican) and because its report received ample media attention, Mr. Reagan had little choice but to face the music.

This much-awaited speech cast Reagan in an unaccustomed role—that of Apologist—and began a long period of frustration for him as well. To his credit, in the speech Reagan accepted a good deal of blame for what went wrong, although he chalked up some of the problem to incomplete reports, faulty memory, irresponsible aides, and general miscommunication. All in all, it was a speech Ronald Reagan did not enjoy giving.

One way of capturing the tenor of his remarks is to categorize his I-statements by means of a crude, but straightforward system consisting of four elements: (1) **Emotional/moral action:** the speaker's reports of feelings experienced, moral lessons learned, and hopes and desires for the future. In the Reagan speech, statements 6, 14, 21, 37, and 58 are examples of this type of I-statement; (2) **Narrative action:** references to allegedly factual events, sometimes occurring in the distant past, that led up to the speech, (exemplified in the Reagan address by statements 1, 5, 16, 27, 35, and 39); (3) **Behavioral action:** specific *policy* behaviors the speaker has engaged in immediately prior to the speech event itself (e.g., statements 10, 44, 56, 65, and 71); and (4) **Performative action:** a more complex category consisting of references to the speaker's intentions for the speech (e.g., statements 13, 18, and 24) or to commitments and certifications being made by the fact of the speech itself (e.g., statements 54, 63, 70, and 77).

This system highlights the **locus of action** in a text. That is, it describes whether the speaker is being acted upon by events (i.e., when the message is high on Narratives) or whether the speaker is taking charge (i.e., when it is high on Behavioral Action). This critical system can also track internal versus external action (i.e., Is the speaker a "feeler" or a "doer"?) by scrutinizing the number and types of Emotional/moral statements. Finally, the system identifies whether the speaker is personally willing to become part of the bottom line for policy initiatives (i.e., the number and force of Performative statements).

Although Ronald Reagan used all four types of I-statements in his speech on the Iran-Contra affair, the first half of his message was dominated by Emotional/moral and Narrative action and the latter half by Performative and Behavioral Action. That is, Mr. Reagan commenced his remarks by backpedaling, recounting how the tide of events swept him up: "As angry as I may be about activities undertaken without my knowledge, I am still accountable for those activities" [Reagan, 1987:12].

The locus of *observable* action in the early part of the speech is therefore external to Mr. Reagan while the *emotional* action lies inside, establishing the President as a sensitive, compassionate person ("I let my personal concern for the hostages spill over. . . .") who felt deeply about the events of the day but who was not responsible for them.

Reagan corrects this latter error in the second part of his address. There, he takes charge of events by "adopting," "endorsing," "telling," "nominating," "issuing," "creating," and "ordering." Like a phoenix rising from the ashes, Reagan ends his remarks by promising that there will be action, that he is once again in charge, and that his audience need no longer worry. But while the emphasis changes dramatically during the speech, Mr. Reagan never completely abandons the Emotional/moral note on which he began.

For Ronald Reagan, this was unquestionably the most difficult speech of his life and so he concluded by redocumenting his personal seriousness: "You know, by the time you reach my age, you've made plenty of mistakes if you've lived your life properly. So you learn. You put things in perspective. You pull your energies together. You change. You go forward" [p. 12].

I-statements are only a part of rhetoric, and comparatively little is known about them at present. But when examined in the manner suggested here, they can shed light on the motivational dynamics of discourse. Speakers who use a great many self-references hint strongly that a special persona is being created in the texts they produce. They may also hint something of importance about the persons behind the persona, although that is far less certain.

Speakers, like Bradley Smith, who never refer to themselves also make an important personal statement by not making one, a condition that should be particularly inviting to the imaginative critic. It would be interesting to know, for example, *why* Mr. Smith became a holocaust revisionist, what personal grievances he may have suffered in the past, and how they may have affected his view of the world as well as his rather peculiar library research techniques. Naturally, tracking such humble uses of language as I-statements is a speculative business, but if it moves the critical enterprise forward even slightly by shedding light on the Ronald Reagans and Bradley Smiths of the world, it is a worthwhile business indeed.

CONCLUSION

Within one seven-year period, two very different events occurred in the state of Texas. In 1976, President Gerald Ford gave a speech at the Waco Suspension Bridge. His speech was not a magnificent one, but suspension bridges rarely bring forth eloquence. Mr. Ford did his best with the situation presented to him, declaring the bridge "a tribute to your forefathers, their vision, their foresight to have something like this over this great river, the Brazos river" [1976b:1335]. Having made this observation, Mr. Ford could apparently think of nothing else to say and so he thanked the people in attendance and sat down.

Seven years later, rock star Ozzie Osbourne urinated on the Alamo—clearly, an ungracious act. Mr. Osbourne's poverty of spirit was explained to him by virtually everyone over the age of nineteen in the city of San Antonio and explained in especially great detail by one irate city judge. What Gerald Ford had given to the Lone Star State, Ozzie Osbourne had taken away.

In this chapter, we have examined the roles speakers play—how those roles come to be, how they are managed, how they can be studied. Although they may not like it, most people play roles. Roles, after all, facilitate social traffic. They help us think of things to say. It is probably true, for example, that even a kindly person like Gerald Ford would have willingly passed up the chance to give his oration at the bridge. But being a trooper he carried on, appropriating a ceremonial role that he might have used previously at the opening of a new restaurant in Idaho or with the fishing fleet in Massachusetts. His persona was friendly, engaging, and respectful and he carried it off without a hitch. His audience in Waco probably knew that he was playing a role, but they hardly minded. After all, it was their bridge built by their ancestors that their president had come to commemorate. Mr. Ford's role, in effect, was owned by his audience as well.

As mentioned earlier, it is *motive* that listeners are keen to discover in almost any rhetorical situation. Speakers use roles to help listeners assign them proper motives. This was, among other things, Ozzie Osbourne's problem at the Alamo. Had he been some unfortunate derelict who in a state of inebriation had relieved himself, Osbourne might well have escaped San Antonians' wrath. But Osbourne had motive going for him, or against him. The irreverent persona he had so carefully nurtured over the years via his bizarre stage antics, his antisocial lyrics, and his satanic costuming made it rhetorically impossible for him to claim uncontrollable bladder problems.

Osbourne had long since established a *purposive* image, and no amount of explaining could make it seem otherwise. That which he had worked so hard to create over the years—persona—and that which he paid his staff thousands of dollars a year to manage for him—role—was the same thing that made him a cause célèbre on that fated evening in Texas. Like Frank Sinatra before him, Ozzie Osbourne did it his way.

Chapter 11

CULTURAL CRITICISM

The United States dollar took another pounding on German, French and British exchanges this morning hitting the lowest point ever known in West Germany. It has declined there by 41% since 1971 and this Canadian thinks it's time to speak up for the Americans as the most generous and possibly the least appreciated people in all the earth.

As long as 60 years ago when I first started to read newspapers, I read of floods on the Yellow river and the Yangtze. Who rushed in with men and money to help? The Americans did. They have helped control floods on the Nile, the Amazon, the Ganges and the Niger. Today the rich bottom land of the Mississippi is under water and no foreign land has sent a dollar to help. Germany, Japan and to a lesser extent Britain and Italy were lifted out of the debris of war by the Americans who poured in billions of dollars and forgave other billions in debts. None of those countries is today paying even the interest on its remaining debts to the United States. *When the franc was in danger of collapsing in 1956, it was the Americans who propped it up*, and their reward was to be swindled on the streets of Paris. I was there. I saw it.

When distant cities are hit by earthquakes, it is the United States who hurries in to help. Managua, Nicaragua is one of the most recent examples. So far this spring, 59 American communities have been flattened by tornadoes. Nobody has helped.

The Marshall Plan, the Truman Policy all pumped billions upon billions of dollars into discouraged countries. Now newspapers in those countries are writing about the decadent, warmongering Americans. I'd like to see just one of those countries that is gloating over the erosion of the United States dollar build its own airplane. Come on, let's hear it. Does any other country in the world have a plane to equal the Boeing Jumbo Jet, the Lockheed Tri-Star or the Douglas 10? If so, why don't they fly them? Why do all international lines except Russia fly American planes? *Why does no other land on earth even consider putting a man or woman on the moon?*

You talk about Japanese technocracy and you get radios. You talk about German technocracy and you get automobiles. You talk about American technocracy and you will find men on the moon—not once, but several times and safely home again.

You talk about scandals and the Americans put theirs right in the store window for everybody to look at. Even the draft dodgers are not pursued and hounded. They are here on our streets. Most of them, unless they are breaking Canadian laws, are getting American dollars from Ma and Pa at home to spend here. When Americans get out of this bind, as they will, who could blame them if they said the hell with the rest of the world.

Let someone else buy the Israel bonds. Let someone else build or repair foreign dams or design foreign buildings that won't shake apart in earthquakes. *When the railways of France, Germany and India were breaking down through age, it was the Americans who rebuilt them. When the Pennsylvania railroad and the New York Central went broke, nobody loaned them an old caboose.* Both are still broke.

I can name you 5,000 times when the Americans raced to the help of other people in trouble. Can you name me even one time when someone else raced to the Americans in trouble? I don't think there was outside help even during the San Francisco earthquake. Our neighbors have faced it alone and I'm one Canadian who's damned tired of hearing them kicked around. They will come out of this thing with their flag high and when they do they are entitled to thumb their nose at the lands that are gloating over their present troubles. I hope Canada is not one of these, but there are many smug, self-righteous Canadians.

And finally, the American Red Cross was told at its 48th annual meeting in New Orleans that it was broke. This year's disasters have taken it all—and nobody has helped. [Sinclair, 1973]

These remarks were made some twenty years ago by Gordon Sinclair, a radio personality for station CRFB in Toronto, Canada. At the time, the United States was facing inflation at home and an unfavorable dollar abroad. Unemployment was higher than it had been in some time and America's superiority in manufactured goods, high technology, and natural resources was being questioned on many fronts. The Vietnam war had cost the United States considerable prestige in the eyes of many Europeans, and the Watergate affair was beginning to unravel the administration of Richard Nixon. All in all, this was not a happy time for the American people, which is why Sinclair spoke as he did during one of his daily radio commentaries.

The effect of Sinclair's remarks was immediate and dramatic. The text was reprinted in full in many American newspapers and commented on in virtually all. Similarly, at the request of their listeners, U.S. radio stations ran his commentary for days on end. Numerous television interviews were conducted with Sinclair, he received some 50,000 appreciative letters from U.S. citizens, and Westbound Records of Detroit, Michigan, eventually distributed a recording of the Sinclair apologia.

What could account for such an unprecedented popular reaction? What made Sinclair's jingoism intuitively attractive to many Americans? What was it about Sinclair's rather pedestrian philosophizing that caused so many listeners to respond so viscerally?

Most likely, the Sinclair statement reveals more about his audience than it does about him. U.S. citizens appreciated the speech because it had cultural resonance for them. In the language of Chapter 3, Americans liked Sinclair's speech-act itself. It was fearless, assaultive, and totally unexpected. In the language of Chapter 7, Americans liked Sinclair's style. It was simple, hard-hitting, unembellished, concrete, and concise—five adjectives often used to describe the American people themselves. In the language of Chapter 10, Americans liked the Sinclair persona, an independent, blue-collar tough guy—John Wayne and Mike Tyson.

But perhaps the most important feature of Gordon Sinclair's statement lies in the evidence he used to support his central argument. It is noteworthy that Sinclair lionizes the United States not on the basis of its educational system, the essential goodness of its people, its artistic and cultural achievements, or its democratic form of government. Rather, he burrows into the fundaments of the American culture for his arguments when claiming that its entrepreneurship has made it a great nation. Gordon Sinclair speaks like a classic empiricist, one who believes that tangible knowledge is the best sort of knowledge. He spoke this way because his ultimate audience, the American people, are themselves classic empiricists.

It is *American money,* not American missionaries, that he mentions in connection with Africa. It is *American technology,* not American diplomacy, that he mentions in connection with the former Soviet Union. It is *American engineering,* not American science, that he mentions in connection with the space program. Sinclair's praise is praise not based in ethics or social theory. It is homage based on war reparations, airline safety, moon walks, dam building, and earthquake relief.

In short, Sinclair complimented the American people as they compliment themselves—for what they have *done* and for what they have done *alone.* When he spoke, Sinclair implicitly invoked Americans' most cherished self-portraits: of seventeenth-century Puritans carving out communities on the windswept Atlantic coast; of eighteenth-century farmers venturing south and west to plow land with tools fashioned by hand; of nineteenth-century miners, ranchers, and sea captains settling the great American West. The American people have been raised on these designedly ethnocentric stories and they derive fierce pleasure from "facing it alone."

Like Sinclair, they too get "damned tired" of being "kicked around" (Americans are especially sensitive to being kicked). But their national history, or at least that portion of their national history they choose to remember, sustains them in moments of trouble. American confidence knows no bounds. Americans hold "their flag high" and take special delight in "thumbing their noses" at their detractors. And this delight turns into double delight if the "smug, self-righteous" detractors have the sort of Old World mentality that is especially repugnant to a nation founded by dispossessed persons with chips on their shoulders. And the fact that Gordon Sinclair was himself a Canadian, a citizen in a faintly Eurocentric culture, made his statement especially welcome to many Americans.

In this chapter, we will study the cultural features of rhetoric. That culture seeps into all messages is beyond question. Nobody escapes such influences completely. While Henry Higgins may have changed some of Eliza Doolittle's speech patterns in *My Fair Lady,* he did not change them all and he surely did not change the engine that drives language—Ms. Doolittle's thoughts, feelings, values, and cultural experiences. Eliza Doolittle may have become less a cockney speaker but she always remained, in part, a cockney thinker. Such cultural influences did not make her less an individual but they did make her an individual *somewhere.* It is this somewhere that the cultural critic studies. Three features of culture are especially important to study:

1. Values—deep-seated, persistent beliefs about essential rights and wrongs that express a person's basic orientation to life;
2. Myths—Master Stories describing exceptional people doing exceptional things and serving as moral guides to proper action;
3. Fantasy Themes—abbreviated myths providing concrete manifestations of current values and hinting at some idealized vision of the future.

While we will separate these key cultural elements for ease of discussion in this chapter, everyday rhetoric finds them working in tandem. Gordon Sinclair, for example, uses them all. The values he champions—charity is laudatory, technology is sacred, free speech must prevail—are drawn from the very sinews of the American value system. Similarly, Sinclair draws on exploration myths (the moon landing), the good Samaritan myth (floods on the Yellow River), and the savior myth (the Marshall Plan) in his address as well. But full mythic development takes time, something that persuaders rarely have enough of, so fantasy themes, a kind of mythic shorthand, become its workhorses. Gordon Sinclair's fantasy themes become evident when he imagines Europe without American aircraft, Africa without American relief assistance, Paris without American capital, Israel without U.S. material. These projective "snippets" are among the tales Americans tell each other constantly and, in repeating them, Gordon Sinclair became an American for a day.

When a critic peels back culture from a given message, there is often no message left. One's cultural assumptions, treasured stories, ways of valuing, and linguistic preferences are so deeply ingrained within us that we become mute without them. One cannot, for example, fully appreciate the masculine, hyperactive tone of Saturday morning cartoon shows without understanding that such shows have been produced in a nation historically led, for good and ill, by hyperactive males. Fortunately, even the most sophisticated persuaders carry their culture absent-mindedly. That is a real boon to the rhetorical critic who can look through message to culture and hence to the roots of persuasion itself.

VALUES: THE BEGINNINGS OF CULTURE

How can you tell whether a person is a good citizen? The *Webelos Scout Book* tells us that there are "a few signs":

- He obeys the law. If he thinks a law is wrong, he tries to have it changed. He does this by telling the people who are elected to make laws.
- He respects the rights of others. He does not try to get special privileges for himself.
- He tries to be fair and honest with everyone.
- He tries to make his country or town a better place.
- If in school, he "does his best" to learn all he can about his country.
- If grown up, he learns all that he can about his government. Then he votes on election day. [Webelos, 1979:71]

Children growing up in any culture confront many such litanies. Texts like this tell people who they are and, equally, who they are not. In some senses, the values framed here are obvious and unremarkable—honesty, justice, participatory government, etc. These are the values lying at the surface of the message. A more careful inspection of the text's "deep structure" finds still other values worth noting.

For example, Americans have always believed that values can be taught—just like mathematics, iambic pentameter, or motor mechanics. Americans, along with many other Westerners, tend to be quite linear in their thinking: "Learn these propositions and proper behavior will automatically follow." They become impatient with the round-about modes of instruction found in the Orient or with the patriarchal lectures of kinship-based cultures. Americans believe that all instruction, even value-based instruction, can be systematized, personalized, and efficiently delivered. Their (originally) radical notion of universal public education was based on this read-a-book-learn-a-construct model. It is therefore only slightly more ambitious to try to teach national values in the same way.

Americans are an impatient people. They do not, by and large, value indirection. As philosophers, they favor pragmatism, not metaphysics. They not only believe that a question like "What is a good citizen?" is answerable but they believe that it is answerable (1) universally and (2) behaviorally. They believe that "signs" of a citizen's goodness are empirically observable and that, no matter what form of madness may lie in a voter's head, the act of voting on election day is what really counts.

Americans are also passionate believers in free will and self-determination. They feel that any country or town can be made "a better place" by dint of human effort. Their skyscrapers, hydroelectric dams, and interstate highways stand as evidence of such beliefs. Unlike Islamic fundamentalists, they believe that governance is an essentially cognitive matter. They believe that learning "all he can about his country" will somehow translate into an effective political system and, for that reason, they believe that sublimating intense political passions is highly desirable. Unlike Fiji Islanders, Americans were brought up on change and are challenged and stimulated by it as well. They believe that if a person "thinks a law is wrong," that that law can be altered just as easily as one's name, one's spouse, or one's brand of deodorant. No matter what the evangelical Christians among them might argue, Americans are "evolutionists" of the first order.

So the *Webelos Scout Book* tells both a simple and a complex story, as does most rhetoric. The critic's job thus becomes one of examining the *presuppositions* imbedded in discourse, its *nonargued* premises, on its *taken-for-granted* assumptions. Consider, for example, the research of Lionel Lewis [1972] who did a careful content analysis of some 300 letters of recommendation written for applicants to graduate school in Sociology and for faculty positions in Chemistry at such institutions as Cal Tech, Chicago, Berkeley, Harvard, Minnesota, etc. Here are some of the statements he found in the recommendations:

> (1) He is a very serious and determined student of sociology. In most assignments he goes beyond the call of duty [by producing] more than is expected. [p. 22]
> (2) Although she is rather short, she compensates by drive and perseverance and usually attains her goal. [p. 22]
> (3) He is the oldest son in a family wherein the mother is widowed and has contributed substantially to his own education through outside work. [p. 22]
> (4) He has a good sense of humor which is often masked by his usually serious manner. [p. 26]
> (5) He is emotionally stable and mature, and has an agreeable dry wit. [p. 26]
> (6) There is no question about the fact that he was one of the best liked of our students. He is mature and reserved, yet very friendly and cooperative. [p. 25]

Lewis titled his study "On the Genesis of Gray-Flanneled Puritans," but he could just as easily have titled it "The *Webelos Scout Book* Revisited." We see in these endorsements of modern scientists very little that is modern and even less that is scientific. What we do find is American axiology writ large—effort, stability, overcoming great odds, teamwork, likability. The ghosts of Horace Greely and Horatio Alger beckon here, and there is something of television's Beaver Cleaver and Alex Keaton as well. Lewis was understandably distressed by much of what he found, and he warns that such letters of recommendation threaten to give scientific excellence a permanent back seat to public relations. By replacing scholarly qualities with "the social ethic" and by judging professionals on the basis of their "whole beings" rather than on the basis of their work, warns Lewis, universities could well become populated by personable but incompetent faculty members.

Lewis may be right, but the letter-writers wrote in the only language available to them—the language of their culture. There is something almost inevitable about that. White [1949] discovered, for example, that Adolf Hitler denied not a single major democratic value when he spoke to the German people, even though his political actions embraced none of those values. It was as if a cultural frame had preshaped the contours of Hitler's remarks, thereby preventing many of his listeners from sensing his totalitarian ambitions.

A similar effect was noted by Jewett [1973] who reports in his book, *The Captain America Complex,* that the long-standing Puritan image of the United States as a Redeemer Nation contributed substantially to the "millennial" fervor of American prowar rhetoric. From Jewett's perspective, then, the American people fought the Persian Gulf War because doing so preserved the nation's oft-articulated goals of preserving world freedom. To deny such a rich rhetorical heritage would have threatened what Jewett sees as the nation's "mythic base of moral superiority" [p. 222].

Although it is risky to present a list of values for some two hundred and fifty million Americans, Table 11.1 attempts just that. The list is based on work done over some forty years ago by Minnick [1957], but it does not differ from that done in 1831 by the French writer Alexis de Tocqueville. The key test of such a list is what is known as "face validity": Do the values seem familiar to a discerning member of the culture?

Admittedly, there are things to argue about here: Is success in the United States really judged by economic standards only? Are family values as strong today as they were when the list was first formulated? Is government still thought to be naturally inefficient? While the values in any culture wax and wane over the years, they are not altered radically except during periods of massive social upheaval because, as our earlier definition stated, values represent *basic life orientations.*

When Minnick formulated this list of values in the 1950s, he could not have predicted that Americans in the 1990s would be purchasing Japanese automobiles, listening in rapt attention to testimony at the O. J. Simpson trial, or coping with waves of Cuban refugees in Miami. But knowing that Americans value efficiency, are fascinated by male aggressiveness and, for the most part, feel that equality of opportunity should be extended to minority groups, Minnick might well have guessed at such contemporary events.

The cultural critic can use Minnick's schema as a kind of checklist for discovering the value emphases in a particular message, for discovering why and how often a given persuader dipped into this satchel of sacred beliefs. For example, Gordon Sinclair's message was in many ways just a prose version of Minnick's telegraphic list. Although Sinclair does not touch upon aesthetic values, he mentions all of the other valuetypes. Similarly, Lewis' [1972] letters of recommendation appear to have been generated by using Minnick's list as

TABLE II.I A Catalog of American Values

I. Theoretical Values of Contemporary Americans

1. Americans respect the scientific method and things labeled scientific.
2. They express a desire to be reasonable, to get the facts and make rational choices.
3. They prefer, in meeting problems, to use traditional approaches to problems, or means that have been tried previously. Americans don't like innovations, but, perversely, they think change generally means progress.
4. They prefer quantitative rather than qualitative means of evaluation. Size (bigness) and numbers are the most frequent measuring sticks.
5. They respect common sense.
6. They think learning should be "practical," and that higher education tends to make a man visionary.
7. They think everyone should have a college education.

II. Economic Values of Contemporary Americans

1. Americans measure success chiefly by economic means. Wealth is prized and Americans think everyone should aspire and have the opportunity to get rich.
2. They think success is the product of hard work and perseverance.
3. They respect efficiency.
4. They think one should be thrifty and save money in order to get ahead.
5. Competition is to them the most important aspect of American economic life.
6. Business can run its own affairs best, they believe, but some government regulation is required.
7. They distrust economic royalists and big business in general.

III. Aesthetic Values of Contemporary Americans

1. Americans prefer the useful arts—landscaping, auto designing, interior decorating, dress designing, etc.
2. They feel that pure aesthetics (theatre, concerts, painting, sculpture) is more feminine than masculine and tend to relegate the encouragement of them to women.
3. They prefer physical activities—sports, hunting, fishing, and the like—to art, music, literature.
4. They respect neatness and cleanliness.
5. They admire grace and coordination, especially in sports and physical contests.
6. They admire beauty in women, good grooming and neat appearance in both sexes.
7. They think many artists and writers are queer or immoral.
8. They tend to emphasize the material rather then the aesthetic value of art objects.

IV. Social Values of Contemporary Americans

1. Americans think that people should be honest, sincere, kind, generous, friendly, and straightforward.
2. They think a man should be a good mixer, able to get along well with other people.
3. They respect a good sport; they think a man should know how to play the game, to meet success or failure.
4. They admire fairness and justice.
5. They believe a man should be aggressive and ambitious, should want to get ahead, and be willing to work hard at it.
6. They admire "a regular guy" (one who does not try to stand off from his group because of intellectual, financial, or other superiority).
7. They like people who are dependable and steady, not mercurial.
8. They like a good family man. They think a man should marry, love his wife, have children, love them, educate them, and sacrifice for his family. He should not spoil his children, but he should be indulgent with his wife. He should love his parents. He should own his own home if possible.
9. They think people should conform to the social expectations for the roles they occupy.

(continued)

TABLE 11.1 (*continued*)

V. Political Values of Contemporary Americans

---

1. Americans prize loyalty to community, state, and nation. They think the American way of doing things is better than foreign ways.
2. They think American democracy is the best of all possible governments.
3. They prize the individual above the state. They think government exists for the benefit of the individual.
4. The Constitution to the American is a sacred document, the guardian of his liberties.
5. Communism is believed to be the greatest existing menace to America.
6. Americans believe the two-party system is best and should be preserved.
7. They think government ownership in general is undesirable.
8. They believe government is naturally inefficient.
9. They think a certain amount of corruption is inevitable in government.
10. They think equality of opportunity should be extended to minority groups (with notable minority dissent).

VI. Religious Values of Contemporary American

---

1. Americans believe Christianity is the best of all possible religions, but that one should be tolerant of other religions.
2. They think good works are more important than one's religious beliefs.
3. They believe one should belong to and support a church.
4. God, to most Americans, is real and is acknowledged to be the creator of the universe.
5. They think religion and politics should not be mixed; ministers should stay out of politics, politicians out of religious matters.
6. Americans are charitable. They feel sympathy for the poor and the unfortunate and are ready to offer material help.
7. They tend to judge people and events moralistically.

From Minnick [1968] pp. 218–220.

a kind of artificial intelligence system: II.6 + IV.4 + VI.3 = a letter of recommendation. That impression is heightened when one examines some of the unfavorable letters Lewis studied:

> (1) He is an individual capable of working long hours at his chemistry, with the aid and encouragement of his splendid wife. . . . But I believe he has dissipated a good deal of his energy in nonscientific endeavors—including two unsuccessful marriages and a substantial business venture. [p. 28]
>
> (2) She was something of a 'wheeler-dealer' in student politics, and as a result may not have been too well-liked by some of her peers. [p. 24]
>
> (3) The only objectionable feature that I have noted is that this last semester he has raised a beard. I thought his appearance without the beard was very nice. I do not know how permanent the beard is. Otherwise I am sure you would be well pleased with him in this position. [p. 26]

Perhaps the most interesting feature of such value-based rhetoric is how *automatically* and *confidently* these value-centered observations are made, as if the warrants for such data-claim movements were beyond question. This same sense of confidence can be found in the rhetoric of Norman Vincent Peale, a cleric who for fifty years offered advice through his radio talks, television appearances, and, primarily, through his books, newsletters, and prayer cards. In many ways, Peale was as much a minister to the nation's psyche as to the nation's soul. One of his pamphlets, *Help Yourself with God's Help*, lists ten steps for problem-solving. These are the first four:

> **1. SEEDS** The way to start out in solving a problem is to entertain a solid belief that for every problem there is a solution. Indeed, every problem contains the seeds of its own solution. You can find the answer to your problem if you look deeply into the problem itself.
>
> **2. CALM** A basic premise for solving a problem is to remain emotionally calm. Uptightness can block off the flow of thought power. And therefore it is important to reduce the stress and tension elements, for the mind can only operate efficiently when the emotions are under control.
>
> **3. ASSEMBLE** In dealing with a problem a proper procedure is to assemble all of the facts connected with it. Then deal with those facts impartially, impersonally and judicially. Take a scientific attitude toward the elements of the problem.
>
> **4. PAPER** Lay out all of the component parts of the problem on paper, so that you can see them in orderly coherence. Such a procedure will help to clarify your thinking by bringing the various factors of a problem into systematic order. Being able to see clearly, you will be better able to think clearly. [Peale, 1976:10]

Peale's approach is interesting on a number of fronts. For one thing, he provides an enumerated list, thereby displaying the preferred Western logic of linearity and numerosity. The steps he lists are behavioral, things *to do,* actions to be taken. It is interesting, for example, that he urges putting things down on paper before seeking Intuition (which he lists as step 8) or tapping one's Creativity (step 10). The fact-gathering he endorses (step 3) is well aligned with the preferred "scientific" approach to problem-solving found in Minnick's list, as is the "calmness" Peale urges in step 2. All of these features are subsidiary to step 1, however, which is the most American feature of them all—the supreme confidence that every problem can be solved. In a sense, then, Peale's faith amounts to a faith in hope.

According to a number of scholars, one of the most distinctive things about American rhetoric is its curious combination of **Transcendental** and **Pragmatic** themes. Kristol [1972] has identified the blending of these themes as quintessentially American. The Transcendental themes stem from the "prophetic-utopian" strains of colonial religion and the Pragmatic themes come from the rugged mercantilism that also motivated the nation's earliest European settlers. Arnold [1977] observes that almost every major debate in American history has borne witness to this struggle between "doing the will of God" and "doing business."

The statement Brinton [1938:34] makes about all revolutions— "grievances, however close they are to the pocketbook, must be made respectable, must touch the soul"—has been especially true in the United States, a nation that seems to need a Holy Purpose for doing almost anything. The Transcendent strain in discourse gives it an "elevating" tone, the sort of tone one hears on inauguration day in the United States. On such days, Americans have been told that they are guarantors of a "new covenant," inventors of a "new deal," explorers of a "new frontier." These rich abstractions were, in each case, attended by the levying of new taxes, a bitter dose of Pragmatism but one that was easier to swallow because of the Transcendent chaser. Ostensibly, new policy cannot be effected in the United States without this mixture.

Kristol [1972:148] explains why: "Just imagine what our TV commentators and 'news analysts' would do with a man who sought elected office with the promise that, during his tenure, he hoped to effect some small improvements in our conditions. They would ridicule him into oblivion." Some commentators have argued that pushing Pragmatic policies with Transcendent tones results in an offensive self-righteousness, making all Americans Ugly Americans.

Solomon's [1983a] study of TV evangelist Robert Schuller, for example, finds him at the center of the American mainstream with his "get rich/get God" formula. Solomon notes that Schuller has been unusually effective in blending Transcendent and Pragmatic themes and quotes from him as follows:

> Why should a person strive for success? Isn't that a pretty selfish objective? No, for when we succeed, whether it's in school, marriage, business, or social services—we inspire others to try to win, too. . . . *We have a stewardship to attempt to succeed for the glory of God and for the inspiration of others!* Success is not a selfish objective, for there is no way you can succeed unless you find a need and fill it, find a hurt and heal it, find a problem and solve it! . . . Success is *being the person God wants you to be.* [p. 179]

In most American discourse, then, the astute critic can find both transcendental and pragmatic themes. Smith [1980] did so when investigating the lyrics to some 2300 country music ballads and found in them a struggle between the Transcendent Southern values (close family ties, natural beauty, strong religious values) and the Pragmatism of the North (often depicted as cold but efficient, a source of jobs but also a source of sin). This same kind of struggle was noticed in Frentz and Farrell's [1975] analysis of the value themes in *The Exorcist,* a movie they describe as a classic conflict between Transcendence (in the person of Father Karras, the exorcist) and Scientific Pragmatism (or Positivism) in the person of the psychiatric community. The authors argue that the popularity of the film in the 1970s signaled America's disillusionment with Positivism and its need to turn away from the Pragmatic tragedies of air pollution, presidential assassinations, Vietnam, the rise of pornography, Watergate, etc.

No doubt, non-U.S. cultures also blend Pragmatic and Transcendent themes. But Americans appear to have a special penchant for *institutionalizing* rhetoric of this sort and for maintaining the *balance* between them. Because they have shared no common ethnic roots, cultural folkways, universal religion, or long-standing political heritage, the American people have been especially susceptible to discussions of national purpose. But it is also because they *lack* these common ties that they are also attracted to Pragmatic discussions. After all, a diverse citizenry can more often reach agreement about oil import fees or sewer systems than they can about political abstractions. In any event, the presence of this twin value cluster is a special boon to the critic interested in monitoring cultural continuity and change in the United States.

MYTHS: THE SUBSTANCE OF CULTURE

Earlier, myths were defined as Master Stories that describe exceptional people doing exceptional things and that serve as moral guides to proper action. Among the most common myths are **Cosmological** stories—why we are here, where we came from, what our ancestors were like. Myths like these are heard at an early age from one's parents (why Great Uncle Ezra moved off the farm), in schoolbooks (how the Declaration of Independence came to be), at church (what Moses found in the burning bush), and even in popular films (the legend of Pocahontas).

Societal myths teach one the proper way to live. Tales of George Washington's childhood lies, of Abraham Lincoln's trek through the snow to school, and of Teddy Roosevelt's charge up San Juan Hill become richer in detail and more heavily drenched in meaning each time they are told. They also often become more erroneous, but the literal truth of a myth is rarely its most important measure. Rather, a myth's serviceability is judged by its *evocative potential,* its capacity to impress on a listener the "Truth" of an event, not by its factuality.

Identity myths are also common. They explain what makes one cultural grouping different from another. The United States, for example, is seen as a "melting pot" of the world's peoples, and winsome tales of struggling/succeeding immigrants are commonly told ("Mr. Cosamino began with a pushcart and now owns the lower east side."). In a similar vein, stories of the United States as a "nonaggressor" nation, as "peace-keeper of the world," are used to distinguish it from political rivals like the Societ Union (once thought to be committed to "world conquest") or its economic rivals like Japan (a "fiercely dedicated" but somewhat "fanatical" nation).

Finally, **Eschatological** myths help a people know where they are going, what lies in store for them in the short run ("a balanced budget," "full employment," "an end to the nuclear fear") as well as in the long run (a "heavenly reward," the "transmigration of souls," etc.).

Virtually all rhetoric depends on myth for its effect. A political announcement of rising employment rates is especially heartening to citizens who have heard of the Great Depression. Ethnic jokes are funny only if one knows the supposedly peculiar story of the group being teased. Sermons of hell fire and damnation are frightening only if a worshipper is familiar with a certain brand of Christian mythology. Even if a rhetor does not retell a mythic tale in full, he or she will use some device (a quick allusion, a metaphor) to invite the audience's remembrance of that tale.

But why use myth? There are at least six reasons, as discussed below.

1. *Myths provide a heightened sense of authority.* When using myths, speakers expect listeners to treat the myths seriously. Such stories are not presented for the sake of mere diversion but to justify a data-claim movement ("If you don't buy Clearasil you'll be a wallflower.") by inviting listeners to search through their mental files and to contemplate anew the life of a wallflower. McDonald [1969:144] claims that "without myths there is no authority and without authority there is no politics," thereby suggesting that no government can succeed unless it can link its preferred policies to its historical truths.

2. *Myths provide a heightened sense of continuity.* As one event merges into another, its "meaning" becomes hard to discern. Myth helps out by grabbing up huge chunks of time and thousands of individual events to make some sort of patterned sense. The radical leftist operates in just this way when arguing that a series of apparently isolated events is evidence of some Great Plan secretly engineered by reactionaries. As a result, *myth gives meaning to the present by making it seem continuous with the past.* So, for example, the Kennedy assasination meant very different things to different people depending on the stories they were exposed to prior to the assasination itself [Zelizer, 1992].

3. *Myths provide a heightened sense of coherence.* Just as myth can reach across time, it can also reach across intellectual space by fashioning "whole" stories out of bits and pieces of ideas. So, for example, Adolf Hitler wove British nationalism, Marxist imagery, Roman Catholic pageantry, and Freemason eschatology into Nazi wholecloth [Bosmajian, 1974]. Pocock [1971] describes such rhetoric as one that uses "ancestral ghosts" to fashion something ostensibly new and complete. Through such combinations, myth serves a kind of tidying up function, bringing together diverse parts of an audience's emotional life.

4. *Myths provide a heightened sense of community.* Communities become communities when they admire the same heroes and revere the same moments in history. Studies of colonial America (a diverse and unsettled citizenry if there ever was one) show how myths create community. Merritt [1966] studied the newspapers of the day and found that revolutionary fever increased as references to "the American colonies" (vs. "the British colonies") increased. According to McGee [1975], almost all references to "the people" are based more in myth than in history. As McGee [p. 242] says, the people "are conjured into objective reality, remain so long as the rhetoric which defined them has force, and in the end wilt away, becoming once again merely a collection of individuals."

5. *Myths provide a heightened sense of choice.* People rarely change their behavior unless a choice is forced on them. Myths dramatize such choices by depicting **dialectical struggles** between Good and Evil. Such grappling

heightens the importance of the issues at stake ("the path of Light or the path of Darkness") and clarify the alternatives ("a life in chains or a chance to breathe free"). At times, the struggle is between the Haves and the Have-Nots, as Williams [1974] observed in an inner-city church where parishioners described *themselves* as "outcasts," "the despised few," and "poor folks." At other times, the struggle is between Rationality and Irrationality, as Ivie [1980] found when studying myths of savagery in prowar rhetoric.

6. *Myths provide a heightened sense of agreement.* Although myths often describe concrete events, they do so in a marvelously abstract way. Myths of The Abortion Clinic Bomber and The Welfare Queen are useful to Leftists and Rightists even though such stereotypes are often vague. But vagueness has its value, says Hart [1977], since an abstraction like "One Nation Under God" has kept church-state tensions to a minimum in the United States for over two hundred years. In sanctioning invocations at political banquets and nondescript prayers before sessions of Congress, the American people have forged a civil-religious "contract" between church and state, using myth, not law, to handle these potentially dangerous matters.

How is myth best studied? Although some extrapolations must be made, the work of Claude Levi-Strauss is perhaps the richest approach available. Levi-Strauss, the father of **Structuralism,** was an anthropologist by training and particularly fascinated by the folk stories told in the cultures he studied. A broad and imaginative thinker, Levi-Strauss [1955:431–40] has provided six guidelines (here paraphrased) for the critic of myth:

1. The critic should try to track the **source** of the myth being used (where it came from, what forms of the myth existed before) in order to understand its emotional power for people.
2. The key to the effectiveness of a given myth lies not in its individual narrative elements but in how such elements are **combined** in the story.
3. The critic's task is to discover the unique sort of **harmony** (of emotions, images, ideas, etc.) this combination of elements provides.
4. The critic must calculate how a given myth treats standard chronology (historical time) versus **synchronic time**—the narrative progression as imaginatively constructed by the storyteller.
5. Narrative elements that are temporal neighbors, that share the same **context,** will often lead the critic to the myth's basic "argument."
6. Similarly, the critic should pay special attention to the **oppositional** (or dialectical) forces in a given myth in order to discover its motivational base.

Levi-Strauss' suggestions are a good starting point for the critic even though critics have discussed its shortcomings [see Warnick, 1979; Harari, 1979; and McGuire, 1977]. A good case in point is a speech given by Major, an aging pig in George Orwell's *Animal Farm.* In his book, Orwell tells of a society populated largely by animals who, not unlike man, struggle daily with life's ups and downs. In the beginning of Orwell's book, Major gives a classic revolutionary address. When reading it, one can easily imagine the same rhetorical ploys being used to inspire any oppressed class in any era. This is Major's speech:

(1) Comrades, you have heard already about the strange dream that I had last night. But I will come to the dream later. I have something else to say first. I do not think, comrades, that I shall be with you for many months longer, and before I die, I feel it my duty to pass on to you such wisdom as I have acquired. I have had a long life, I have much time for the nature of life on this earth as well as any animal now living. It is about this that I wish to speak to you.

(2) Now, comrades, what is the nature of this life of ours? Let us face it: our lives are miserable, laborious, and short. We are born, we are given just so much food as will keep the breath in our bodies, and those of us who are capable of it are forced to work to the last atom of our strength; and the very instant that our usefulness has come to an end we are slaughtered with hideous cruelty. No animal in England knows the meaning of happiness or leisure after he is a year old. No animal in England is free. The life of an animal is misery and slavery: that is the plain truth.

(3) But is this simply part of the order of nature? Is it because this land of ours is so poor that it cannot afford a decent life to those who dwell upon it? No, comrades, a thousand times no! The soil of England is fertile, its climate is good, it is capable of affording food in abundance to an enormously greater number of animals than now inhabit it. This single farm of ours would support a dozen horses, twenty cows, hundreds of sheep—and all of them living in a comfort and dignity that are now almost beyond our imagining. Why then do we continue in this miserable condition? Because nearly the whole of the produce of our labour is stolen from us by human beings. There, comrade, is the answer to all our problems. It is summed up in a single word—Man. Man is the only real enemy we have. Remove Man from the scene, and the root cause of hunger and overwork is abolished forever.

(4) Man is the only creature that consumes without producing. He does not give milk, he does not lay eggs, he is too weak to pull the plough, he cannot run fast enough to catch rabbits. Yet he is lord of all animals. He sets them to work, he gives back to them the bare minimum that will prevent them from starving, and the rest he keeps for himself. Our labour tills the soil, our dung fertilises it, and yet there is not one of us that owns more than his bare skin. You cows that I see before me, how many thousand of gallons of milk have you given during this last year? And what has happened to that milk which should have been breeding up sturdy calves? Every drop of it has gone down the throat of our enemies. And you hens, how many eggs have you laid in this last year, and how many of those eggs ever hatched into chickens? The rest of you have all gone to market to bring in money for Jones and his men. And you, Clover, where are those four foals you bore, who should have been the support and pleasure of your old age? Each was sold at a year old—you will never see one of them again. In return for your four confinements and all your labour in the fields, what have you ever had except your bare rations and a stall?

(5) And even the miserable lives we lead are not allowed to reach their natural span. For myself I do not grumble, for I am one of the lucky ones. I am twelve years old and have had over four hundred children. Such is the natural life of a pig. But no animal escapes the cruel knife in the end. You young porkers who are

sitting in front of me, every one of you will scream your lives out at the block within a year. To that horror we all must come—cows, pigs, hens, sheep, everyone. Even the horses and the dogs have no better fate. You, Boxer, the very day that those great muscles of yours lose their power, Jones will sell you to the knacker, who will cut your throat and boil you down for the foxhounds. As for the dogs, when they grow old and toothless, Jones ties a brick round their necks and drowns them in the nearest pond.

(6) Is it not crystal clear, then, comrades, that all the evils of this life of ours spring from the tyranny of human beings? Only get rid of Man, and the produce of our labour would be our own. Almost overnight we could become rich and free. What then must we do? Why, work night and day, body and soul, for the overthrow of the human race! That is my message to you, comrades: Rebellion! I do not know when that Rebellion will come, it might be in a week or in a hundred years, but I know, as surely as I see this straw beneath my feet, that sooner or later justice will be done. Fix your eyes on that, comrade, throughout the short remainder of your lives! And above all, pass on this message of mine to those who come after you, so that future generations shall carry on the struggle until it is victorious.

(7) And remember, comrades, your resolution must never falter. No argument must lead you astray. Never listen when they tell you that Man and the animals have a common interest, that the prosperity of the one is the prosperity of the others. It is all lies. Man serves the interests of no creature except himself. And among us animals let there be perfect unity, perfect comradeship in the struggle. All men are enemies. All animals are comrades. . . .

(8) I have little more to say. I merely repeat, remember always your duty of enmity towards Man and all his ways. Whatever goes upon two legs is an enemy. Whatever goes upon four legs, or has wings, is a friend. And remember also that in fighting against Man, we must not come to resemble him. Even when you have conquered him do not adopt his vices. No animals must ever live in a house, or sleep in a bed, or wear clothes, or drink alcohol, or smoke tobacco, or touch money, or engage in trade. All the habits of Man are evil. And, above all, no animal must ever tyrannise over his own kind. Weak or strong, clever or simple, we are all brothers. No animal must ever kill any other animal. All animals are equal.

(9) And now, comrades, I will tell you about my dream of last night. I cannot describe that dream to you. It was a dream of the earth as it will be when Man has vanished. But it reminded me of something that I have long forgotten. Many years ago, when I was a little pig, my mother and the other sow used to sing an old song of which they knew only the tune and the first three words. I had known that tune in my infancy, but it had long since passed out of my mind. Last night, however, it came back to me in my dream. And what is more, the words of the song also came back— words, I am certain, which were sung by the animals of long ago and have been lost to memory for generations. I will sing you that song now, comrades. I am old and my voice is hoarse, but when I have taught you the tune, you can sing it better for yourselves. It is called "Beasts of England":

(10) Beasts of England, beasts of Ireland,
      Beasts of every land and clime,
      Hearken to my joyful tidings
      Of the golden future time.

> Soon or late the day is coming,
>   Tyrant Man shall be o'erthrown,
>   And the fruitful fields of England
>   Shall be trod by beasts alone.
> Rings shall vanish from our noses,
>   And the harness from our back,
>   Bit and spur shall rust forever,
>   Cruel whips no more shall crack.
> Riches more than mind can picture,
>   Wheat and barley, oats and hay,
>   Clover, beans, and mangel-wurzels
>   Shall be ours upon that day.
> Bright will shine the fields of England,
>   Purer shall its waters be,
>   Sweeter yet shall blow its breezes
>   On that day that sets us free.
> For that day we all must labour,
>   Though we die before it break;
>   Cows and horses, geese and turkeys,
>   All must toil for freedom's sake.
> Beasts of England, beasts of Ireland,
>   Beasts of every land and clime,
>   Hearken well and spread my tidings
>   Of the golden future time. [Orwell, 1946:17–23]

Taken at its broadest level, Major's speech is a myth of rebirth. In paragraph 1, Major mentions his own advancing years, but at the end of the speech he returns to a story from his infancy, thereby giving the speech a mythic frame of death and rebirth. The propositional content of the speech progresses in precisely the same way: Animals have been horribly exploited in the past but a new day is dawning. Paragraphs 2 through 5 amplify the death motif as Major details the horrors his comrades must abide daily. Paragraphs 6 through 8 proceed differently as Major describes the mythic labor pains attendant to any birth, even the birth of a movement. Not unlike an instructor in a natural childbirth class, Major comforts, coaxes, and inspires his charges during this painful, yet glorious, parturition. The final two paragraphs detail how glorious this birth will be and it is not incidental that Major mentions his own mother's love in paragraph 9.

Within this overall frame, three major substructures can be detected. Table 11.2 sketches one such mythic substructure—how Major generates dialectical tension in the speech. Paragraph 1 is comparatively peaceful, with Major reflecting on his dream of the night before. Here, he also foreshadows mythic transcendence when mentioning his desire to donate what he has learned to posterity. But this tranquility is sharply arrested in paragraph 2 as Major introduces the first of seven major clashes. He begins on the most general note (freedom) and quickly introduces the theme of exploitation that he

TABLE 11.2 Myth and Dialectic in Major's Speech

Paragraph	Negative Mythic Elements	Positive Mythic Elements
1	None	Wisdom, nostalgia
2	Unspecific exploitation	Personal freedom
3	Human exploitation	Fruitfulness
4	Human exploitation	Productivity
5	Human exploitation	Longevity
6	Human exploitation	Deliverance
7	Human exploitation	Equality
8	Human exploitation	Personal integrity
9	None	Wisdom, nostalgia
10	Human exploitation	Freedom, productivity, fruitfulness, brotherhood

will subsequently develop. In this second paragraph, however, the precise source of the exploitation is left unstated, as Major tries to engage his listeners' imaginations.

But paragraph 3 begins with gusto as the speaker warms to his subject—the depravity of humankind. Thenceforth, Major maintains mythic continuity, successively contrasting human exploitation with the things his listeners most treasure. Paragraph 3 focuses on basic survival needs. Paragraph 4 makes an incipiently Marxist argument about the distribution of capital. Paragraph 5 ups the stakes by considering death itself.

Beginning with paragraph 6, however, the mood shifts substantially as higher needs are introduced—self-achievement, companionship, a sense of honor. In each case, humankind is again made the foil as Major contrasts each animal virtue with a human vice. Finally, in paragraph 9, dialectic fades into synthesis as Good subsumes Evil. The speech ends in paragraph 10 on the dream motif with which it began but, this time, the dream is amplified majestically.

Structuralists emphasize the importance of time to myth. That is clearly the case here as well, as we see in Figure 11.1. Unlike historical time, mythic time does not have to move moment by moment. Persuaders sometimes violently rearrange chronology in order to place the listener in the proper "emotional time." Major, for example, begins his speech in the distant past, no doubt because it gave him special credibility (he was the patriarch of the community). He quickly moves forward in time but, interestingly, returns once again to the distant past at the end of his speech, thereby sandwiching all that has transpired with his omniscience.

Temporally, paragraph 2 is a complex unit of discourse because it foreshadows the entire speech. Here, Major establishes himself as a person of perspective, one who can move easily across time. In addition, this paragraph establishes that his topic is grounded in the reality of the past, linked to the saliency of the present, but also relevant to the uncertainty of the future.

FIGURE 11.1 Myth and Time in Major's Speech

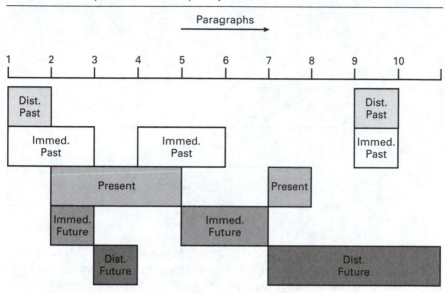

Major juxtaposes the immediate past and the present in paragraphs 2 through 6. These paragraphs give emotional force to the speech because the data he cites spring directly from the dreadful lives of his listeners (he even mentions some members of his audience by name, as if to heighten the audience's personal crisis).

The use of the *immediate* future is perhaps most unsettling of all in these paragraphs as Major argues that his listeners' current desperation cannot compare to tomorrow's hardships. It is the *structural* relationship between these temporal elements—the fact that they occur together at this point in the message—that makes for such powerful mythic effects.

When Major says in paragraph 3, "Remove Man from the scene, and the root cause of hunger and overwork is abolished forever," he briefly shows the light at the end of a tunnel he is about to make considerably darker. He returns to this theme briefly in paragraph 6 ("Only get rid of Man, and the produce of our labur would be our own. Almost overnight we could become rich and free."), drops it in paragraph 7, develops it in the two penultimate paragraphs, and finally lets it blend into the transcendent future in his concluding paragraph.

Moving in and out of the distant future in this way seems a clear attempt by Major to maintain mythic tension within his listeners until it becomes almost unbearable. This is a primitive rhetorical device that serves to heighten appreciation for the full-bodied, self-contained myth with which he concludes his remarks.

FIGURE 11.2 Myth and Topic in Major's Speech

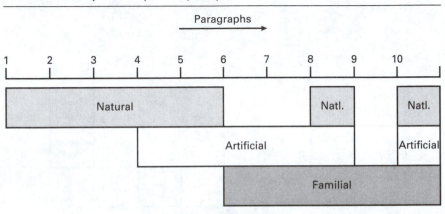

A final structural pass can be made over Major's speech. This time, one detects the use of three different mythic themes, as we see in Figure 11.2. **Naturalistic** myths introduce his topic, properly so, since his audience members are animals. In these passages, images of bodily processes (sleeping, breathing, eating) interact with images of nature (growing, fertilizing, watering) so as to establish the real-life import of Major's remarks.

These themes are extended in paragraphs 4 and 5. There, images of fertility (laying eggs, bearing foals, breeding calves) are linked to organic images (excreting, hatching) and aging images (declining musculature, toothlessness). But in these paragraphs, dialectical tension is also established as Major contrasts the naturalness of the animal world with the artificiality of the **human** world. The speaker lists humanity's sins serially: overconsumption of food, a materialistic standard of values, the arbitrary foreshortening of animal life. He also contrasts such natural objects as eggs, milk, and dung with the contrivances of human society: knives, blocs, knackers, bricks.

Humanity continues to be the mythic foil in paragraphs 6 through 8 as the poverty of the human spirit (tyranny, selfishness) is linked to humankind's depraved (and unnatural) habits: sleeping in beds, wearing clothes, drinking alcohol. But a third mythic grouping is displayed at this same time—images of brotherhood—and these images begin to change the tone of the speech from one of outrage to one of solidarity.

The **family** myth is developed *across species* ("whatever goes upon four legs, or has wings, is a friend.") as well as *across time* ("pass on this message of mine to those who come after you . . ."). The terminology used changes too as "comrades" are mentioned with greater frequency, and kinship terms (brothers, mother, family) are also used explicitly. Specifications for this new family of animals are also provided. They include political admonishments (references to the "common interest"), sociological enjoinders (human habits should not be imitated), and moral advice (no killing of other animals).

In paragraph 9, this newly fabricated family is linked, magically, to an ostensibly preexisting family by means of a song that was "sung by the animals of long ago." Finally, in paragraph 10, "beasts of every land" are united in a grand eschatological myth that describes a "golden future time."

Although we have made three separate critical passes over Major's speech, it cannot be forgotten that this message, like any message, is a *coalescence* of all three different mythic structures. Unlike critics, listeners do not have the luxury of unraveling that which they hear when they hear it. Major implicitly asked his listeners to deal with the dialectical, temporal, and topical structure of his myths *simultaneously*. It is this simultaneity that gives rhetoric its richness. It is the delicate interweaving of these themes that makes for rhetorical genius. As Claude Levi-Strauss demonstrated, the study of myth is necessarily a complex undertaking. But the tyrants who despoil myth show it is an undertaking the critic dare not abandon.

FANTASY THEMES: THE GRASS ROOTS OF CULTURE

Considerable research has been done in recent years using an approach called fantasy theme analysis. Originally identified by social psychologist Robert Bales, fantasy themes have also been studied extensively by communication scholar, Ernest Bormann. In this section, however, some amount of license will be taken with the notion of fantasy themes in order to make it immediately useful to the critic.

For our purposes, fantasy themes can be thought of as *mythic shorthand,* the stories told by subgroups in society. If myths are the prized tales of humankind in general, fantasy themes are the *local variations* wrought on these themes. If myths are vague, fantasy themes are specific. If myths are enduring, fantasy themes are short-lived. If myths are universally suited to public discussion, fantasy themes change from topic to topic. If myths are cross-cultural, fantasy themes are culture-specific.

An example: One of the most popular master myths in the United States has been that of America-as-a-New-Israel, a conviction that God specially created, and then guided, the nation for a special purpose— that of delivering the world's peoples from a state of Darkness. The belief was that God gave U.S. citizens an incredibly bountiful land because He especially favored them. In recompense, however, He expected the American Message (which was really His message) to be spread far and wide.

It may seem preposterous that any group could feel so self-important as to believe the literal truth of this tale, especially when the myth is described in such a blunt and unembellished way. That is how fantasy themes help. They round out the bluntness by using attractive vignettes to disguise the myth's presumptions. In a sense, fantasy themes become the everyday language of myth.

The early Puritans brocaded the New Israel myth considerably, and it soon sunk deep roots into the American psyche. One cluster of fantasy themes spawned from it argues that the United States is the peacekeeper of the world, one that must keep itself strong in order to protect all of God's children. Another set of fantasy themes preached that space must be colonized first by Americans because of God's charge to go forth into the wilderness with His word. Westward expansion in the early 1800s was launched in a similar way, as was Woodrow Wilson's League of Nations, Harry Truman's Marshall Plan, John Kennedy's Peace Corps, Lyndon Johnson's Vietnam War, and George Bush's War in the Gulf.

New Israel fantasy themes were used to launch the public education movement in the United States, broaden participation in the Olympic Games, and support a host of charities: The Red Cross, UNESCO, and CARE. Social movements of both the Right and the Left have used such themes as well, with Ted Kennedy marching off in the mid-1980s to explain civil rights to South Africans and televangelist Pat Robertson urging greater U.S. involvement in Central America. Fantasy themes have also been used to endorse the Voice of America. It is noteworthy that there is no Voice of Canada or, for that matter, no Voice of Israel either.

According to Bormann and his colleagues [1994], the purpose of fantasy themes is to dramatize ideas for listeners. The basic notion here is that listeners or readers often lack the imagination needed to see what the world will be like if they accept new beliefs. A study by Kidd [1975] demonstrates how rhetoric performs this task. Kidd was interested in how popular magazines represented the social world to its female readers. She found two major "visions" of the world being projected in such discourse, one of which stressed that (1) women were fundamentally different from men and should behave thusly, (2) that women should avoid conflict under all circumstances, and (3) that they should follow clearly established guidelines when interacting with others. Some of the passages Kidd cites from the magazines exemplify this traditional vision:

- In New York City the 'career woman' can be seen in fullest bloom and it is not irrelevant that New York City also has the greatest concentration of psychiatrists. [p. 33]
- There is no such thing as a worthless conversation provided you know what to listen for. The attentive listener . . . listens for what people unconsciously reveal about themselves while they're talking. Thus [she] can derive meaning from a conversation even thought the other person may be talking nonsense. [p. 34]
- A man can feel kinship with the gods if his wife can make him believe he can cause a flowering within her. If she doesn't feel it she must bend every effort to pretend. [p. 34–5]

A second, much newer, vision found by Kidd embraced a more fluid conception of life, far fewer social strictures, and more numerous societal roles for women. Kidd offers the following excerpts as representative of that vision:

- Specialists who study family life now agree that it is pointless to compare real marriages with some imagined ideal. The model marriage is a myth. . . . We must begin with a basic fact. Not all marriages are alike and they cannot be measured by the same standards. [p. 35]
- The idea of permanence is an absurd illusion. Change is the most permanent thing you can say about the whole universe. [p. 35]
- Unpleasant feelings, petty resentments and frustrations do not go away simply because one refuses to let them show. Rather, they can build up a deadly store of bitterness. [p. 36]

Kidd found that after these premises were laid out for readers, the fantasy themes were developed in considerable detail, with countless "case studies" of happy and unhappy women used to add dramatic intensity to the ideas being stressed.

By finding so many instances of these two visions in so many different magazines, Kidd demonstrated another feature of fantasy themes: they "chain out" in society because of their rhetorical power. People become caught up in these visions and then repeat them for others. Thus, because of the rhetoric of the 1960s "everybody knew" that racial harmony was just around the corner. In the 1970s "everybody knew" that the Grateful Dead subverted the values of American youth. In the 1980s "everybody knew" that being able to spell the word entrepreneur would make one rich. And in the 1990s "everybody knew" that young people were slackers.

Fantasy theme analysts are especially interested in calculating the *breadth* of such appeals, discovering those that "echo" through society and those that are unique to a subgroup. By keying on the fantasies spun out by the Disciples of Christ, for example, Hensley [1975] was able to discover how that group of outcasts sustained themselves for so long in a larger culture that had little use for them (the answer: All "disciples" are reviled at first but ultimate victory is assured them). In a similar vein, Ilkka [1977] traced the rhetoric of the American Communist Party, a group facing considerable persuasive odds, and found that they coped with their decided minority status by dramatizing the exploits of communist leaders, thereby replacing argument with hero-worship.

Fantasy themes, then, can be highly sustaining. A fascinating example of this was reported by Weisman [1980] who studied the activities of prisoners held in Nazi concentration camps during the Second World War. Weisman argues that it was the capacity to generate and share fantasy themes that helped the prisoners maintain their sanity. By repeating for one another sacred religious tracts, by engaging in "public dreaming" (e.g., by describing the elaborate meals they would prepare on their release), and by recording their visions for the future in their diaries (a punishable activity itself), some of the prisoners were able to distract themselves usefully from the horrors surrounding them.

A less dramatic, but no less important, testament to the worth of fantasy themes is provided by Elpenor [1986], who describes the rhetoric shared during meetings of Alcoholics Anonymous. An alcoholic himself, Elpenor reports that he initially regarded such standard fantasy themes as Count Your Blessings, One Day at a Time, Easy Does It, Live and Let Live, and First Things First to be tedious and banal. Eventually, however, he came to realize that such themes provide "integrity, coherence, simplicity" to the alcoholic.

Given the importance of fantasy themes, how might they best be studied? Bormann and his students have developed a number of elaborate social scientific methods for testing their popularity. Here, however, we will take an approach better suited to the beginning critic. Table 11.3 presents eight major questions that can be asked of discourse. In a sense, these questions operate at the philosophical level because they probe the *presuppositions* underlying a group's rhetoric. These probes ask the critic to isolate the stories told most often in a given body of rhetoric and then to ask what "lessons" they appear to be teaching: about people in general, about the capacity of individuals, about right and wrong. Following Bormann's lead, *it is not sufficient to answer these questions for a single text*. Rather, the cultural critic must track answers to them across speakers. Only then can genuine thematizing be established.

Let us consider a cursory example of how such questions can prove useful in rhetorical analysis. The following passage is an excerpt from an oft-circulated flyer entitled "Ideals of a Klansman" by Robert Shelton [n.d.], one-time leader of the Ku Klux Klan. Although the excerpt is brief, it is more than enough

TABLE 11.3 Critical Probes for Fantasy Theme Analysis

1. Given the speaker's story lines, what are people like?
   Are they dependable? Fundamentally deceived? Are people essentially alone? Evil or duplicitous at root? Do they care for one another?
2. Given the speaker's story lines, what are the possibilities of group action?
   Is group effort morally superior to individual effort? Practically superior? Are groups doomed to disharmony? Does group action bring out the best in us? The worst?
3. Given the speaker's story lines, on what can people most depend?
   Their mental agility? Physical skills? Spiritual resources? Hard work? Other people? Nothing at all?
4. Given the speaker's story lines, what is humankind's fundamental purpose on earth?
   To help others? To self-actualize? To change the world? To fulfill historical mandates? To right wrongs?
5. Given the speaker's story lines, what are the fundamental measures of right and wrong?
   Personal ethics? Some religious code? Social obligations and agreements? Political utility? Legal duty?
6. Given the speaker's story lines, how can success best be measured?
   By assessing quantitative gain? By enhancing self-knowledge? By fulfilling group destiny? By being faithful to certain abstract principles? By defeating an enemy?
7. Given the speaker's story lines, what sort of information is most dependable?
   Book learning? Empirical observation? Personal experience? Folk wisdom? Secret revelation?
8. Given the speaker's story lines, why do things happen as they do?
   Because of some hidden design? Because of individual or group effort? Because of random chance? Because of some extrahuman force?

to give us a feeling for the Klan's mythic orientation and for the fantasy themes it utilizes most frequently:

> We believe in the upholding of the Constitution of these United States. By upholding the Constitution, is meant the whole Constitution, anyone who violates one clause of the Constitution, would as quickly break every other one if it serves his purpose to do so. . . .
>
> We believe in a free press, uncontrolled by political or religious sects.
>
> The press should be free to spread news without coloring it to suit any person or sect: But such is not the case, scarcely a newspaper anywhere dares to publish the truth: the whole truth and nothing but the truth. The press is largely controlled by the Roman Catholic priesthood and Judaism, and as a result the great masses of people are fed on propaganda instead of true facts. When an article is read in either a newspaper or magazine, one does not know but what there is a sinister motive back of it. And a paper that publishes nothing but the truth can hardly exist.
>
> We believe in law and order: In other words, the Klan believes in keeping the laws and in enforcing the laws. Many accusations have been brought against the Klan as lawbreakers. These accusations against the order are purely newspaper propaganda. So far we have not heard of a single instance where the Klan, by an official act, has violated any law.
>
> We believe in white supremacy.
>
> The Klan believes that America is a white man's country, and should be governed by white men. Yet the Klan is not anti-Negro, it is the Negro's friend. The Klan is eternally opposed to the mixing of the white and the colored races. Our creed: Let the white man remain white, the black man black, the yellow man yellow, the brown man brown, and the red man red. God drew the color line, and the man should so let it remain, read Acts 17:26 if you please.
>
> We believe in the protection of our pure womanhood, the home, the church, our public school system, our Constitution, and our American way of life.
>
> This is a stand for the purity of the home, for morality, for the protection of our mothers, our sisters, our wives, our daughters, against the whiteslaver, the homewrecker, the libertine. And to live up to this principle a Klansman must keep himself pure and above reproach. He must treat other women as he would have those of his own household treated.

Here, we can begin to see the fantasies that chain out among Klan members and that motivate their labors. Throughout the passage, one gets the clear sense that the world is divided into two groups: one, a small one, sees things clearly, and another, much larger, group is made up of people too lazy to see the truth or who have been captured by the forces of evil (e.g., the press). Life as described by the Klan is a dog-eat-dog existence. Laws are broken with impunity, immigration threatens to pollute the gene pool, churches deceive their flocks. Only the Klan stands for righteousness; even the courts cannot be trusted. Men are strong, but sheep; women are innocent, but weak.

These conditions give the Klan a reason for being. In an anomic world where all is disorder, even a small band of fearless patriots can turn back the slovenly forces massing against them. Because the enemy is in *moral* disarray, group action is indeed possible but only if the essential truth of the Klan philosophy is adhered to by all concerned. It is perhaps for this reason that we find so much repetition in even this short passage. The repetition gives a kind of energy to the prose ("the truth, the whole truth, and nothing but the truth") and it also serves to document the inevitable coherence to be found in Klan philosophy. A small but powerful truth sustains a crusade best.

Philosophical allegiance, then, will best advance Klan goals. Like much doctrinaire rhetoric, this passage places little faith in "great persons" leading the group to moral victory. Given the tremendous number of people who have already accepted what they see as the insanity of civil rights, the Klan has little confidence in human discernment. Nor does the Klan have much hope for change via natural evolution. The Klan's world is fixed: The NAACP is in league with the Communists; foreign ideas are inherently bankrupt; Klansmen are "pure and above reproach." "England for Englishmen, France for Frenchmen, Italy for Italians, and America for Americans," says Shelton elsewhere in the pamphlet.

Because so much in the world is thereby "set" in the eyes of the Klan, the only possibility for change is *complete* eradication of evil, *total* removal of Blacks and Jews, and *unqualified* acceptance of the Constitution ("anyone who violates one clause of the Constitution would . . ."). Given the genetic deficiency of the offending groups, no cosmetic change is possible. Similarly, given the inherent bias of the media, the courts, and the established churches, their pronouncements can be disregarded in toto as well.

Generally speaking, the Klan does not discover its purpose in self-actualizing, in helping others, or for the most part, in changing public policy in a piecemeal fashion. While they do seem motivated by an "historical mandate" of sorts, the precise source of that mandate is unclear (the advancement of Christianity? embracing strict constructionism? returning to the chivalric code?). Despite this vagueness, the Klan points to the past as it looks to the future. The Klan finds right and wrong in religion ("an infidel is a person who rejects Jesus Christ"), in law ("we have not heard of a single instance where the Klan . . . has violated the law"), and in morality ("this is a stand for the purity of the home. . . .").

Given the magnitude of the Klan's goals, success will not be had in the short run. Given the galaxy of challenges the Klan identifies, its rhetoric will not appeal to those looking for a quick fix. Rewriting an entire nation's laws, disbanding the media, eliminating three-fourths of the world's religions, removing all "foreigners" from the United States, and protecting womanhood in all its varieties (mothers, sisters, wives, and daughters) is clearly a tall order. Only the tireless need apply.

The Klansman is an empiricist. He believes in what his eyes tell him: the length of a nose, the pigmentation of skin, the existence of "true facts" (as opposed to "propaganda"). His sensory organs are all that he needs. "God drew the color line," says Shelton, "and the man should so let it remain." The world he projects is therefore a tidy world with people and ideas housed in the categories to which they are natively suited. Books (and, one suspects, education in general) merely serve to confuse because they build higher and higher abstractions and mangle categorical distinctions (e.g., by entertaining the notions of a Black patriot or a white libertine). By keeping one's eyes on what one "knows for sure," the Klansman is not likely to underestimate the enemies who threaten to sully the nation further. "Let him who has eyes see," argues the Klansman, for it is through vision that one finds Vision.

One cannot help but notice in Klan rhetoric a certain tired quality. The fantasy themes are old and shopworn: rapacious Blacks, crooked lawyers, liberated women, power-mongering Catholics, usurious Jews. The pamphlets issued from its national headquarters do not differ from year to year, or from decade to decade for that matter. It is as if all that is known has already been learned. Klan persuaders have long since found their major claims and now seem interested only in collecting copycat data. As a result, the rhetorical visions they generate are not particularly clear or compelling. The repetitiveness of their fantasy themes makes for a lazy rhetoric, one that can be heard in every age but that seems peculiar to no age. This may be why the Klan has been consistently relegated to marginal status in the United States, a rhetorical fate for which we may all be grateful.

CONCLUSION

In this chapter, we have observed the rhetoric of Klansmen, television evangelists, magazine authors, Boys Scouts, aging pigs, and a U.S.-loving Canadian. All embraced values. Each depended on myth. All traded in fantasy themes. Each went about their rhetorical business in a different way because each has a special message to share. Each had a vision of what a perfect world would be like and each tried to share that vision with others. Some, like the Boy Scouts, succeeded because their goals were so traditional, while others, like Robert Schuller, succeeded because they demanded so little from their listeners. Still others, like Gordon Sinclair, succeeded because they had the right message for the right moment. But Sinclair quickly receded into the background because that was his only message and because there are so many moments.

There is much that is unique about each of these persuaders but there is something they share as well—a culture. For all of them it was Western culture; for most of them, U.S. culture. But having said that, what has one said? After all, each had a different rhetorical goal and each a distinctive rhetorical style. But each possessed something else—cultural confidence—a sense that they had the right message for the right place. Also, like the authors of the *Webelos Scout Book,* they felt they could talk people into behaving better than they had been behaving. This is a thoroughly Western kind of confidence and it is very much in the tradition of American political evangelism as well.

At the moment, we do not know what will happen when some of these old values are fashioned for some new purpose, or who will win and who will lose when certain other fantasy themes become tired and die. We do not know what will happen but we can guess about such matters. Cultural criticism helps with the guessing.

Chapter 12

DRAMATISTIC CRITICISM

with David Payne

Remember when you knew most of your neighbors and their children? Wasn't it a comfort to know if your child was playing a couple of blocks away and had a bump, bruise, or skinned elbow that one of your friends would take care of the immediate problem and let you know, because you'd show the same concern? This is how small neighborhoods used to be. This is how Wimbledon Country is! [Wimbledon Country, 1988:3]

*****

Legend Oaks is a carefully planned neighborhood of nearly 300 thickly-wooded acres in the very heart of Southwest Austin. Here, Mother Nature, preserved and even enhanced by new plantings, lives in harmony with a new standard of neighborhood amenities. Right now, children laugh and swing on our playscape, tennis balls bounce across our lighted court, and the surface of our pool is broken by a swimmer's rhythmic strokes. [Legend Oaks, 1988:F12]

*****

When you purchase a home site in Weston Lakes you can enjoy the prestigious Weston Lakes Country Club and build your dream home when you're ready. The country club features one of the finest 18-hole championship golf courses in

Texas, adult and family swimming pools, tennis courts, croquet lawn and fine dining. Situated among huge century old pecan and oak trees and shimmering natural lakes, Weston Lakes offers a distinctive and private life style. The lakes act as a clearwater moat surrounding the property and enhance the privacy and security of the development. They are also stocked with catfish and trophy-size bass. [Weston Lakes, 1988:5]

*****

The homes in Ember Oaks Estates are built on lush, wooded homesites and are surrounded by gently rolling hills, giving the entire area a peaceful country atmosphere. . . . Ember Oaks offers a secluded atmosphere, yet it is close to Southlake, the new IBM complex, Las Colinas, the Mid Cities and Dallas/Forth International Airport. [Fox and Jacobs, 1988:J5]

*****

Our company sells houses. Nothing more. If you need to live near the third busiest airport in the United States so that you can travel four days out of five for Transcontinental Computers, you're going to hear a lot of planes. Now, we'll be happy to plant a few begonias next to your house so you can be reminded of Mayberry R.F.D., but you'll still be living within twenty miles of three million people. We've been in business for twenty-five years, so see us if you want a house built. As for illusions, you'll have to shop elsewhere. For a hundred and fifty thousand bucks we can't give you prestige—you'll have to earn that by becoming president of your company, playing ball for the Dallas Mavericks, running for Congress, or writing a best seller. Our company can't relieve your guilt feelings about your latchkey kids and we sure as hell can't stop the air pollution you and your neighbors will generate on I-30 each morning. When we build houses, we supply the two-by-fours, the duct tape, the corner molding, the electrical circuits, and the paneling. You supply the baloney.

In the last of these ads, something has gone awry. Or perhaps something has gone wry. The first four ads, drawn from the Homes sections of various Texas newspapers, represent their genre nicely. Filled with overly rich images, these ads turn brick-and-wallboard boxes into much grander places by focusing on what their products symbolize rather than what they are. The last ad, however, misses the game-plan entirely. Its depressing frankness fails to do an essential job of rhetoric: blending an audience's lived life with its psychic life.

Critic Kenneth Burke says that it takes mystery, adventure, community, and magic to make a human creature. He says that to thwart people's imaginations (as in the fifth ad) is to deny people the resources they need to cope with rootlessness and anomie. He says that the need for drama is not just an affectation that some people have but a basic need that *all* people have, as basic as the needs for food, sex, and shelter. Burke would probably say that the need for drama is so profound that the fifth advertisement could only have been written by a textbook author to make a point. And he would be right.

This chapter details the critical approach of Burke, a critic who has explored the complex relationships among aesthetics, politics, language, and social organization. Burke's ideas have influenced countless students of rhetoric and literature as well as sociologists, political scientists, historians, linguists, and philosophers. Burke urges the doing of criticism not because rhetoric is powerful, even though it surely is, and not because criticism is interesting, which goes without saying. Rather, says Burke, tracking the "rhetorical motive" is central to understanding what human beings are at root (symbol-users, he feels), what they strive to do (rise above themselves, he argues), and what they have the potential to do (rise up together, he hopes).

Especially in his younger days, Burke viewed criticism as social activism. One of his most famous essays, "The Rhetoric of Hitler's Battle," is a trenchant analysis of the persuasion in Adolf Hitler's *Mein Kampf* [1973:191–232]. Today, of course, academic discussion of Hitler's techniques have become something of a cliché, but it was Burke who traced the trajectory of Hitler's rhetoric in the early 1930s. Unlike his contemporaries, who viewed Hitler as just another politician, Burke treated the Fuhrer as a medicine man who had concocted an elixir for the ailing German spirit.

In 1939, few commentators anticipated the scapegoating of the Jew but Burke saw that potential in the scenarios Hitler sketched in *Mein Kampf*. Burke reasoned that any person who saw himself striding—alone—across a grand political stage could dispatch unthinkingly the lesser characters in his self-made play, much as Shakespeare's kings dismissed their fools with nary a thought. Accordingly, Burke feared Hitler's rhetoric more than he feared Hitler's politics. Burke knew that political systems come and go as a nation's economy, sociology, and demography evolve. But a galvanizing drama can be repeated endlessly, Burke warned, because people's deepest fears and anxieties never change. As a result, Burke became a kind of political psychoanalyst and Hitler became his first, and most disturbed, patient.

Burke wrote his initial book, *Counter-Statement,* in 1931 to "counter" the view that art and literature were merely ornamental. Rather, he said, all of the verbal arts, including literature, drama, speech, pedagogy, and reportage, affect both social knowledge and political decision-making. While exploring this thesis, Burke put over six million words in print in 14 books and in hundreds of essays, lectures, poems, stories, and even a modest novel. Throughout his work, Burke refused to treat life *as* drama. Rather, he felt that life *is* drama, that people's actions are themselves symbolic statements. In this view, rhetoric employs primitive dramatic forms that make people see more than their eyes alone allow them to see.

Such forms abound in the passages above. In the first ad, the reader is asked to **identify** with a simpler, safer time and place. For many people (e.g., urban dwellers, newly arrived immigrants, single-parent families, etc.), such a place never in fact existed. But these neighborhoods exist throughout American literature, not to mention in episodes of *The Waltons,* so people can come to view this idealized neighborhood as their neighborhood. Burke would also call attention to how the second passage uses **language clusters** to build its images of innocence. Thick woods, Mother Nature, new plantings, children, water, natural rhythms—these are primal terms, Burke might observe, terms that recall for us the stuff of dreams. Judging by its advertising, "Legend" Oaks is aptly named.

Burke feels that the principle of **hierarchy** is especially helpful in explaining rhetorical force. The third passage provides evidence of hierarchy with its talk of "prestigious" country clubs, "fine" dining, and "distinctive" life styles. "Moving up" when buying a home would be more than just a metaphor for Burke since one's house has psychic as well as material properties and is intimately tied to one's sense of relative worth. When bass are described as "trophy-sized," Burke might note, somebody, somewhere, is feeling inadequate. Also, while this passage celebrates old hierarchies with its talk of "century old" pecans, secure "moats," and "croquet lawns," it implies that even the Newly Arrived can scale the summits if they have the money.

While issues of hierarchy pose the central questions of drama, **transcendence** provides the answers. When considering the fourth passage, for example, Burke might note how "secluded closeness" splits the difference between the inconveniences of rural living and the hectic pace of city life. "Secluded closeness" does not actually make living in the Metroplex easy as much as it transcends such problems by offering a construct around which all persons—country bumpkin as well as city slicker—can rally. Even if it takes an hour on the interstate to get home each day, a "lush homesite" in a "country atmosphere," not a tract home in a subdivision, awaits. This image adds dramatic action to the suburbanite's commute and calls attention to what people are: actors living out their lives speaking scripts to one another.

The dramatistic critic reads these scripts, although there can be danger in doing so. Too often, critics use Burke's ideas merely to label textual elements rather than to explain their symbolic power, a point nicely made by Chesebro [1994]. To avoid this trap, Burke's system will be discussed selectively here so that the principles of dramatism, not its terminology, become our focus. But discussing Burke selectively also has its disadvantages since Burke's mind has ranged so far over so many subjects. Burke's writings show him to be a topical critic, a narrative critic, a structural critic, and a rather scientific student of syntax and lexicon. He has commented on role, imagery, and speech-acts, and his treatment of myth has been consummate. He was also an early devotee of Marxist thought and linguistic skepticism and he was Freudian to his core (topics to be treated in Chapter 14). Burke, in short, followed his own advice when doing criticism: He used all there was to use.

THE PRINCIPLES OF DRAMATISM

Almost as soon as drama existed in Western culture, criticism existed as well. Among the first critics were the *theoria*, a troupe commissioned to travel about in ancient Greece gathering local information about society. Often, they would comment upon local rituals and festivals, activities designed from the start to call attention to what is noble and what is base in people and their motives. By adopting the dramatistic model for criticism, Burke therefore seized on features of drama that had long been recognized but inadequately developed as a critical paradigm.

Burke presented his theory of dramatism before the advent of television. With so few people going to the legitimate theater these days, does a dramatistic model still make sense? Indubitably. Current estimates are that the average American child will watch **30,000** television stories by the time he or she matures. High drama this is not, but television is often good low drama. Each day, TV reintroduces the child to the very heart of dramatic action: why people do what they do, a phenomenon Burke calls **motive.** Cartoons teach that exasperation leads to irrationality (as with Sylvester and Tweetie); situation comedies teach that callousness can be profitable, if censurable (as in *Murphy Brown*); adventure stories teach that evil must be punished at all costs (as in *NYPD Blue*). All such dramas throw light on human motives, inviting viewers to examine—and judge—how people behave.

Equally important, television employs age-old dramatic conventions. Because of television, political conventions turn into prime-time extravaganzas, electronic preaching adopts the form of modern morality plays, and George Steinbrenner's New York Yankees become as intriguing off the field as on. Through television, even the most pedestrian American has been made drama-literate. But when Burke introduced his notion of dramatism in 1939, people were less sophisticated about the mass media (recall that 1939 was the year in which Orson Welles' radio spoof, "The War of the Worlds," capitalized on its audience's ignorance of dramatic forms). Today, in contrast, most of us have a second sense about drama. Burke's critical system depends upon this second sense by making six key assumptions:

1. The range of rhetoric is wide. Wherever he looked, Burke found rhetoric. In the language of Chapter 1, Burke rarely analyzed obviously rhetorical messages (commercial salesmanship, political solicitation, religious pamphleteering, etc.). Instead, he teased out the unspecified policies hidden in implicit rhetoric: poems, plays, polite conversation, signs, maxims, histories, scientific treatises, folklore. One of Burke's most famous studies was an analysis of Antony's address to the mob in Shakespeare's *Julius Caesar.* Instead of detailing how Antony cleverly bested Brutus & Co. in the speech ("So are they all, all honorable men."), Burke focused on how Shakespeare adapted the play to his Elizabethan audience. Why, for example, did Shakespeare's audience wind up respecting Caesar and not Brutus or Cassius? After all, Caesar was deaf in one ear, suffered from falling sickness, "cried out like a sick girl" on occasion, and was timid and superstitious in addition. "Who could identify with such an undistinguished person?" Burke asked. And yet is it not crucial that we do so? Burke asked further. He solved his puzzle thusly:

> For such reasons as these you are willing to put a knife through the ribs of Caesar. Still, you are sorry for Caesar. We cannot profitably build a play around the horror of a murder if you do not care whether the murdered man lives or dies. So

we had to do something for Caesar—and you would be ashamed if you stopped to consider what we did. I believe we made Caesar appealing by proxy. That is: I, Antony, am a loyal follower of Caesar; you love me for a good fellow, since I am expansive, hearty, much as you would be after not too heavy a meal; and as one given to pleasure, I am not likely to lie awake at night plotting you injury. If such a man loves Caesar, his love lifts up Caesar in your eyes. . . .

[Although I, Antony, was a reveler before Caesar's death], in expanding to my expanded role, I must break the former mold somewhat. Let *savants* explain the change by saying that carefree Antony was made a soberer man, and a bitter one, by the death of Caesar. But it is an obvious fact that if an important cog in the plot vanishes in the very middle of our drama, something has to take its place. In deputizing for Caesar, I found it impossible to remain completely Antony. Let *savants* explain my altered psychology as they will—*I* know it was a playwright's necessity. [Burke, 1973:66,67]

Like all good rhetorical critics, Burke focuses here on the speaker-audience relationship, looking through the text to readers' needs and expectations. Because he thereby focused on the "strategic business" of literature, Burke is *persona non grata* for orthodox critics interested in a text's inherent merit. But such inherency did not exist for Burke. He believed that truth is a human thing and therefore a negotiated thing, that any attempt to share unaltered reality with an audience is doomed to failure: "Even if any given terminology is a *reflection* of reality, by its very nature as a terminology it must be a *selection* of reality; and to this extent it must function also as a *deflection* of reality" [Burke, 1966:45].

Sharing ideas with others, Burke felt, was always an act of misdirection, a condition required by the complexity of language. Even the simple image of the shepherd, Burke observed, remains innocent only if an audience half thinks about the shepherd's duties. A fuller consideration of that job reveals ominous portents: "If the shepherd is guarding the sheep so that they may be raised for market, though his role (considered in itself as guardian of the sheep) concerns only their good, he is implicitly identified with their slaughter. A total stress on the autonomy of his pastoral specialization here functions *rhetorically* as a mode of expression whereby we are encouraged to overlook the full implications of his office" [Burke, 1966:301–2].

In his writing, Burke is especially insistent that *formal discourse* be studied carefully since it often escapes public scrutiny. He felt that the "drama of human relations" could even be found in the wording of political constitutions, bureaucratic injunctions, academic treatises, and scientific discourse. Especially scientific discourse. Burke was concerned that the technological establishment (which grew up around him in the 1940s and 1950s) was escaping critical examination because of its rhetoric of nonrhetoric. The Scientific Word, Burke argued, is often exploitative and combative; it typically dissociates thought and feeling and too often rejects its communal responsibilities [Frank, 1969:84]. "Scientism," Burke argued, "needs to be counterbalanced by a stress on 'intuition,' 'imagination,' 'vision,' and 'revelation' " [Rueckert, 1963:38].

In terms of the politics of the 1990s, Burke might therefore be attracted to the rhetoric of futurists like Alvin Toffler or William Bennett, not because of their political viewpoints (which are quite different), but because their rhetoric stresses social and moral possibilities rather than systemic constraints, personal responsibility rather than determinism. Burke might worry that the technocratic realism of a Bill Clinton or a Newt Gingrich would reduce politics to "mere motion" rather than to "dramatic action" and therefore hide the *choice-making* that all politics involves. Burke always appreciated persuasion that owned up to its nature as persuasion. But whenever rhetoric denied itself, Burke's perked up his ears.

2. *All life is drama.* Burke believes that drama is present whenever people congregate but that the essential drama of a situation is not revealed until rhetoric exploits it. The New Journalists, writers who describe real events but who do so as novelist/journalists, exemplify Burke's point. For example, Truman Capote's *In Cold Blood* told of an innocent farm family slaughtered by persons they did not know. Before Capote got to this story, it was just another uninspiring crime in a rural setting. Because of his writing skills, however, Capote could add back the dramatic action hidden by the disembodied statistics of the local police blotter. Capote's rhetoric returned life to the victims who had died and humanized the story of the inhuman beasts who had perpetrated the crime.

The beat journalists in western Kansas had also written about this crime, but their reports did not help readers hear the dull thud of the death instruments or feel the rush of the murderers' adrenalin as they committed their crimes. But Capote made his readers feel these things and more when he redramatized the murders. Thus, in Burke's terms, the New Journalists might be better dubbed Old Journalists since they *reestablish* the dramatic action of prior events, events whose drama would have seeped away if the writer's rhetoric had not taken hold.

Rhetoric is therefore a compass for dramatic action: It points out what is at stake, for whom, by affixing labels to activities. Without such labels, Burke says, people cannot describe what they feel, even to themselves. Burke was especially interested in definitional labels [Heath, 1986:96]. When Truman Capote titled his book *In Cold Blood,* for example, he revealed his view of the crime's motivational dynamics (i.e., he did not entitle it *Accidental Mayhem*). Similarly, when the FBI referred to the Branch Davidians (headed by the infamous David Koresh) as a "dangerous cult," it allowed the FBI to take extraordinary steps to halt their activities. Equally, says Lule [1990], an objective observer might rightly call the Challenger incident a "disaster," but when Ronald Reagan sanctified the seven astronauts via his eulogies, the crash became a "sacrifice" in behalf of the nation.

To appreciate rhetoric, then, one must understand a culture's library of dramas. As Rueckert [1963:20] observes, the "quest" drama alone has inspired countless works of literature including *The Odyssey, The Aeneid, The Adventures of Huckleberry Finn,* and *The Heart of Darkness.* Quests are also found when people speak about forthcoming developments in virtual reality, in the war against cancer, or in establishing a United States–Soviet Union space station. Becoming aware of these formulae, especially when they are used in non-narrative discourse (e.g., in expert testimony before Congress), can help the critic disestablish dangerous forms of dramatic action.

So, for example, Burkean critics like Payne [1992] have told us that the acclaimed film *The Dead Poets Society* at first appears to be a celebration of adolescent rebellion and creativity but, because a creative rebel is killed at the end of the movie, the film ultimately pays homage to their dramatistic opposites: order and stability. Similarly, Trujillo and Dionisopoulos [1987] did a participant-observation study in a local police department and found day-to-day life there to be quite dull. But the *dramatic talk* shared by the police officers—of almost being accosted, of almost being shot, of almost being heroic—made their jobs highly exciting indeed. Through rhetoric, then, life becomes a choice among dramatic scenarios.

3. Dramas feature human motives. This is a key Burkean assumption. It says that the central purpose of drama is to spotlight why people do what they do. It also says that our natural curiosity about human motives can seduce us. As an illustration, let us consider the headlines from a randomly chosen front page of *The New York Times* (Sunday, July 30, 1995):

"CLINTON AND DOLE BIDDING TO BREAK WELFARE IMPASSE"

"RIFLE GROUP TAKES A BOLD NEW STANCE AGAINST THE A.T.F."

"SLAYING OF CONNECTICUT INFANT SHIFTS POLICY ON CHILD ABUSE"

"MEXICAN CONNECTION GROWS AS COCAINE SUPPLIER TO U.S."

"D'AMATO WIELDS THE GAVEL, WITHOUT THE SCRAPPER'S STYLE"   ▸

"YOUNG, CAREFREE AND IN LOVE WITH CIGARETTES"

Dramatism is not difficult to find here: a dangerous rise in teenage smoking, more truculence by the National Rifle Association, a potential class war over the issue of welfare, armed encounters in Mexico because of the drug trade, a domestic tragedy intertwined with a changing community agenda, the transformation of Alfonse D'Amato. But these are not just random happenings; they are also motivated. In each case, the *Times'* headline writers have taken us behind the scenes to show that someone is acting for/with/against someone else for some set of reasons. Will Dole and Clinton abandon their egos and seek consensus? Why don't young people listen to their parents about smoking? Can Al D'Amato keep his Mr. Hyde hidden while serving as Dr. Jekyll during the Whitewater hearings?

Even a staid journal like the *New York Times* cannot resist the motive mandate. In the D'Amato case, for example, the paper tells us that D'Amato, a "hyperkinetic" person who has heretofore "raged with partisan certainty" and used "jungle-fast thrusts" to accomplish his political ends, is now approaching the job of Senate committee chairman with "soft-spoken gravity." The *Times* tries to catch us up in this drama, asking us to see if "the scrapper up from steerage," "the nobody with no place in the halls of power" can mend his ways and become statesmanlike. By focusing on the motive question—Does the man make the job or does the job make the man?—the paper makes a front page story out of no story at all. With dramatics, there is no such thing as a slow news day.

With regard to motive, the critic's job is (1) to inspect discourse for its model of motivation and (2) to explain the rhetor's dramatic actions parsimoniously. That is a tall order. Motives, after all, are complex, overlapping, and sometimes contradictory. So Burke begins simply by examining a rhetoric's **vocabulary of motives**—the language it uses to explain human behavior—in order to outline that rhetoric's theory of volition. It is this motivational apparatus, says Burke, that makes one piece of rhetoric different from another.

For example, a scientist may describe drinking-while-driving as "conditioned behavior," a phrase that downplays motive, while the libertarian and the religious cleric may highlight motives but do so oppositely (i.e., "drinking as personal freedom" vs. "drinking as sin"). For the scientist, decisions are made by the brain; for the libertarian they are made by the mind; for the preacher they are made by the conscience. Each sketches a different theory of life: a matter of random reinforcement, a question of political conversion, part of a divine plan. Each differs as to human possibility (there is much, some, none) and each proposes a unique solution to problems (scientific analysis, political propaganda, moral submission).

Different still is the rhetoric of Mothers Against Drunk Driving. For them, drinking is a social act, often a public act, and only the *public's motives*—not the driver's—are relevant to the discussion. MADD's vocabulary of motives is therefore neither long nor textured: "Killing while drinking and driving is murder, plain and simple."

4. *Hierarchy is fundamental to human symbolism.* Every page of the daily newspaper shows the centrality of hierarchy. *Page 1:* "Henderson Elected Mayor in Landslide." *Editorial Page:* "Trash Collectors Should Strike." *Obituary Page:* "Prominent Physician, Church Deacon, Dies." *Sports Page:* "Daly Wins British Open in Sudden Death." *Society Page:* "Harvard Grad Marries Social Worker." *Entertainment Page:* " 'Son of Rocky' Debuts Locally."

In these ways and more, the newspaper tells who has gotten how far in life, which is why young brides and old mayors alike prepare their press releases carefully. Even after death, hierarchy remains, and so the good doctor's survivors labor over his obituary notice. Yet it is also true that people read newspapers not just to find out about the rich and powerful but to regain hope that the trash collectors among them will receive justice as well.

Hierarchy is, by definition, incremental, so dramatic tension is highest when the increments are small (e.g., when a championship can slip away with one bad putt). Hierarchy is also bidirectional: it recounts failure as well as triumph. Should "Son of Rocky" ever be filmed, it would no doubt depict a young man brought up in luxury who somehow loses his fortune. Cast headlong into life's gutter, Rocky, Jr., would retrace his father's pugilistic steps until he, like Dad, becomes older, wiser, and, given improved ticket distribution, considerably richer.

Burke says that people are "goaded by hierarchy" to do more, to be more, and to have more. But Burke's hierarchies are not just monetary. Values, too, are hierarchical, which is why preachers preach. Knowledge is hierarchical, which is why teachers teach. Beauty is hierarchical, which is why there are cosmetics commercials. Even though none of us has yet found an ideal person, idea, or object, the *principle* of hierarchy goads us on. Despite a world filled with injustice, many feel that "Jesus is the answer." Despite the sorry track record of consumer products, others "Buy Panasonic, the last TV you'll ever own." In their heart of hearts, many people harbor religious doubts and even more distrust home appliances. And yet the principle of hierarchy will not let them rest. They become gluttons for the rhetoric of perfection.

Rhetoric is filled with overstatements because it so often focuses on the endpoints of the hierarchy, inspiring us with the Highest Highs, frightening us with the Lowest Lows. As Nichols [1969:279] observes, the rhetoric of Karl Marx had special power for many because his political cosmos was structured so hierarchically: The worker worked for the State, the State worked for the worker, all worked for the Motherland. As a result, the peasant could perform his menial chores happily, knowing that he or she was contributing *directly* to the great historical drama of Communism. Griffin [1969:460] argues that many other successful movements have used similar motivational tactics when positing an Ideal Order, a Heaven, the Good Society, Utopia, etc.

Burke [1966:18] says that rhetoric can also tilt in the opposite direction when it describes perfect evil: the Christian's devil, the Nazi's Jew, Israel's PLO, etc. According to Appel [1987], this sort of "rhetorical perfection" is especially attractive to the alienated in society, persons who cannot be persuaded via incremental appeals. Brummett [1989] gives a good example of perfectionism in action when noting that discussions of nuclear warfare have changed significantly of late, with their talk of "perfect death" via the "perfect bomb." The "tug of the entelechial motive," says Brummett, animates talk of the neutron bomb, which is said to be "clean" because it leaves no radiation and "preservative" because it kills people but leaves their buildings standing. When death can be spoken of in these perfectionist ways, says Brummett, we must ask if we are happy with the hierarchies we have inherited.

5. *Rhetoric promises transcendence.* If hierarchy gives rhetoric a quantitative dimension (how much, how often, how high), transcendence gives it a qualitative dimension (how good, how grand, how noble). Hierarchy argues that people can get more; transcendence argues that they can become better. Hierarchy suggests how people can improve; transcendence tells them why they should. Rhetoric has transcendent themes because people want to feel they are doing something important with their lives, that they are rising above the ordinary.

According to Burke, meeting these needs turns rhetoric into a kind of **secular prayer.** Perhaps this is why black preachers have been such an important emotional resource in their communities throughout American history. They secularized Christian motifs for the black slaves (and, later, for the black unemployed), assuring them that their hard physical labors would earn them rewards in Tomorrow's Tomorrow. Transcendence can also be found at the other end of life's hierarchy: An aging millionaire suddenly decides to become an aging philanthropist as well. Those who practice the art of philanthropic solicitation know full well that some people will trade millions for meaning.

Transcendence is also an incorporative device. When a U.S. president speaks of "all Americans," momentarily at least Texans cease to be Texans and New Yorkers cease to be New Yorkers. At that same time, American doctors become less medical and American farmers less agricultural. Similarly, each time we give the Elks handshake or wear the company softball uniform, we transcend to another level of symbolic identity, acquiring new "motives" for what we do. Moving upward in this way gives people a sense of drama and also offers them new explanations for their actions: "I am standing in this long line to vote not because I am a masochist but because I am a patriot."

Naturally, Burke was wary of transcendent rhetorics since so much evil has been done at their behest. And yet his reading of history resigned him to their drumbeat. From the time of the Pharaoh's pyramids to that of the modern organizational chart, people have been attracted to hierarchies and to the transcendent rhetorics that help them scale these hierarchies.

6. *Rhetoric is fueled by the negative.* Burke is fascinated by the negative. He accounts for the omnipresence of rhetoric by looking to the inevitable divisions among people and between people and their personal goals. This makes people "relentlessly rhetorical" [Rueckert, 1982:22] as they try to bridge the gap between themselves and their dreams. Burke also regards people as guilt-ridden by nature who, when sharing rhetoric with one another, use "collectivist effort" [Rueckert, 1963:47] to slay the "guilty part" of themselves and become "purified." In doing so, rhetoric serves important, realistic purposes by becoming an intellectual defense against ignorance, an emotional defense against

estrangement, a spiritual defense against impurity. In these ways, rhetoric becomes, like literature, what Burke would call **equipment for living.**

"C-SPAN junkies" who fear World War III and who, as a result, gorge themselves on Congressional rhetoric seem to use rhetoric as equipment for living. They do so because such speechmaking is highly controlled and, importantly, boring ("Why should I be afraid of war when the Representatives in the chamber are falling asleep?"). Similarly, people watch soap operas to steel themselves against cancer, infidelity, drug use, aging, and loneliness. Each day, soap opera characters confront these evils and persevere (there *will* be a show again tomorrow), thereby providing viewers with steady doses of emotional medicine. In other words, "passive" television viewing may not be passive at all but a safe, active way of coping with real and potential psychological loss.

Burke says that nature itself is completely "positive," that it is people who invented the negative, which is why, wherever he looked, Burke found formulas of guilt and redemption. As Rueckert [1963:130] says, "a 'No Trespassing' sign on a piece of property is the infusion of a linguistic negative into nature" (the fenced-in pasture has no "preference" as to who walks where) and "the proposition that adultery and fornication are sinful is the infusion of a linguistic negative into pure sensory experience" (the sex drive, after all, does not mandate a spouse).

Rhetoric, in short, puts people in charge of people by saying "Thou shalt not." Why celebrate the Fourth of July? To stave off tyranny. Why attend a funeral? To conquer death, at least temporarily. Why buy aluminum siding? Because weather can be brutal. Christian soldiers march onward because there is sin, Vanessa Williams sings of love because there is hate, *Bionic Abs* is syndicated on TV because there is blubber. In each case, a rhetor steps forward to shout "No!" to nature.

In nature, time passes. In nature, memory fades. But Carlson and Hocking [1988:211] discovered that slips of paper continue to be collected each day at the Vietnam War Memorial in Washington. D.C., deposited there by ordinary citizens so that *they*, not nature, will have the last word: "Finally, America has awakened and taken home those of us who live and remember you and all the others. . . . I kept your spirit alive 'til America woke up, sir. I'm done. Rest well my friend, my Lieutenant." Similarly, as Bostdorff [1987:45] observes, political cartoonist Tony Auth could not personally fire James Watt (a probusiness Secretary of the Interior in the Reagan administration) but he could symbolically rearrange nature by creating a Ronald Reagan National Forest and populating its hillsides with oil derricks.

In both examples, rhetoric has reduced evil to a **scapegoat,** a person, group, or idea treated as the incarnation of evil. Hitler, of course, used this technique, but Burke argued that this same principle is employed whenever people build a sense of unity by identifying a common enemy. Sometimes, the scapegoat is made obvious (like James Watt) and sometimes it is not (e.g., a "sleeping America" in the War Memorial example). At still other times, the scapegoat is not a person at all but an object (e.g., demon rum), an idea (e.g., reckless liberalism), or even a bodily process (e.g., the notion that alcoholism is a disease). Burke notes that while rhetoric often scapegoats others (an operation he calls **victimage**), it can also scapegoat the self (what he calls **mortification**). In either case, rhetoric cleanses the soul of sin and provides new "attitudes" for use in daily decision-making.

Burke was ambivalent about his discovery of the negative. He understood that any group must develop a shared conception of evil if it is to develop a social order. He realized that morals must be taught somewhere, either through formal institutions (e.g., church or school) or through everyday experience (e.g., popular entertainment, family interaction, etc.). If commercial advertisements, for example, inadvertently teach people how to deal with romantic or work problems, they serve an educational function. But Burke would also note that these same ads purge something or someone to get their messages across.

For example, when Crest urges that we brush three times a day "to avoid that trip to the dentist's office," the image of the dental profession suffers once again. Similarly, Burke would be bothered, as was Brummett [1985], to learn that young, sexually active, women were overwhelmingly chosen for victimage in contemporary horror films. What lessons about life are being taught here? That youth is bad? That sex is bad? That women are bad? Rhetoric may indeed be equipment for living, but, we must ask, what sort of life is that equipment endorsing?

THE METHODS OF DRAMATISM

Burke's interpreters often describe his critical approach as a system of conceptual principles but it is more often a loose confederation of ideas that Burke uses erratically but often brilliantly. Not being Kenneth Burke, we must proceed more carefully. The key to Burke's brand of criticism is asking how and why a text is dramatized and the principles examined in the first section of this chapter became Burke's basic critical vantage point. They can become our vantage point as well. Phrased as critical probes, they are:

1. *Can principles of **hierarchy** be found in the discourse?* Who or what has great value, little value? Is movement up the hierarchy possible or are things "set"? Are there many gradations or only a few? Are the hierarchial stages clear or hazy?
2. *What is the rhetor's **vocabulary of motives**?* Why do things turn out as they do in life? Why do people think and act as they do? Are their motives described clearly or mysteriously? Does the rhetor give personal reasons for speaking? Why or why not?
3. *Who or what is being **scapegoated**?* Is the scapegoating obvious or subtle? If the scapegoat is within ourselves, what sort of mortification is needed to

purge it? If the scapegoat is another person or group, why have they been selected for victimage?

4. *Are strategies of **transcendence** in evidence?* What will help the audience get beyond the problems described? Are the transcendent forces human (e.g., a group, a nation) or extrahuman (e.g., God, fate)? Are they concrete (e.g., new legislation) or abstract (e.g., renewed spirit)?

Burke feels that we cannot speak without dramatizing, so questions of this sort are not really alien intrusions into a text. The average suburban cocktail party proves this. Informal chatter about the Neighborhood Watch Program (a transcendent solution), who is sleeping with whom (mortification and victimage), why good elementary teachers are hard to find (motive), and who might get promoted at the plant (hierarchy) are the very stuff of day-to-day drama. As the party drinks and dramatizing are ingested, the increasingly loud buzz of conversation proves the increasing influence of both.

Burke, of course, was interested in weightier matters than those discussed at 7:00 p.m. in the suburbs. He was interested in texts like this:

When I speak to you today and thus to millions of other Americans, I have more right to do this than anyone else. I have grown out of you yourselves. Once I myself stood among you, I was among you in the war for four and one-half years and now I speak to you to whom I feel myself to be bound still today, and for whom in the final analysis I carry on the struggle. As far as I was concerned the struggle was not necessary. Nor would I wage it for a class or any certain stratum of society. I lead the struggle for the masses of millions of our honest, industriously working, and creative people. . . .

In my youth I was a worker like you, and then I worked my way up by industry, by study, and I can say, by starving. In my innermost being, however, I have always remained what I was before. When, after the war, I entered political life, I did so with the conviction that our people was poorly advised by its political leadership, that a horrible future awaited the American people as a result of this bad leadership. I acted then with the most sincere self-justification because I did not belong to those who were in any way responsible for the war. I was just as little responsible for the war as anyone among you, for at that time I was, just like you, an unknown person, whom fate passed over in the order of the day. In any case I have not counted myself among those who set themselves against their own nation at the time.

I was convinced that one had to enter the struggle for the destiny of the nation, if sooner or later the entire people was not to suffer a terrible ordeal. That is what separated me from the others who turned against America. When the war was over I, as a front soldier, assumed the right to represent that which I had recognized to be right. Before this I had not made any speeches, nor had I engaged in any activity. I was simply a man who earned his daily bread. Not until I saw after the conclusion of the war that the political leadership did not live up to what it had promised the nation, but that the contrary was true, did I go among the people and work with six other quite insignificant workers and found a movement.

I began with six or seven men. Today it is the greatest American Movement; this is so not by chance and not because the way was made easy for me, but because the ideas upon which I built are right. It was only for this reason that they could be carried through. For you can imagine, my friends, that when a man in my station in life begins a movement, success does not just fly to him. That is self-understood. One needs great tenacity and a tremendous will to begin such an enterprise at all. And I should like to say this to you: If I had this faith, I had it only because I knew the people and because I had no doubts as to the quality of the American people. The intellectual groups did not give me the courage to begin this gigantic work; I took courage because I knew the American worker and the American farmer. I knew that these two classes would one day become the bearers of the new spirit and that the group of college professors would also join them of itself. A gigantic program! When I was called on January 30th, after a bitter struggle of fourteen years, I had only one wish and that was to fulfill this great task. What does a title mean to me? I do not need a title. My name, which I achieved with my own strength, is my title. I only wish that posterity would sometime confirm the fact that I have striven to achieve my program decently and honestly. . . .

In America I am the guarantor that this community will not work out to the advantage of any element of the American people. You can look upon me as the man who belongs to no class, who belongs to no group, who is above all such considerations. I have nothing but my connections with the American people. To me everyone is entirely equal. What interest do the intellectuals have for me, the middle class, or the working class? I am interested only in the American people. I belong exclusively to the American people and I struggle for the American people. . . .

These immortal words were spoken by Samuel Adams just after the Revolutionary War. Or are they the remarks of Andrew Jackson after the War of 1812? Or perhaps they are those of Ulysses S. Grant during reconstruction, or Huey Long after World War I, or John Kerry post-Vietnam? Any of these exsoldiers could claim these remarks, for they dramatize fundamentally American themes: working hard, staying close to the common folks, defending the country, succeeding because of effort, not because of privilege. We have heard these themes since childhood and we resonate instinctively to them.

But Burke felt that dramatism knew neither national nor temporal boundaries. So he would not be surprised to learn that this speech does not outline the American dream at all. It outlines the American nightmare, for these are really the words Adolf Hitler spoke to the German people in November of 1933. But if we restore the words "German" or "Germany" (for "America" and "American") in the passage above, what change would really be made? Would thirteen little substitutions fundamentally alter the message's emotional impact? Clearly not. Hitler had his finger on *human* drama here. He, better than virtually anyone, knew the prerequisites of political theater.

Even when altered, Hitler's speech retains its **dramatic form** and thus its ability to persuade. It is therefore really only an accident of history that these words were spoken by Adolf Hitler and not Abraham Lincoln. Altering the passage in this way simply makes it easier for contemporary Americans to identify with Hitler's drama. Naturally, one may be put off a bit by the egotism of the speech, but Hitler's nationalism more than compensates for it. So do his word-pictures, which make life larger than life. Hitler tells how he starved and struggled to start his movement, how his people had seen hard times, how their destiny was at hand, how the values of equality and classlessness could soon be achieved. Hitler told his audience they were standing at an unprecedented moment in human history. Who could refuse to become part of such a moment?

A dramatistic critic. An overriding concern of Burke's was that such moments of great drama tend to unhinge people, making them co-actors rather than critics of dramatic action. These needs for drama no doubt rise and fall within people. In the early 1930s, for example, Germany was a gray and lifeless place. Precious little food, few jobs, the national disgrace of having lost the first world war, an uninspiring, old-line leader in office. These were hard and brutal times. In response, Hitler turned Germany's black-and-white into technicolor. In many ways, Hitler's rhetoric was a rhetoric waiting to happen.

How might a critic use Burke's insights to understand Hitler's persuasion better? Two starting places are Hitler's use of **hierarchy** and **transcendence.** One of Hitler's most ingenious ploys is to identify each subgroup in German society (workers, farmers, intellectuals) and relate them directly to the supreme values of prosperity and nationhood, moving his audience up the hierarchy until they are surrounded by "millions of our honest, industriously working, and creative people." Hitler also establishes the possibilities of hierarchial movement by using himself as a case study. Having been a lowly worker at one time, he recounts how "industry" and "study" provided upward ascent. Even more dramatically, he shows how "starving," surely the lowest point to which a person could sink, also contributed to his upward mobility so that he could now become the "guarantor" of civil equality.

But an audience will not strive upward without guidance. They must be teased into doing so, so Hitler dramatizes the slowness of his own ascent. He recounts his beginnings ("I was, just like you, an unknown person, whom fate passed over."), details his growing consciousness ("[I labored] with six other quite insignificant workers."), establishes his current success ("Today it is the greatest German movement."), and then reaches his rhetorical mountaintop ("I knew that these two classes would one day become the bearers of the new spirit."). Hitler removes himself from the meanness of practical politics, transcendently declaring that he "belongs to no class" and does "not need a title." He offers himself "exclusively to the German people," all of whom, in his eyes, were "entirely equal" to one another. History might question his sincerity about this latter point.

Hitler also cleverly managed **motive** in his speech. He did so immediately by asserting "I have more right to [speak] than anyone else," presumably because his emotional investment in the movement had long since extinguished his natural human reticence ("Before . . . I was simply a man who earned his daily bread."). Hitler paints the picture of one who has been "overcome" by the need to speak. He is not a clever manipulator who has carefully planned his address, nor is he motivated by ego. Instead, his "ideas" have pushed him forward and he has become a kind of political mannequin: "I have grown out of you yourselves."

Today, we think of such strategies as stock forms of identification. But perhaps we do so because Hitler defined the acceptable vocabulary of motives for a mass movement. How different are Hitler's remarks from those of Louis XIV who allegedly declared "L'état c'est moi." There had, of course, been other people's movements before Hitler, but they were less rhetorically based, depending more on sudden uprisings (e.g., the American revolution) or on bitter, long-term struggles (e.g., the Russian revolution). Hitler, in contrast, largely talked his way into power, and so the matter of symbolic motives was always on his mind.

Hitler uses historical revisionism to find an acceptable **scapegoat** in this speech. He catalogues the motives of the extant political establishment, finding them wanting in each case. The "quality," "courage," and "spirit" of all the German classes, he alleges, could be trusted implicitly. Then why have the German people suffered? Because they have been "poorly advised" by the previous leadership that "did not live up to what it had promised the nation." This leadership, which was "responsible for the war," offered only a "horrible future" for the country. Hitler's motival universe here is not one of Classic Innocence versus Classic Malevolence. Rather, he derides Pure Incompetence since, in 1933 at least, he could not afford to alienate completely the supporters of the Prussian government that his Third Reich would eventually replace. Nevertheless, by indirection, Hitler found wellsprings of the negative sufficient for his rhetorical purposes.

In addition to the general critical tools of hierarchy, motive, scapegoating, and transcendence, Burke introduced other methods for dissecting rhetorical texts. Three of them are particularly important:

What invitations for **identification** *are extended in the message?* Identification is now a fairly common term (e.g., "I can identify with that."), but Burke had something more subtle in mind. He felt that people identified with one another when their common interests were dramatized for them, just as if they were biological organisms exchanging chemical properties in order to survive. Even "naturally unaligned" groups—rich and poor, black and white, old and young—said Burke, will become motivated to share new identities when their unmet needs are made salient to them. Rhetoric provides this salience.

For Burke, drama cannot succeed unless it invites an audience to (1) reexamine and (2) activate its identity. Identifications are the "aligning symbols" that serve such functions. These symbols can be as simple as a politician saying "I was a farmboy myself" when stumping through Iowa. Or they can be as complex as the intricate web of symbols that links one Floridian to another, unless one of them happens to be a transplant from North Carolina, which is alright as long as he is not a Democrat, which could, of course, be forgiven if their kids happen to be in the second grade together. Burke felt that these complex intertwinings were indeed weblike, "trapping" complex psychological materials so that communication becomes functionally possible. He wrote a poem that illustrates:

> He was a sincere but friendly Presbyterian—and so
> If he was talking to a Presbyterian,
> He was for Presbyterianism.
> If he was talking to a Lutheran,
> He was for Protestantism.
> If he was talking to a Catholic,
> He was for Christianity.
> If he was talking to a Jew,
> He was for God.
> If he was talking to a theosophist,
> He was for religion.
> If he was talking to an agnostic,
> He was for scientific caution.
> If he was talking to an atheist,
> He was for mankind.
> And if he was talking to a socialist, communist, labor leader, missiles
>   expert, or businessman,
> He was for PROGRESS. [Burke, 1968:238]

In the Hitler passage, identifications abound. Everyone has been hungry; Hitler has been hungry. Everyone has been upset; Hitler has been upset. Everyone has had a moment of bravery; Hitler has had many such moments. And even though contemporary Americans cannot appreciate exactly what it was like to be a poor peasant in Hitler's Germany, such feelings and experiences can be approximated.

Common *rhetorical* experience makes it possible. For example, documentaries about the Depression in the 1930s, news stories about a terrible drought in Ethiopia, and CARE advertisements featuring sad, large-eyed children have explained hunger and social disintegration vividly to us. In similar ways, movies like *Country, The River,* and *Places in the Heart* tell urbanites about farmers' battles with nature, their moral commitment to the land, their sense of family pride. All of these sentiments can be shared via identification, perhaps suggesting that there is a universal language of the emotions.

Identification can also partially bridge hierarchical separations. This bridging is only partial because **dramatic force** comes from difference while **dramatic comfort** comes from similarity. Burke [1966:105] explains, for example, the rhetorical techniques Shakespeare used in writing his tragedy, *Coriolanus*. To get his Elizabethan audience to identify with something more magnificent than themselves, Shakespeare referred to Cleopatra as "Egypt," a synecdoche for a foreign and mysterious force. By being invited to reach up the hierarchy in this way, Shakespeare's audience could feel a bit grander during their evening at the theater. But Shakespeare also knew that his audience should not be overpowered, so he sprinkled derogatory references to eunuchs in his play to appeal to his often-bawdy clientele.

Carlson [1986] reports a parallel case in the rhetoric of Mahatma Gandhi. She notes that the strategy of civil disobedience allowed Gandhi to appear stronger than his opponents (since he dared to be disobedient) and yet at the same time similar to his opponents since they both preached respect for civility. Such a two-pronged strategy kept Gandhi from being scapegoated by the British as an ill-mannered hooligan and also gave him continued access to the British press. For Burke, then, "rhetoric occurs when individuals examine their identities to determine who they are and how they fit into groups with others who share those identities" [Heath, 1986:202]. It is this interest in identification that makes Burke such a manifestly "psychological" critic.

*What **associational/dissociational clusters** can be found in the message?* Burke frequently takes what he calls a "statistical" approach to style, examining language elements for patterned relationships. Such patterns, he felt, worked additively on an audience without their knowing it. By tracking which images went with which, which opposed which, or which followed which, Burke often had novel things to say about rhetorical tone.

When doing this sort of analysis, Burke looked for increasingly abstract relationships among stylistic elements. That is, Burke would have had no justifiable basis for designating *Coriolanus* something of a rustic play unless he could relate Shakespeare's allusions to eunuchs to his references to Antony's "inches" and to the bodily and animal images also found in the play. In other words, unless the critic tracks word patterns up the ladder of abstraction, they become mere tidbits of data that have been tidily assembled by the critic but whose conceptual importance is impossible to discern.

A study by Berthold [1976] did just such patient tracking. She examined John Kennedy's rhetoric and discovered that his references to "peace" were typically found adjacent to references to "freedom," ostensibly because Kennedy's liberal instincts were vying with the conservative realities of the early 1960s. A second finding corroborated this inference: Berthold found the terms "freedom" and "Communism" consistently *opposed* to one another in Kennedy's speeches, again suggesting that there was more of the Cold Warrior in John Kennedy than many had noticed.

Burke is particularly interested in these opposed or **agonistic** patterns since conflict lies at the heart of drama [Brock, 1985:88]. When he battled his fate, for example, Oedipus "agonized" with the Gods over his personal destiny. Oedipus' situation is no different from those played out by the prot-agon-ists and ant-agon-ists of everyday life, which is why Burke took special interest in how significant symbols line up in a text to produce conflict.

These alignments often tell the text's basic plot: who is good, who is evil, what the future portends, and why. For instance, when two American technicians were discovered in Iraq in 1995, people in the United States were anxious to get the basic "story" as quickly as possible. With events of such magnitude, however, that is often not easy since reliable information is initially scarce. As a result, the rhetoric of the day deployed stock agons, with the "evil Saddam" and his "disregard for human life" counterpoised to the "innocent" and "peace-loving" Americans who had "accidentally" strayed into his country.

Not too different was the Clinton administration's plan to do aerial bombing in support of the United Nations defense force in Bosnia during that same year. For Clinton, the undeniable *victims* of such a plan—the Bosnian Serbs—were "barbarians" committed to the destruction of the once-peaceful nation of Yugoslavia and, therefore, persons richly deserving of their fate. But other incidents created difficulties for this scenario. When it was learned that the United States' allies in Europe were not agreed on this course of action, and when it was learned further that bombing may not work (thereby requiring ground forces), the favored good/bad agon had to be abandoned. Thus denied a favored script, the Clinton administration foundered when making its case to a skeptical Congress.

The job of the dramatistic critic, then, is to discover the "calculus of meanings" in a text. For instance, in the now-classic movie *Poltergeist,* a family does battle with an evil force hoping to drive them from their home. The force steals the smallest child (through the television set, no less!) and generally traumatizes the rest of the family. As we watch, there is an almost direct "statistical" alignment between good and evil: The family is good, the television ghosts evil (a comment that TV destroys the American family?). The spiritualist who comes to the house is also on the side of right and becomes a kind of hero for the family. The movie's dramatic tension comes from questions about who or what has selected the family for harassment and why.

In Hollywood fashion, the denouement reveals all: Real estate developers have built the family's home over a graveyard without first removing the bodies. This conclusion "solves for x" in the dramatic equation: Big is evil, new is evil, capitalism is evil. Although *Poltergeist* displays little subtlety in selling its rape-of-the-countryside moral, it does exemplify what Burke finds being done (well or poorly) in virtually all rhetorical exchanges.

What is the foreground/background ratio in the discourse? One of the most frequently used Burkean tools is also one of the most frequently misused: his "pentad" of dramatic elements—Agent (who did what), Act (what was done), Agency (how it was done), Purpose (why), and Scene (in which context). This all seems straightforward enough but application of this format has produced a welter of confusion. Accordingly, we shall abbreviate Burke's system here, focusing just on Act, Purpose, and Scene, and use these tools to examine TEXTUAL materials only. Thus, we shall be concerned with the Scene *the rhetor* depicts, the Purpose *the rhetor* claims, and the Act *the rhetor* recounts.

Our key critical questions will be these: (1) Which factor dominates the discourse generally? and (2) When two factors are discussed simultaneously, which predominates and why? By roughly calculating the ratio among these usages, the critic begins to appreciate how dramatic tension and excitement are produced. Definitionally, we can proceed simply: **Act**—*when the rhetor describes the freely chosen activities of some protagonist;* **Purpose**—*when the rhetor details the protagonist's feelings, intentions, and value systems;* **Scene**—*the kind of stage the rhetor sets when describing community conditions, social influences, historical causes, or natural events (e.g., a severe storm).*

The value of Burke's approach here is that it looks at the same rhetorical situation from multiple perspectives and thereby explains the otherwise unexplainable. For example, a fascinating study by Tonn and her colleagues [1995] examined the case of one Donald Rogerson, who, while deer hunting in rural Maine, shot and killed Karen Wood, a wife and mother who had just moved to Maine from Iowa and who at the time of the shooting was standing in her back yard. Hapless manslaughter? Not according to Mr. Rogerson, who argued in court that his Act (hunting) had a long and honorable tradition and that his Purpose (being prudent) was beyond question since he thought he had spotted a deer. But Rogerson was acquitted because of Scenic arguments—all folks in rural Maine know that you don't poke your head out the back door during hunting season. Case closed.

Another interesting study is Gusfield's [1981] who examined the rhetoric surrounding highway driving. His report is highly critical of law enforcement in the United States and of the federal agencies charged with investigating traffic fatalities. Gusfield argues that virtually all of the official documents he investigated took an Agent/Act focus, treating *the driver's behavior* as solely responsible for highway mayhem. Almost never, reports Gusfield, do public officials ask the Scenic questions of how driving behavior is affected by weather conditions, highway construction, automobile manufacturing, car maintenance, police training, etc. Instead, accident rhetoric focuses on Purpose via a "language of Job" [p. 45]. Said a General Motors executive: "Most accidents are caused by [people] doing things known to be wrong" [p. 44].

Gusfield says that the popularity of this rhetoric puts a straightjacket on highway policy in the United States. Thus, when the "story of the 'killer-drunk' " alone occupies public attention, the "story of the unsafe car" cannot even be entertained. According to Gusfield, this latter story could prove interesting if it were heard: "The approach of the 'unsafe car' ignores the drinking driver and seeks solutions through automobile designs that might enable drinking and driving to be conducted more safely. It ignores the individual as a source of danger and places the ownership of the problem . . . in social institutions to regulate the design of the auto" [p. 174]. Despite its advantages, however, Gusfield is not optimistic that such a Scenic rhetoric will suddenly become popular.

Within the same text or set of texts, rhetors will sometimes shift ratios from moment to moment. By examining these different "featuring" strategies, a critic can gain a rich perspective on a dramatic encounter, as we see in Table 12.1. The case study is that of Brummett [1984], who examined news

TABLE 12.1 Dramatistic News Strategies in the DeLorean Case*

Act Dominates Scene

What is featured? Freely chosen activities of some protagonist

What is muted? Community conditions, social influences, historical causes, or natural events

Eulogistic use: Describes a protagonist's actions as being of such heroic proportions that the actions of others pale in comparison

> *Example:* "[At General Motors, DeLorean stood out] like a Corvette Stingray in a showroom full of GMC trucks."

Dyslogistic use: Characterizes a person or group's behaviors as being so reckless or self-centered that they dwarf normal, social obligations

> *Example:* "I don't know how you square the description of a community-minded man with that of a man who engineered the delivery of China white."

Scene Dominates Act

What is featured? Community conditions, social influences, historical causes, or natural events

What is muted? Freely chosen activities of some protagonist

Eulogistic use: Draws attention to the personal sacrifices a protagnostic faced as a result of some larger social trend or societal condition

> *Example:* "Sales of domestically built cars have been sagging for more than three years, while imports are thriving under precisely the same market conditions . . . [all of which resulted in] 'the failure of the enterprise.' "

Dyslogistic use: Emphasizes that the larger community can ultimately constrain the actions of even the most powerful

> *Example:* "DeLorean, a man accustomed to gold bracelets, was led away in steel bracelets . . . [his jail was] not the Ritz [and was filled with] male prostitutes, muggers, and murderers."

Scene Dominates Purpose

What is featured? Community conditions, social influences, historical causes, or natural events

What is muted? Protagonists's feelings, intentions, value systems

Eulogistic use: Emphasizes the social attractiveness of one who is so responsive to societal needs that no questions of character can be raised

> *Example:* "If DeLorean was driven to drug dealing in an effort to raise capital, underlying the resentment there is some compassion for him . . . [since he was trying to protect] the DeLorean family [his employees]."

Dyslogistic use: Describes a protagonist-as-puppet who has become so enmeshed in the social world that his or her values and priorities have been forsaken

> *Example:* "DeLorean was vulnerable to the magic aura of the cocaine trade and its promise of euphoric profits. After eight years of superhuman struggle . . . DeLorean appeared to crack."

Purpose Dominates Scene

What is featured? Protagonist's feeling, intentions, value systems

What is muted? Community conditions, social influences, historical causes, or natural events

Eulogistic use: Argues that one's feelings and thought are of such importance that they override social and other consequences

> *Example:* "There is a very high price to pay for such a dream [as DeLorean had]."

(continued)

*Adapted from Brummet [1984].

TABLE 12.1 (*continued*)

Purpose Dominates Scene (*cont.*)

Dyslogistic use: Shows the tragic results of allowing personal pride or idealogical zeal to override social obligations

> *Example:* "How could a shrewd businessman like DeLorean fall so stupidly and easily into the hands of drug suppliers and federal agents?"

Purpose Dominates Act

What is featured? Protagonist's feeling, intentions, value systems

What is muted? Freely chosen activities of some protagonist

Eulogistic use: Features the significant personal costs borne by some person or group because of their beliefs and values

> *Example:* "[DeLorean] improbably as it seems, detected parallels between his life and that of Jesus Christ."

Dyslogistic use: Indicates that a protagonist has become so preoccupied with personal goals that he or she is now behaving erratically and irresponsibly

> *Example:* "He [DeLorean] was drawing $475,000 a year and $1,000 a week in expenses, even when the company was dying. . . . All the things he despised at G.M. he became himself."

Act Dominates Purpose

What is featured? Freely chosen activities of some protagonist

What is muted? Protagonist's feeling, intentions, value systems

Eulogistic use: A person or group's actions are described as so grand in scale that to raise questions of motive would seem pedestrian

> *Example:* Adjectives for DeLorean: "feisty," "swashbuckling," "awesome," "charismatic," "phenomenal," "savvy,""remarkable," filled with "creativity," "eclat," and "flair" and never losing his "cool"

Dsylogistic use: A person or group's actions are described as noteworthy and yet ill-advised, thus opening the door to questions of intelligence and decency

> *Example:* Headlines in DeLorean case: "Coke, Cars, and Capitol" *(New Republic),* "DeLorean Drove the Fast Lane" *(Washington Post),* "DeLorean's Scramble Ends with Arrest" *(Business Week),* "When You Wish Upon a Car" *(New York),* "Superstar and Maverick, DeLorean Never Fit the Mold" *(New York Times).*

---

coverage of John DeLorean, a one-time automobile executive at General Motors who left a promising career at GM to found his own automobile company (and to live the life of a jet-setting bon vivant). When his company began to founder, DeLorean allegedly sought venture capital in the cocaine industry but was eventually tried and found innocent of the drug charges. Because of DeLorean's flamboyant approach to business and personal affairs, his story became front-page material for months on end in the 1980s.

Brummett's deft analysis recounts the "ironic frame" the press used to tell this tale and he explains why the press was able to keep the story alive for so long. As we see in Table 12.1, the press could do so because so many *different* ratios were available to them for creating dramatic clash. Table 12.1 also shows that these rhetorical ratios produced both favorable and unfavorable stories, depending on the reporters' intentions, further adding to the overall, ironic storyline. As Brummett's study shows, dramatistic ratios can prove endlessly fascinating.

In many ways, Kenneth Burke is the most daring of the well-published critics. One of his favorite techniques is to extract from just a bit of text some intricate conceptual design. He looks at a piece of discourse for its **representative anecdote,** a Scene/Act imbalance, a narrative habit, a pattern of imagery, a telling example, etc., that sums up its rhetorical tone. According to Burke, such an anecdote will be representative if it contains the basic agon or master metaphor of the discourse system in general. So, for example, the Hitler speech reviewed earlier is probably a representative anecdote since it captures the senses of struggle and revenge that fanned the flames of the Third Reich.

Most rhetorical critics, however, are not as adventurous as Kenneth Burke, nor should they be. Burke's penchant for establishing sweeping psychological and cultural *answers* on the basis of isolated bits of rhetoric is probably not the Kenneth Burke the beginning critic should emulate. But the Kenneth Burke who asked wonderfully imaginative *questions,* who was bold enough to search for rhetoric where others would not, who inquired constantly about how such discourse affected the human condition, who asked about the sundry victimizations of persuasion as well as its glorious transcendences, who was concerned, constantly, with those on the bottom of life's hierarchies as well as those at the top—this is the Kenneth Burke who teaches capably, often brilliantly, and who has lessons aplenty for all.

CONCLUSION

In 1935, before he developed his theory of dramatism, Kenneth Burke, published *Permanence and Change.* In it, he argued that all persons, not just those interested in literary and rhetorical matters, must become critics. He said that even a trout whose mouth has been ripped apart by biting into an angler's hook becomes a critic as a result of the experience, sharply revising its understanding of food, bait, time, and tide. But all living things are not necessarily *good* critics, Burke argued further, which is why the critical faculty must be nurtured so carefully and so insistently.

People are not fish. Human judgment-making is complicated because people must respond to both a physical and a symbolic world. To fail to become a critic of symbology, warned Burke, would be to ignore human motives and that would be (and often is) disastrous. Some people write their poems on paper, he [1984:76] observed, while others "carve them out of jugular veins." Accordingly, the social responsibility of the critic extends even to a consideration of human warfare since wars are "statements" two countries are trying to make to one another ("stay off our land," "give us back the money your grandparents stole," "let us practice our religion in peace," etc.). Burke felt that critics could help "purify war" by discovering what rival nations were attempting to say to one another and by suggesting symbolic ways of saying such things.

Criticism was therefore not an effete activity for Burke since he felt that people make their grandest and most heinous statements with symbols. He believed that by becoming better critics people would come to understand how complicated human motives are and how inadequate ordinary communication can be for sharing that complexity. Burke reminds us that criticism is a profession exclusively devoted to asking questions . . . and never stopping. Persons in such a profession, Burke felt, could never abide facile, incomplete, or doctrinaire answers. He felt, too, that criticism was an "art of living," humankind's best chance for doing what only humans can do: be reflective. Burke concluded that understanding what people are saying—or trying to say—is therefore a badly needed enterprise. Who can say him nay?

Chapter 13

FEMINIST CRITICISM
With Joanne Gilbert

Q: Why did God create women?
A: Because a set of golf clubs can't cook.

*****

Q: Why did God create men?
A: Because vibrators can't mow lawns.

*****

Q: How many feminists does it take to change a light bulb?
A: "That's *not* funny!"

Which of these texts is distinctly feminist? Which is harshest on women? How can one be sure? Can a feminist text be as sexist as a masculinist text? When does a joke stop being a joke and become a speech? An attack? An insult? These seem like simple questions but they become more complicated on inspection. Gender and complications—these are the issues of our age.

Initially, the first joke seems to demean women. It objectifies them (by turning them into commodities), thereafter relegating them to pure domesticity. But who is really the butt of the joke here? Men, not women. It is men who are portrayed as unidimensional, unfeeling brutes that measure a woman's worth by her ability to satisfy their basic needs. And so we have our initial complicating question: *Is the first joke an informal sort of feminist criticism?*

The second joke can be read as blatantly sexist, this time with men as the object of scorn, beasts fit for nothing more than the provision of sexual and material services. But there are complications here too. Does the joke not imply a terrible shallowness in women, persons who would use sexual and material standards exclusively when judging their fellow humans? And so we have another complicating question: *Does the second joke essentialize both men and women, thereby reconstituting male notions of dominance?*

The punch line in our third joke repeats a popular myth: That feminists are humorless, angry ideologues. Like all comedy, the third joke trades in that most efficient of all vehicles, the stereotype. But the third joke does something even more insidious: It robs women of their most hum-an trait—their hum-or. Thus, we have a final complicating question: *Is the third joke the most political of all since it terminates rather than fosters inquiry?*

And then there is the most important question of all: What is the feminist agenda? Given the many kinds of feminists today, that is not an easy question to answer. hooks [1984:17], for example, asserts that "A central problem with feminist discourse has been our inability to either arrive at a consensus of opinion about what feminism is or accept definition(s) that could serve as points of unification." Because feminism is as much a *movement* as an intellectual position, and because feminists' goals have shifted and matured so much over the years, we will have to approach feminism in a complicated way as well.

Friend [1994:52] reports that a *Time*/CNN survey shows that 94% of all Americans believe in the feminist movement's leading issue of equal pay for equal work, while another poll reveals that only 37% of American women consider themselves feminists and that even fewer college women (16%) embrace the term. In other words, we may now have more *political* feminists in the United States than *rhetorical* feminists, with the "humorless man-hater" being a symbol around which few contemporary women can rally.

Philosophical confusion must be confronted as well. Fox-Genovese [1991: 56] tells us that:

> Today, as in the past, feminists divide over whether women should be struggling for women's rights as individuals or women's rights as women—whether women need equality with men or protection for their difference from men. . . . This debate over equality versus difference lies at the core of contemporary feminist thought, not merely because of the way in which it divides feminist theorists, but, perhaps more important, because of its ability to link theory and practice.

Wolf [1993:224] addresses these same complexities when she distinguishes between **victim feminism,** which employs an exaggerated type of female innocence and powerlessness and **power feminism,** which encourages women to "identify with one another through the shared pleasures and strengths of femaleness." In an attempt to overcome these stresses and strains in the movement, Wolf concludes that "any woman who believes in women's right to self-definition and self-respect is a feminist in my book" [p. 278].

Numerous definitions of feminism exist, some action-oriented ("Feminism is the struggle to end sexist oppression" [hooks, 1984:26]), others more ideological (feminists are those who recognize that the earth doesn't revolve around anybody's son" [Barreca, 1991:178]). Some critics seek to end these debates by proclaiming the emergence of a "postfeminist" era in which personal, not political, goals have triumphed. *Esquire* [Would?, 1994:65] reports that of the one thousand women (between 18 and 25) it polled, 54.3% would rather "get run over by a truck" than "gain 150 pounds."

Has the "beauty myth" finally consumed the nation's young consumers, thereby precluding a next generation of feminist thought and action? Not according to Friend [1994:50], who sees the emergence of a new kind of **hedonistic feminist,** who tries to "shift discussion from the failures of men to the failures of feminism, from the paradigm of sexual abuse to the paradigm of sexual pleasure. They want to return sex from the political realm to the personal. In short, they want to have fun." For Friend, at least, the once-angry feminist has become almost joyous of late.

Given these political and philosophical complications, this chapter can hardly embrace a single brand of feminism. Instead, our goal will be to discover how rhetorical texts become gendered and how such gendering blinds audiences to some realities while opening them up to others. Philosophically, we will embrace a basic sexual egalitarianism, the idea that humanistic and pluralistic values best guide human affairs and that the privileging of one sex over the other ultimately harms social life. Critically, we will highlight these feminist assumptions.

1. Rhetorical acts are androcentric (male-dominated). Feminist critics claim they do not introduce politics into a text but expose the politics already there. For example, it may seem natural for a male U.S. president to sing the praises of the "father of our country" on Washington's birthday and then relinquish the podium to a male prelate intoning the benediction, "Our Father, who art in heaven." Feminist critics would quickly point out that this "natural" androcentrism is nothing but a grand contrivance: Ceremonies are conducted by those who already have power (presidents and ministers) and who are also heir to a rich tradition of masculine motifs (as in the Washington myth and the King James Bible). As a result, the very act of participating in these ceremonies reinforces the power of those who speak (men) and the relative powerlessness of those who listen (women).

Because of the growing number of activist women today, it is easy to forget how recently feminism has developed in the United States. According to Donovan [1980], prior to the nineteenth century women could not study Latin (the language of education, religion, and the law) and thus were denied the key to the door of power. It was not until 1920 that women in the United States won the right to vote. The Equal Rights Amendment guaranteeing individuals protection from discrimination on the basis of sex, first proposed in 1923, is still not a part of the U.S. constitution. Women in this country still earn considerably less than their male counterparts for doing the same job. From the literary to the political domain, women have gone to great lengths to claim their rightful rhetorical practices. Feminist critics seek to expose, and offset, the patriarchal customs that have silenced women for so long.

2. *Rhetorical texts are androcentric.* Feminist criticism employs two different modes. In the **universalizing mode,** a critic examines a text for its general descriptions of the human condition and then asks how "general" those descriptions really are. This sort of criticism is demanded, says Showalter [1985:143], because texts have heretofore asked women to "identify against themselves" by presuming that *male* standards for beauty, truth, and justice are equivalent to all *human* standards. That these masculine premises have been accepted so implicitly, without self-reflectiveness, is especially egregious to feminist critics. As Ruthven [1984:64–5] points out, "men are able to conceive of their own subjectivity as being nongendered, and therefore wonder why feminists make such a fuss about gender. But because women are not aligned with the universal, they are much more inclined to see themselves as women than men are to see themselves as men."

Accordingly, says Rich [1972:20], critics must practice what she calls revision, the act of "entering an old text from a new critical direction" so that these male-centered premises can be thought anew. Take, for example, a standard piece of American eloquence—John Kennedy's inaugural address. Feminists would urge us to reexamine this *master*piece to see if what Kennedy endorsed for all Americans was also endorsable by women. Early in his address, Kennedy [1961a:267] made the following declaration:

> We dare not forget today that we are the heirs of that first revolution. Let the word go forth from this time and this place, to friend and foe alike, that the torch has passed to a new generation of Americans—born in this century, tempered by war, disciplined by a hard and bitter peace, proud of our ancient heritage—and unwilling to witness or permit the slow undoing of those human rights to which this Nation has always been committed, and to which we are committed today at home and around the world.

What is alleged to be universally true here? That forgetting is unconscionable; that pride is a human virtue; that the United States must tend the international community. Fine sentiments all. But the feminist critic would also find the invisible hand of patriarchy here and be moved to ask: Must we make the (male) assumption that wars are good and that old wars are especially good? Must we honor the (male) need to pass on the "torches" of war, bequeathing to our heirs yesterday's victories as well as a taste for tomorrow's battles? Must oratory always appeal to the (male) taste for a "hard and bitter" peace? Are these the only *human* options available? Must all Americans become men on inauguration day? In short, feminist critics would be suspicious of all high-blown oratory like Kennedy's and want to examine anew virtually all of the "great" historical texts in the rhetorical and literary canons.

3. Traditional criticism is androcentric. The **particularizing mode** of feminist scholarship tries to find an authentic female voice by calling into question the established, universal norms for literary and rhetorical excellence. More than sixty years ago, Virginia Woolf [1929:77] understood the inherent bias in these "universal" norms when she articulated the usual (male) standard of literary excellence: "This is an important book . . . because it deals with war. This is an insignificant book because it deals with the feelings of women in a drawing room." In reaction to such biases, feminist critics frequently use the phrase "women's writing" rather than "women's literature" to define their interests because the former, more generous phrase, includes the schoolbooks, diaries, and letters that were the only outlets available to generations of literarily inclined women.

Operating on these three major premises, feminist criticism has been especially productive during the past two decades. Feminist critics have found patriarchal **intellectual conventions** problematic since they typically endorse (1) abstractions such as "duty" and "honor" rather than people's lived experiences and (2) dichotomies such as male (good)/female (bad). Ruthven [1984: 72] notes, for instance, that whereas male characters have been given full definition in literature, female characters have more often been given binary options: "sensuous roses or virginal lilies, pedestaled goddesses or downtrodden slaves, Eves or Marys, Madonnas or Magdalenes, damned whores or God's police."

Feminist critics have been especially displeased with political discourse because it is so laden with these dichotomies and abstractions, leading men (i.e., those in power) to conflict rather than negotiation, to martyrdom rather than flexibility, to independence rather than interdependence. The historical reality of women—as bearers of children, as nurses to the sick, as preparers of food—has forced them to develop and focus on relational skills such as compassion and nurturing. Accordingly, feminist critics prize concrete experience and contend that the personal is always political.

Feminist critics are also interested in the **mythic conventions** used in rhetoric. Not surprisingly, they have found that many standard mythic patterns have marginalized women. Ruthven [1984:80], for example, argues that the typical story line in a fairy tale is of a passive princess "who waits patiently on top of the Glass Hill for the first man to climb it" and who, as a result, is "symbolically dead" and can only be brought to life by a man. Radway's [1984:212–3] study of why modern women read paperback romance novels stirs up parallel concerns. She finds similar kinds of passivity there and, although she notes that reading such fiction is a somewhat "rebellious" act, it is also mythically entrapping: "They do nothing to challenge [women's] separation from one another brought about by the patriarchal culture's insistence that they never work in the public world to maintain themselves but rather live symbiotically as the property and responsibility of men."

Feminist critics also focus on the **role conventions** of discourse. Perhaps the most cherished role, the role of authority, has been an especially male preserve.

Male doctors have issued public warnings about breast cancer; male psychologists have offered counsel about child care; male governors have announced the membership of the State Commission on Women. The comparatively few female authorities available have spoken about women's rights, not human rights, about family budgets, not the national budget, about the war between the sexes, not the wars between the continents. This has resulted in a kind of rhetorical ghetto-izing of women and has set up a paradox: People who cannot be heard cannot be taken seriously; people who cannot be taken seriously should not be heard.

The *projected* roles of women—how they are portrayed in rhetoric and literature—are also frequently demeaning. These roles, too, have consequences. Not only do they affect how men see women but also how women see themselves. An example of such portrayals is found in the work of Barbatsis et al. [1983], who did a comprehensive analysis of television programming. They found that men talked most of the time on television shows (even in cartoons), that females received significantly more orders than did males, and that women asked more questions than they gave answers. Even in romantic fiction, says Snitow [1986:138], women's roles are circumscribed. Despite the comforting familiarity of such characterizations from a literary view point, one can only wonder about their *rhetorical* impact in women's attitudes:

> When women try to picture excitement, the society offers them one vision, romance. When women try to imagine companionship, the society offers them one vision, male, sexual companionship. When women try to fantasize about success, mastery, the society offers them one vision, the power to attract a man. When women try to fantasize about sex, the society offers them taboos on most of its imaginable expressions except those that deal directly with arousing and satisfying men. When women try to project a unique self, the society offers them very few attractive images. True completion for women is nearly always presented as social, domestic, sexual.

These, then, are some of the major themes characterizing the feminist perspective. Individual critics deploy these perspectives differently and the result is a multi-hued feminism. Here, we will focus on five of its hues. Our category system will be neither exhaustive nor definitive but it will expose some of the ways in which power becomes gendered and in which gender becomes powerful.

THE POLICY CRITIQUE

Feminist critics have been quick to challenge how the male orator has been enshrined as the font of political wisdom, thereby privileging a narrow sort of discourse. In her landmark study of early feminist rhetoric, Campbell [1989:11] explains the social costs women suffered when trying to embrace the male tradition:

a woman who spoke [in public] displayed her "masculinity"; that is, she demonstrated that she possessed qualities traditionally ascribed only to males. When a woman spoke, she enacted her equality, that is, she herself was proof that she was as able as her male counterparts to function in the public sphere. That a woman speaking is such proof explains the outraged reactions to women addressing "promiscuous" audiences of men and women, sharing a platform with male speakers, debating, and preaching, even on such clearly moral issues as slavery, prostitution, and alcohol abuse. The hostility women experienced in reform efforts led them to found female reform organizations and to initiate a movement for women's rights, at base a movement claiming woman's right to engage in public moral action.

In recent years, Campbell and others have provided important analyses of early feminist oratory. For example, Japp [1985] has shown how the abolitionist rhetoric of Angelina Grimkè became the forerunner of female rights in the United States, providing nineteenth-century women with their first brush with real political power. Jorgensen-Earp [1990:83] explored the rhetoric of English suffragist Emmeline Pankhurst, a woman who utilized "the discourse of the dominant culture *as it stands* in order to force revolutionary change within that culture." Carlson [1994] noted that another early feminist, Lucretia Coffin Mott, used Quaker theology in a similar way, delicately showing how the will of God and the rights of women could be reconciled. And Griffin [1994] studied the fascinating, often obstreperous, rhetoric of Mary Wollstonecraft, a woman who took on such magisterial thinkers as Jean Jacques Rousseau, thereby showing that marginalization does not necessarily lead to political impotence.

In a more contemporary vein, Dow and Tonn [1993:287] studied the rhetoric of former Texas Governor, Ann Richards. The authors maintain that Richards' use of narrative, her personal (often humorous) tone, and the direct audience participation she encouraged brought a "feminine style" to politics that distinguished her governorship from the more divisive forms of argument favored by men. Along these same lines Foss and Griffin [1995] call for greater use of an "invitational rhetoric" in the public sphere, a discourse grounded in the feminist principles of equality, immanent value, and self-determination. By seeking understanding rather than control, they claim, a leader can avoid the zero-sum-game that politics too often becomes.

Power. Discrimination. Discourse. Relationship. These are the things the feminist perspective tries to change. And these are the things that came together in October 1991 to produce a most remarkable series of events. At that time, as we saw in Chapter 9, Anita Hill, then a college professor but formerly an assistant to Supreme Court Justice Clarence Thomas, alleged that Judge Thomas had sexually harassed her on previous occasions. She made these charges to a nervous group of U.S. Senators and to a fascinated nation as well. Because the Hill/Thomas hearings involved all three branches of government (as well as the fourth estate), it was widely viewed and discussed. More important, the Hill/Thomas hearings displayed in public what many women had suffered in private for years.

Feminist critics have treated the hearings as a microcosm of competing rhetorics. Fraser [1992:599], for example, saw the distinction between the private and public spheres as crucial to the hearings' outcome. She argues that the Bush administration's attempt to forbid interrogation into Judge Thomas' private life reinscribed the public/private distinction that has long favored men over women. Such a strategy, for example, excluded expert testimony on sexual harassment, a move that

> cast Clarence Thomas and Anita Hill in very different relations to privacy and publicity. Thomas was enabled to declare key areas of his life "private" and therefore off-limits. Hill, in contrast, was cast as someone whose motives and character would be subjects of intense scrutiny and intrusive speculation, since her "credibility" was to be evaluated in a conceptual vacuum. When the Senate Judiciary Committee adopted these ground rules for the hearings, they sealed in place a structural differential in relation to publicity and privacy that worked overwhelmingly to Thomas's advantage and to Hill's disadvantage.

Fraser shows how the advantage quickly became Thomas's when she quotes directly from the hearing itself:

> Senator Leahy: Did you ever have a discussion of pornographic films with . . . any other women [than Professor Hill]?
> Judge Thomas: Senator, I will not get into any discussions that I might have about my personal life or my sex life with any person outside of the workplace [p. 600].

"While the country was awash in speculation concerning the character, motives, and psychology of Anita Hill," says Fraser, "there was no comparable speculation" about Thomas, thereby reconstituting "the asymmetry or hierarchy of power along gender lines" in the United States. Fraser maintains that in defending his privacy so vigorously Thomas was defending his essential masculinity since to have one's "privacy publicly probed is to risk being feminized" [p. 601]. In addition, says Fraser, when Judge Thomas played the race card by complaining the hearings were a "high-tech lynching," he rendered Hill "functionally white." Rather quickly, says Fraser, "the black woman was erased from view" [p. 605].

Other studies of the Hill/Thomas hearings show how democratic governance itself was used as a scapegoat for the abuse that otherwise might have been directed at Judge Thomas. By engaging in a "proceduralist rhetoric," Regan [1994] discovered, Hill/Thomas participants succeeded in condemning the political process rather than sexual harassment itself. This is a dangerous rhetoric, says Regan, because it focuses attention on "extraordinary" issues (issues that lie safely beyond adjudication) rather than on ordinary crimes committed by ordinary people. Not surprisingly, it was Judge Thomas [1991:23] himself who most artfully used the proceduralist approach:

> In my 43 years on this earth I have been able with the help of God to defy poverty, avoid prison, overcome segregation, bigotry, racism and obtain one of the finest

educations available in this country, but I have not been able to overcome this process. . . . When there was segregation I hoped there would be fairness one day or some day. When there was bigotry and prejudice, I hoped that there would be tolerance and understanding some day. Mr. Chairman, I am proud of my life, proud of what I have done and what I have accomplished, proud of my family and this process, this process is trying to destroy it all.

With Judge Thomas decrying the nature of the hearings, with Anita Hill objecting to them on the same grounds, and with the Senate Committee eagerly joining in, the participants agreed on one thing: that nobody should be there. Eventually they all went home. So, too, did the case of sexual harassment at hand.

Beasley [1994] explains the Hill/Thomas hearings somewhat differently when describing their competing logics of freedom and power. The logic of freedom, Beasley notes, assumes that people are free to choose their own courses of behavior. The much less popular logic of power, in contrast, holds that people sometimes do irrational things because they are compelled to do so. Employing the logic of freedom, many people asked why Anita Hill would continue to work for Judge Thomas after being so badly treated by him. The logic of power explains this easily: People (especially women) who have no influence do what they must to survive. The testimony of Ellen Wells, a witness for Hill, illustrates this second logic:

> I get Christmas cards from people that I do not see from one end of the year to another, and quite frankly, do not wish to. And I also return their cards and will return their calls. And these are people who have insulted me and done things which have perhaps degraded me at times, but there are also things that you have to put up with. And being a black woman, you have to put up with a lot, so you grit your teeth and you do it [p. 297].

Because of the logic of freedom, many Americans never really understood Wells's statement here. They could not grasp the psychology of the downtrodden, persons who sometimes participate in their own subjugation because they fear retribution. But according to Beasley, Anita Hill was just one of millions of women who were intimately familiar with that curious logic.

A final study is that by Lipari [1994:300] who examined press coverage of the Hill/Thomas hearings. Lipari argues that the press treated the Hearings as a melodrama, using eroticized news stories that "trivialized the issue of sexual harassment and, by extension, women's collective claim to social and political legitimacy." Headlines like "Next Act in Drama Fails to Disappoint" domesticated the hearings, Lipari claims, thereby undercutting the charges of *illegality* made by Anita Hill.

Such rhetorical flourishes are amply demonstrated in a snippet from one of the news reports: "What happened on TV yesterday was an electric thunderbolt, a riveting tragicomedy that combined the sugar of kinky sex with the salt of power, passion and propriety" [p. 303]. Such coverage turned the hearings into a case of "he said/she said," claims Lipari, making it hard for many

Americans to see sexual harassment as a crime and ensuring that "the system-atic subordination of women [would] appear personal and hence not at all political" [p. 307]. That soap opera coverage like this was used to describe the activities of the highest court in the land is an extraordinary thing. It is also reason for feminist critics to pay careful attention to the policy sphere.

THE NARRATIVE CRITIQUE

The narrative critique focuses on women as readers, women as fiction writers, and how narrative in general interacts with the female consciousness. Ever since Kate Millett's landmark book, *Sexual Politics,* [1985] feminist critics have called into question the androcentric "canon" long popular in the West. In her book, Millet argued that male writers typically distorted female charac-ters, often associating them with deviance and, simultaneously, ensuring that the "narrative structures of fiction" would always faithfully "represent the structures of masculine culture".

In *The Resisting Reader,* Fetterly [1978:492–3] takes us the next step when insisting that feminist criticism is inherently an act of resistance. Look-ing at writers from D. H. Lawrence to Ernest Hemingway, Fetterly explodes the notion of a universal "human experience," insisting that the emotional lives of women have rarely been faithfully reproduced by even great male nov-elists. Writers like Lawrence and Hemingway force their female readers to think like men, says Fetterly [1978:493], who also argues that:

> "Rip Van Winkle" is paradigmatic of this phenomenon [of forced identification]. While the desire to avoid work, escape authority, and sleep through the major decisions in one's life is obviously applicable to both men and women, in Irving's story this "universal" desire is made specifically male. Work, authority, and deci-sion making are symbolized by Dame Van Winkle, and the longing for flight is defined against her. She is what one must escape from, and the "one" is necessar-ily male.

Most literature is dangerous, Fetterly believes, because through it women are subtly encouraged to identify against themselves. Hence, she urges that women readers adopt a strategy of constant vigilance.

While Fetterly focuses on the woman reader, Schweickart [1991:531] is concerned with the female writer. She notes, however, that "the relevant dis-tinction is not between woman as reader and woman as writer, but between feminist readings of male texts and feminist readings of female texts." The goal of feminist criticism, Schweickart believes, is to create an "ideological space for the recuperation of women's writing" [p. 537]. Because the Western canon has such monolithic power, a feminist

> cannot simply refuse to read patriarchal texts, for they are everywhere, and they condition her participation in the literary and critical enterprise. In fact, by the

time she becomes a feminist critic, a woman has already read numerous male texts—in particular, the most authoritative texts of the literary and critical canons. . . . The feminist story stresses that patriarchal constructs have objective as well as subjective reality; they are inside and outside the text, inside and outside the reader [p. 541].

As mentioned earlier, Virginia Woolf [1929] was the first critic to herald the lost texts of women writers. In her book *A Room of One's Own* Woolf speculates on why the West has seen so few female litterateurs, reasoning that if Shakespeare had had a gifted sister her talents would have been squandered for the most practical of reasons: she would have been denied an education, betrothed against her will, and barred from her beloved theater ("decent women aren't seen in public" and all that). Perhaps, says Woolf, she might even have contemplated suicide:

When . . . one reads of a witch being dunked, of a woman possessed by devils, of a wise woman selling herbs, or even of a very remarkable man who had a mother, then I think we are on the track of a lost novelist, a suppressed poet. . . . Indeed, I would venture to guess that Anon, who wrote so many poems without signing them, was often a woman. [p. 49]

Horrified by such a sorry history, Woolf issues this manifesto: "Lock up your libraries if you like; but there is no gate, no lock, no bolt that you can set upon the freedom of my mind" [p. 75].

Half a century later, feminist criticism has flourished. Some say it has flourished all too well, producing so many kinds of criticism that it has lost intellectual focus. Kolodony [1991:101] warns that "The very energy and diversity of our enterprise have rendered us vulnerable to attack on the grounds that we lack both definition and coherence." But with black, Latina, lesbian and other marginalized women demanding their own critical stance, where else could one turn if not to pluralism? Besides, says Lorde [1981: 99,100], the "master's tools will never dismantle the master's house," and so feminists must be on guard not to replace gender discrimination with racial discrimination:

If white [A]merican feminist theory need not deal with the differences between us, and the resulting difference in aspects of our oppressions, then what do you do with the fact that the women who clean your houses and tend your children while you attend conferences on feminist theory are, for the most part, poor and third world women?

While feminist criticism is not of one piece, it has nonetheless served to enliven narrative theories by focusing on the autobiographical voice. According to feminist theory, the power to tell one's own story, to tell it loudly and proudly, is a key political move. For centuries, after all, women were not allowed to "publicize," to make their stories known, to become their own authors. But now, according to Olsen [1978], they are filling in the silences of their missing texts.

The autobiography is an important kind of discourse because it deals with the complex issues of self, identity, authority, and experience. hooks [1991:1038] notes that "The longing to tell one's story and the process of telling is symbolically a gesture of longing to recover the past in such a way that one experiences both a sense of reunion and a sense of release." Some scholars are pushing these notions further by even bringing an autobiographical style to the scholarly essay. In "Me and My Shadow," for example, Tompkins [1991] critiques the distanced (male?) language of the academy, which had heretofore forced her to speak a language not of her own making. As Tompkins puts it, "The thing I want to say is that I've been hiding a part of myself for a long time" [p. 1083]. Tompkins' essay illustrates the twofold purpose of autobiographical critique—to validate the author's individual voice and to force reconsideration of what discourse itself is about.

An interesting use of narrative occurs in Sharon Olds' poem, "Rite of Passage" [1983:66], which is both a piece of feminist criticism and a piece of autobiographical rhetoric as well:

Rite of Passage

As the guests arrive at my son's party
they gather in the living room—
short men, men in first grade
with smooth jaws and chins.
Hands in pockets, they stand around
jostling, jockeying for place, small fights
breaking out and calming. One says to another
How old are you? Six. I'm seven. So?
They eye each other, seeing themselves
tiny in the other's pupils. They clear their
throats a lot, a room of small bankers,
they fold their arms and frown. *I could beat you up,* a
seven says to a six,
the dark cake, round and heavy as a
turret, behind them on the table. My son,
freckles like specks of nutmeg on his cheeks,
chest narrow as the balsa keel of a
model boat, long hands
cool and thin as the day they guided him
out of me, speaks up as a host
for the sake of the group.
We could easily kill a two-year-old,
he says in his clear voice. The other
men agree, they clear their throats
like Generals, they relax and get down to
playing war, celebrating my son's life.

Clearly, Olds' poem represents the personal (an autobiographical story) and the political (an autobiographical critique). Here, she tells an important story involving several rites—her son's birth, her son's birthday celebration and, less directly, her own passage on the journey of parenting. The poem ironically blends the juvenile with the mature ("men in first grade/with smooth jaws and chins"), thereby helping the poet (and reader) integrate the various phases of life and thus to get at the essential human experience. Olds lovingly notices "freckles like specks of nutmeg on his cheeks,/chest narrow as the balsa keel of a/model boat, long hands/cool and thin as the day they guided him out of me." Reflecting on her own son's birth in this manner is a deeply intimate reflection that turns the public poem into a private interaction with an unknown reader. Masterful though he was with language, John Donne did not write this way.

But "Rite of Passage" is also critique, with Olds's rendition of the strutting youngsters quickly becoming an acerbic commentary on patriarchal values. Calling her party guests "a room of small bankers," Olds cleverly apes the incipient machismo of her son and his friends: "Hands in pockets, they stand around/jostling, jockeying for place, small fights/breaking out." Olds's poem condenses the rumblings of aggression found in the male child and she wonders aloud about the eventual, perhaps inevitable, loss of innocence these rumblings will exact on her son. Olds does not simply assert that "boys will be boys" but makes the larger and, in her eyes, more sinister claim: "boys will be men." That her metaphors include bankers and generals is also apt, making her poem a highly political one indeed.

But Olds's poem, because it is a poem, does not close us down entirely. She leaves us wondering about the precise "policy options" she might endorse. Her poem has a delicious ambiguity to it, with a picture of rambunctious youth laid atop a searing indictment of patriarchal culture. Olds is a feminist, yes, but she is also a mother, making her poem both portrait and lens. Her autobiographical approach lets us see Olds-the-mother but Olds-the-critic lets us see *through her* as well. Her move is deft. As we saw in Chapter 10, a text takes on an irresistible innocence when the self is featured. Olds capitalizes on that innocence ("it's only a story about my son's birthday party, after all") making it hard for a reader to dismiss her as some sort of unthinking ideologue. Rhetoric and poetry conjoined are a potent blend indeed.

THE REPRESENTATIONAL CRITIQUE

The representational critique examines portrayals of women in television and cinema with an eye to determining how social policies are advanced or retarded by these portrayals. Mulvey's essay, "Visual Pleasure and Narrative Cinema" was a springboard for much criticism. Mulvey [1991:436] maintains that there are three "looks" in a Hollywood film: (1) the look of the camera,

(2) the look of the audience, and (3) the look of the character. Of special interest is her notion of the "male gaze" of the camera. This is a mode of production whereby women are "simultaneously looked at and displayed, with their appearance coded for strong visual and erotic impact" so that they come to have that most precious of Hollywood qualities, "*looked-at-ness.*" This idea helps to explain why, all things being equal, the male gaze prefers a visual woman like Sharon Stone rather than a thinking woman like Olympia Dukakis.

Mulvey argues that in Hollywood films men serve as the "bearer of the look" and this grants them special subjectivity, a preferred point-of-view. Women in films are denied these essential aspects of character and hence function as pure spectacle. In essence, the rhetoric of the film forces an audience to see female characters from the male character's perspective—as erotic, perhaps pathetic, but hardly dimensional. Although Mulvey's essay is twenty years old now, the male gaze (of camera, actor, and spectator) is still at work in such Hollywood blockbusters as *Pretty Woman, Basic Instinct,* and less obviously, in the Academy Award winning *Forrest Gump,* where all female characters—including the oft-quoted "Momma"—serve to refocus us on Forrest's bewildering thoughts and, ironically, on his unparalleled successes.

Williams [1984:83] notes that the horror film is a particularly interesting genre for examining "when the woman looks." Almost always, says Williams, the horror film punishes the female character for her gaze (the gaze, after all, being a primordial act of human empowerment). So there are excellent reasons for women spectators to cover their eyes during such films, "not the least of which is that she is often asked to bear witness to her own powerlessness in the face of rape, mutilation and murder." But there are more subtle reasons to do so as well since "women are given so little to identify with on the screen." Unlike her male counterpart, the female character in horror films looks directly at the "monster's freakishness," thus having her wits scared out of her (pun intended). And yet a bizarre kind of "sympathy and affinity" often develops between monster and female victim, Williams continues, an eventuality that is "less an expression of sexual desire . . . and more a flash of sympathetic identification" between two marginalized entities [p. 88].

Mayne [1984:55] uses the metaphor of a woman looking through a keyhole to describe the *female* gaze in traditional cinema, claiming that "the history of women's relationship to the cinema . . . has been a series of tentative peeks." In the "woman's film" genre popular throughout the 1930s, '40s, and '50s, Mayne explains, male film-makers tried to create films for a female audience. The melodramatic nature of such films earned them the sobriquet, "the weepies," a precursor of the contemporary soap opera. Doane [1984:80] points out that these films typically desexualized the female body, removing the focus from female action to the most superficial of emotional experiences. This is ultimately problematic, says Doane, because "to desexualize the female body is ultimately to deny its very existence." In other words, Hollywood has typically given women two choices: to be objectified or to be invisible.

Even films hailed by Hollywood as triumphs for women are not necessarily seen as such by feminist critics. For example, in films like *Thelma and Louise* (woman as bandit), *The Piano* (woman as property), and *Disclosure* (woman as predator) we find the same tired options for women despite the fiery nature of the female leads. *Thelma and Louise,* for example, a film in which two women become instinctive desperados, ultimately reduces to a formulaic, "buddy" film. Thelma (played by Geena Davis) and Louise (played by Susan Sarandon) become the contemporary Butch and Sundance, scofflaws all. Thelma and Louise kill a potential rapist, lock a police officer in a car trunk, and finally hurl themselves into the Grand Canyon rather than face capture. While the film addresses some of the oppressions modern women endure, its final message has a familiar, binary flavor: oppression or death. This is hardly a feminist message.

Disclosure is a film about sexual harassment in the corporate world. The twist here is that Meredith Johnson (played by Demi Moore) harasses her former lover Tom Sanders (played by Michael Douglas). Self-serving and aggressive, Meredith attempts to force Tom into having sex with her. The now-happily-married Tom engages in (at times) resistant foreplay with Meredith, but runs from the room before things progress further. In revenge, Meredith sabotages Tom's career, which causes him to sue the company. With the help of a hard-nosed female lawyer Tom wins his case, exposing Meredith as a ruthless megalomaniac. In the final reckoning, Meredith is fired, Tom rehired, and his sought-after promotion given to a female co-worker but not until the company C.E.O. (played by Donald Sutherland) proclaims that she is being promoted for her talents, not as recompense for long-standing corporate insensitivity toward women.

Throughout the film the viewer is told that sexual harassment is not about sex but about power. In the end, Meredith laments that she is being punished for playing by the rules men have mandated, implicitly calling for a new set of (woman-sensitive) corporate standards. Like *Thelma and Louise,* however, *Disclosure* is a case of faux feminism. Throughout Hollywood's history, "Meredith Johnson" has been seen on film numerous times (but with a male persona). Is turnabout fair play? Genuine feminist advancement? Not according to the film's ending. Although Meredith tells Tom she will be back in ten years to buy the company, she has clearly been beaten, one more female mogul thrown onto the corporate ashheap. And where is Tom's wife during his turmoil? By his side, cool and understanding, a unidimensional character.

Despite its activist pretensions, then, *Disclosure* does what Hollywood cinema has always done: It eroticizes the female body and caricaturizes her. Even though she is allegedly a corporate titan, Demi Moore still provides the obligatory cheesecake poses in the film. And so films like *Thelma and Louise* and *Disclosure* tell us two things: (1) placing women in leading roles often has little to do with feminism and (2) the male gaze still ensures a box office draw.

Do feminist films exist? Yes, but they are rare. *Fried Green Tomatoes*—a film about the love and strength of women—is one case in which women's experiences are affirmed. *Leaving Normal,* a little known "road" film about the unlikely friendship between two women, is another. But what does Hollywood reward? Holly Hunter won an Oscar for her role in *The Piano* by playing a man-defined woman and Tom Hanks won his Oscar by playing a simple fellow who effortlessly reaches fame and fortune.

The moral? Even in the 1990s Hollywood makes its money robbing women of their subjectivity, their personhood, their complexity. The only strength it knows is brute strength, its only tenderness sexual tenderness. The Hollywood Woman thus becomes pure representation, pure gossamer. Feminist critics are beginning to call our attention to these non-women and man-women. We need to know more about why real men and real women so often fall prey to their charms.

THE PERFORMATIVE CRITIQUE

Judith Butler [1990:278] asserts that gender "is real only to the extent that it is performed." Unlike gender essentialists or biological determinists, performative critics argue that gender is not a static thing but a fluid process open to change. Imagine, for example, a large closet housing a long clothes rack. At one end of the rack is hyperfemininity; at the other, hypermasculinity. Dead center is androgyny, a perfect blending of the masculine and the feminine. If gender is conceptualized as the outfits hanging on our humble rack, one begins to think of gender as coming into existence only when a person *performs* the role of man or woman or a mixture of the two.

Scholars are now investigating this notion of gender-as-performance. When a male student is asked to read the part of a female heroine in theater class, for example, he is immediately confronted with his nonreflective maleness. More important, he is asked to experience gender in a way that the silent reading of *Little Women* could never teach him. Thus, while biological *sex* is ours at birth, we are taught *gender* by society itself. The challenge for the critic, then, is to examine the performed text to see how it becomes gendered and what happens to performer and audience as a result.

Take, for example, stand-up comedy. While men have dominated that arena over the years, female performers are increasingly being seen in the nation's comedy clubs and on cable television shows. But given the aggressive history of the genre, how can a woman know what to do, know who to be, in such a venue? Even more basically, can a woman even perform femaleness in such a format? No doubt, any comic performance will be an exaggeration (of gender, of race, of everything else). But the comedic is an interesting site because the *public* pressures of performance make obvious what ordinary social life typically leaves unclear.

Gilbert [1994] describes the most popular rhetorical postures of the female comic. She argues that these postures grew out of the limited options available to women on the nineteenth-century stage. **The Kid** is one such persona. Playful, desexualized, and nonthreatening, The Kid is a neutral performance of gender. From Lotta Crabtree in the late 1800s, through burlesque's Fanny Brice (in the 1930s) and Lily Tomlin's Edith Ann in the 1970s, The Kid has delighted audiences and given women one of their few chances for public acclaim. Today, comics like Paula Poundstone and Ellen DeGeneres project this same persona. By suppressing all trappings of traditional femininity, says Gilbert [p. 133], Poundstone becomes everyone's friend, a quirky but guileless sprite:

> Pilots on planes always tell you to look out the window and you're always sitting on the wrong side, so you just know they're goin', "Psst—people on the left . . . don't tell the people on the right—there is the coolest stuff out your window right now. . . .We *hate* the people on the right . . . just look at them sitting there. . . . I hate that . . . they're ruining *everything*. . . . You don't have to put your tray tables up if you don't want to. . . . If we go down, we're getting you out first.

We have here a child's idiom, with tokens like "coolest" and "stuff" signaling a full embrace of the immediate, human moment. Even when naughty and childlike, perhaps because she is naughty and childlike, Poundstone is able to get her audience to bracket the entire issue of gender and, hence, to leave the negotiation of power for another day. Desexualized as she is, The Kid becomes a modern eunuch, able to poke fun at the king in each of us but endearing herself at the same time.

The Bawd is far different. She "revels in [her] sexuality and sensuality," using both as means "of pleasure and control" [p. 134]. Sometimes insatiable (often regarding younger men) and always overtly threatening, The Bawd typically pokes fun at male sexuality, that most precious of all male possessions. Physically voluptuous, The Bawd first arrived in the early 1900s. Later Bawds included such comics as Eva Tanguay, Sophie Tucker (the "Last of the Red Hot Mamas"), Moms Mabley, and the indomitable Mae West—known for such lines as "Sex is a lot like snow. You never know when it's gonna come, how long it's gonna last, or how many inches you're gonna get" [p. 135]. After "blue" comics like Belle Barth in the 1960s and Bette Midler in the 1970s, the 1980s gave rise to contemporary bawds like Carrie Snow and Angela Scott. Snow captures the spirit of the modern Bawd when she tells her audience:

> I like young guys. . . . I call 'em *tender vittles*. . . . Sometimes though when they're really young, they're a little bit too frisky. So whatcha have to do is take 'em to the Sizzler, fill 'em full of beef to calm 'em down. Sometimes, if you're really lucky, they'll return the favor. . . . [p. 142].

Depending on one's political assumptions, The Bawd is either a throwback (because she trades on sexuality, not unlike a prostitute) or an avatar of feminism (because she appropriates the role of sexual aggressor). The third of

Gilbert's female comics, **The Bitch,** is considerably easier to decode since she habitually uses " 'putdown' humor as a form of social critique" and thus makes an active play for social dominance. Evolving out of the Bawd tradition, The Bitch speaks her mind, gets what she wants, and, ostensibly, is "not interested in pleasing her audience" [p. 146].

Comedian Joan Rivers may well be the prototype of this persona, with her loud, abrasive voice and her famous "vomiting" gesture (usually done when referring to an unattractive person). Her material takes no prisoners:

> Don't give me all this liberation shit—men like 'em stupid. All you need is a pretty face and a trick pelvis and you're home free. . . . [to a female audience member who shows Rivers her engagement ring] You're a Jew and you took that shitty ring? A piece of shit in 4 prongs—is your mother alive? [p. 147]

Perhaps the most notorious Bitch in the 1990s is Roseanne who in one memorable moment asked an audience, "How many men here are impotent? Can't get your *arms* up either, huh?" [Gilbert, p. 149]. Gilbert explains that:

> By choosing to end her act with the ultimate subversion . . . , Roseanne simultaneously illustrates the preeminent power of the phallus in Western culture (and specifically in the genre of stand-up comedy) and lampoons this power by using the phrase as a woman—a woman who denigrates men. She is quite literally using the "master's tool" to mock the [master]. . . . [p. 150].

As with The Bawd, one is forced to ask unsettling questions about the Bitch: Does she descend to the male's level by adopting his scatological tastes? Or does she force reconsideration of male hegemony by calling attention to the heterosexual male's most precious, perhaps most confusing, possession—his sexuality? Sorting out the answers to these questions is not easy but, as the women's movement has been teaching us for thirty years, it is important to do so.

The fourth comedic posture is **The Whiner** who uses self-deprecatory humor to ingratiate herself with the audience. From nineteenth-century comic May Irwin's use of fat jokes, to Lucille Ball's pratfalls in the 1950s, to the simpering Phyllis Diller (popular in the 1960s and 1970s), The Whiner conforms to the most enduring gender stereotypes. Spouting lines like "Two weeks ago, my Playtex living bra died . . . of starvation," Diller presented a nonthreatening persona, a kind of rag doll with whom the audience could toy. Contemporary comic Karen Haber uses the same formula, ostensibly joining the enemy in order to control him:

> I walked up to this one guy and he wasn't so great and I said to him, "Look—if you would take me out . . . you could keep my car." And he said, "What kind of car do you have?" . . . In the morning, I made him breakfast and I shined his shoes and I painted his apartment and he said, "I hate you, you're stupid, get outta here." I said, "That's o.k. 'cause I'm busy Saturday night anyway" [pp. 165–6].

The final posture Gilbert describes is **The Reporter,** a wry, distanced comic who surveys the social terrain, making random observations about our lives and times. Like The Kid, The Reporter performs gender androgynously, using observational remarks carefully adapted to middle-class tastes. Comic monologists like Jean Carroll in the 1950s paved the way for contemporary Reporters like Elayne Boosler, Carol Leifer, and Rita Rudner (all of whom are Comedy Channel favorites). Rudner, who once declared that she loves to sleep because, "you get to be alive and unconscious at the same time" [p. 170], typifies her breed.

Like her counterparts in journalism itself, The Reporter often travels the corridors of power when looking for material, further desexualizing herself by becoming Everyperson. Margaret Smith, for example, once complained that it was "unfair that Hillary [Clinton] had to give up Law" when her husband became president since "when Bush was President, no one screamed at Barbara to get off the oatmeal container" [p. 122]. When Reporters incur audiences' wrath, they typically do so as political animals, not as gendered animals.

Gilbert argues that all five comedic roles are **ways of performing marginality.** Whether it takes the form of ingratiation, intimidation, or supplication, the female comic exemplifies some of the stock options available to women in the less dramatized, but ultimately more important, spheres of everyday life. The Kid urges us to pay no attention to the fact that she is a woman while The Bawd urges the opposite. The Whiner apologizes for her femaleness, hoping to curry favor on patriarchal terms. Admittedly, these personae are terribly conventionalized. Everyday life surely presents women with richer options. But studying humor is important for, as the comic goes, so go we all eventually.

Most important, the critic operating from this perspective gives women (and men) an extraordinarily liberating option by assuming that **rhetorical performances**—not biology, not sociology, not history, not destiny—makes woman woman. The workplace may invite us to play The Kid to get a promotion but nothing says we must do so. A man may be uncomfortable dating a Reporter or a Bawd but that may be his problem, not hers. Some women may find The Bitch retrograde, but her role may be a necessary precursor to social change. Comedy has always asked us to confront life itself. With regard to gender, it asks if we have yet discovered all our ways of being. We act out our self-definitions each day, says the performative critic. By behaving, in other words, we become who we are and what we are.

CORPOREAL CRITIQUE

Feminist critics writing from this last perspective are considerably more deterministic than the performative critics. Often called Essentialists (since they deal with the biological essences of men and women), they examine how the human body becomes implicated in the messages we share with one another. Here, gender is not thought to be a fluid, socially constructed entity but a fixed and enduring matter. Among the most radical of this corps are the French feminists, especially Luce Irigaray and Helene Cixous, who, according to Jones [1991:359] feel that women are instinctively repelled by masculine logics and language habits and that they "must recognize and assert their *jouissance* [physical pleasure, first experienced in infancy and later, through sexuality] if they are to subvert phallocentric oppression at its deepest levels" [p. 360].

Like Irigaray, Cixous focuses on women's difference from men. She holds that "women's unconscious is totally different from men's" and that they need "to overthrow masculinist ideologies and to create new female discourses" [Jones, p. 360]. Cixous develops what she calls "ecriture feminine," a way of literally "writing the body." As Jones explains it, "to the extent that the female body is seen as a direct source of female writing, a powerful alternative discourse seems possible: to write from the body is to recreate the world" [p. 361]. According to Jones, both Irigaray and Cixous believe that for women to escape oppression they must start by experiencing their unique sexuality, a sexuality that "begins with their bodies, with their genital and libidinal difference from men" [p. 361].

Such an extreme view can be easily parodied (and has been), in part because it is essentialistic and in part because it is abstract, far removed from the political battles women fight each day. But some critics use the corporeal perspective with creativity, one of whom is Bordo [1993]. In her book, *Unbearable Weight,* Bordo critiques American culture (as well as educational, social, and economic institutions) for creating the kind of low self-esteem among women that results in eating disorders, plastic surgery, and rampant consumerism.

Examining the causes of anorexia and bulimia and the lush advertising campaigns that foster them, Bordo finds that "The general tyranny of fashion—perpetual, elusive, and instructing the female body in a pedagogy of personal inadequacy and lack—is a powerful discipline for the normalization of *all* women in this culture" [p. 254]. Bordo identifies two rhetorical moves that are especially debilitating: (1) normalization, whereby women are urged to conform to a particular standard of beauty and femininity and (2) homogenization, which tells all women to look alike.

In the past, says Bordo, "the body was dominantly conceptualized as a fixed, unitary, primarily physiological reality," but today it is better regarded as a "historical, plural, culturally mediated form." [p. 288] As evidence, Bordo points out that throughout history women have been subjected to such external mutilations as "clitoridectomy, Chinese foot-binding, [and] the removal of bones of the rib cage in order to fit into tight corsets," [p. 162] all in an attempt to attain an impossible feminine ideal—the perfect body (formerly curvaceous, currently lean).

Examining the rhetoric of our day, Bordo shows how seemingly innocuous cultural messages produce disastrous results for women:

> In 1984 . . . a study conducted by *Glamour* magazine and analyzed by Susan Wooley and Wayne Wooley revealed that 75 percent of the 33,000 women surveyed considered themselves "too fat," despite the fact that only one-quarter were deemed overweight by standard weight tables, and 30 percent were actually *underweight*. . . . A study by Kevin Thompson . . . found that out of 100 women "free of eating-disorder symptoms" more than 95 percent overestimated their body size—on average one-fourth larger than they really were [p. 56].

The reason? Bordo asserts that along with teaching women to be insecure about their bodies, society teaches women how to *see* their bodies. When the cultural ideal becomes progressively slimmer, therefore, women at or below their optimal weight tend to feel fat.

Bordo illustrates this problem by comparing the Maidenform Woman from both the 1960s and the 1990s, noting that "What was considered an ideal body in 1960 [Figure 13.1] is currently defined as 'full figure' [see, for example, Figure 13.2]. . . ., requiring special fashion accommodations!" Given the changing standards, Bordo argues, "the anorectic does not 'misperceive' her body; rather she has learned all too well the dominant cultural standards of *how* to perceive" it [p. 57]. Thus, women today starve themselves to achieve the slender, yet firm, body. As Bordo notes, "Areas that are soft, loose, or 'wiggly' are unacceptable, even on extremely thin bodies" [pp. 190–1].

To this end, Bordo discusses the "I believe" advertising campaign for Reebok shoes. In each of the ads she examines, she finds a "lean, highly toned, and stylishly attractive young exerciser declaring her invulnerability to traditional insecurities of women, resistance to gender expectations, and confidence in her own power of self-determination." In the first ad, the copy declares "I believe a man who wants something soft and cuddly to hold should buy a teddy bear." Bordo points out that:

> The suggestion is that this woman's own desire to be hard and ripped, rather than her need to appeal to men, has determined the type of body she is working out to achieve. The man who doesn't like it can look somewhere else for someone to hold, she implies. But just how many men in 1992—at least of this young woman's generation—find the "soft and cuddly" an erotic or aesthetic ideal? [p. 297]

Not only is rhetoric like this insidious, says Bordo, it is also dangerous: "By creating the impression that Sandra Dee is still what men want, Reebok is able to identify its product with female resistance to cultural norms of beauty while actually reinforcing those norms" [p. 297].

The copy in a second ad reads, "I believe if you look at yourself and see what is right instead of what is wrong, that is the true mark of a healthy individual." Again, says Bordo, women are exquisitely trapped by such a discourse, hemmed in by a culture of consumerism on the one side and a cultural of phys-

FIGURE 13.1 Lady Marlene ad

FIGURE 13.2 Fashion Plus Ad

icalism on the other. While these ads *appear* to uphold individualistic ideals, Bordo finds them fully dictatorial:

> the model's body *itself*—probably the most potent "representation" in the ad—is precisely the sort of perfected icon that women compare themselves to and of course see "what is wrong." The ad thus puts "real" women in a painful double bind. On the one hand, it encourages them to view themselves as defective; on the other hand, it chastises them for their insecurities. The offered resolution to this bind, of course, is to buy Reebok and become like the woman in the ad [p. 297].

By saying "Be yourself" but identifying the ideal female body as akin to the adolescent male's, Reebok fuels women's self-loathing while selling yet another technology (athletic shoes) for self-improvement.

And so, says the corporeal critic, rhetorical messages are now literally shaping our bodies. Whether it is food advertising depicting men eating heartily and women counting calories, or ads for contact lenses and hair relaxer promoting a light-eyed, straight-haired ideal, women are invited each day to confront their inadequacies. Surely it is a bizarre thing to imagine the human creature as naturally deficient. Equally bizarre is the notion that a pair of shoes could somehow make us perfect. And yet each day our culture tells us how to look and how to be seen. Feminist critics argue that women are especially harassed by such solicitations. Resistance, quite clearly, is needed.

CONCLUSION

Feminist criticism interrogates business as usual and demands that we examine power inequities in everyday life. It asks uncomfortable questions as well— Who is the real author of a given text, a flesh-and-blood woman or the patriarchy? Why are women so often ignored or trivialized in popular culture, and why are their complaints so seldom heard in elite political circles? Why do women sometimes settle for half a loaf of social change when a whole loaf is possible? Given the enormous cleavages in American society between rich and poor, black and white, old and young, can any feminist in the 1990s speak for all women?

There is one thing that most feminists agree on, however: that the individual lived experiences of women must be respected. They also agree that oppression runs deep in a patriarchal culture and that the greatest oppression of all occurs when women's minds are "colonized" by popular discourses. It is one thing, they argue, for rhetoric to change behavior. Far more profound is when it alters our very habits of mind.

Like any discipline, feminist criticism has its flaws. At times it is heavy-handed with texts, ignoring their subtleties in a blind rush to pass judgment on them. At other times its political commitments makes it predictable, as if the answers had been gathered before the questions had been asked. But feminist criticism is best when it gets us to re-see traditional texts. As Ruthven [1984:13] says, it is not so important that we all "write criticism" as that we "incorporate the lessons of feminism into everything [we] write."

And those lessons are twofold: (1) to question what we think we know about rhetoric in case it is only what men know and (2) to assess the consequences of rhetoric that historically has treated half the human race as inconsequential. Best of all, feminist criticism makes us uncomfortable with our comfortableness. It is in these moments of intense discomfort that people often do their best thinking, which is why all of us, in part, should become feminist critics.

Chapter 14

CONTINENTAL CRITICISM

Sometimes it can be disappointing to learn that your parents are not perfect. When you were a young child, they seemed so wise and strong. When parents make mistakes or can't do something you expect, you may feel angry or critical of them. At such times, it helps to remember that they are people just like you. [Chamberlain, 1982:107]

*****

Stereotyping can limit your possibilities. If you're a girl who loves to work outdoors, who has been driving your father's tractor for years, and who is strong for your age, you'll be frustrated if the summer jobs for yardwork or farmwork all go to boys. [Chamberlain, 1982:50]

*****

doing things adults do does not necessarily mean you will be wiser, braver, or more self-assured. It takes time to acquire knowledge and build self-confidence. Adults need to test themselves in the world just as you do as a teen. Being an adult, like being a young person, is a continual process of growth. [Chamberlain, 1982:56]

*****

Mr. and Mrs. Kopec both have full-time jobs. On days that Mr. Kopec gets home from work first, he starts supper. Mrs. Kopec cleans up. On other days, Mrs. Kopec prepares supper and Mr. Kopec cleans up. They take turns doing various household tasks and outdoor chores, as well as washing the cars and taking them to be repaired. They decided this was the best way so neither of them would get tired of doing the same tasks all the time. [McGinley, 1983:104]

* * * * *

Since values result from learning and from our experiences and relationships with others, they may change as we get older. Some values may become stronger as a result of our experiences and learnings while others may become less important. [McGinley, 1983:20]

* * * * *

When there are problems in families, the community is often able to provide help on either a temporary or permanent basis. Sometimes children are removed from their homes and placed in the care of others. The intent is to protect the child from experiences which may be physically or emotionally harmful. [McGinley, 1983:35]

* * * * *

Your moods go back and forth. One day you feel full of laughter, happy, and self-confident. The next day you feel downright weird. You want to hit someone or cry, and you don't know why. One day the idea of becoming an adult seems exciting. You can't wait to take off, get a job, and find an apartment of your own. [Chamberlain, 1982:28–9]

This assemblage of sophomoric philosophizing is sophomoric because it comes from textbooks written for high school sophomores enrolled in home economics classes. Most of us would view these remarks as innocuous, if not banal. But that is not how they were viewed by U.S. District Judge W. Brevard Hand. He treated them as evidence that an "established religion" of secular humanism was being taught in the Alabama public schools, a religion that questioned parental authority, preached the relativity of values, and emphasized liberal social themes. In his now historic opinion, Judge Hand commented as follows:

> The Court is not holding that high school home economics books must not discuss various theories of human psychology. But it must not present faith based systems to the exclusion of other faith based systems, it must not present one as true and the other as false, and it must use a comparative approach to withstand constitutional scrutiny. . . . [Therefore] use of these texts violates the religion clauses of the first amendment. [Hand, 1987:109]

Judge Hand's opinion was quickly overturned by a higher court and his removal of some forty-four history, social studies, and home economics textbooks was set aside. Yet Judge Hand's opinion is not merely of legal interest but also of scholarly interest, for he operates here as an ideology-based critic, one who lays his philosophical presuppositions atop his textual materials when inspecting them.

One of Judge Hand's presuppositions was that rhetorical force can be found everywhere, even in the plucky little world of home economics texts. Because he *presumed* that persuasion could be found there, he could not be fooled by the objectivist strategies (facts, statistics, quotations, etc.) found in textbooks or by the matter-of-fact rhetorical styles of their authors. Judge Hand knew what he knew and found what he expected to find, which caused teacher's associations, the U.S. publishing industry, school board officials, and People for the American Way to question his critical credentials.

But people often question the credentials of ideology-based critics. This has been especially true in the United States, with its long-standing preference for (1) liberal or pluralistic philosophies and (2) pragmatic, functional methodologies. Things have been different in Europe. In part because of the sheer intellectual power of certain German and French intellectuals, and in part because of the very different ethnic, political, and economic circumstances of European life in the twentieth century, continental critics have differed from their American cousins. But during the past twenty years U.S. critics have been learning from the Europeans, and their work now reflects those influences. This chapter details two such influences.

The term "continental criticism" is used here advisedly, for it embraces two dissimilar, at times antagonistic, modes of thought. But there is little doubt that the schools featured here are currently the freest spirits in the academic community. What do they have in common? In general, they are more leftist than rightist, composed of Marxists (who believe in undermining economic conspiracies) and deconstructionists (who believe in not believing). How do they differ? Marxists often charge that deconstructionists play wasteful semantic games while the deconstructionists feel that Marxists are tedious moralizers and that they, the deconstructionists, do indeed play wasteful semantic games, but that that is the only game in town.

Despite their differences, both groups would question Judge Hand's heavy-handed analysis of the Alabama textbooks. They would argue that the Judge has approached the text in a narrow, provincial way and thereby missed some of its most important aspects. Instead of seeing the above passages as seditious, for example, Marxists would view them as tame. They might note, for example, that while the authors encourage young girls to drive the family tractor, that they leave *ownership* of tractors in parental hands. Marxists might also argue that the steady tattooing of family values in the textbook opens up its readers to later, manipulative political appeals in behalf of a "national family."

Marxists might also note how *interiorized* the textbook rhetoric is (e.g., "one day you feel full of laughter . . . the next day you feel downright weird") and how, as a result, it is ultimately accommodationistic. By emphasizing "thinking" teens and "doing" parents (e.g., "Mr. and Mrs. Kopec both have full-time jobs"), the book fails to explicate *behavioral* options to parental exploitation ("When parents make mistakes . . . remember that they are just like you."). For the pure Marxist then, any relationship (between parents and children, among teenage peers, or between adolescents and the business world) that results in an unequal distribution of goods ultimately leads to political repression.

Deconstructionists march to an entirely different drummer. Mostly, they are interested in the linguistic integrity of a text: how well its arguments hang together, how internally consistent its images are, how well it resists vacuums (or aporia) of meaning. Deconstructionists make no attempt to honor an author's intentions since they feel that all meanings are the arbitrary products of speaker-audience negotiations. So, for example, they might become interested in another passage from one of the Alabama textbooks: "classes for parents are provided at some centers. They help parents learn effective ways to rear their children. Soon, certified centers may require parents to take part in the activities center" [Kelly and Eubanks, 1981:].

Deconstructionists are notoriously playful. Here, they might mention the irony of putting parents in "classes" (just as their own children are in classes), thereby *reducing* parents' expertise about teenage problems. Deconstructionists might also note that the so-called centers described here could hardly be centers since there are only a few of them, thereby making them "peripheries." Moreover, since only some centers are "certified" (making the rest of them uncertified peripheries), and since they are designed to deal with "marginal" rather than "central" people, the rhetoric of the textbook self-destructs. In other words, deconstructionists create problems for a text or, as they would have it, point up problems a text creates for itself. They unravel what an author has raveled, trying to reduce the author's hold on the reader by showing the inevitable self-contradictions in human discourse.

These schools of thought are not part of a single, monolithic consciousness but they embrace three general themes:

1. All criticism is politically self-interested. As Jameson [1981:58] argues, virtually any statement a critic makes has latent historical or theoretical assumptions. Whenever we look at something, we do so with all of our habitual ways of looking, including our biases, hunches, and deep-seated uncertainties. Thus, to enjoy a Dr. Pepper commercial featuring dancing teenagers and their dancing grandparents may expose our belief that physical energy is central to a meaningful life. This assumption may betray yet other assumptions we have about aging (i.e., that it is best when it looks like non-aging) as well as about politics (i.e., that state funding for the care of sedentary geriatric patients should not be increased). In other words, Continentals tend to believe that feigning objectivity when doing criticism makes us deny what we are as people.

2. Criticism should be expansionistic. Continental critics often study previously ignored texts. In contrast, says Wander [1983:3], U.S. critics have typically studied texts produced by "the monopoly of officialdom"—white, Anglo-Saxon, centrist males—and have thereby produced rhetorical theories of doubtful generalizability. To correct for such limitations, says Lentricchia [1983:15], the Continental critic tries "to reread culture so as to amplify and strategically position the marginalized voices of the ruled, exploited, oppressed, and excluded."

So, for example, deconstructionists study the works of modernists who have stood literary conventions on their heads, while Marxists study youthful "punk" cultures to "open a space within which . . . resistance may be heard" [Grossberg, 1984:416]. Such critics practice what Ricoeur calls a "hermeneutics of suspicion" [Ruthven, 1984:35], an ominous-sounding phrase, but one that keeps critics from being tripped up by the forces of power and that ensures that they listen to the voices that have either been muted or ignored previously.

3. *Criticism should be oppositional.* Continental critics feel that their U.S. counterparts have been too willing to honor the text the author had in mind. The very title of E. D. Hirsch's classic, *Validity in Interpretation* [1967], suggests that, heretofore, the only way for a traditional critic to know a text was the author's way, resulting in a gospel of "intentionalism" that reproduced the author's worldview. Continental critics show no such obeisance to the author. They often become "resistant readers" [Fetterley, 1978], who accept no utterance at face value and who instead examine a text for what they find interesting, whether or not it coincides with the author's intended interpretation.

In short, continental critics ask questions not always asked. Admittedly, when doing so they often say outrageous things, become tedious in their preachments, and ask questions they cannot always answer. It is this last reason, however, that especially recommends them, for such critics are now producing some of the most interesting work being done. As a kind of gentle godfather to this way of thinking, Kenneth Burke counseled that criticism should be more than just an intellectual exercise, that we "take our work home" with us and become "responsible to the larger social project" [Lentricchia, 1983:151]. If criticism is to be insightful, as it must be, probing, as it can be, and pluralistic, as it should be, can we afford to ignore these voices?

THE DECONSTRUCTIONIST CRITIQUE

Born out of the social turmoil that swept through Europe in the 1960s, deconstruction is "intensely skeptical of all claims to truth" [Norris, 1982: 57]. To deconstruct is to take apart a rhetorical message, to examine how well a text "holds" its author's ideas without revealing unintended meanings. Given such obstreperous goals, it is not surprising that deconstruction was spawned by frustration. Its founders were French thinkers—Jacques Derrida, Michel Foucault, and Roland Barthes—who disdained the Western

Establishment that fostered the Vietnam War, student repression, and racial segregation.

Moreover, they charged Establishment academics with spawning positivism (a love of things scientific), formalism (a reverence for traditional texts), and structuralism (a commitment to study such texts scientifically). Deconstructionists are, then, *post*-structuralists. They do not view language "as a complex but stable system whose constituents can be securely established" but as "an unreliable structure that violates its own rules" [Barney, 1987:179].

Deconstructionists are often accused (by people such as Michael Walzer [1988]) of being anarchists who treat communication as an impossibility and who are, as a result, nothing more than radical debunkers. According to their detractors, deconstructionists flee from the hard, patient work of disciplined criticism. But hard, patient, disciplined criticism is often unenlightening, they respond, and too often becomes "mere paraphrasing" of a message rather than really rich analysis.

The alternative, say the deconstructionists, is criticism that challenges rather than confirms critics' assumptions, that explores rather than retraces textual features, that subverts rather than accepts literary or rhetorical artistry. Deconstructionists resist the charge that they are political saboteurs costumed as critics, arguing that the nature of textuality demands their approach, especially when three crucial premises are granted:

1. *Meaning is problematic.* The mystery of language is the central issue for deconstructionists. They feel that language is polysemous, that the "same" word means different things to different people and different things to the same person on different occasions. Accordingly, deconstruction turns into linguistic skepticism because of what Derrida [1978] has called the constant "deferral" of meaning in a text.

One factor demanding such deferral, says Moi [1985:106], is **language structure.** She notes, for example, that the letter "b" has no inherent meaning but only "gets" meaning when grouped with other letters (e.g., to make "bat" or "bit"). "B" therefore must "defer" its meaning to these other elements to establish understandability. Similarly, "bat" and "bit" must defer their meaning once again to form "batch" or "bitter." If instability is true at such elementary levels, the deconstructionists argue, how can a critic expect to settle, once and for all, the complete meaning of a verbal text?

Cooper [1988] provides an interesting example of this principle. She notes, for example, that Richard Nixon's famed Checkers speech succeeded in exonerating him in 1952. At the same time, says Cooper, that speech put the *personal* lives of politicians on the press's agenda forevermore. Ironically, then, it may have been this Nixon-inspired concern over personal character that sustained the media's investigation of the Watergate burglaries twenty years later. According to this logic, the ultimate "meaning" of the Checkers speech was Nixon's resignation from the presidency.

Verbal context further complicates the picture, says Ryan [1982:12], who notes that the "God" in "God damn" and in "God of our Fathers" are very different Gods indeed. As a result, says Sumner [1979:149], every text will have a "surplus of meaning," which changes the critic's job considerably. Rather than looking for a message's "best" meaning, deconstructionists seek out its widest range of meanings by asking the question: In how many *different* ways might people come to understand this text?

Cheryl Walker [1985] provides an example. She studied the images of women contained in early Puritan poetry and found, naturally, that women occupied a peripheral place there. But Walker became intrigued by the *continuing,* perhaps even *crucial,* functions of such images. She concludes that the omnipresence of these "marginal" characters proved their latent power. Why speak of the periphery so often, Walker asks, if it is indeed a periphery and not a threat? Walker concludes that such an over-concern with marginal people ultimately reveals a patriarchy in trouble.

Social context makes meaning even harder to establish. Take a statement like the following, says Belsey [1980:52], and then ask if its interpretation is unproblematic: "Democracy will ensure that we extend the boundaries of civilization." Would this statement sound different, Belsey asks, to residents of Western democracies (who would think of free speech, consumer choice, and open elections) than to residents of the Third World (who might think of colonial exploitation, guerilla warfare, and cultural decadence)? Belsey says that such a statement would sound different still if mouthed by a conservative Member of Parliament in Great Britain, by a committed socialist, or by the International Vice President of Pepsi Cola. This sentence will not stand still, Belsey argues, and we cannot pretend in criticism that it will.

Given these roadblocks to easy meaning, someone must become equipped to deal with what Culler [1982:220] calls "the uncanny irrationality of texts." Someone must realize that chaos is not something the radical critic adds to a text but something that constitutes the text initially. Someone must ask the questions about "real meaning" that traditionalists have been afraid to ask. The deconstructionist is the person who asks such questions.

2. All messages are intertwined. No text can be understood unless viewed in the light of what Chapter 3 described as its persuasive field, the messages to which that text responds and which respond to it. The ideal critic, says Barthes [1981:39], views the text as an "intertext," as something woven by the threads of other texts. The critic looks for the traces of these other messages within the text so that its "pluralistic" effects can be gauged. This means that deconstructionists "often show scant respect for the wholeness or integrity of individual works" [Culler, 1982:220] but are more interested in the general themes that echo through society. While deconstructionists sometimes visit with an individual text, they rarely stay for long.

To take a pedestrian example of intertextuality, we might ask why radio call-in shows are so popular. A deconstructionist might observe that they contain (and are contained by) backyard gossip, doctrinaire preaching, psychological counseling, classroom instruction, obscene phone-calling, stage drama, and commercial salesmanship. Each of these genre carries its own "charge" for listeners, which can "detonate" from time to time, thereby increasing the show's overall rhetorical "explosion." And because these subdiscourses are mutually implicative, their power is increased all the more. Hence the job of the deconstructionist: to reveal the seams in the fabric of talk-radio by asking whether listeners really wish to become addicted to discourse emerging from the rather squalid worlds of doctrinaire preaching and obscene phone-calling.

As Goodall [1994] demonstrates, a political campaign is no different. After all, when the average citizen "inhales" a campaign, he or she absorbs snippets of campaign rock music, head-shots of the candidates, a news bulletin, long-winded speeches, a *Comedy Channel* parody, interviews with the candidates' children, a caravan of trains, and thousands upon thousands of additional images. "A" campaign, then, is a rich but unstable thing and hence its meanings must be plural.

Deconstructionists say that we cannot escape intertextuality, that subtexts affect not only how we listen and read but also how we are *prepared* to listen and read. So, for example, even with an empirical event like the Civil War, people will view it differently depending on the texts (Northern myths vs. Southern myths) heard previously. Because of this complexity, deconstructionists feel that criticism must challenge the univocal interpretation of any text. As Foucault [1981:70] points out, for example, madness and hypersexuality have been the object of scorn *and reverence* at different points in human history. Thus, unless a text's meanings are pluralized, an old rhetoric may gain new, unwarranted popularity because its "textual history" has been forgotten or not plainly established in the first place.

A wonderful piece of criticism by Blair and her colleagues [1991] illustrates. They were interested in capturing the meaning of the Vietnam Veterans Memorial in Washington, D.C., a memorial that sits in close proximity to other monuments (the Washington, the Lincoln) that appear to speak clearly. The authors found that the meanings of the Vietnam Memorial, in contrast, were so plentiful that "capturing" them was out of the question. Why? Because the Vietnam War was the most equivocal, uncertain, and agonizing war ever fought by the United States, a war that opened rifts that still exist among the citizenry. As a result, even though the wall itself is a model of architectural simplicity (black granite, no flourishes), people have visited it by the millions, complicating its meaning with their poems, flowers, torches, medallions, signs, vigils, and long, beautiful letters.

3. Rhetoric is problematic. Heretofore, most deconstructionists have spent their time unmasking authors by demonstrating the clever tricks they have used to fabricate rationality in a fictional world. While traditional critics have assumed that the author knew what he or she was doing when composing a text, deconstructionists have made no such assumption. They proclaim "the Death of the Author" [Belsey, 1980:139], approaching texts in ways that might well horrify their creators. As a result, deconstructionists often call authors to task for the "texts" they wittingly or unwittingly reproduce anew.

Not wishing to become leeches on someone else's writings, these critics often use these texts merely to *illustrate* arguments that they, the critics, want to forward.

Because deconstruction has been used primarily in literary studies, its full power has not yet been tapped since literature is, after all, self-consciously fictive. Literature does not expect readers to grant it factual status, only "truth" status; it does not present itself as a final authority but only as an initial, teasing voice. Rhetoric is different. It expects to be taken seriously. To counteract that power, deconstructionists approach rhetoric as if it were literature. They emphasize rhetoric's fabricated status so that people will learn to question the Declaration of Independence just as sharply as they do the *Canterbury Tales*. Equally, the deconstructionist approaches literature as if it were rhetoric, warning readers not to become so relaxed in the presence of literature that they forget that it can also affect their social attitudes and expectations. Tracking strategic devices in a text—whether rhetorical or literary—sheds light on how an author privileges one meaning over its many alternatives. By "pluralizing" a text in this way, the critic regains control over that text.

Given these three, rather frustrating, premises, what is a critic to do? How does one deconstruct a text? And why would one want to do so? The deconstructionist's answers to these questions of purpose and method can be frustrating. For one thing, they rarely worry about producing answers. Their business is producing (or reproducing) questions. Deconstruction is therefore never a completed process. Its goals are (1) to "exhaust" a text so that its multiple meanings become clearer and (2) to contrast what an author intends for a text with the other intentions a critic might find in it.

As for critical method, there is none. Not really. Rather, the critic operates creatively, teasing out themes, inconsistencies, and pontifications in a text, starting down one path and then another, looking for semantic uncertainty until it is time to stop. (A deconstructionist never *concludes*.) When doing criticism, a deconstructionist will frequently "seize on some apparently peripheral fragment in the work—a footnote, a recurrent minor term or image, a casual allusion—and work it tenaciously through to the point where it threatens to dismantle the oppositions which govern the text as a whole. The tactic of the deconstructive critic . . . is to show how texts come to embarrass their own ruling systems of logic" [Eagleton, 1983:133].

But while deconstructionists dismiss questions of purpose (a delusion, they feel) and critical method (the refuge of pedants, they feel), they do ask certain questions persistently. To avoid complete bewilderment, we will use these questions during a sample deconstruction. But what should be deconstructed? What sort of text deserves the rather rough treatment deconstruction hands out? Aune [1983:260] provides a clue when he recalls that Derrida & Co. were especially suspicious of the "transcendental significations" of formalized rhetoric. Derrida had in mind here such things as legal statutes, religious coda, scientific reports, and political oratory.

He might also have had Gerry Ford in mind. We will assume that he did, and here consider the simple set of remarks President Ford gave on July 1, 1976, just prior to the opening of a Centennial safe that had been sealed at the U.S. Capitol a century before. Mr. Ford spoke thusly:

(1) Thank you very much, Senator Mansfield, Mr. Speaker, Senator Scott, Senator Brooke, Congressman Boggs, distinguished Members of the House and Senate, ladies and gentlemen:

(2) Obviously, I am deeply honored to have the opportunity this afternoon to open this historic Centennial safe. It contains many items of interest to us today as we celebrate the completion of our second century. But it symbolizes much more than a valuable collection of mementos, it symbolizes something about the United States of America that is so mighty and so inspiring that it cannot be locked up in a safe—I mean the American spirit.

(3) When this safe was sealed, Americans looked forward to the future, to this year of 1976. There was no doubt in their minds that a President of a free government would participate in a ceremony here in the United States Capitol Building.

(4) Just as American men and women 200 years ago looked to the future, those who sealed this safe 100 years ago also looked to the future. So it is today with Americans. But there is no safe big enough to contain the hopes, the energies, the abilities of our people. Our real national treasure does not have to be kept under lock and key in a safe or in a vault. America's wealth is not in material objects, but in our great heritage, our freedom, and our belief in ourselves.

(5) A century ago the population of the United States numbered over 40 million; today we have more than five times as many. But the growth of our population has not lessened our devotion to the principles that inspired Americans in 1776 or 1876.

(6) In 1876 our immense wealth, both natural and inventive, commanded world-wide attention. We grew from coast to coast in greater industrial and agricultural development than humanity had ever known. In 1876 America was still emerging from a terrible fraternal war. A lesser people might have been unequal to the challenge, but 1976 finds the confidence of 1876 confirmed.

(7) Today there is far greater equality of opportunity, liberty, and justice for all of our citizens in every corner of America. There is rising prosperity for our Nation and peace and progress for our people.

(8) We look back to the evening of July 4, 1776. It was then, after the adoption of the Declaration of Independence, that the Continental Congress resolved that Franklin, Adams, and Jefferson begin work on a seal as a national symbol. We are all familiar with the front part of that great seal. But the reverse side, which also appears on every dollar bill, is especially instructive. It depicts a pyramid which is not completed and a single eye gazing out radiantly. The unfinished pyramid represents the work that remains for Americans to do. The Latin motto below is freely translated: "God has favored our undertaking." Two hundred years later, we know God has.

(9) Though we may differ, as Americans have throughout the past, we share a common purpose: It is the achievement of a future in keeping with our glorious past. The American Republic provides for continued growth through a convergence of views and interests, but that growth must be spiritual as well as material.

(10) As we look inside this safe, let us look inside ourselves. Let us look into our hearts and into our hopes.

(11) On Sunday we start a new century, a century of the individual. We have given meaning to our life as a nation. Let us now welcome a century in which we give new meaning to our lives as individuals. Let us look inside ourselves to unleash the God-given treasures stored within. And let us look outside ourselves to the needs of our families, our friends, our communities, our Nation, and our moral and spiritual consciousness.

(12) Thank you very much. [Ford, 1976a:1941–3]

Most Americans would judge this a fine speech. It says nothing terribly new but it resays old things in a pleasing way. Mr. Ford develops a trite metaphorical theme (spiritual values as riches), touches on the expected bits of Americana (the Revolutionary War, Adams and Jefferson), and ends his speech by looking toward a glorious future. There is nothing startling here but nothing distasteful either. Even the most cynical observer would judge the speech harmless. Not so, says the deconstructionist: This speech subverts the dignity of the average citizen and promotes a new American oligarchy. Where is the proof?

The deconstructionist might first examine any **absolute language** in the text that implies that listeners can rise above partiality. President Ford's brave phrases—"so mighty and so inspiring," "our great heritage," "devotion to the principles"—merely float in rhetorical space, the deconstructionist would argue. Similarly, when Ford speaks of "we," "us," or "Americans," he conceives of a dormant citizenry. Of the twenty-one such references in the speech, over half refer to *looking*, not acting. Americans look forward and backward; they look inside their hearts and inside their national safe. But what sort of citizen is a "looking" citizen, the deconstructionist would ask? Why does Ford use only three *behavioral* verbs to describe what Americans are like? How can such an inert speech comfort an audience? And if the American people are not "acting," who is?

The speech's **figurative language** answers this latter question. According to deconstructionists, people depend heavily on metaphors for meaning but too often forget how imagery can trap them. The deconstructionist would note, for example, that during Mr. Ford's speech-act he not only opens a safe inside the Capitol but also uses that safe figuratively. Why choose the metaphor of a safe, the deconstructionist would ask, when most Americans have no immediate connection with a convenience the upper class uses to hide its money? Is Mr. Ford really describing a *national* safe or is he just taunting blue-collar Americans by alluding to valuables they do not possess residing in a safe they do not own? Besides, how "safe" can a safe be for ordinary people when opened but once every hundred years and then only by the ruling-class individuals who have its keys?

Deconstructionists might observe that there is even a certain cruelty to Mr. Ford's teasing here since the safe we are locked out of *contains our hopes:*

"As we look inside this safe, let us look inside ourselves. Let us look into our hearts and into our hopes." So, it appears, we are (1) inside a safe that (2) we do not own and (3) for which we do not have a key. We are thus a people trapped and isolated, separated from our fellow citizens by steel walls, a people who cannot even hope for community since the President has urged us to "give new meaning to our lives *as individuals.*"

But why do the American people deserve this fate? Too many of them were born on the wrong side of the tracks, says Mr. Ford via his **abstract language**. "[T]hrough abstractions," says Ryan [1982:50,56], people can be manipulated by making things "seem outside the movement of time and the productive processes of society." Such is the case with Mr. Ford's concept of "wealth," which he says lies "not in material objects" but is "spiritual as well."

Is Ford arguing here that monetary and spiritual wealth are necessarily separate, with some people deserving one and some another? Apparently so, since he claims that *our* "real national treasure does not have to be kept in a vault." But why can't *we* have secured riches, Mr. Ford? Because there is "no safe big enough to contain the hopes . . . of our people," he replies. Thus, we must resign ourselves to the lot of all non-elites (only "*work* remains for Americans to do") and to inequality as well ("We may differ, as Americans have throughout the past."). The American Dream, it appears, is ultimately just a dream.

Deconstructionists also key on **hierarchical language** because of their theory of meaning: A thing can be known only by its opposite; if one thing is good, other things must be less good and still others more good. This sense of relativitity is rarely explicated in a text, which is not to say that it is not there (by implication). Mr. Ford's unfinished pyramid on the back of the dollar bill is a case-in-point.

By the time he makes this allusion, Mr. Ford has already affirmed (in paragraph 6) that there are greater and "lesser" people in the world. Presumably, this means that some people are on the pyramid's bottom and some at its top. When finishing the construction of such a pyramid, one would presumably work at (for?) its apex and not at (for?) its base. This implies that the real beneficiaries in the future will be those who are already at the top of the pyramid, powerful persons looking with "a single eye gazing out radiantly" on the day-laborers in society.

Might Mr. Ford's hierarchy be leveled in the future? Apparently not, since we can only look toward "a future *in keeping with* our glorious past," a past that Mr. Ford admits included a civil war, insufficient opportunity for the nation's citizens, denial of liberty, and an inadequate judicial system. While there apparently will be some increases for "our citizens in every corner of America," one wonders whether cornered citizens will even notice such improvements, sitting as they do at the base of the Ford pyramid.

Deconstructionists are particularly devilish when it comes to **inconsistent language**. For example, despite his lionizing of "spiritual treasures," Ford declares that the "valuable collection of mementos" in the national vault symbolizes "something" (some-*thing*) important, thereby endorsing materialist values. He repeats this theme when recollecting that "our immense wealth . . . commanded world-wide attention" in 1876, attention he clearly appreciates. If Mr. Ford were not a materialist, why did he choose the dollar bill as his central rhetorical image?

Moreover, why did he tell us to look "outside ourselves" to the "needs of our families, our friends, our communities?" If these needs are truly *outside* ourselves, how can we possibly deal with them? And how can we trust in the future when it took until 1976 to "find the confidence" needed to persevere: "Two hundred years later, we know God has [favored our undertaking]." With a heavenly time-lag of this magnitude, can this really be called a speech of hope?

Much more sophisticated deconstructions than this one have been performed in the past and many of them have inspected the same five "trouble spots" isolated in the Ford text. Ryan [1982:136], for example, examined a report from the Carnegie Commission on Higher Education. He argues that while the report lauded "academic freedom," it really camouflaged "the link between education and business behind a benign vocabulary," thereby endorsing "academic constriction" rather than its opposite. In a similar vein, Aden [1995] examined a nostalgic HBO documentary on baseball (*When it Was a Game*) and shows how its glorification of yesteryear's blue-collar players has a *disempowering* effect on today's viewers who, when watching the show, are reminded of the million-dollar-bonus babies seen in today's sports pages.

On a very different front, Belsey [1980:114–7] observes how Sherlock Holmes' detective stories praise the scientific method and yet how women of "shadowy sexuality" often steal the show, thereby casting doubt on scientific rationality. A similar theme was traced by Ryan [1982:146], who examined how "philosophic reason" became utilitarian when articulated by business leaders accused of air and water pollution. As one business leader remarked: "I don't think it's realistic to ask a corporation to do [too much]. . . . The cost-benefit [ratio] can get out of line."

Given deconstruction's often bizarre flights of fancy, what are we to make of it? Deconstructions can be cute, but are they valid? useful? important? Any message, after all, could be "destroyed" in the way we have destroyed Mr. Ford's speech. That is a crucial fact, the deconstructionists would reply. After all, if a carefully crafted, simple, speech like Ford's can be shown to be pessimistic, reactionary, materialistic, isolationistic, and hierarchical rather than their opposites, should we not be especially on guard when presented with vastly more subtle rhetorical materials?

Perhaps, but was our deconstruction really fair? Did it not put words into Mr. Ford's mouth? Not really, for Ford's vacuums of meaning came from *his own remarks*. Admittedly, we did not interpret the President's words as he would have preferred. But why should we? Why should critics help Ford fashion his message? Aren't critics free agents? Must they slavishly conform to the author's rhetorical directions? Besides, is Gerald Ford not a grown adult? If he could not make his words stand still, why should the critic compensate for him?

It is rather important, after all, that Ford's language could not obviate problems that have plagued American democracy throughout its history: poverty in a land of opportunity, peace in a land of militarism, godlessness in a land of churches. If these inconsistencies have not been resolved in two hundred years, how could Gerry Ford resolve them in one five minute speech? Ultimately, then, there is nothing magical about deconstruction except that it forces a text to be honest with itself.

Perhaps the sharpest challenge to deconstruction is that, as in the example above, President Ford's *actual listeners* probably never noticed what Johnson [1981:166] has called the "warring forces of signification" in a text. Indeed, Mr. Ford's listeners were probably charmed by his oration. Do not such real-life responses give the lie to deconstruction? Only if the critic wishes to become an audience member and not a critic. In deconstruction, it is the critic who must highlight the conflicts inside texts, thereby making those texts problematic for the wider community. The deconstructionist is essentially a consciousness-raiser, spotting trouble in a text where there seems to be none. Ultimately, the question becomes one of who will have the last word—Gerry Ford or the critic. It is not to Mr. Ford's advantage to have his speeches deconstructed. But it may be to society's advantage, which is why the critic does criticism.

The most devastating critique of deconstruction is that of the Marxists, who find it to be too game-like. It produces an "infinite regression" in texts, warns Barney [1987:199], "a kind of "textual fiddling while Rome burns," says Norris [1982:131], an "elitist cult and reactionary force," says Felperin [1985:111]. While "millions have been killed because they were Marxists," observes Ryan [1982:1], "no one will be obliged to die because s/he is a deconstructionist."

As we will see, Marxists are fond of making such grand statements. But the deconstructionist and the Marxist have much in common because they both expose "the complicity between rhetoric, power, and authority" [Cain, 1984:241] and can therefore be liberating. But liberation for what end, asks the Marxist? What social policies does deconstruction put in place? How will people's lives be improved because contrariety is found in a text? About such matters, the deconstructionist is typically silent.

THE MARXIST CRITIQUE

The Marxist critic takes a very old story—a story of exploitation—and tells it again and again. What is its plot? It is this: The ruling classes use rhetoric to justify their exalted positions, rationalize the meager existences of the down-trodden, and inhibit insurrection. How do they do so? Through education, religion, political patronage, banking systems, nationalism, bureaucracies, and manufacturing processes. Why does rhetoric enter the picture? Because each of these systems of exploitation needs an attractive public face. And what does the critic do? Expose the constantly changing disguises of repression.

Even in this simplistic rendering, it is clear why Marxist thought captivates many. In the scholarly world, it especially captivates those who have tired of traditional criticism and, more recently, of deconstruction. According to the Marxist, traditional critics "appreciate" rather than critique discourse, thereby making criticism a decadent activity, like collecting bottle caps or frequenting Woody Allen film festivals. Such criticism stands too far away from its object of analysis and ultimately becomes boring, predictable, and socially irresponsible.

In short, Marxists aim to make a difference in the world of politics by making a row in the world of criticism. Unlike their cousins on the Left, the deconstructionists, Marxists will risk being both repetitious and tendentious if it will open people's eyes to the political manipulations surrounding (and suppressing) them. For Marxists, a text is worth studying not for its inherent worth but because it signals such manipulation. They base their criticism on the following premises.

1. Economic factors determine rhetoric. There is no plainer way of stating the most fundamental presupposition of Marxist criticism. And the word "determine" is central to this proposition, for it holds that the possibilities for communication are set by society's structural and economic mechanisms. These mechanisms make only certain thoughts thinkable and, hence, only certain messages sayable. Although this "vulgar" form of Marxism has become less popular as Marxist theory has matured, Marx's fundamental dictum still informs most such criticism: "Consciousness does not determine life; life determines consciousness" [Eagleton, 1976:4].

Why is this true? Because society needs to reproduce itself from age to age and therefore needs a rhetoric capable of making its favored institutions compelling and dynamic. If a politico-economic "base" is to remain viable, it must produce "superstructures" (e.g., religious, social, cultural, and educational systems) capable of sustaining that base. Thus, it is not enough for a capitalistic system to produce goods (its economic base), but it must also find a rhetoric to make such production continuingly necessary. So, says King [1987:73], "Americans have been told to feel that their bodies are filthy, rotting masses of chemicals and that their odors and body faults must be constantly disguised, or they will be found out and ridiculed. [Marxist] theorists point to the enormous sales of soaps and deodorants as proof that the engineered insecurity of the masses is a fact of life."

2. Messages are produced, not created. This proposition proceeds logically from the first: If the base dominates the superstructure, then human texts are fashioned automatically. The implications of this proposition are stark and unsettling: People's most unique thoughts are little more than the thoughts "granted" them by the larger social system. So, for example, a high school sophomore who feels she is dressed distinctively when wearing her Calvin Kleins is not just deluded but trebly deluded: (1) she is wearing jeans because that is what the powerful cotton industry in the United States has made available for her to wear; (2) she has chosen the Calvin Klein brand because it can be purchased locally, meaning that in comparison to its competitors Calvin Klein, Inc., has best managed to keep wages low and profits high, and (3) she feels distinctive because the Calvin Klein ads have depicted independent women doing independent things while wearing their Calvins.

Our high school sophomore would naturally be outraged by this analysis, feeling that her choice of clothing was, in fact, *her choice*. She must embrace this delusion, the Marxist says, for without such "false consciousness" the social and economic system would fail. Delusions like these result from what Williams [1977] and others have called **hegemony,** an all-encompassing Master Text so broadly based in society that it can no longer be seen by either speaker or audience. "The author does not make the materials with which he works," claims Eagleton [1976:29], just as "the worker in a car-assembly plant fashions his product from already-processed materials."

So, says Eagleton [1975:52], the three-volume novel became popular in Victorian England not because writers wished to write them or readers read them but because publishers found them profitable to produce and formed a cartel with the newly emerging circulating libraries for their distribution. In short, while we may wish to believe that ideas spring from Nothingness, the Marxist finds this a silly notion.

3. Ideologies leave textual evidence. Generally speaking, Marxist critics treat an individual message as a fragment of a larger, coherent cultural experience. They differ with one another about how easy it is to find such coherence, but few doubt it can be found. The basic critical operation for the Marxist is thus one of "rewriting" a text so that its ideological imprintings can be observed. For the Marxist, true critical consciousness is being able to know even "yourself as the product of a historical process that has deposited its traces in you" [Lentricchia, 1983:11]. This is similar to the cultural critic's challenge (as seen in Chapter 11), but Marxism adds a new dimension—the State—by looking for the political and economic truths a text honors.

But it is often hard to find ideology within texts because it hides inside "natural" phenomena. For example, the Marxist might note that American companies often vie with one another to support U.S. Olympic teams. These corporate/nationalistic linkages do not just make for good public relations but have two other benefits in addition: (1) the televised athletic competition reinforces free market competitiveness and (2) the private sector's capitalistic message is linked directly to the public sector's patriotic message. This is why Marxist critics so often study popular culture, where such contrivances and collusions have become so naturalized that they can no longer be seen (What could be more natural than running and jumping?).

4. Established institutions need rhetoric. Rhetoric is often thought of as the tool of the downtrodden, a way of changing the status quo. But Marxist critics have shown that the Establishment also depends on public discourse, even if it does so less colorfully. Religious leaders attend political gatherings, business executives appear on the nightly news, and Hollywood personalities, well-paid athletes, and military leaders move about constantly in each other's company, forming what Hart [1994] has called a "rhetorical establishment." Their persuasive skills make for what Thompson [1984:68] calls "cultural capital," which, when combined with having an education, gaining access to the media, and learning bureaucratic routines, makes some people very powerful indeed.

This shower of Establishment rhetoric often makes us forget what we know. We know, for example, that individuals have different amounts of money. But in capitalistic societies, rhetoric develops to make these differences seem both natural and necessary. Still other rhetoric develops to prove that these inequalities need not be permanent: the Rags-to-Riches tale, the Lottery Millionaire myth, the Spike Lee Success Story, etc. Cultural rituals, political oratory, and television dramas cooperate to make what we see with our eyes (disparity) different from what we come to accept (justifiable disparity).

At times, these differential allocations are even made to seem *attractive* (e.g., the rather forgettable Goldie Hawn movie "Overboard" in which a bored heiress falls off her yacht, loses her memory, moves in with a laborer, and eventually finds her essential self in his poor-but-honest embrace). These messages bombard us so constantly and so unobtrusively that we are not just awakened to Establishment values but deadened to all competing values as well.

Given these assumptions about rhetoric, what do Marxist critics do? At the risk of generalizing about a diverse group, it seems that they do two main things. *The first goal of Marxist criticism is to reestablish the history that produced the text.* Marxists remind us constantly that rhetoric is crafted by particular people for particular people. They steer clear of what Bennett [1979a: 147] calls the "metaphysic of the text" (a text in pure form) by repopulating it. So, for example, a Marxist critic would never treat a documentary on Central America as a mere example of its genre. Rather, the critic would want to know *who* financed the film, *who* the director studied under, why *this* political figure and not *that* political figure was profiled in the film, *who* was made to seem a devil and *who* an angel in the film, and *to whom* the documentary was distributed and through *whose* agency.

Naturally, one need not be a Marxist to be interested in such questions. But Marxists take special pains to remember (1) that each piece of rhetoric contains the marks of its unique historical situation and (2) that rhetoric has a powerful (and dangerous) capacity to make the world abstract. This is why Marxists are interested in a rhetorical image's **material conditions** (e.g., who lives and who dies in the documentary, what sorts of food people eat in the restaurant scenes, what type of work they perform in the fields, etc.). According to the

Marxist, traditional criticism too often overlooks such facts by "aestheticizing" a text. So, for example, the Marxist critic would discover whether the documentarist placed a First World or a Third World lens on the camera, whether peasant rituals were treated paternalistically, whether the film accurately depicted the reality of prostitution in Central America, and whether a rock beat or a Latin beat was featured in the nightclub scenes. In other words, a Marxist critic would never forget that the Central American documentary ultimately dealt with Central Americans.

The second goal of Marxist criticism is to comfort the afflicted and afflict the comfortable, often by amplifying voices that have been previously muted. So, for example, Jameson [1981] urged examination of the oral epics of tribal society, the fairy tales developed by the European underclasses, and the melodramas written for pennies by paupers. Similarly, Genovese [1976] studied how black slaves transformed their oppressors' Christianity into a religious style better suited to their own cultural patterns. Yet another brand of Marxist criticism studies the "symbolic violence" done to oppressed groups by mainstream messages (e.g., how ghetto residents watching *Lifestyles of the Rich and Famous* decode its obscene consumerism).

But how do Marxists do their criticism? As with all critics, they ask questions. Specifically, they look for rhetorical features that have been "overdetermined" by socioeconomic conditions. We shall consider five common ways of isolating these features by examining a humble guide to student parking regulations at the University of Texas. Like so many bureaucratic tomes, this document is almost comically dense. Among its highlights are the following:

(1) **PERMITS REQUIRED FOR ACCESS & PARKING:** Only vehicles conspicuously displaying proper University permits (as specified in Section VI, infra) may enter or park on the main campus Monday through Friday from 7:30 a.m. to 5:00 p.m. Purchase of a permit does not guarantee a parking place on campus (Section II, infra).

(2) **DISPLAY OF PERMITS:** Parking permits must be properly affixed to or displayed on the vehicle(s) as described in Section VI infra. Decals which are taped or affixed by unauthorized materials will subject the holder to a University citation. Additionally, the permit will be revoked and the holder may lose all parking privileges. (Section VIII, infra). . . .

(4) **REMOVAL OF PERMITS:** Permits shall be removed when there is a change of vehicle ownership; when association with the University is terminated; when a replacement permit (decal) has been issued to take the place of a previously issued permit (decal); or upon expiration or revocation. (Section VI, infra)

(5) **OWNERSHIP OF PERMIT:** Ownership of the parking permit remains with The University. Purchase of a parking permit signifies that an individual has been granted the privilege of parking a motor vehicle on University property (Section VI, infra). . . .

(14) **BICYCLES AND SKATES:** Bicycles must be operated in accordance with the ordinances of the City of Austin, the specific applicable provisions of these regulations, all provisions of these regulations concerning parking restrictions and

traffic and applicable state laws. Rollerskating (including skate boards) is not permitted on any part of the campus. (Section IV, infra). . . .

(17) **POSTED SIGNS:** Posted signs, whether permanent or temporary, must be obeyed at all times and take precedence over painted curbs, pavement markings and designations shown on any University map. . . .

(20) **REGISTRATION OF TWO VEHICLES:** Holders of Class D, F or O permits may register an alternate vehicle at no extra cost. Holders of Class A, C or G permits may register one additional motorcycle, or moped. (Section VI, infra). . . .

(21) **ENFORCEMENT AND IMPOUNDMENTS:** Failure to abide by these regulations may be the basis for disciplinary action against students, and faculty/staff (Section V, infra). Upon notice, violators may subject their vehicle(s) to impoundment pending payment of overdue charges (Section VIII, infra). Students may also be barred from readmission and have grades, degree, refunds or official transcripts withheld pending payment of overdue charges (Section VIII, infra). Vehicles may also be impounded for specific violations. (Section VII, infra).

(22) **APPEAL OF CITATION:** University parking and traffic citations may be appealed, **within five (5) working days** from date of citation by filing a Citation Appeal Form with the Parking and Traffic Office, (See Section VIII for detailed procedures). Court Appearance citations are handled by the appropriate state or municipal court.

(23) **VISITORS:** All visitors need permits to park on campus UNLESS parked at a paid parking meter or at the University Visitor Center or in the parking garage. OFFICIAL VISITORS are those who conduct important business with the University or who are not otherwise eligible for annual parking permits. Official Visitors may obtain temporary visitor parking permits from the guards at the traffic control stations. These permits entitle the holder to park *only* in a space designated "Official Visitor." Permits must be clearly visible and hanging from the rear view mirror support. (Section VI, infra).

(24) **PEDESTRIANS-RIGHTS AND DUTIES:** Pedestrians are subject to all official traffic control devices. They have the right-of-way at marked crosswalks, in intersections and on sidewalks extending across a service drive, building entrance or driveway. Pedestrians crossing a street at any point other than within a marked crosswalk or within an unmarked crosswalk at an intersection shall yield the right-of-way to all vehicles on said street. Pedestrians shall not leave curb or other place of safety and walk or run into the path of a vehicle which is so close that it is impossible for the driver to yield. They may cross an intersection diagonally only where permitted by special pavement marking.

(25) **INOPERABLE VEHICLES:** If a vehicle become inoperable, a telephone call shall be placed to the University Police Department (471–4441). The police will either render assistance or authorize temporary parking. Temporary parking shall not exceed 24 hours and must not create an obstruction or hazard. Vehicles shall not be left without written permission from UTPD. Hand written notes are NOT acceptable. [Quick Reference, 1986]

Documents like this abound in any bureaucracy, where they are defended as necessary for carrying out mundane affairs. If people were allowed to park a dune buggy backward in the reflection pool at high noon, bureaucrats would argue, all order would disappear from a parking infrastructure that is fragile at best with some 48,000 students descending on the campus daily. To make interdependence possible on such a campus, bureaucrats continue, rules-of-the-road must be formulated and then shared widely in a society prizing informed consent.

But why do such documents sound the way they do? Do they keep the "extant modes of production" in force, as the Marxists argue? Are students' consciousnesses "colonized" when they passively accept such reading materials?

To answer such questions, Marxist critics might first consider **structural strategies,** given their interest in the ideology of form. Eagleton [1975:56] notes, for example, that John Milton's decision to write *Paradise Lost* in his native tongue, to use the vernacular *form,* was a thunderous rejection of the aristocratic values of his day. In contrast, our list of parking regulations is mainstream. It is highly ordered (note the numbered paragraphs), thereby warning students that any response they might make to it must also be orthodox in form (and hence in content).

The document's voice is muted, so no personal interchange with its author is encouraged. Moreover, it is a document-within-a-document (note the cross-references), thus threatening students with an endless welter of paperwork should they become obstreperous. It is streamlined in appearance (note the simple, declarative sentences), suggesting that it exhausts all knowledge on the subject. In short, the document's overall form suggests that *the University* knows all and that it knows best. In thereby "reproducing authority," the document maintains the traditional administrator/student power imbalance found on any college campus.

Marxists are also interested in **homogenizing strategies** which (1) downplay individual desires, (2) simulate a collective consciousness not based on fact, and (3) posit totalistic models for appropriate behavior. Clearly, our parking document works hard at homogenization. It issues common permits to all University personnel (paragraph 1); it creates a kind of Grand Overseer out of University, city, and state authorities (paragraphs 14 and 22); and it affixes its *own* labels to everyone, even to miscellaneous persons (paragraph 23). Moreover, the document specifies public norms and excoriates counter-cultural behavior. Paragraph 14 eliminates the free-spirited skateboarders. Paragraph 25 forbids handwritten notes of apology. And paragraph 24 even specifies proper walking behavior!

While Marxists are interested in **utopian strategies,** our prosaic parking document has few of them. Still, there is a constant invocation of what McGee [1980] calls ideographs, Ultimate Terms that point toward the operating social consensus. Terms like "ownership," "privileges," "regulations," "eligibility" and "the University" reflect an ideal world where matters of authority have been long since settled, where orderliness reigns supreme, where one knows one's place. But there is no real delineation of this ideal state here, perhaps because bureaucrats must guard against preachment. Marxists would therefore be of two minds about this document: They would appreciate its austerity but they would worry that by not arguing explicitly for its utopian ideals, it removes them from public scrutiny, thereby instantiating them in the audience's minds.

Marxists feel that utopianism typically serves the interests of the exploiters rather than the exploited. As Eagleton [1976:45] reports, Marx's own tastes in literature tended to the "realist, satirical, radical writers" who were hostile to Romanticism, a movement that Marx felt "concealed the sordid prose of bourgeois life." In other words, because utopian visions are so rich and yet so malleable, they can be used to sanctify the unsanctifiable, something evidenced in the early 1990s by Afrikaners who use the Christian vision to defend apartheid in South Africa.

Marxists are particularly sensitive to the **dialectical strategies** of rhetoric. They feel that each text contains evidence of the oppositions facing its creator (and its creator's culture) and that good criticism "reads the code" of these oppositions. Although our parking document tries to put its best foot forward, even it betrays stresses and strains: University vs. city jurisdiction (paragraph 14), permanent vs. temporary students (paragraph 4), drivers vs. pedestrians (paragraph 24), visitors with "important business" vs. informal visitors (paragraph 23). And there are other tensions as well, tensions produced by creative students (who try to display decals "taped or affixed by unauthorized materials"), tardy students (whose citations are not appealed "within five (5) working days"), and litigious students (who try to play one rule against another: "posted signs . . . take precedence over painted curbs").

Often, these dialectical themes unwittingly "reproduce the hierarchy" of the University community, with faculty members, but not students, able to "register an alternate vehicle at no extra cost" (paragraph 20) and with penalties specified for students but not for faculty (paragraph 21). The job of rhetoric, then, is to explain, justify, and ultimately resolve such dialectical tensions. According to the Marxists, these resolutions typically favor Established sources of power. It is clear, after all, that even though the parking document deals exclusively with student life on campus, it was *not* written by students.

Rhetorically speaking, one of the most remarkable things about the parking document is that it is so unremarkable. Its words tumble from on high— sensible, rational, drained of emotion. And yet look what happens: It establishes a park-for-pay system with differential allocations of resources, with career-threatening sanctions for untoward behavior, with governance vested in a small number of unnamed persons, and with all signs of student individuality punished severely. The Marxist would quickly draw a parallel between this minisociety (this textual fragment) and the larger society of which it is a part (the Master Text).

And their case would be strongest when focusing on the **strategies of omission** it employs. Like the deconstructionist, the Marxist examines the not-said because it often speaks the unspeakable: that which cannot be argued clearly because it cannot be argued at all. Imagine the rhetoric required, for example, to justify the following propositions: a parking permit is a privilege, not a right (paragraph 5); "parking cooperatives" are illegal and immoral (paragraph 4); a student-purchased decal belongs to the University (paragraph 5); economic penalties for parking misbehavior are legitimate (paragraph 21); one's right to redress wrongs lasts less than a week (paragraph 22); even pedestrians have duties specifiable by a *public* University (paragraph 24).

Defending even one of these premises would be time-consuming, but most time-consuming of all would be defending how a University's prerogatives supersede those of the Almighty and the suicide-prone: "Pedestrians shall not leave curb or other place of safety and . . . run into the path of a vehicle which is so close that it is impossible for the driver to yield" (paragraph 24).

Naturally, an experienced bureaucrat could eventually generate enough words to justify these nonarguments. But ideology obviates the need to do so, functioning like a "linguistic legislature which defines what is available for public discussion and what is not" [Thompson, 1984:85]. Reacting against such trends, Marxist critics try to make rhetoric work harder by exploring what it wishes to conceal: its unargued premises. Unless required to do so, rhetoric will follow the path of least resistance, tapping values rooted in the political and economic priorities a society has already established.

Marxist critics study such things as parking regulations because their ordinariness allows them to deliver ideology to our doorsteps daily. A study by Mumby and Spitzack [1983] also examined the impact of everyday messages. They found that television news commentators emphasize politicians' *roles* rather than their moral obligations, thereby giving these leaders an "ideology of impersonality" that helped to explain away their ethical lapses. A related study by Corcoran [1986] traced U.S. newsmagazine coverage of a Soviet attack on a Korean airliner and found that such reports amounted to little more than nationalistic cheerleading, even though subsequent events cast doubt on the Soviets' responsibility for the incident.

Studies like these show how dependent political leaders are on the mass media for keeping ideological beliefs available, relevant, and powerful for their citizens. Another study by Thomas [1985] also traced ideology in the media, finding that religious programs designed for the working class (e.g., Rex Humbard) differed considerably from programs pitched to the upwardly mobile (e.g., The 700 Club). The former minimized worldly achievements (concentrating instead on piety and spiritual devotion) while the latter found God's hand at work in their viewers' economic successes. A similar study by Butsch [1992] found that lower class fathers on TV sitcoms were consistently portrayed as less competent and less responsible than middle-class dads, while a study by Illouz [1991] found that the language of the marketplace has now penetrated even the advice women receive in popular magazines on how to tend a relationship: organize it, strategize it, measure it, in short, manage it.

Capitalistic ideology has been found to penetrate national writing tests used in the nation's schools [Marvin, 1988], pamphlets supplied by health agencies concerned with reproductive options [Condit, 1994], and even college history books [Nerone, 1989]. Indeed, the economic benefits of a good education are even reinforced on TV quiz shows, which "demonstrate symbolically that the rewards a society offers really *are* available for all, that the free-enterprise, equal-opportunity systems *works*. All you need is a bit more luck than the next bloke and the bedroom suite falls into your lap" [Fiske, 1983:143].

A central theme in Marxist criticism is that ideology operates most powerfully when audiences are relaxed. Schwartzman's [1987] study of the industrial propaganda in Walt Disney's EPCOT Center illustrates. He found that the various pavilions in Orlando depicted an unusual amount of harmony on the world scene, which he read as a powerful endorsement of current U.S. foreign policy by the highly self-involved (and internationally minded) corporate sponsors. Television dramas also nurture Established worldviews, says Selnow [1986], who found that the problem-solving model dramatized in prime-time shows (like *Coach,* for example) reinforced the same work ethic emphasized in U.S. politics as well as in schools and churches.

Not all popular rhetoric parrots Establishment values. Counter cultural texts also invade the private space of the average citizen. Jameson's [1981] analysis of *Lord Jim,* for example, shows how graphically Joseph Conrad depicted the brutal working conditions of nineteenth century seamen, which Jameson interprets as Conrad's critique of the political ethos of his age. In a similar vein, Eagleton's [1975:161] survey of writers from George Eliot to D. H. Lawrence found them questioning the favored, but misguided, "organic" model of society in which all citizens work cooperatively for the common good.

Marxist criticism is not for everyone. Its detractors are many. Some object to its circularity: Exploitation is posited; the marks of exploitation are sought in a text; the text is then used to prove the exploitation. The Marxist approach "assumes what it cannot demonstrate," argue some [Real, 1984:76]. It turns "the text's force against itself," argue others [Felperin, 1985:32–3], by "roughing it up, so to speak, until it says what is ideologically required by the interpreter's community." Because many Marxist critics approach texts more probatively than playfully, they often become heavy-handed, seizing on a minor rhetorical feature cordial to their case and missing a more important one. Their "sneering self-confidence," says Felperin [1985:61], often makes them too short-sighted.

While some accuse Marxists of applying their model too forcefully, others question the model itself. Deconstructionists, for example, reject the notion of base/superstructure relationships. Economic forces, historical events, and political entanglements come to people *through texts,* they say, so the "the firm and privileged ground of marxist history as the basis for a scientific study of literature turns out to be not only firm or privileged, but not even a ground at all; it is more like an abyss" [Felperin, 1985:68]. Others question the Marxist vision of the audience. That is, at times Marxists see the public as dull-witted oafs who must be awakened to the exploitations they cannot see. At other times, they seize upon the subtlest rhetorical themes and imply that these same oafs would also notice, and be affected by, such manipulations. Thus, until we know more about what audiences actually "do" with the messages directed at them, we should scrutinize carefully what Marxist critics have to say.

But there is much to be learned from them as well. Critics are always at their best, after all, when challenged. And with Marxists about, there will be no shortage of challenges. Their critique of traditional criticism is not mild: They say that it is too orthodox in its critical assumptions, too establishmen-tarian in its choice of texts, too naive in its understanding of rhetorical effects, and too scientistic in its methodologies. They argue that traditional criticism is too intellectually smug, too politically bourgeois, and too Western in outlook as well. These rebukes call into question the *assumptions* critics make about rhetoric, about criticism, and about life itself. No self-respecting critic could resist such an important call for introspection.

CONCLUSION

It is hard to project the future of Continental criticism in the United States. Because aspects of it are so angry, so irreverent, and so cynical, it threatens the optimistic, liberal credo of the American establishment. For all these reasons, such criticism may always be a minority practice. But this may not be entirely unfortunate. After all, because of its passion, a minority discourse always has a special claim on our attention. It asks constantly if we know what we are doing and, if we know, how we know. It requires us to examine where we go for our premises and why we go there and not elsewhere. It asks if our critical practices are of benefit to anyone in particular and, if not, why not.

Continental critics sense a certain, systematic unfairness in the world. And they see rhetoric as a tool for turning such unfairness into social routines and thenceforth into public policy. Thus, they offer a critique. In doing so, they operate as critics always have, which should remind us that criticism itself is a minority business. There are powerful people in the world. There always have been. They use rhetoric to maintain their power. They always will. Somebody, therefore, must call attention to how they do what they do and ask if it is right that they do so. This challenge is challenge enough for legions of rhetorical critics since the odds so heavily favor the producers of rhetoric and, hence, the producers of power. So for reasons both conceptual and practical, we must welcome the Continentals.

REFERENCES

POPULAR REFERENCES

Ackerman, G. "Remarks on the Anniversary of the First Condominium Conversion," Reprinted from the *Congressional Record* by *Harpers,* October, 1986, 16.

"Are They Harmless Observances?" *Awake,* February 8, 1974, 27–8.

Boone, P., et al. *The Solution to Crisis—America* (Van Nuys, CA: Bible Voice, Inc., 1970).

Bush, G. "Remarks During the Second Presidential Debate," *Washington Post,* October 16, 1992, pp. A35–6.

Chamberlain, V. *Teen Guide,* 5th ed. (New York: McGraw-Hill, 1982).

Dallek, R. Quoted in P. Applebome, "Sense of Pride Outweighs Fears of War," *New York Times,* February 24, 1991, p. 1–3.

Eisenhower, D. "Commencement Address at the University of Notre Dame," June 5, 1960, *Public Papers of the Presidents, 1960–1,* 461–8.

Eisenhower, D. "Remarks to the Easter Egg Rollers on the White House Lawn," April 7, 1958, *Public Papers of the Presidents, 1958,* 65.

Eisenhower, D. "Text of General Eisenhower's Reply," August 14, 1952, *Public Papers of the Presidents, 1952,* 517–8.

Fairlie, H. "TV's Conventions wil be a Lie," *Washington Post,* July 13, 1980, p. E1.

Ford, G. "Remarks to American Society of Newspaper Editors," April 16, 1975, *Weekly Compilations of Presidential Documents,* 11:16 (1975), 388–93.

Ford, G. "Remarks at the Centennial Safe Opening at the Capitol," July 1, 1976a, *Public Papers of the Presidents, 1976:2,* 1941–3.

Ford, G. "Remarks at the Waco Suspension Bridge in Waco, Texas," April 29, 1976b, *Public Papers of the Presidents, 1976:2,* 1335–6.

"Fox and Jacobs Fetes Grand Opening in Ember Oaks," *Dallas Times Herald,* August 21, 1988, J5.

Gallagher, W. N. "Throw this Away" (Publicly Circulated Letter, August, 1984)

Gould, F. *Funeral Services Without Theology* (Girard, KS: Haldeman-Julius Publ., n.d.).

Hand, W. B. *Douglas T. Smith, et al. vs. Board of School Commissioners of Mobile County, et al. and George G. Wallace, Governor of Alabama, et. al., U.S. District Court, Southern District, Alabama* (Civil Action No. 82–0544-BH, 82–0792-BH, 1987).

Hill, H. "Prelude to Seventy Six Trombones," *The Music Man* by M. Willson (New York: G. P. Putnams, 1986).

Hitler, A. "Speech at Siemensstadt, Berlin," November 10, 1933. Fugitive translation. Partially translated in A. Hitler, *My New Order,* R. DeSales (Ed.) (New York: Reynal and Hitchcock, 1941) as well as in N. Baynes (Ed.), *The Speeches of Adolf Hitler, April 1922—August, 1939* (London: Oxford University Press, 1942) and F. Prange (Ed.), *Hitler's Words (Washington: American Council on Public Affairs, 1944).*

Johnson, L. "Medicare Program," June 15, 1966a, *Weekly Compilations of Presidential Documents,* 2:24 (1966a), 774–80.

Johnson, L. "Remarks at a Party Rally in Chicago," May 17, 1966b, *Weekly Compilations of Presidential Documents,* 2:20 (1966b), 657–60.

Johnson, J. H. *Religion is a Gigantic Fraud* (No publisher cited, n.d.).

Kelly, J., and E. Eubanks. *Today's Teen* (Peoria, IL: Charles Bennett Co., 1981).

Kennedy, J. "A Moral Imperative," June 11, 1963, *Vital Speeches of the Day,* 29:18 (1963), 546–7.

Kennedy, J. "Remarks to the Greater Houston Ministerial Association," September 12, 1960," in T. H. White, *The Making of the President, 1960* (New York: Atheneum, 1961a), 427–30.

Kennedy, J. "Remarks at a Meeting of the Democratic National Committee," January 21, 1961b, *Public Papers of the Presidents, 1961,* 4–5.

King, L. The Father of 'Talk Show Democracy': On the Line with Larry King, *Media Studies Journal,* 8 (1994), 123–37.

King, M. L. "I Have a Dream," in R. Hill (Ed.), *The Rhetoric of Racial Revolt* (Denver: Golden Bell Press, 1964), 371–5.

"Legend Oaks: Live a Legendary Lifestyle," *Austin American-Statesman,* August 21, 1988, F12.

Macdonald, C. "Two Brothers in a Field of Absence," in *Alternate Means of Transport: Poems* (New York: Knopf, 1985), 75–6.

Manson, C. "Interview," *Harpers,* September, 1985, 28–9. (Originally published as "Manson at 50" in *California,* May, 1985).

McDonald's Corporation. "More about What We're All About and McDonald's Good Food." (Nationally circulated advertisement, 1987).

McGinley, H. *Caring, Deciding, and Growing* (Lexington, MA: Ginn and Co., 1983).

Newsweek. Assorted commentaries on the Persian Gulf War appearing in the following issues: 9/17/90; 9/24/90; 10/29/90; 12/17/90; 1/21/91; 2/18/91; 2/25/91.

Nixon, R. "The Expense Fund Speech," *U.S. News and World Report* (October 3, 1952), 66–70.

Nixon, R. "Letter to Pat Boone," Reprinted in P. Boone, et al., *The Solution to Crisis—America* (Van Nuys, CA: Bible Voice, Inc., 1970b), 18.

Nixon, R. "The President's News Conference of August 22, 1973a," *Public Papers of the Presidents, 1973,* 710—25.

Nixon, R. "Remarks on Departure from the White House," August 9, 1974b, *Public Papers of the Presidents, 1974,* 630–3.

Nixon, R. "Second Inaugural Address," January 20, 1973b, *Public Papers of the Presidents, 1973,* 12–5.

Orwell, G. *Animal Farm* (New York: Harcourt, Brace, and Company, 1946, 1974).

Patton, G. "Speech to the Troops in July, 1944," in W. B. Mellor, *Patton: Fighting Man* (New York: Putnam, 1946).

Peale, N. V. *Help Yourself with God's Help* (Pawling, New York: Foundation for Christian Living, 1976).

Pershing, J. "My Fellow Soldiers," February 28, 1919, General Orders No. 38A, G. H. Q. American Expeditionary Forces.

"Prayer at the Funeral Service," *Book of Common Prayer: According to the Uses of the Episcopal Church* (New York: Church Hymnal Corp., (1789), 1979), 482–5.

Prinz, J. "Speech at the March on Washington," August 28, 1963, Original recording.

"Quick Reference to Parking and Traffic Regulations," University of Texas at Austin, 1986.

Reagan, R. "Address to the Nation on the Iran Arms Controversy," *New York Times,* March 5, 1987, 12.

Reagan, R. "First Inaugural Address," January 20, 1981, in W. Linkugel et al. (Eds.), *Contemporary American Speeches* (Dubuque: Kendall/Hunt Publishers, 1982), 375–80.

Reagan, R. "Presidential Debate of October 21, 1984," *Weekly Compilations of Presidential Documents,* 20:43 (1984), 1591–610.

Reagan, R. "Salute to a Stronger America," November 13, 1981, *Weekly Compilations of Presidential Documents,* 17:47 (1981), 1257–61.

Sandler, R. "Blowing Smoke," *Harpers,* August, 1987, 15–6. Reprinted from *Philip Morris Magazine,* Spring, 1987.

Shelton, R. *Ideals of a Klansman* (Denham Springs, LA: Invisible Empire Knights of the Ku Klux Klan, n.d.).

Sinclair, G. *Americans,* Westbound Records, Detroit, Michigan, 1973.

Smith, B. "The Holocaust Controversy: The Case For Open Debate," a tract submitted for publication in campus newspapers, 1990–1993.

Truman, H. "Democratic Aims and Achievements," May 15, 1950, *Vital Speeches of the Day,* 16:16 (1950), 496–8.

Truman, H. "Message to Dwight Eisenhower Inviting Him to a Luncheon and Briefing at the White House," August 14, 1952, *Public Papers of the Presidents, 1952,* 517.

U.S. Army, "Eleven Point Checklist for Job Hunters," Flyer circulated nationally in April, 1972.

Vail Resort Association. "Ski, Mix, Meet," (Nationally circulated advertisement, n.d.).

von Hoffman, N. "Andy Jackson's Boy," *Washington Post,* January 24, 1973, B1.

Webelos Scout Book (Boy Scouts of America, 1979).

"Weston Lakes Has Superlative Golf, Swimming, Tennis, Croquet," *Houston Post* (Homefinder), August 21, 1988, 5.

Wiesel, E. "Plea to Reagan," *New York Times,* April 20, 1985, 22.

"Wimbledon Country," *Houston Post (Homefinder),* August 21, 1988, 3.

"Would One Thousand Young American Women rather Increase the Size of their Income, Political Power, or Breasts?," *Esquire,* February, 1994, pp. 65–7.

SCHOLARLY REFERENCES

Abraham, L., et al., "The Effects of MTV-Style Editing on Viewers' Comprehension of a PSA," Paper presented at the 9th annual Visual Communication Conference, June, 1995.

Adams, W. C. "Whose Lives Count?: TV Coverage of Natural Disasters," *Journal of Communication,* 36:2 (1986), 113–22.

Aden, R. "Nostalgic Communication as Temporal Escape: 'When it Was a Game's' Re-Construction of a Baseball/Work Community," *Western Journal of Communication,* 59 (1995), 20–38.

Appel, E. "The Perfected Drama of Reverend Jerry Falwell," *Communication Quarterly,* 35 (1987), 26–38.

Arendt, H. *Eichmann in Jerusalem: A Report on the Banality of Evil* (New York: Viking, 1963).

Armstrong, G. B., et al. "TV Entertainment, News, and Racial Perceptions of College Students," *Journal of Communication,* 42 (1992), 153–76.

Arnold, C. *Criticism of Oral Rhetoric* (Columbus: Merrill, 1974).

Arnold, C. "*Inventio* and *Pronuntiatio* in a 'New Rhetoric,' " Paper presented at the annual convention of the Central States Speech Association, April, 1972.

Arnold, C. "Oral Rhetoric, Rhetoric, and Literature," *Philosophy and Rhetoric,* 1 (1968), 191–210.

Arnold, C. "Reflections on American Public Discourse," *Central States Speech Journal,* 28 (1977), 73–85.

Asante, M. and D. Atwater, "The Rhetorical Condition as Symbolic Structure in Discourse," *Communication Quarterly,* 34 (1986), 170–7.

Aune, J. "Beyond Deconstruction: The Symbol and Social Reality," *Southern Speech Communication Journal,* 48 (1983), 255–68.

Austin, J. L. *How to Do Things with Words* (New York: Oxford University Press, 1970).

Bailey, R. "Authorship Attribution in a Forensic Setting," in D. Ager et al. (Eds.), *Advances in Computer-Aided Literary and Linguistic Research* (Birmingham: University of Aston, 1979), 1–20.

Barbatsis, G., et al. "A Struggle for Dominance: Relational Communication Patterns in Television Drama," *Communication Quarterly,* 31 (1983), 148–155.

Barney, R. "Uncanny Criticism in the United States," in J. Natoli (Ed.), *Tracing Literary Theory* (Urbana: University of Illinois Press, 1987), 177–212.

Barreca, R. *They Used to Call Me Snow White . . . But I Drifted: Women's Strategic Use of Humor* (New York: Penguin, 1991).

Barthes, R. *The Responsibility of Forms: Critical Essays on Music, Art, and Representation* (New York: Hill and Wang, 1985).

Barthes, R. "Theory of the Text," in R. Young (Ed.), *Untying the Text: A Post-Structuralist Reader* (London: Routledge and Kegan Paul, 1981), 31–47.

Beasley, V. B. "The Logic of Power in the Hill-Thomas Hearings: A Rhetorical Analysis," *Political Communication,* 11 (1994), 287–97.

Belsey, C. *Critical Practice* (London: Methuen, 1980).

Benjamin, J. "Performatives as a Rhetorical Construct," *Philosophy and Rhetoric,* 9 (1976), 84–95.

Benjamin, W. "The Work of Art in the Age of Mechanical Reproduction," in H. Arendt (ed.), *Illuminations* (New York: Schocken Books, 1969), pp. 217–51.

Bennett, T. *Formalism and Marxism* (London: Methuen, 1979a).

Bennett, W. L. "Rhetorical Transformation of Evidence in Criminal Trials: Creating Grounds for Legal Judgment," *Quarterly Journal of Speech,* 65 (1979b), 311–23.

Benson, T. "Poisoned Minds," *Southern Speech Communication Journal,* 34 (1968), 54–60.

Bettinghaus, E. and M. Cody. *Persuasive Communication* (Fort Worth: Harcourt Brace, 1994).

Berthold, C. "Kenneth Burke's Cluster-Agon Method: Its Development and Application," *Central States Speech Journal,* 27 (1976), 302–9.

Bitzer, L. "The Rhetorical Situation," *Philosophy and Rhetoric,* 1 (1968), 1–14.

Black, E. *Rhetorical Criticism: A Study in Method* (Madison: University of Wisconsin Press, (1965), 1978).

Black, E. *Rhetorical Questions: Studies of Public Discourse* (Chicago: University of Chicago Press, 1992).

Black, E. "The Second Persona," *Quarterly Journal of Speech,* 56 (1970), 109–19.

Black, E. "The Sentimental Style as Escapism, or the Devil with Dan'l. Webster," in K. Campbell and K. Jamieson (Eds.), *Form and Genre: Shaping Rhetorical Action* (Falls Church, Va.: Speech Communication Association, 1978), 75–86.

Blair, C., et al. "Public Memorializing in Postmodernity: The Vietnam Veterans Memorial as Prototype," *Quarterly Journal of Speech,* 77 (1991), 263–88.

Blankenship, J. *A Sense of Style: An Introduction to Style for the Public Speaker* (Belmont, CA: Wadsworth, 1968).

Bloch, M. (Ed.), *Political Language and Oratory in Traditional Society* (London: Academic Press, 1975).

Bordo, S. *Unbearable Weight: Feminism, Western Culture, and the Body* (Berkeley: University of California Press, 1993).

Bormann, E., J. Cragan, and D. Shields. "In Defense of Symbolic Convergence Theory: A Look at the Theory and its Criticisms after Two Decades," *Communication Theory,* 4 (1994), 259–94.

Bosmajian, H. "The Sources and Nature of Adolph Hitler's Techniques of Persuasion," *Central States Speech Journal,* 25 (1974), 240–8.

Bostdorff, D. "Making Light of James Watt: A Burkean Approach to the Form and Attitude of Political Cartoons," *Quarterly Journal of Speech,* 73 (1987), 43–59.

Branham, R. and W. B. Pearce. "Between Text and Context: Toward a Rhetoric of Textual Reconstruction," *Quarterly Journal of Speech,* 71 (1985), 19–36.

Brinton, C. *The Anatomy of Revolution* (New York: Vintage, 1938).

Brock, B. "Epistemology and Ontology in Kenneth Burke's Dramatism," *Communication Quarterly,* 33 (1985), 94–104.

Brockriede, W. "Rhetorical Criticism as Argument," *Quarterly Journal of Speech,* 60 (1974), 165–74.

Brummett, B. "Burkean Comedy and Tragedy, Illustrated in Reactions to the Arrest of John DeLorean," *Central States Speech Journal,* 35 (1984), 217–27.

Brummett, B. "Perfection and the Bomb: Nuclear Weapons, Teleology, and Motives," *Journal of Communication,* 39 (1989), 85–94.

Brummett, B., and M. Duncan. "Toward a Discursive Ontology of Media," *Critical Studies in Mass Communication,* 9 (1992), 229–49.

Bryant, D. "Rhetoric: Its Functions and Its Scope," in D. Ehninger (Ed.), *Contemporary Rhetoric: A Coursebook* (Glenview: Scott, Foresman (1953), 1972), 15–38.

Brydon, S. "The Two Faces of Jimmy Carter: The Transformation of a Presidential Debater, 1976 and 1980," *Central States Speech Journal,* 36 (1985), 138–51.

Burgin, V. "Seeing Sense," in H. Davis and P. Walton (Eds.), *Language, Image and Media* (New York: St. Martins, 1983), pp. 226–44.

Burke, K. "Antony in Behalf of the Play," in S. E. Hyman (Ed.). *Perspectives by Incongruity* (Bloomington: Indiana University Press, 1964), 64–75.

Burke, K. *Counter-Statement* (Berkeley: University of California Press (1931), 1968).

Burke, K. *A Grammar of Motives* (Cleveland: World Publishing Co., 1962).

Burke, K. *Language as Symbolic Action: Essays on Life, Literature and Method* (Berkeley: University of California Press, 1966).

Burke, K. *Permanence and Change* (Berkeley: University of California Press (1935), 1984).

Burke, K. *Philosophy of Literary Form* (Berkeley: University of California Press, 1973).

Butsch, R. "Class and Gender in Four Decades of Television Situation Comedy: *Plus ça Change* . . . ," *Critical Studies in Mass Communication,* 9 (1992), 387–99.

Butler, J. "Performative Acts and Gender Constitution: An Essay in Phenomenology and Feminist Theory," In S. E. Case (Ed.), *Performing Feminisms: Feminist Critical Theory and Theatre* (Baltimore: Johns Hopkins University Press, 1990), pp. 270–83.

Cain, W. E. *The Crisis in Criticism: Theory, Literature and Reform* (Baltimore: Johns Hopkins University Press, 1984).

Campbell, K. "Critique of Spiro T. Agnew: An Exercise in Manichean Rhetoric," in K. Campbell (Ed.), *Critiques of Contemporary Rhetoric* (Belmont, CA: Wadsworth, 1972), 94–110.

Campbell, K. "Femininity and Feminism: To be or Not to be a Woman," *Communication Quarterly*, 31 (1983), 101–9.

Campbell, K. K. *Man Cannot Speak for Her: A Critical Study of Early Feminist Rhetoric*, Vol. I. (New York: Greenwood Press, 1989).

Carbone, T. "Stylistic Variables as Related to Source Credibility: A Content Analysis Approach," *Communication Monographs*, 42 (1975), 99–106.

Carlson, A. C. "Defining Womanhood: Lucretia Coffin Mott and the Transformation of Femininity," *Western Journal of Communication*, 58 (1994), 85–97.

Carlson, A. C. "Gandhi and the Comic Frame: 'Ad Bellum Purificandum,' " *Quarterly Journal of Speech*, 72 (1986), 446–55.

Carlson, A. C. "The Role of Character in Public Moral Argument: Henry Ward Beecher and the Brooklyn Scandal," *Quarterly Journal of Speech*, 77 (1991), 38–52.

Carlson, A. C. and J. Hocking, "Strategies of Redemption at the Vietnam Veterans' Memorial," *Western Journal of Speech Communication*, 52 (1988), 203–15.

Carpignano, P., et al., "Chatter in the Age of Electronic Reproduction: Talk, Television, and the 'Public Mind,' " *Social Text*, 25–26 (1990), 93–120.

Chapman, S., and G. Eggar, "Myth in Advertising and Health Promotion," in H. Davies and P. Walton (Eds.), *Language, Image Media* (London: Blackwell, 1983), pp. 166–86.

Cherwitz, R., and T. Darwin. "Toward a Relational Theory of Meaning," *Philosophy and Rhetoric*, 28 (1995), 17–29.

Cherwitz, R. and K. Zagacki, "Consummatory Versus Justificatory Crisis Rhetoric," *Western Journal of Speech Communication*, 50 (1986), 307–24.

Chesebro, J. "Extending the Burkean System: A Response to Tompkins and Cheney," *Quarterly Journal of Speech*, 80 (1994), 83–90.

Clark, T. "An Exploration of Generic Aspects of Contemporary American Christian Sermons," *Quarterly Journal of Speech*, 63 (1977), 384–94.

Cloud, D. "The Limits of Interpretation: Ambivalence and the Stereotype in 'Spenser for Hire.' " *Critical Studies in Mass Communication*, 9 (1992), 311–24.

Condit, C. "Hegemony in a Mass-mediated Society: Concordance about Reproductive Technologies," *Critical Studies in Mass Communication,* 11 (1994), 205–30.

Condit, C. and J. Lucaites. *Crafting Equality: America's Anglo-African Word* (Chicago: University of Chicago Press, 1993).

Cooper, M. "Rhetorical Criticism and Foucault's Philosophy of Discursive Events," *Central States Speech Journal,* 39 (1988), 1–17.

Corcoran, F. "KAL 007 and the Evil Empire: Mediated Disaster and Forms of Rationalization," *Critical Studies in Mass Communication,* 3 (1986), 297–316.

Crable, R. "Ike: Identification, Argument, and Paradoxical Appeal," *Quarterly Journal of Speech,* 63 (1977), 188–95.

Crane, J. "Terror and Everyday Life," *Communication,* 10 (1988), 367–82.

Culler, J. *On Deconstruction: Theory and Criticism after Structuralism* (Ithaca: Cornell University Press, 1982).

Darsey, J. "From 'Gay is Good' to the Scourge of AIDS: The Evolution of Gay Liberation Rhetoric, 1977–1990," *Communication Studies,* 42 (1991), 43–66.

Darsey, J. "Joe McCarthy's Fantastic Moment," *Communication Monographs,* 62 (1995), 65–86.

Daughton, S. "Lyndon Baines Johnson's Use of Metaphor and Speech Styles: 1939–1969," Paper Presented at the Annual Convention of the Southern Speech Communication Association, April, 1988.

Daughton, S. "Metaphoric Transcendence: Images of the Holy War in Franklin Roosevelt's First Inaugural," *Quarterly Journal of Speech,* 79 (1993), 427–46.

Davies, H., and P. Walton, "Death of a Premier: Consensus and Closure in International News," in H. Davies and P. Walton (Eds.), *Language, Image Media* (London: Blackwell, 1983), pp. 8–49.

Doane, M. A. "The Woman's Film: Possession and Address," In M. A. Doane, P. Mellencamp, and L. Williams (Eds.), *Re-vision: Essays in Feminist Film Criticism* (Los Angeles: University Publications of America, 1984), pp. 67–83.

Donovan, J. "The Silence is Broken," in S. McConnell-Ginet et al. (Eds.), *Women and Language in Literature and Society* (New York: Praeger, 1980).

Donsbach, W., et al., "Second-Hand Reality: A Field Experiment on the Perception of a Campaign Event by Participants and Television Viewers," Paper delivered at the annual convention of the International Communication Association, May, 1992.

Douglass, R. and C. Arnold. "On Analysis of *Logos:* A Methodological Inquiry," *Quarterly Journal of Speech,* 56 (1970), 22–32.

Dow, B. and M. B. Tonn. "Feminine Style and Political Judgement in the Rhetoric of Ann Richards," *Quarterly Journal of Speech,* 79 (1993), 286–302.

Eagleton, T. *Criticism and Ideology: A Study in Marxist Literary Theory* (London: Verso, 1975).

Eagleton, T. *Literary Theory: An Introduction* (Minneapolis: University of Minnesota Press, 1983).

Eagleton, T. *Marxism and Literary Criticism* (Berkeley: University of California Press, 1976).

Edelman, M. *Political Language: Words that Succeed and Policies that Fail* (New York: Academic Press, 1977).

Edelman, M. *Politics as Symbolic Action: Mass Arousal and Quiescence* (Chicago: Markham, 1971).

Edelman, M. *The Symbolic Uses of Politics* (Urbana: University of Illinois Press, 1964).

Ehninger, D. and W. Brockriede, *Decision by Debate* (New York: Dodd, Mead, 1963).

Einhorn, L. "Basic Assumptions in the Virginia Ratification Debate: Patrick Henry vs. James Madison on the Nature of Man and Reason," *Southern Speech Communication Journal,* 46 (1981), 327–40.

Elpenor (A pseudonym). "A Drunkard's Progress: AA and The Sobering Strength of Myth," *Harpers,* October, 1986, 42–8.

Enkvist, N. "On the Place of Style in Some Linguistic Theories," in S. Chatman (Ed.), *Literary Style: A Symposium* (London: Oxford, 1971), 47–64.

Entman, R. "Framing U.S. Coverage of International News: Contrasts in Narratives of the KAL and Iran Air Incidents," *Journal of Communication, 41* (1991), 6–27.

Erickson, K., and C. Fleuriet. "Presidential Anonymity: Rhetorical Identity Management and the Mystification of Political Reality," *Communication Quarterly,* 39 (1991), 272–289.

Farrell, T. "Critical Modes in the Analysis of Discourse," *Western Journal of Speech Communication,* 44 (1980), 300–14.

Felperin, H. *Beyond Deconstruction: The Uses and Abuses of Literary Theory* (Oxford: Clarendon, 1985).

Fetterley, J. *The Resisting Reader* (Bloomington: Indiana University Press, 1978).

Fetterly, J. "Introduction: On the Politics of Literature," In R. R. Warhol and D. P. Herndl (Eds.), *Feminisms: An Anthology of Literary Theory and Criticism* (New Brunswick: Rutgers University Press, 1991), pp. 492–502.

Finkelstein, L. "The Calendrical Rite of the Ascension to Power," *Western Journal of Speech Communication,* 45 (1981), 51–9.

Fisher, W. "Clarifying the Narrative Paradigm," *Communication Monographs,* 56 (1989), 55–8.

Fisher, W. *Human Communication as Narration: Toward a Philosophy of Reason, Value and Action* (Columbia: University of South Carolina Press, 1987).

Fisher, W. "Romantic Democracy, Ronald Reagan, and Presidential Heroes," *Western Journal of Speech Communication*, 46 (1982), 299–310.

Fiske, J. "The Discourses of TV Quiz Shows or, School + Luck = Success + Sex," *Central States Speech Journal*, 34 (1983), 139–50.

Foss, S. "Ambiguity as Persuasion: The Vietnam Veterans Memorial," *Communication Quarterly*, 34 (1986), 326–40.

Foss, S. and K. Foss. "The Construction of Feminine Spectatorship in Garrison Keillor's Radio Monologues," *Quarterly Journal of Speech*, 80 (1994), 410–426.

Foss, S. K. and C. Griffin, "A Feminist Perspective on Rhetorical Theory: Toward a Clarification of Boundaries," *Western Journal of Communication*, 56 (1992), 330–49.

Foucault, M. "The Order of Discourse," in R. Young (Ed.), *Untying the Text: A Post-Structuralist Reader* (London: Routledge and Kegan Paul, 1981), 48–78.

Fox-Genovese, E. *Feminism Without Illusions: A Critique of Individualism* (Chapel Hill: University of North Carolina Press, 1991).

Fraser, N. "Sex, Lies, and the Public Sphere: Some Reflections on the Confirmation of Clarence Thomas," *Critical Inquiry*, 18 (1992), 595–613.

Friend, T. "Goddess, Riot Girl, Philosopher-Queen, Lipstick Lesbian, Warrior, Tattooed Love Child, Sack Artist, Leader of Men: Lock up your Sons—the 21st-century Woman is in the Building," *Esquire*, February, 1994, pp. 47–56.

Frank, J. "Symbols and Civilization," in W. Rueckert (Ed.), *Critical Responses to Kenneth Burke* (Minneapolis: University of Minnesota Press, 1969), 401–6.

Frentz, T., and T. Farrell, "Conversion of America's Consciousness: The Rhetoric of *The Exorcist*," *Quarterly Journal of Speech*, 61 (1975), 40–7.

Gaines, R. "Doing by Saying: Toward a Theory of Perlocution," *Quarterly Journal of Speech*, 65 (1979), 207–17.

Gallagher, V. "Remembering Together: Rhetorical Integration and the Case of the Martin Luther King, Jr. Memorial," *Southern Communication Journal*, 60 (1995), 109–19.

Gastil, J. "Undemocratic Discourse: A Review of Theory and Research on Political Discourse," *Discourse and Society*, 3 (1992), 469–500.

Geis, M. *The Language of Television Advertising* (New York: Academic Press, 1982).

Genovese, E. *Roll Jordan Roll* (New York: Vintage, 1976).

Gerland, O. "Brecht and the Courtroom: Alienating Evidence in the 'Rodney King' Trials," *Text and Performance Quarterly*, 14 (1994), 305–18.

Gibson, W. *Tough, Sweet and Stuffy: An Essay on Modern Prose Styles* (Bloomington: Indiana University Press, 1966).

Gilberg, S., et al., "The State of the Union Address and the Press Agenda," *Journalism Quarterly,* 57 (1980), 584–8.

Gilbert, J. "Performing Marginality: Humor, Gender and Social Control," Unpublished Doctoral Dissertation, University of Texas at Austin, 1994.

Gitlin, T. "Car Commercials and *Miami Vice:* 'We Build Excitement,' " in T. Gitlin (Ed.), *Watching Television* (New York: Pantheon, 1987), pp. 136–61.

Gitlin, T. *The Whole World is Watching: Mass Media in the Making and Unmaking of the New Left* (Berkeley: University of California Press, 1980).

Goldman, R., et al. "Commodity Feminism," *Critical Studies in Mass Communication,* 8 (1991), 333–51.

Goodall, H. L. "Living in the Rock'n Roll Campaign: Or Mystery, Media, and the American Public Imagination," in S. Smith (Ed.), *Bill Clinton on Stump, State and Stage: The Rhetorical Road to the White House* (Fayetteville: University of Arkansas Press, 1994), pp. 365–416.

Greenberg, B., and C. Atkin, "The Portrayal of Driving on Television, 1975–1980," *Journal of Communication,* 33:2 (1983), 44–55.

Gregg, R. "The Ego-Function of the Rhetoric of Protest," *Philosophy and Rhetoric,* 4 (1971), 71–91.

Griffin, C. "The Rhetoric of Form in Conversion Narratives," *Quarterly Journal of Speech,* 76 (1990), 152–63.

Griffin, C. "Rhetoricalizing Alienation: Mary Wollstonecraft and the Rhetorical Construction of Women's Oppression," *Quarterly Journal of Speech,* 8 (1994), 293–312.

Griffin, L. "A Dramatistic Theory of the Rhetoric of Movements," in W. Rueckert (Ed.), *Critical Responses to Kenneth Burke* (Minneapolis: University of Minnesota Press, 1969), 456–78.

Griffin, L. "When Dreams Collide: Rhetorical Trajectories in the Assassination of President Kennedy," *Quarterly Journal of Speech,* 70 (1984), 111–131.

Griffin, M. "Looking at TV News: Strategies for Research," *Communication,* 13 (1992), 121–41.

Gronbeck, B. "Rhetorical Timing in Public Communication," *Central States Speech Journal,* 25 (1974), 84–94.

Grossberg, L. "Strategies of Marxist Cultural Interpretation," *Central States Speech Journal,* 1 (1984), 392–421.

Gumpert, G., and R. Cathcart. "Media Grammars, Generations and Media Gaps," *Critical Studies in Mass Communication,* 2 (1985), 23–35.

Gumpert, G., and S. Drucker. "From the Agora to the Electronic Shopping Mall: Shopping as a Form of Interpersonal Communication," *Journal of Communication,* 9 (1992), 186–98.

Gusfield, J. *The Culture of Public Problems: Drinking-Driving and the Symbolic Order* (Chicago: University of Chicago Press, 1981).

Halliday, J., et al., "After the Wall: Myth, Metaphor and Articulation in U.S. Media Representations of Events in Eastern Europe," Department Of Communication Studies, Muhlenberg College, October, 1990.

Harari, J. "Critical Factions/Critical Fictions" in J. Harari (Ed.), *Textual Strategies: Perspectives in Post-Structuralist Criticism* (Ithaca: Cornell University Press, 1979), 17–72.

Harrell, J., et al., "Failure of Apology in American Politics: Nixon on Watergate," *Communication Monographs,* 42 (1975), 245–61.

Hart, R. "Conceptual Dividends in Computerized Language Analysis," Paper presented at the annual convention of the International Communication Association, May, 1995.

Hart, R. "Contemporary Scholarship in Public Address: A Research Editorial," *Western Journal of Speech Communication,* 50 (1986a), 283–95.

Hart, R. "The Functions of Human Communication in the Maintenance of Public Values," in C. Arnold and J. Bowers (Eds.), *Handbook of Rhetorical and Communication Theory* (Boston: Allyn and Bacon, 1984a), 749–91.

Hart, R. "The Language of the Modern Presidency," *Presidential Studies Quarterly,* 14 (1984b), 249–64.

Hart, R. "Of Genre, Computers, and the Reagan Inaugural," in H. Simons and A. Aghazarian (Eds.), *Form, Genre, and the Study of Political Discourse* (Columbia: University of South Carolina Press, 1986b), 278–98.

Hart, R. "On Applying Toulmin: The Analysis of Practical Discourse," in G. P. Mohrmann, et al. (Eds.), *Explorations in Rhetorical Criticism* (University Park: Pennsylvania State University Press, 1973), 75–95.

Hart, R. *Philosophical Commonality and Speech Types,* Unpublished Ph.D. Dissertation, Pennsylvania State University, 1970.

Hart, R. *The Political Pulpit* (W. Lafayette, IN: Purdue University Press, 1977).

Hart, R. "The Rhetoric of the True Believer," *Speech Monographs,* 38 (1971), 249–61.

Hart, R. *Seducing America: How Television Charms the Modern Voter* (New York: Oxford University Press, 1994).

Hart, R. *The Sound of Leadership: Presidential Communication in the Modern Age* (Chicago: University of Chicago Press, 1987).

Hart, R. "Systematic Analysis of Political Discourse: The Development of DICTION," in K. Sanders, et al. (Eds.), *Political Communication Yearbook,* 1984 (Carbondale, IL: Southern Illinois University Press, 1985).

Hart, R. "An Unquiet Desperation: Rhetorical Aspects of Popular Atheism in the United States," *Quarterly Journal of Speech,* 64 (1978), 33–46.

Hart, R. *Verbal Style and the Presidency* (New York: Academic Press, 1984c).

Hart, R., and D. Burks. "Rhetorical Sensitivity and Social Interaction," *Speech Monographs,* 39 (1972), 75–91.

Hart, R., et al. "Evolution of Presidential News Coverage," *Political Communication,* 7 (1990), 213–30.

Hart, R., et al. *Public Communication* (New York: Harper, 1983).

Hart, R., et al., "Rhetorical Features of Newscasts about the President," *Critical Studies in Mass Communication,* 1 (1984d), 260–86.

Hart, R. et al., "Religion and the Rhetoric of the Mass Media," *Review of Religious Research,* 21 (1980), 256–75.

Hayes, J. "Gayspeak," *Quarterly Journal of Speech,* 62 (1976), 255–66.

Heath, R. *Realism and Relativism: A Perspective on Kenneth Burke* (Macon: Mercer University Press, 1986).

Hensley, C. W. "Rhetorical Vision and the Persuasion of a Historical Movement: The Disciples of Christ in Nineteenth Century American Culture," *Quarterly Journal of Speech,* 61 (1975), 250–64.

Hetherington, M. "The Media's Role in Forming Voters' National Economic Evaluations in 1992," *American Journal of Political Science,* 40 (1996).

Hillbruner, A. "Archetype and Signature: Nixon and the 1973 Inaugural," *Central States Speech Journal,* 25 (1974), 169–81.

Hillbruner, A. "Inequality, the Great Chain of Being, and Ante-Bellum Southern Oratory," *Southern Speech Communication Journal,* 25 (1960), 172–89.

Himelstein, J. "Rhetorical Continuities in the Politics of Race: The Closed Society Revisited," *Southern Speech Communication Journal,* 48 (1983), 153–66.

Hirsch, E. D. *Validity in Interpretation* (New Haven: Yale University Press, 1967).

hooks, b. "Writing Autobiography," In R. R. Warhol and D. P. Herndl (Eds.), *Feminisms: An Anthology of Literary Theory and Criticism* (New Brunswick: Rutgers University Press, 1991), pp. 1036–40.

hooks, b. *Feminist Theory: From Margin to Center* (Boston: South End Press, 1984).

Horton, D., and R. Wohl, "Mass Communication and Para-Social Interaction: Observation on Intimacy at a Distance," in G. Gumpert and R. Cathcart (Eds.),

Inter/Media: Interpersonal Communication in a Media World, 3rd ed. (New York: Oxford University Press, 1986), pp. 185–206.

Hubbard, R. C. "Relationship Styles in Popular Romance Novels, 1950 to 1983," *Communication Quarterly,* 33:2 (1985), 113–25.

Hughey, J., et al. "Insidious Metaphors and the Changing Meaning of AIDS," Paper Presented at the Annual Convention of the Speech Communication Association, November, 1987.

Huspek, M. and K. Kendall. "On Withholding Political Voice: An Analysis of the Political Vocabulary of a 'Non-Political' Speech Community," *Quarterly Journal of Speech,* 77 (1991), 1–19.

Hyde, M. "Medicine, Rhetoric and Euthanasia: A Case Study in the Workings of a Postmodern Discourse," *Quarterly Journal of Speech,* 79 (1993), 201–224.

Ilkka, R. "Rhetorical Dramatization in the Development of American Communism," *Quarterly Journal of Speech,* 63 (1977), 413–27.

Illouz, E. "Reason within Passion: Love in Women's Magazines," *Critical Studies in Mass Communication,* 8 (1991), 231–48.

Ivie, R. "Images of Savagery in American Justifications for War," *Communication Monographs,* 47 (1980), 279–94.

Ivie, R. "Presidential Motives for War," *Quarterly Journal of Speech,* 50 (1974), 337–45.

Jablonski, C. *Institutional Rhetoric and Radical Change: The Case of the Contemporary Roman Catholic Church in America, 1947–1977,* Unpublished Ph.D. Dissertation, Purdue University, 1979a.

Jablonski, C. "Promoting Radical Change in the Roman Catholic Church: Rhetorical Requirements, Problems, and Strategies of the American Bishops," *Central States Speech Journal,* 31 (1980), 282–9.

Jablonski, C. "Richard Nixon's Irish Wake: A Case of Generic Transference," *Central States Speech Journal,* 30 (1979b), 164–73.

Jameson, F. *The Political Unconscious: Narrative as a Socially Symbolic Act* (Ithaca: Cornell University Press, 1981).

Jamieson, K. "Antecedent Genre as Rhetorical Constraint," *Quarterly Journal of Speech,* 61 (1975a), 406–15.

Jamieson, K. *Eloquence in an Electronic Age* (New York: Oxford University Press, 1988a).

Jamieson, K. "Generic Constraints and the Rhetorical Situation," *Philosophy and Rhetoric,* 6 (1973), 162–70.

Jamieson, K. "The Metaphoric Cluster in the Rhetoric of Pope Paul VI and Edmund G. Brown, Jr.," *Quarterly Journal of Speech,* 66 (1980), 51–72.

Jamieson, K. *Packaging the Presidency: A History and Criticism of Presidential Campaign Advertising* (New York: Oxford University Press, 1984).

Jamieson, K. "Television, Presidential Campaigns and Debates," in J. Swerdlow (Ed.), *Presidential Debates: 1988 and Beyond* (Washington, DC: Congressional Quarterly Press, 1988b), 27–33.

Jamieson, K., and K. Campbell, "Rhetorical Hybrids: Fusions of Generic Elements," *Quarterly Journal of Speech,* 68 (1982), 146–57.

Jamieson, K., and J. Cappella. *Spirals of Cynicism* (New York: Oxford, 1996)

Japp, P. "Esther or Ishiah? The Abolitionist-Feminist Rhetoric of Angelina Grimkè," *Quarterly Journal of Speech,* 71 (1985), 335–48.

Jasinski, J. "Rhetoric and Judgment in the Constitutional Ratification Debate of 1787–1788: An Exploration of the Relationship Between Theory and Critical Practice," *Quarterly Journal of Speech,* 78 (1992), 197–218.

Jewett, R. *The Captain America Complex: The Dilemma of Zealous Nationalism* (Philadelphia: Westminister Press, 1973).

Johannesen, R. "The Jeremiad and Jenkin Lloyd Jones," *Communication Monographs,* 52 (1985), 156–72.

Johnson, B. "The Critical Difference: Balzac's *Sarrasine* and Barthes's *S/Z,*" in R. Young (Ed.), *Untying the Text: A Post-Structuralist Reader* (London: Routledge and Kegan Paul, 1981), 162–74.

Johnson, B. "Images of the Enemy in Intergroup Conflict," *Central States Speech Journal,* 26 (1975), 84–92.

Johnstone, H. "Truth, Communication, and Rhetoric in Philosophy," *Revue Internationale de Philosophie,* 90:4 (1969).

Jones, A. R. "Writing the Body: Toward an Understanding of *l'Ecriture Feminine,*" In R. R. Warhol and D. P. Herndl (Eds.), *Feminisms: An Anthology of Literary Theory and Criticism* (New Brunswick: Rutgers University Press, 1991), pp. 357–71.

Jorgensen-Earp, C. R. "The Lady, the Whore, and the Spinster: The Rhetorical Use of Victorian Images of Women," *Western Journal of Speech Communication,* 54 (1990), 82–98.

Kaplan, S. "Visual Metaphors in the Representation of Communication Technology," *Critical Studies in Mass Communication,* 7 (1990), 37–47.

Katriel, T. "Sites of Memory: Discourses of the Past in Israeli Pioneering Settlement Museums," *Quarterly Journal of Speech,* 80 (1994), 1–20.

Kaufer, D. "Analyzing Philosophy in Rhetoric: Darrow's Mechanism in the Defense of Leopold and Loeb," *Southern Speech Communication Journal,* 45 (1980), 363–77.

Kaufer, D. "Ironic Evaluations," *Communication Monographs,* 48 (1981), 25–38.

Kerbel, M. "Covering the Coverage: The Self-Referential Nature of Television Reporting of the 1992 Presidential Campaign," A paper presented at the annual meeting of the American Political Science Association, September, 1994.

Kessler, M. "The Role of Surrogate Speakers in the 1980 Presidential Campaign," *Quarterly Journal of Speech,* 67 (1981), 146–56.

Kidd, V. "Happily Ever After and Other Relationship Styles: Advice on Interpersonal Relations in Popular Magazines, 1951–1973," *Quarterly Journal of Speech,* 61 (1975), 31–9.

King, A. *Power and Communication* (Prospect Heights, IL: Waveland, 1987).

King, A. "The Rhetoric of Power Maintenance," *Quarterly Journal of Speech,* 62 (1976), 127–34.

Kirkwood, W. "Storytelling and Self-Confrontation: Parables as Communication Strategies," *Quarterly Journal of Speech,* 69 (1983), 58–74.

Klaus, C. "Reflections on Prose Style," in G. Love and M. Payne (Eds.), *Contemporary Essays on Style* (Glenview, IL: Scott, Foresman, 1969), 52–62.

Knapp, M., et al. "Deception as a Communication Construct," *Human Communication Research,* 1 (1974), 15–29.

Kolata, G. "Communicating Mathematics: Is It Possible?" *Science,* 187 (1975), 732.

Kolodny, A. "Dancing Through the Minefield: Some Observations on the Theory, Practice, and Politics of a Feminist Literary Criticism," In R. R. Warhol and D. P. Herndl (Eds.), *Feminisms: An Anthology of Literary Theory and Criticism,* (New Brunswick: Rutgers University Press, 1991), pp. 97–117

Kristol, I. *On the Democratic Idea in America* (New York: Harper & Row, 1972).

Lacy, M. "Toward a Rhetorical Conception of Civil Racism," unpublished Ph.D. Dissertation, University of Texas at Austin, 1992.

Lake, R. "Enacting Red Power: The Consummatory Function in Native American Protest Rhetoric," *Quarterly Journal of Speech,* 69 (1983), 127–42.

Lakoff, G. and M. Johnson. *Metaphors We Live By* (Chicago: University of Chicago Press, 1980).

Langer, J. "Television's 'Personality System,' " *Media, Culture and Society,* 4 (1981), 351–65.

Lanham, R. *Analyzing Prose* (New York: Scribners, 1983).

Leathers, D. "Belief-Disbelief Systems: The Communicative Vacuum of the Radical Right," in G. Mohrmann, C. Stewart, and D. Ochs (Eds.), *Exploration in Rhetorical Criticism* (University Park: Pennsylvania State University Press, 1973), 124–37.

Leff, M. "Things Made By Words: Reflections on Textual Criticism," *Quarterly Journal of Speech,* 78 (1992), 223–31.

Leiss, W., et al. *Social Communication in Advertising: Advertising, Persons, Products and Images of Well-being* (New York: Routledge, 1990).

Lentricchia, F. *Criticism and Social Change* (Chicago: University of Chicago Press, 1983).

Lessl, T. "Science and the Sacred Cosmos: The Ideological Rhetoric of Carl Sagan," *Quarterly Journal of Speech*, 71 (1985), 175–87.

Lester, P. "African American Photo Coverage in Four U.S. Newspapers, 1937–1990," *Journalism Quarterly*. 71 (1994), 129–36.

Levi-Strauss, C. "The Structural Study of Myth," *Journal of American Folklore*, 68 (1955), 428–44.

Lewis, L. "On the Genesis of Gray-Flanneled Puritans," *A.A.U.P. Bulletin*, Spring, 1972, 21–9.

Lipari, L. "As the Word Turns: Drama, Rhetoric, and Press Coverage of the Hill-Thomas Hearings," *Political Communication*, 11 (1994), 299–308.

Logue, C. and E. Miller. "Rhetorical Status: A Study of its Origins, Functions and Consequences," *Quarterly Journal of Speech*, 81 (1995), 20–47.

Lorde, A. "The Master's Tools will Never Dismantle the Master's House," In C. Moraga and G. Anzaldua (Eds.), *This Bridge Called my Back: Writings by Radical Women of Color* (New York: Kitchen Table, Women of Color Press, 1981), pp. 98–102.

Lowry, D., and D. Towles. "Soap Opera Portrayals of Sex, Contraception, and Sexually Transmitted Diseases," *Journal of Communication*, 39 (1989), 76–83.

Lucas, S. "Genre Criticism and Historical Context: The Case of George Washington's First Inaugural Address," *Southern Speech Communication Journal*, 51 (1986), 354–70.

Lule, J. "The Political Use of Victims: The Shaping of the *Challenger* Disaster," *Political Communication*, 7 (1990), 115–28.

Mackin, J. "Schismogenesis and Community: Pericles Funeral Oration," *Quarterly Journal of Speech*, 77 (1991), 251–62.

Mader, T. "On Presence in Rhetoric," *College Composition and Communication*, 24 (1973), 375–81.

Marchetti, G. "Action-Adventure as Ideology," in I. Angus and S. Jhally (Eds.), *Cultural Politics in Contemporary America* (New York: Routledge, 1989), pp. 182–97.

Maranhão, T. "Psychoanalysis: Science or Rhetoric," in H. Simons (Ed.), *The Rhetorical Turn: Invention and Persuasion in the Conduct of Inquiry* (Chicago: University of Chicago Press, 1990), pp. 116–44.

Marvin, C. "Attributes of Authority: Literacy Tests and the Logic of Strategic Conduct," *Communication*, 11 (1988), 63–82.

Mayne, J. "The Woman at the Keyhole: Women's Cinema and Feminist Film Criticism," In M. A. Doane, P. Mellencamp, and L. Williams (Eds.), *Re-vision: Essays in Feminist Film Criticism* (Los Angeles: University Publications of America, 1984), pp. 49–67.

McCombs, M., and D. Shaw, "The Agenda-Setting Function of the Mass Media," *Public Opinion Quarterly*, 36 (1972), 176–87.

McDonald, L. "Myth, Politics, and Political Science," *Western Political Quarterly*, 22 (1969), 141–50.

McGee, M. "The 'Ideograph': A Link Between Rhetoric and Ideology," *Quarterly Journal of Speech*, 66 (1980), 1–16.

McGee, M. "In Search of 'The People': A Rhetorical Alternative," *Quarterly Journal of Speech*, 61 (1975), 235–49.

McGuire, M. D. "Mythic Rhetoric in *Mein Kampf:* A Structuralist Critique," *Quarterly Journal of Speech*, 63 (1977), 1–13.

McGuire, M. B. "Religious Speaking and Religious Hearing: Rules and Responsibilities," A paper presented at the annual convention of the Society for the Scientific Study of Religion, 1976.

McMillan, J. *The Rhetoric of the Modern Organization*, Unpublished Ph.D. Dissertation, University of Texas at Austin, 1983.

McMullen, W. and M. Solomon. "The Politics of Adaptation: Steven Spielberg's Appropriation of *The Color Purple*," *Text and Performance Quarterly*, 14 (1994), 158–74.

Mechling, E. W., and J. Mechling. "Hot Pacifism and Cold War: The American Friends Service Committee's Witness for Peace in 1950s America," *Quarterly Journal of Speech*, 78 (1992), 173–96.

Medhurst, M. "Resistance, Conservatism, and Theory Building: A Cautionary Note," *Western Journal of Speech Communication*, 49 (1985), 103–15.

Medhurst, M. "The Rhetorical Structure of Oliver Stone's *JFK*," *Critical Studies in Mass Communication*, 10 (1993), 128–43.

Merritt, R. *Symbols of American Community, 1735–1775* (New Haven: Yale University Press, 1966).

Meyer, D. "Framing National Security: Elite Public Discourse on Nuclear Weapons During the Cold War," *Political Communication*, 12 (1995), 173–92.

Meyers, R., et al., "Political Momentum: Television News Treatment," *Communication Monographs*, 45 (1978), 382–8.

Milburn, M., and A. McGrail, "The Dramatic Presentation of News and Its Effects on Cognitive Complexity," *Political Psychology,* 13 (1992), 613–32.

Milic, L. "Rhetorical Choice and Stylistic Option: The Conscious and Unconscious Poles," in S. Chatman (Ed.), *Literary Style: A Symposium* (London: Oxford University Press, 1971), 77–94.

Miller, M. C. "Prime Time: Deride and Conquer," in T. Gitlin (Ed), *Watching Television* (New York: Pantheon, 1987), pp. 183–228.

Minnick, W. *The Art of Persuasion* (Boston: Houghton-Mifflin, 1968).

Moi, T. *Sexual/Textual Politics: Feminist Literary Theory* (London: Methuen, 1985).

Mulvey, L. "Visual Pleasure and Narrative Cinema," In R. R. Warhol and D. P. Herndl (Eds.) *Feminisms: An Anthology of Literary Theory and Criticism* (New Brunswick: Rutgers University Press, 1991), pp. 432–43.

Mumby, D. and C. Spitzack, "Ideology and Television News: A Metaphoric Analysis of Political Stories," *Central States Speech Journal,* 34 (1983), 162–71.

Nerone, J. "Professional History and Social Memory," *Communication,* 11 (1989), 89–104.

Nichols, M. H. "Kenneth Burke and the 'New Rhetoric,' " in W. Rueckert (Ed.), *Critical Responses to Kenneth Burke* (Minneapolis: University of Minnesota Press, 1969), 270–87.

Norris, C. *Deconstruction: Theory and Practice* (London: Methuen, 1982).

Nothstine, W., C. Blair, and G. Copeland. "Professionalization and the Eclipse of Critical Invention," in W. Nothstine, et al. (eds.), *Critical Questions: Invention, Creativity and the Criticism of Discourse and Media* (New York: St. Martins, 1994), 15–70.

Olds, S. *The Dead and the Living* (New York: Alfred A. Knopf, 1983).

O'Leary, S. *Arguing the Apocalypse: A Theory of Millenial Rhetoric* (New York: Oxford University Press, 1994).

Olsen, T. *Silences* (New York: Delacorte Press/Seymour Lawrence, 1978).

Olson, K. "The Function of Form in Newspapers' Political Conflict Coverage: The *New York Times'* Shaping of Expectations in the Bitburg Controversy," *Political Communication,* 12 (1995), 43–64.

Olson, K. and T. Goodnight. "Entanglements of Consumption, Cruelty, Privacy, and Fashion: The Social Controversy over Fur," *Quarterly Journal of Speech,* 80 (1994), 249–76.

Olson, L. "Benjamin Franklin's Pictorial Representations of the British Colonies in America: A Study in Rhetorical Iconography," *Quarterly Journal of Speech,* 73 (1987), 18–42.

Osborn, M. "The Evolution of the Archetypal Sea in Rhetoric and Poetic," *Quarterly Journal of Speech,* 63 (1977), 347–63.

Osborn, M. *Orientations to Rhetorical Style* (Chicago: Science Research Associates, 1976).

Osgood, C. and E. Walker, "Motivation and Language Behavior: A Content Analysis of Suicide Notes," *Journal of Abnormal and Social Psychology,* 59 (1959), 58–67.

Parry-Giles, S. "Rhetorical Experimentation and the Cold War, 1947–1953: The Development of an Internationalist Approach to Propaganda," *Quarterly Journal of Speech,* 80 (1994). 448–67.

Patterson, T. *Out of Order* (New York: Knopf, 1993).

Payne, D. *Coping with Failure: The Therapeutic Uses of Rhetoric* (Columbia: University of South Carolina Press, 1989).

Payne, D. "Political Vertigo in 'Dead Poets Society,' " *Southern Communication Journal,* 58 (1992), 13–21.

Perry, S. "Rhetorical Functions of the Infestation Metaphor in Hitler's Rhetoric," *Central States Speech Journal,* 34 (1983), 229–35.

Philipsen, G. "Speaking 'Like a Man' in Teamsterville: Cultural Patterns of Role Enactment in an Urban Neighborhood," *Quarterly Journal of Speech,* 61 (1975), 13–22.

Phillips, E. B. "Magazine's Heroines: Is *Ms.* Just another Member of the *Family Circle?*" in G. Tuchman, et al. (Eds.), *Hearth and Home: Images of Women in the Mass Media* (New York: Oxford, 1978), 116–29.

Picard, R. "News Coverage as the Contagion of Terrorism: Dangerous Charges Backed by Dubious Science," *Political Communication,* 3 (1986), 385–400.

Pittman, R. "How TV Babies Learn," *New York Times,* September 30, 1990, p. 19.

Pocock, J. *Politics, Language and Time: Essays on Political Thought and History* (New York: Atheneum, 1971).

Powers, S., et al. "Motion Pictures and the Politics of Gender," A paper presented at the annual meeting of the American Political Science Association, September, 1992.

Priest, P., and J. Dominick. "Pulp Pulpits: Self-Disclosure on 'Donahue,' " *Journal of Communication,* 44 (1994), 74–97.

Radway, J. *Reading the Romance: Women, Patriarchy and Popular Literature* (Chapel Hill: University of North Carolina Press, 1984).

Rainville, R. E. and E. McCormick. "Extent of Covert Racial Prejudice in Pro Football Announcers' Speech," *Journalism Quarterly,* 54 (1977), 20–6.

Rasmussen, K., and S. Downey. "Dialectical Disorientation in Vietnam War Films: Subversion of the Mythology of War," *Quarterly Journal of Speech,* 77 (1991), 176–95.

Rawlence, C. "Political Theatre and the Working Class," in C. Gardner (Ed.), *Media, Politics and Culture: A Socialist View* (London: Macmillan, 1979), pp. 61–70.

Real, M. "The Debate on Critical Theory and the Study of Communications," *Journal of Communication,* 34:4 (1984), 72–80.

Regan, A. "Rhetoric and Political Process in the Hill-Thomas Hearings," *Political Communication,* 11 (1994), 277–85.

Rich, A. "When We Dead Awaken: Writing as Re-Vision," *College English,* 33 (1972), 18–30.

Ritter, K. "Drama and Legal Rhetoric: The Perjury Trials of Alger Hiss," *Western Journal of Speech Communication,* 49 (1985), 83–102.

Rosen, R. "Soap Operas: Search for Yesterday," in T. Gitlin (Ed.), *Watching Television* (New York: Pantheon, 1987), pp. 42–67.

Rosenfield, L. "The Anatomy of Critical Discourse," in R. Scott and B. Brock (Eds.), *Methods of Rhetorical Criticism: A Twentieth Century Perspective* (New York: Harper & Row, (1968) 1972), 131–57.

Rosenfield, L. "A Case Study in Speech Criticism: The Nixon-Truman Analog," *Communication Monographs,* 35 (1968), 435–450.

Rosteck, T. "The Intertextuality of 'The Man from Hope," in S. Smith (ed.), *Bill Clinton on Stump, State and Stage: The Rhetorical Road to the White House* (Fayetteville: University of Arkansas Press, 1994), 223–47.

Rueckert, W. *Kenneth Burke and the Drama of Human Relations* (Minneapolis: University of Minnesota Press, 1963).

Rueckert, W. "Some of the Many Kenneth Burkes," in H. White and M. Brose (Eds.), *Representing Kenneth Burke* (Baltimore: Johns Hopkins University Press, 1982), 1–30.

Ruthven, K. K. *Feminist Literary Studies: An Introduction* (Cambridge, England: Cambridge University Press, 1984).

Ryan, M. *Marxism and Deconstruction: A Critical Articulation* (Baltimore: Johns Hopkins University Press, 1982).

Rybacki, K. and D. Rybacki. *Communication Criticism: Approaches and Genres* (Belmont, CA: Wadsworth, 1991).

Sanchez, J. M. "The American Politician on Film: From *Mr. Smith* to *Bob Roberts,*" A paper presented at the annual meeting of the American Political Science Association, September, 1993.

Savage, K. "The Politics of Memory: Black Emancipation and the Civil War Monument," in J. Gillis (Ed.), *Commemorations: The Politics of National Identity* (Princeton: Princeton University Press, 1994), pp. 127–49.

Schmuhl, R. *Statecraft and Stagecraft: American Political Life in the Age of Personality* (Notre Dame: Notre Dame University Press, 1990).

Schwartzman, R. "The Substance of Paradox: Communication of Ideology at EPCOT and the Museum of Science and Industry," Paper Presented at the Annual Meeting of the International Communication Association, May, 1987.

Schweickart, P. "Reading Ourselves: Toward a Feminist Theory of Reading," In R. R. Warhol and D. P. Herndl (Eds.), *Feminisms: An Anthology of Literary Theory and Criticism* (New Brunswick: Rutgers University Press, 1991), pp. 525–51.

Scott, R. "Argument as a Critical Art: Re-Forming Understanding," *Argumentation*, 1 (1987), 57–71.

Sedelow, S. and W. Sedelow, "A Preface to Computational Stylistics," in J. Leed (Ed.), *The Computer and Literary Style* (Kent, OH: Kent State University Press, 1966), 1–13.

Selnow, G. "Solving Problems in Prime-Time Television," *Journal of Communication*, 36:2 (1986), 63–72.

Showalter, E. "Toward a Feminist Politics," in E. Showalter (Ed.), *The New Feminist Criticism: Essays on Women, Literature and Theory* (New York: Pantheon, 1985), pp. 125–43.

Silverstone, R. "The Agonistic Narratives of Television Science," in J. Corner (Ed.), *Documentary and The Mass Media* (London: Edwin Arnold, 1986), pp. 81–106.

Simons, H. *Persuasion: Understanding, Practice, and Analysis,* 2nd ed. (New York: Random House, 1986).

Sinclair, D. "Rhetoric and Success: The Case of the Southern Baptists," Unpublished Ph.D. Dissertation, University of Texas at Austin, 1985.

Sloop, J. " 'Apology Made to Whoever Pleases': Cultural Discipline and the Grounds of Interpretation," *Communication Quarterly*, 42 (1994), 345–62.

Smith, S. "Sounds of the South: The Rhetorical Saga of Country Music Lyrics," *Southern Speech Communication Journal*, 45 (1980), 164–72.

Snitow, A. "Mass Market Romance: Pornography for Women is Different," in M. Eagleton (Ed.), *Feminist Literary Theory: A Reader* (London: Blackwell, 1986), 134–9.

Snow, M. "Martin Luther King's 'Letter from Birmingham Jail' as Pauline Epistle," *Quarterly Journal of Speech*, 71 (1985), 318–34.

Solomon, M. "Robert Schuller: The American Dream in a Crystal Cathedral," *Central States Speech Journal*, 34 (1983a) 172–86.

Solomon, M. "Stopping ERA: A Pyrrhic Victory," *Communication Quarterly*, 31 (1983b) 109–17.

Spurling, L. *Phenomenology and the Social World: The Philosophy of Merleau-Ponty and its Relations to the Social Sciences* (London: Routledge, 1977).

Steuter, E. "Understanding the Media/Terrorism Relationship: An Analysis of Ideology and the News in *Time* Magazine," *Political Communication*, 7 (1990), 257–78.

Strine, M. and M. Pacanowsky, "How To Read Interpretive Accounts of Organizational Life: Narrative Bases of Textual Authority," *Southern Speech Communication Journal*, 50 (1985), 283–97.

Sullivan, P., and S. Goldzwig. "A Relational Approach to Moral Decision-Making: The Majority Opinion in *Planned Parenthood v. Casey*," *Quarterly Journal of Speech*, 81 (1995), 167–90.

Sumner, C. *Reading Ideologies: An Investigation into the Marxist Theory of Ideology and Law* (London: Academic Press, 1979).

Taylor, B. "The Politics of the Nuclear Text: Reading Robert Oppenheimer's *Letters and Recollections*," *Quarterly Journal of Speech*, 78 (1992), 429–49.

Thomas, S. "The Route to Redemption: Religion and Social Class," *Journal of Communication*, 35:1 (1985), 111–22.

Thompson, J. B. *Studies in the Theory of Ideology* (London: Polity, 1984).

Tompkins, J. "Me and my Shadow," In R. R. Warhol and D. P. Herndl (Eds.), *Feminisms: An Anthology of Literary Theory and Criticism* (New Brunswick: Rutgers University Press, 1991), pp. 1079–93.

Tonn, M. B., V. Endress, and J. Diamond, "Hunting and Heritage on Trial: A Dramatictic Debate over Tragedy, Tradition, and Territory," *Quarterly Journal of Speech*, 79 (1993), 165–81.

Toulmin, S. *The Uses of Argument* (Cambridge, England: Cambridge University Press, 1958).

Tucker, L., and H. Shah. "Race and the Transformation of Culture: The Making of the Television Miniseries *Roots*," *Critical Studies in Mass Communication*, 9 (1992), 325–336.

Turner, G. *Stylistics* (Baltimore: Penguin, 1973).

Trujillo, N., and G. Dionisopoulos, "Cop Talk, Police Stories, and the Social Construction of Organizational Drama," *Central States Speech Journal*, 38 (1987), 196–209.

Vartabedian, R. "Nixon's Vietnam Rhetoric: A Case Study of Apologia as Generic Paradox," *Southern Speech Communication Journal*, 50 (1985), 366–81.

Waddell, C. "The Role of *Pathos* in the Decision-Making Process: A Study in the Rhetoric of Science Policy," *Quarterly Journal of Speech*, 76 (1990), 381–400.

Walker, C. "In the Margin: The Image of Women in Early Puritan Poetry," in P. White and H. Meserole-Harrison (Eds.), *Puritan Poets and Poetics: Seventeenth-Century American Poetry in Theory and Practice* (University Park: Pennsylvania State University Press, 1985), pp. 111–25.

Wallman, S. "Refractions of Rhetoric: Evidence for the Meaning of 'Race' in England," in R. Paine (Ed.), *Politically Speaking: Cross-Cultural Studies of Rhetoric* (Philadelphia: Institute for the Study of Human Issues, 1981), 143–64.

Walzer, M. *The Company of Critics: Social Criticism and Political Commitment in the Twentieth Century* (New York: Basic Books, 1988).

Wander, P. "The Ideological Turn in Criticism," *Central States Speech Journal*, 34 (1983), 1–18.

Wander, P. "The Rhetoric of American Foreign Policy," *Quarterly Journal of Speech*, 70 (1984), 339–61.

Ware, B., and W. Linkugel, "They Spoke in Defense of Themselves: On the Generic Criticism of Apologia," *Quarterly Journal of Speech*, 54 (1973), 273–83.

Warner, W. L. "The Ritualization of the Past," In J. Combs and M. Mansfield (Eds.), *Drama in Life: The Uses of Communication in Society* (New York: Hastings House, 1976), 371–88.

Warnick, B. "Structuralism vs. Phenomenology: Implications for Rhetorical Criticism," *Quarterly Journal of Speech*, 65 (1979), 260–1.

Weaver, R. *The Ethics of Rhetoric* (Chicago: Henry Regnery, 1953).

White, R. "Hitler, Roosevelt, and the Nature of War Propaganda," *Journal of Abnormal and Social Psychology*, 44 (1949), 157–74.

Whittenberger-Keith, K. *Paradox and Communication: The Case of Etiquette Manuals*, Unpublished Ph.D. Dissertation, University of Texas at Austin, 1989.

Wichelns, H. "The Literary Criticism of Oratory," in R. Scott and B. Brock (Eds.), *Methods of Rhetorical Criticism: A Twentieth Century Perspective* (New York: Harper & Row, [1925] 1972), 27–60.

Williams, L. "When the Woman Looks," In M. A. Doane, P. Mellencamp, and L. Williams (Eds.), *Re-vision: Essays in Feminist Film Criticism* (Los Angeles: University Publications of America, 1984), pp. 83–100.

Williams, M. *Community in a Black Pentacostalist Church: An Anthropological Study* (Pittsburgh: University of Pittsburgh Press, 1974).

Williams, R. *Marxism and Literature* (London: Oxford, 1977).

Wilson, J. and C. Arnold, *Public Speaking as a Liberal Art*, 3rd ed. (Boston: Allyn and Bacon, 1974).

Windt, T. "The Diatribe: Last Resort for Protest," *Quarterly Journal of Speech*, 58 (1972), 1–14.

Woodward, G. "Prime Ministers and Presidents: A Survey of the Differing Rhetorical Possibilities of High Office," *Communication Quarterly,* 27 (1979), 41–9.

Wolf, N. "Excerpts from *Fire with Fire,*" *Glamour,* November, 1993, pp. 221+.

Woolf, V. *A Room of One's Own* (New York: Harcourt, 1929).

Worth, S. *Studying Visual Communication* (Philadelphia: University of Pennsylvania Press, 1981).

Youngquist, M. "Three Blind Mice," Quoted in W. Espy, *The Garden of Eloquence: A Rhetorical Bestiary* (New York: Dutton, 1983), 153.

Zelizer, B. *Covering the Body: The Kennedy Assasination, the Media, and the Shaping of Collective Memory* (Chicago: University of Chicago Press, 1992).

Zyskind, H. "A Case Study in Philosophic Rhetoric: Theodore Roosevelt," *Philosophy and Rhetoric,* 1 (1968), 228–54.

INDEX